Tales from the Land of Saints & Scholars

Traditional tales, fables and sagas from Ireland

4th edition revised and updated

Compiled, adapted & edited by Clive Gilson

Tales from the World's Firesides

Tales From The Land Of Saints & Scholars © 2019 - 2025 Clive Gilson

First published in 2019 by Clive Gilson, Bath, UK: Clivegilson.com

This 4th edition published in 2025 by Clive Gilson, Bath, UK

The right of Clive Gilson to be identified as the author of this work has been asserted in accordance with the Copyright, Designs and Patents Act 1988.

All rights reserved. No part of this publication may be reproduced, stored in a retrieval system, or transmitted in any form or by any means, electronic, mechanical, photocopying, recording or otherwise, without prior written permission of the publisher, except for brief quotations in reviews or academic critique.

ISBN (paperback): 978-1-915081-68-1

ISBN (eBook): 978-1-915081-66-7

ISBN (hardback): 978-1-915081-67-4

This is a work of fiction. Names, characters, places and incidents are products of the author's imagination or are used fictitiously. Any resemblance to actual persons, living or dead, events or locales is entirely coincidental.

Cover design by Clive Gilson.

A catalogue record for this book is available from the British Library.

Printed on demand.

For permissions and foreign rights: gilson.clive@gmail.com

ISBN: 978-1-915081-68-1

Contents

Preface
A Legend of Knockmany
Andrew Coffey
Bewitched Butter
Conall Yellowclaw
Diarmid Bawn, The Piper
Fair, Brown and Trembling
Far Darrig in Donegal
Fior Usga
Hookedy-Crookedy
King Iubdan and King Fergus
King O'Toole and St Kevin
Legend of Bottle Hill
Lough Leagh
Morraha
Munachar and Manachar
Ned Sheehy's Excuse
Rent-Day
The Amadan of the Dough
The Banshee of the Mac Carthys
The Birth of Bran
The Boyhood of Fion
The Brewery of Eggshells
The Carving of Mac Datho's Boar
The Countess Kathleen O'Shea
The Demon Cat
The Enchanted Cave of Cesh Corran

The Enchantment of Gearoidh Iarla
The Fairy Greyhound
The Fate of Frank M'Kenna
The Field of Boliauns
The Good Woman
The Haughty Princess
The Headless Horseman
The Hill-Man and the Housewife
The Horned Women
The Jackdaw
The King of the Black Desert
The Lad with the Goat-Skin
The Lazy Beauty and her Aunts
The Legend of Knockfierna
The Legend of Knockshegowna
The Legend of O'Donoghue
The Little Weaver of Duleek Gate
The Mad Pudding of Ballyboulteen
The Plaisham
The Pursuit of the Gilla Dacker
The Quest of the Sons of Turenn
The Red Pony
The Secret of Labra
The Snow, the Crow, and the Blood
The Spirit Horse
The Story of Deirdre
The Story of the Children of Lir
The Storyteller at Fault
The Three Crowns

The Three Wishes

The Vengeance of Mesgedra

The Witches' Excursion

The Wonderful Tune

The Wooing of Becfola

Historical Notes

About the Editor

Reviews

Preface

This fourth edition of *Tales from the Land of Saints & Scholars* marks a significant step forward in a project that has occupied me for many years: the gathering and re-telling of the world's old stories, shaped for a modern reader yet faithful to their deep, original pulse. In this volume, devoted to Ireland, I have revisited every tale, revising the language, expanding the historical context, and adding new notes on sources, collectors, and cultural background. Much has been re-examined, and where necessary, re-balanced. These stories have been retold many times before, and this edition honours that living tradition by letting them breathe again.

I have been collecting and telling stories for more than two decades now, writing across many forms but always drawn to the edge between the real and the marvellous. Folktales and fairy tales have long been my foundation. Through them, I have built an ever-growing library of thousands of tales gathered from around the world. Each new edition in this series seeks to give these stories a home, a space where they can speak for their places and peoples, their joys and fears, their wit and wonder.

The drive behind this work remains simple: to keep alive stories that might otherwise fade into obscurity. Most of the material here comes from the pioneering collectors of the eighteenth, nineteenth, and early twentieth centuries, whose vision was extraordinary but whose language and assumptions now often feel distant from our own. My task has been to adapt these older texts with care, to preserve their meaning and music while recognising that some of the views once woven into them no longer sit easily with us. The aim is always to hold the spirit of the story intact while letting it meet the light of today.

As ever, I want to stress that these retellings are not acts of ownership but of preservation. Many early collectors brought their own biases to the page, so I try to meet their work with gratitude and caution. Each story here carries full attribution, naming the original collector or source, the collection title, publication details, and, where possible, a note on cultural or regional origins. These notes are more extensive than in previous editions, offering context for how these tales were gathered and how they have travelled.

Ireland's storytelling tradition is one of the richest in the world, lyrical, layered, and profoundly human. Its myths speak of gods who fall and rise again, of saints who borrow the language of sorcery, of lovers bound by fate, of the small people who slip between light and shadow. These are tales of courage and cunning, beauty and melancholy, shaped by a landscape that seems always half in this world and half in another. They remind us that the sacred and the ordinary have never been far apart on Irish soil.

The Tales from the World's Firesides series, now grown to include volumes from across the British and Irish isles and beyond, continues to evolve. New research, better sources, and a shifting sense of how to tell old stories faithfully ensure that each edition becomes both archive and renewal. Even so, I know I am only tracing a small arc across the vast sky of human imagination.

Storytelling remains one of our oldest instincts. Around firelight, across centuries, we have spoken our fears, our hopes, our love of life through the shapes of myth. Beneath all the variations of place and tongue, the patterns remain astonishingly alike. The faces change, but the heart that speaks through them is the same.

These Irish tales, wild, tender, humorous, and strange, still carry that heartbeat. I have loved working with them again. I hope, as you read, you'll hear the echo of the seanchaí, the storyteller, drawing breath before another turning of the world.

Clive

Bath, 2025

Tales From The Land Of Saints & Scholars

A Legend of Knockmany

"A Legend of Knockmany" is an Irish folktale originally written and popularised by William Carleton (1794–1869), later reprinted and adapted by W. B. Yeats in his Fairy and Folk Tales of the Irish Peasantry (1888, The Walter Scott Publishing Company, London).

The story belongs to Carleton's lively body of Irish peasant tales that blend humour, myth, and local superstition. Set around Knockmany Hill in County Tyrone, a real place in Ulster associated with ancient passage tombs and mythic figures, it reimagines one of Ireland's oldest mythological rivalries: that of Fionn mac Cumhaill (Finn McCool) and Cú Chulainn, two legendary heroes from different cycles of Irish mythology.

What Irish man, woman, or child has not heard of our renowned Hibernian Hercules, the great and glorious Fin M'Coul? Not one, from Cape Clear to the Giant's Causeway, nor from that back again to Cape Clear. And, by-the-way, speaking of the Giant's Causeway brings me at once to the beginning of my story. Well, it so happened that Fin and his gigantic relatives were all working at the Causeway, in order to make a bridge across to Scotland; when Fin, who was very fond of his wife Oonagh, took it into his head that he would go home and see how the poor woman got on in his absence. To be sure, Fin was a true Irishman, and so his sense of sorrow at their separation made him want to go home to see that Oonagh was snug and comfortable, and, above all things, that she got her rest well at night; for he knew that the poor woman, when he was with her, used to be subject to nightly qualms and configurations, that kept him very anxious and made him strive all the harder to keep her up to the good spirits and health that she had when they were first married. So, accordingly, he pulled up a fir-tree, and, after lopping off the roots and branches, made a walking-stick of it, and set out on his way to Oonagh.

Oonagh and Fin lived at this time on the very tip-top of Knockmany Hill, which faces a cousin of its own called Cullamore, that rises up, half-hill, half-mountain, on the opposite side - east-east by south, as the sailors say, when they wish to puzzle a landsman.

Now, the truth is, for it must come out, that honest Fin's affection for his wife, though cordial enough in itself, was by no manner of means the real cause of his journey home. There was at that time another giant, named Cucullin - some say he was Irish, and some say he was Scotch - but whether Scotch or Irish, sorrow doubt of it but he was a targer (loud, obnoxious and confrontational). No other giant of the day could stand before him; and such was his strength, that, when well vexed, he could give a stamp that shook the country about him. The fame and name of him went far and near; and nothing in the shape of a man, it was said, had any chance with him in a fight. Whether the story is true or not, I cannot say, but the report went that, by one blow of his fists he flattened a thunderbolt, and kept it in his pocket, in the shape of a pancake, to show to all his enemies, when they were about to fight him. Undoubtedly he had given every giant in Ireland a considerable beating, barring Fin M'Coul himself; and he swore, by the solemn contents of Moll Kelly's Primer, that he would never rest, night or day, winter or summer, till he would serve Fin with the same sauce, if he could catch him. Fin, however, who no doubt was the cock of the walk on his own dunghill, had a strong disinclination to meet a giant who could make a young earthquake, or flatten a thunderbolt when he was angry; so he accordingly kept dodging about from place to place, not much to his credit as a Trojan, to be sure, whenever he happened to get the hard word that Cucullin was on the scent of him. This, then, was the marrow of the whole movement, although he put it on his anxiety to see Oonagh; and I am not saying but there was some truth in that too. However, the short and long of it was, with reverence be it spoken, that he heard Cucullin was coming to the Causeway to have a trial of strength with him; and he was naturally enough seized, in consequence, with a very warm and sudden sit of affection for his wife, poor woman, who was delicate in her health, and leading, besides, a very lonely, uncomfortable life of it (he assured them) in his absence. He accordingly pulled up the fir-tree, as I said before, and having snedded it into a walking-stick, set out on his affectionate travels to see his darling Oonagh on the top of Knockmany, by the way.

In truth, to state the suspicions of the country at the time, the people wondered very much why it was that Fin selected such a windy spot for his dwelling-house, and they even went so far as to tell him as much.

"What can you mean, Mr. M'Coul," said they, "by pitching your tent upon the top of Knockmany, where you never are without a breeze, day or night, winter or summer, and where you're often forced to take your nightcap without either going to bed or turning up your little finger; ay, an' where, besides this, there's the sorrow's own want of water?"

"Why," said Fin, "ever since I was the height of a round tower, I was known to be fond of having a good prospect of my own; and where the dickens, neighbours, could I find a better spot for a good prospect than the top of Knockmany? As for water, I am sinking a pump, and, please goodness, as soon as the Causeway's made, I intend to finish it."

Now, this was more of Fin's philosophy; for the real state of the case was, that he pitched upon the top of Knockmany in order that he might be able to see Cucullin coming towards the house, and, of course, that he himself might go to look after his distant transactions in other parts of the country, rather than - but no matter - we do not wish to be too hard on Fin. All we have to say is, that if he wanted a spot from which to keep a sharp look-out - and, between ourselves, he did want it grievously - barring Slieve Croob, or Slieve Donard, or its own cousin, Cullamore, he could not find a neater or more convenient situation for it in the sweet and sagacious province of Ulster.

"God save all here!" said Fin, good-humouredly, on putting his honest face into his own door.

"Musha, Fin, an' you're welcome home to your own Oonagh, you darlin' bully." Here followed a smack that is said to have made the waters of the lake at the bottom of the hill curl, as it were, with kindness and sympathy.

"Faith," said Fin, "beautiful; an' how are you, Oonagh - and how did you sport your figure during my absence, my bilberry?"

"Never a merrier - as bouncing a grass widow as ever there was in sweet 'Tyrone among the bushes."

Fin gave a short, good-humoured cough, and laughed most heartily, to show her how much he was delighted that she made herself happy in his absence.

"An' what brought you home so soon, Fin?" said she.

"Why, avourneen," said Fin, putting in his answer in the proper way, "never the thing but the purest of love and affection for yourself. Sure you know that's truth, anyhow, Oonagh."

Fin spent two or three happy days with Oonagh, and felt himself very comfortable, considering the dread he had of Cucullin. This, however, grew upon him so much that his wife could not but perceive something lay on his mind which he kept altogether to himself. Let a woman alone, in the meantime, for ferreting or wheedling a secret out of her good man, when she wishes. Fin was a proof of this.

"It's this Cucullin," said he, "that's troubling me. When the fellow gets angry, and begins to stamp, he'll shake you a whole townland; and it's well known that he can stop a thunderbolt, for he always carries one about him in the shape of a pancake, to show to anyone that might misdoubt it."

As he spoke, he clapped his thumb in his mouth, which he always did when he wanted to prophesy, or to know anything that happened in his absence; and the wife, who knew what he did it for, said, very sweetly,

"Fin, darling, I hope you don't bite your thumb at me, dear?"

"No," said Fin, "but I bite my thumb, acushla," said he.

"Yes, jewel; but take care and don't draw blood," said she. "Ah, Fin! don't, my bully - don't."

"He's coming," said Fin, "I see him below Dungannon."

"Thank goodness, dear! an' who is it? Glory be to God!"

"That baste, Cucullin," replied Fin, "and how to manage I don't know. If I run away, I am disgraced; and I know that sooner or later I must meet him, for my thumb tells me so."

"When will he be here?" said she.

"To-morrow, about two o'clock," replied Fin, with a groan.

"Well, my bully, don't be cast down," said Oonagh, "depend on me, and maybe I'll bring you better out of this scrape than ever you could bring yourself, by your rule o' thumb."

This quieted Fin's heart very much, for he knew that Oonagh was hand and glove with the fairies; and, indeed, to tell the truth, she was supposed to be a fairy herself. If she was, however, she must have been a kind-hearted one, for, by all accounts, she never did anything but good in the neighbourhood.

Now it so happened that Oonagh had a sister named Granua, living opposite them, on the very top of Cullamore, which I have mentioned already, and this Granua was quite as powerful as herself. The beautiful valley that lies between them is not more than about three or four miles broad, so that of a summer's evening, Granua and Oonagh were able to hold many an agreeable conversation across it, from the one hill-top to the other. Upon this occasion Oonagh resolved to consult her sister as to what was best to be done in the difficulty that surrounded them.

"Granua," said she, "are you at home?"

"No," said the other, "I'm picking bilberries in Althadhawan, the Devil's Glen."

"Well," said Oonagh, "get up to the top of Cullamore, look about you, and then tell us what you see."

"Very well," replied Granua; after a few minutes, "I am there now."

"What do you see?" asked the other.

"Goodness be about us!" exclaimed Granua, "I see the biggest giant that ever was known coming up from Dungannon."

"Ay," said Oonagh, "there's our difficulty. That giant is the great Cucullin; and he's now coming up to leather Fin. What's to be done?"

"I'll call to him," she replied, "to come up to Cullamore and refresh himself, and maybe that will give you and Fin time to think of some plan to get yourselves out of the scrape. But" she proceeded, "I'm short of butter, having in the house only half-a-dozen firkins, and as I'm to have a few giants and giantesses to spend the evening with me, I'd feel thankful, Oonagh, if you'd throw me up fifteen or sixteen tubs, or the largest miscaun you have got, and you'll oblige me very much."

"I'll do that with a heart and a-half," replied Oonagh, "and, indeed, Granua, I feel myself under great obligations to you for your kindness in keeping him off of us till we see what can be done; for what would become of us all if anything happened Fin, poor man."

She accordingly got the largest miscaun of butter she had - which might be about the weight of a couple a dozen mill-stones, so that you may easily judge of its size - and calling up to her sister, "Granua," said she, "are you ready? I'm going to throw you up a miscaun, so be prepared to catch it."

"I will," said the other, "a good throw now, and take care it does not fall short."

Oonagh threw it; but, in consequence of her anxiety about Fin and Cucullin, she forgot to say the charm that was to send it up, so that, instead of reaching Cullamore, as she expected, it fell about halfway between the two hills, at the edge of the Broad Bog near Augher.

"My curse upon you!" she exclaimed, "you've disgraced me. I now change you into a grey stone. Lie there as a testimony of what has happened; and may evil betide the first living man that will ever attempt to remove or injure you!"

And, sure enough, there it lies to this day, with the mark of the four fingers and thumb imprinted in it, exactly as it came out of her hand.

"Never mind," said Granua, "I must only do the best I can with Cucullin. If all fail, I'll give him a cast of heather broth to keep the wind out of his stomach, or a panada of oak-bark to draw it in a bit; but, above all things, think of some plan to get Fin out of the scrape he's in, otherwise he's a lost man. You know you used to be sharp and ready-witted; and my own opinion, Oonagh, is, that it will go hard with you, or you'll outdo Cucullin yet."

She then made a high smoke on the top of the hill, after which she put her finger in her mouth, and gave three whistles, and by that Cucullin knew he was invited to Cullamore - for this was the way that the Irish long ago gave a sign to all strangers and travellers, to let them know they were welcome to come and take share of whatever was going.

In the meantime, Fin was very melancholy, and did not know what to do, or how to act at all. Cucullin was an ugly customer, no doubt, to meet with; and, moreover, the idea of the confounded "cake" aforesaid flattened the very heart within him. What chance could he have, strong and brave though he was, with a man who could, when put in a passion, walk the country into earthquakes and knock thunderbolts into pancakes? The thing was impossible; and Fin knew not on what hand to turn him. Right or left - backward or forward - where to go he could form no guess whatsoever.

"Oonagh," said he, "can you do nothing for me? Where's all your invention? Am I to be skewered like a rabbit before your eyes, and to have my name disgraced forever in the sight of all my tribe, and me the best man among them? How am I to fight this man-mountain - this huge cross between an earthquake and a thunderbolt? - with a pancake in his pocket that was once - - "

"Be easy, Fin," replied Oonagh, "truth, I'm ashamed of you. Keep your toe in your pump, will you? Talking of pancakes, maybe we'll give him as good as any he brings with him - thunderbolt or otherwise. If I don't treat him to as smart feeding as he's got this many a day, never trust Oonagh again. Leave him to me, and do just as I bid you."

This relieved Fin very much; for, after all, he had great confidence in his wife, knowing, as he did, that she had got him out of many a quandary before. The present, however, was the greatest of all; but still he began to get courage, and was able to eat his victuals as usual. Oonagh then drew the nine woollen threads of different colours, which she always did to find out the best way of succeeding in anything of importance she went about. She then plaited them into three plaits with three colours in each, putting one on her right arm, one round her heart, and the third round her right ankle, for then she knew that nothing could fail with her that she undertook.

Having everything now prepared, she sent round to the neighbours and borrowed one-and-twenty iron griddles, which she took and kneaded into the hearts of one-and-twenty cakes of bread, and these she baked on the fire in the usual way, setting them aside in the cupboard according as they were done. She then put down a large pot of new milk, which she made into curds and whey, and gave Fin due instructions how to use the curds when Cucullin should come. Having done all this, she sat down quite contented, waiting for his arrival on the next day about two o'clock, that being the hour at which he was expected - for Fin knew as much by the sucking of his thumb. Now, this was a curious property that Fin's thumb had; but, notwithstanding all the wisdom and logic he used, to suck out of it, it could never have stood to him here were it not for the wit of his wife. In this very thing, moreover, he was very much resembled by his great foe, Cucullin; for it was well known that the huge strength he possessed all lay in the middle finger of his right hand, and that, if he happened by any mischance to lose it, he was no more, notwithstanding his bulk, than a common man.

At length, the next day, he was seen coming across the valley, and Oonagh knew that it was time to commence operations. She immediately made the cradle, and desired Fin to lie down in it, and cover himself up with the clothes.

"You must pass for you own child," said she, "so just lie there snug, and say nothing, but be guided by me." This, to be sure, was wormwood to Fin - I mean going into the cradle in such a cowardly manner - but he knew Oonagh well; and finding that he had nothing else for it, with a very rueful face he gathered himself into it, and lay snug, as she had desired him.

About two o'clock, as he had been expected, Cucullin came in. "God save all here!" said he, "is this where the great Fin M'Coul lives?"

"Indeed it is, honest man," replied Oonagh, "God save you kindly - won't you be sitting?"

"Thank you, ma'am," says he, sitting down, "you're Mrs. M'Coul, I suppose?"

"I am," said she, "and I have no reason, I hope, to be ashamed of my husband."

"No," said the other, "he has the name of being the strongest and bravest man in Ireland; but for all that, there's a man not far from you that's very desirous of taking a shake with him. Is he at home?"

"Why, then, no," she replied, "and if ever a man left his house in a fury, he did. It appears that someone told him of a big basthoon of a giant called Cucullin being down at the Causeway to look for him, and so he set out there to try if he could catch him. Troth, I hope, for the poor giant's sake, he won't meet with him, for if he does, Fin will make paste of him at once."

"Well," said the other, "I am Cucullin, and I have been seeking him these twelve months, but he always kept clear of me; and I will never rest night or day till I lay my hands on him."

At this Oonagh set up a loud laugh, of great contempt, by-the-way, and looked at him as if he was only a mere handful of a man.

"Did you ever see Fin?" said she, changing her manner all at once.

"How could I?" said he, "he always took care to keep his distance."

"I thought so," she replied, "I judged as much; and if you take my advice, you poor-looking creature, you'll pray night and day that you may never see him, for I tell you it will be a black day for you when you do. But, in the meantime, you perceive that the wind's on the door, and as Fin himself is from home, maybe you'd be civil enough to turn the house, for it's always what Fin does when he's here."

This was a startler even to Cucullin; but he got up, however, and after pulling the middle finger of his right hand until it cracked three times, he went outside, and getting his arms about the house, completely turned it as she had wished. When Fin saw this, he felt a certain description of moisture, which shall be nameless, oozing out through every pore of his skin; but Oonagh, depending upon her woman's wit, felt not a whit daunted.

"Arrah, then," said she, "as you are so civil, maybe you'd do another obliging turn for us, as Fin's not here to do it himself. You see, after this long stretch of dry weather we've had, we feel very badly off for want of water. Now, Fin says there's a fine spring-well somewhere under the rocks behind the hill here below, and it was his intention to pull them asunder; but having heard of you, he left the place in such a fury, that he never thought of it. Now, if you try to find it, truth I'd feel it a kindness."

She then brought Cucullin down to see the place, which was then all one solid rock; and, after looking at it for some time, he cracked his right middle finger nine times, and, stooping down, tore a cleft about four hundred feet deep, and a quarter of a mile in length, which has since been christened by the name of Lumford's Glen. This feat nearly threw Oonagh herself off her guard; but what won't a woman's sagacity and presence of mind accomplish?

"You'll now come in," said she, "and eat a bit of such humble fare as we can give you. Fin, even although he and you are enemies, would scorn not to treat you kindly in his own house; and, indeed, if I didn't do it even in his absence, he would not be pleased with me."

She accordingly brought him in, and placing half-a-dozen of the cakes we spoke of before him, together with a can or two of butter, a side of boiled bacon, and a stack of cabbage, she desired him to help himself - for this, be it known, was long before the invention of potatoes. Cucullin, who, by the way, was a glutton as well as a hero, put one of the cakes in his mouth to take a huge whack out of it, when both Fin and Oonagh were stunned with a noise that resembled something between a growl and a yell. "Blood and fury!" he shouted, "how is this? Here are two of my teeth out! What kind of bread is this you gave me?"

"What's the matter?" said Oonagh coolly.

"Matter!" shouted the other again, "why, here are the two best teeth in my head gone."

"Why," said she, "that's Fin's bread - the only bread he ever eats when at home; but, indeed, I forgot to tell you that nobody can eat it but himself, and that child in the cradle there. I thought, however, that, as you were reported to be rather a stout little fellow of your size, you might be able to manage it, and I did not wish to affront a man that thinks himself able to fight Fin. Here's another cake - maybe it's not so hard as that."

Cucullin at the moment was not only hungry, but ravenous, so he accordingly made a fresh set at the second cake, and immediately another yell was heard twice as loud as the first. "Thunder and giblets!" he roared, "take your bread out of this, or I will not have a tooth in my head; there's another pair of them gone!"

"Well, honest man," replied Oonagh, "if you're not able to eat the bread, say so quietly, and don't be wakening the child in the cradle there. There, now, he's awake upon me."

Fin now gave a skirl that startled the giant, as coming from such a youngster as he was represented to be. "Mother," said he, "I'm hungry - get me something to eat." Oonagh went over, and putting into his hand a cake that had no griddle in it, Fin, whose appetite in the meantime was sharpened by what he saw going forward, soon made it disappear. Cucullin was thunderstruck, and secretly thanked his stars that he had the good fortune to miss meeting Fin, for, as he said to himself, I'd have no chance with a man who could eat such bread as that, which even his son that's but in his cradle can munch before my eyes.

"I'd like to take a glimpse at the lad in the cradle," he said to Oonagh, "for I can tell you that the infant who can manage that nutriment is no joke to look at, or to feed of a scarce summer."

"With all the veins of my heart," replied Oonagh, "get up, acushla, and show this decent little man something that won't be unworthy of your father, Fin M'Coul."

Fin, who was dressed for the occasion as much like a boy as possible, got up, and bringing Cucullin out, "Are you strong?" said he.

"Thunder an' hounds!" exclaimed the other, "what a voice in so small a chap!"

"Are you strong?" said Fin again, "are you able to squeeze water out of that white stone?" he asked, putting one into Cucullin's hand. The latter squeezed and squeezed the stone, but to no purpose; he might pull the rocks of Lumford's Glen asunder, and flatten a thunderbolt, but to squeeze water out of a white stone was beyond his strength. Fin eyed him with great contempt, as he kept straining and squeezing and squeezing and straining, till he got black in the face with the efforts.

"Ah, you're a poor creature!" said Fin. "You a giant! Give me the stone here, and when I'll show what Fin's little son can do; you may then judge of what my daddy himself is."

Fin then took the stone, and slyly exchanging it for the curds, he squeezed the latter until the whey, as clear as water, oozed out in a little shower from his hand.

"I'll now go in," he said "to my cradle; for I scorn to lose my time with any one that's not able to eat my daddy's bread, or squeeze water out of a stone. Bedad, you had better be off out of this before he comes back; for if he catches you, it's in flummery he'd have you in two minutes."

Cucullin, seeing what he had seen, was of the same opinion himself; his knees knocked together with the terror of Fin's return, and he accordingly hastened in to bid Oonagh farewell, and to assure her, that from that day out, he never wished to hear of, much less to see, her husband. "I admit fairly that I'm not a match for him," said he, "strong as I am; tell him I will avoid him as I would the plague, and that I will make myself scarce in this part of the country while I live."

Fin, in the meantime, had gone into the cradle, where he lay very quietly, his heart at his mouth with delight that Cucullin was about to take his departure, without discovering the tricks that had been played off on him.

"It's well for you," said Oonagh, "that he doesn't happen to be here, for it's nothing but hawk's meat he'd make of you."

"I know that," says Cucullin, "devil a thing else he'd make of me; but before I go, will you let me feel what kind of teeth they are that can eat griddle-bread like that?", and he pointed to it as he spoke.

"With all pleasure in life," said she, "only, as they're far back in his head, you must put your finger a good way in."

Cucullin was surprised to find such a powerful set of grinders in one so young; but he was still much more so on finding, when he took his hand from Fin's mouth, that he had left the very finger upon which his whole strength depended, behind him. He gave one loud groan, and fell down at once with terror and weakness. This was all Fin wanted, who now knew that his most powerful and bitterest enemy was completely at his mercy. He instantly started out of the cradle, and in a few minutes the great Cucullin, that was for such a length of time the terror of him and all his followers, lay a corpse before him. Thus did Fin, through the wit and invention of Oonagh, his wife, succeed in overcoming his enemy by stratagem, which he never could have done by force, and thus also is it proved that the women, if they bring us into many an unpleasant scrape, can sometimes succeed in getting us out of others that are as bad.

Tales From The Land Of Saints & Scholars

Andrew Coffey

"Andrew Coffey", as adapted by Joseph Jacobs in Celtic Fairy Tales (1892), is a brief but striking Irish ghost story drawn from the oral tradition.

Jacobs's adaptation preserves the tale's sharp rhythm and dark humour, reflecting the Irish talent for mixing the eerie with the comic. Like many traditional ghost stories, Andrew Coffey plays with boundaries between the real and the supernatural, the rational man and the haunted landscape. The story's brevity and matter-of-fact tone heighten its uncanny effect, as if the otherworld brushes past ordinary life in a moment of accidental trespass.

My grandfather, Andrew Coffey, was known to the whole barony as a quiet, decent man. And if the whole barony knew him, he knew the whole barony, every inch, hill and dale, bog and pasture, field and covert. Fancy his surprise one evening, when he found himself in a part of the demesne he couldn't recognise a bit. He and his good horse were always stumbling up against some tree or stumbling down into some bog-hole that by rights didn't ought to be there. On the top of all this the rain came pelting down wherever there was a clearing, and the cold March wind tore through the trees. Glad he was then when he saw a light in the distance, and drawing near found a cabin, though for the life of him he couldn't think how it came there. However, in he walked, after tying up his horse, and right welcome was the brushwood fire blazing on the hearth. And there stood a chair right and tight, that seemed to say, "Come, sit down in me." There wasn't a soul else in the room. Well, he did sit, and got a little warm and cheered after his drenching. But all the while he was wondering and wondering.

"Andrew Coffey! Andrew Coffey!"

Good heavens! who was calling him, and not a soul in sight? Look around as he might, indoors and out, he could find no creature with two legs or four, for his horse was gone.

"ANDREW COFFEY! ANDREW COFFEY! tell me a story."

It was louder this time, and it was nearer. And then what a thing to ask for! It was bad enough not to be let sit by the fire and dry oneself, without being bothered for a story.

"ANDREW COFFEY! ANDREW COFFEY!! Tell me a story, or it'll be the worse for you."

My poor grandfather was so dumbfounded that he could only stand and stare.

"ANDREW COFFEY! ANDREW COFFEY! I told you it'd be the worse for you."

And with that, out there bounced, from a cupboard that Andrew Coffey had never noticed before, a man. And the man was in a towering rage. But it wasn't that. And he carried as fine a blackthorn as you'd wish to crack a man's head with. But it wasn't that either. But when my grandfather clapped eyes on him, he knew him for Patrick Rooney, and all the world knew he'd gone overboard, fishing one night long years before.

Andrew Coffey would neither stop nor stay, but he took to his heels and was out of the house as hard as he could. He ran and he ran taking little thought of what was before till at last he ran up against a big tree. And then he sat down to rest.

He hadn't sat for a moment when he heard voices.

"It's heavy he is, the vagabond." "Steady now, we'll rest when we get under the big tree yonder." Now that happened to be the tree under which Andrew Coffey was sitting. At least he thought so, for seeing a branch handy he swung himself up by it and was soon snugly hidden away. Better see than be seen, thought he.

The rain had stopped and the wind fallen. The night was blacker than ever, but Andrew Coffey could see four men, and they were carrying between them a long box. Under the tree they came, set the box down, opened it, and who should they bring out but—Patrick Rooney. Never a word did he say, and he looked as pale as old snow.

Well, one gathered brushwood, and another took out tinder and flint, and soon they had a big fire roaring, and my grandfather could see Patrick plainly enough. If he had kept still before, he kept stiller now. Soon they had four poles up and a pole across, right over the fire, for all the world like a spit, and on to the pole they slung Patrick Rooney.

"He'll do well enough," said one, "but who's to mind him whilst we're away, who'll turn the fire, who'll see that he doesn't burn?"

With that Patrick opened his lips, "Andrew Coffey," said he. "Andrew Coffey! Andrew Coffey! Andrew Coffey! Andrew Coffey!"

"I'm much obliged to you, gentlemen," said Andrew Coffey from his hiding place in the tree, "but indeed I know nothing about the business."

"You'd better come down, Andrew Coffey," said Patrick.

It was the second time he spoke, and Andrew Coffey decided he would come down. The four men went off and he was left all alone with Patrick.

Then he sat and he kept the fire even, and he kept the spit turning, and all the while Patrick looked at him.

Poor Andrew Coffey couldn't make it all out at all, at all, and he stared at Patrick and at the fire, and he thought of the little house in the wood, till he felt quite dazed.

"Ah, but it's burning me you are!" says Patrick, very short and sharp.

"I'm sure I beg your pardon," said my grandfather "but might I ask you a question?"

"If you want a crooked answer," said Patrick, "turn away or it'll be the worse for you."

But my grandfather couldn't get it out of his head; hadn't everybody, far and near, said Patrick had fallen overboard. There was enough to think about, and my grandfather did think.

"ANDREW COFFEY! ANDREW COFFEY! IT'S BURNING ME YOU ARE."

Sorry enough my grandfather was, and he vowed he wouldn't do so again.

"You'd better not," said Patrick, and he gave him a cock of his eye, and a grin of his teeth, that just sent a shiver down Andrew Coffey's back. Well it was odd, that here he should be in a thick wood he had never set eyes upon, turning Patrick Rooney upon a spit. You can't wonder at my grandfather thinking and thinking and not minding the fire.

"ANDREW COFFEY, ANDREW COFFEY, IT'S THE DEATH OF YOU I'LL BE."

And with that what did my grandfather see, but Patrick unslinging himself from the spit and his eyes glared and his teeth glistened.

It was neither stop nor stay my grandfather made, but out he ran into the night of the wood. It seemed to him there wasn't a stone but was for his stumbling, not a branch but beat his face, not a bramble but tore his skin. And wherever it was clear the rain pelted down and the cold March wind howled along.

Glad he was to see a light, and a minute after he was kneeling, dazed, drenched, and bedraggled by the hearth side. The brushwood flamed, and the brushwood crackled, and soon my grandfather began to feel a little warm and dry and easy in his mind.

"ANDREW COFFEY! ANDREW COFFEY!"

It's hard for a man to jump when he has been through all my grandfather had, but jump he did. And when he looked around, where should he find himself but in the very cabin he had first met Patrick in.

"Andrew Coffey, Andrew Coffey, tell me a story."

"Is it a story you want?" said my grandfather as bold as may be, for he was just tired of being frightened. "Well if you can tell me the rights of this one, I'll be thankful."

And he told the tale of what had befallen him from first to last that night. The tale was long, and may be Andrew Coffey was weary. It's asleep he must have fallen, for when he awoke he lay on the hill-side under the open heavens, and his horse grazed at his side.

Tales From The Land Of Saints & Scholars

Bewitched Butter

"Bewitched Butter" is a lively folk tale originally written by William Carleton and later included by W. B. Yeats in Fairy and Folk Tales of the Irish Peasantry (1888). The story reflects rural Irish beliefs about witchcraft, envy, and the fragile luck of household prosperity.

Like many of Carleton's tales, Bewitched Butter blends everyday rural life with the supernatural logic of Irish peasant belief. Yeats's 1888 adaptation softened Carleton's dialect but preserved his humour and irony, showing how the folk imagination explained misfortune through patterns of magic rather than economics or chance.

Not far from Rathmullan lived, last spring, a family called Hanlon; and in a farmhouse, some fields distant, people named Dogherty. Both families had good cows, but the Hanlons were fortunate in possessing a Kerry cow that gave more milk and yellower butter than the others.

Grace Dogherty, a young girl, who was more admired than loved in the neighbourhood, took much interest in the Kerry cow, and appeared one night at Mrs. Hanlon's door with the modest request, "Will you let me milk your Moiley cow?"

"An' why would you wish to milk wee Moiley, Grace, dear?" inquired Mrs. Hanlon.

"Oh, just because you're so busy at the present time."

"Thank you kindly, Grace, but I'm no too busy to do my own work. I'll no trouble you to milk."

The girl turned away with a discontented air; but the next evening, and the next, found her at the cow-house door with the same request.

At length Mrs. Hanlon, not knowing well how to persist in her refusal, yielded, and permitted Grace to milk the Kerry cow.

She soon had reason to regret her want of firmness. Moiley gave no more milk to her owner.

When this melancholy state of things lasted for three days, the Hanlons applied to a certain Mark McCarrion, who lived near Binion.

"That cow has been milked by someone with an evil eye," said he. "Will she give you a wee drop, do you think? The full of a pint measure would do."

"Oh, aye, Mark, dear; I'll get that much milk from her, anyway."

"Well, Mrs. Hanlon, lock the door, an' get nine new pins that was never used in clothes, an' put them into a saucepan with the pint o' milk. Set them on the fire, an' let them come to the boil."

The nine pins soon began to simmer in Moiley's milk.

Rapid steps were heard approaching the door, agitated knocks followed, and Grace Dogherty's high-toned voice was raised in eager entreaty.

"Let me in, Mrs. Hanlon!" she cried. "Take off that cruel pot! Take out them pins, for they're pricking holes in my heart, an' I'll never offer to touch milk of yours again."

Conall Yellowclaw

"Conall Yellowclaw", as retold by Joseph Jacobs in Celtic Fairy Tales (1892), is a rich example of the old Gaelic hero tale reshaped into a folk narrative of wit, endurance, and justice.

Jacobs's adaptation retains the flavour of oral storytelling, with the rhythm and understatement of a tale told by firelight. It blends mythic heroism with moral charm: the sense that intelligence, courage, and a clear conscience can outmatch fate. Beneath the adventure lies a moral circle typical of Celtic narrative, where acts of bravery and mercy ultimately return to reward the hero.

Conall Yellowclaw was a sturdy tenant in Erin. He had three sons. There was at that time a king over every fifth of Erin. It fell out for the children of the king that was near Conall, that they themselves and the children of Conall came to blows. The children of Conall got the upper hand, and they killed the king's big son. The king sent a message for Conall, and he said to him—"Oh, Conall! what made your sons go to spring on my sons till my big son was killed by your children? but I see that though I follow you revengefully, I shall not be much better for it, and I will now set a thing before you, and if you do it, I will not follow you with revenge. If you and your sons will get me the brown horse of the king of Lochlann, you shall get the souls of your sons."

"Why," said Conall, "should not I do the pleasure of the king, though there should be no souls of my sons in dread at all. Hard is the matter you require of me, but I will lose my own life, and the life of my sons, or else I will do the pleasure of the king."

After these words Conall left the king, and he went home. When he got home he was under much trouble and perplexity. When he went to lie down he told his wife the thing the king had set before him. His wife took much sorrow that he was obliged to part from herself, while she knew not if she should see him more.

"Oh, Conall," said she, "why did not you let the king do his own pleasure to your sons, rather than be going now, while I know not if ever I shall see you more?"

When he rose on the morrow, he set himself and his three sons in order, and they took their journey towards Lochlann, and they made no stop but tore through ocean till they reached it. When they reached Lochlann they did not know what they should do. Said the old man to his sons, "Stop ye, and we will seek out the house of the king's miller."

When they went into the house of the king's miller, the man asked them to stop there for the night. Conall told the miller that his own children and the children of his king had fallen out, and that his children had killed the king's son, and there was nothing that would please the king but that he should get the brown horse of the king of Lochlann.

"If you will do me a kindness, and will put me in a way to get him, for certain I will pay you for it."

"The thing is silly that you are come to seek," said the miller, "for the king has laid his mind on him so greatly that you will not get him in any way unless you steal him; but if you can make out a way, I will keep it secret."

"This is what I am thinking," said Conall, "since you are working every day for the king, you and your gillies could put myself and my sons into five sacks of bran."

"The plan that has come into your head is not bad," said the miller.

The miller spoke to his gillies, and he said to them to do this, and they put them in five sacks. The kings' gillies came to seek the bran, and they took the five sacks with them, and they emptied them before the horses. The servants locked the door, and they went away.

When they rose to lay hand on the brown horse, said Conall, "You shall not do that. It is hard to get out of this; let us make for ourselves five hiding holes, so that if they hear us we may go and hide." They made the holes, then they laid hands on the horse. The horse was pretty well unbroken, and he set to making a terrible noise through the stable. The king heard the noise. "It must be my brown horse," he said to his gillies, "find out what is wrong with him."

The servants went out, and when Conall and his sons saw them coming they went into the hiding holes. The servants looked amongst the horses, and they did not find anything wrong; and they returned and they told this to the king, and the king said to them that if nothing was wrong they should go to their places of rest. When the gillies had time to be gone, Conall and his sons laid their hands again on the horse. If the noise was great that he made before, the noise he made now was seven times greater. The king sent a message for his gillies again, and said for certain there was something troubling the brown horse. "Go and look well about him." The servants went out, and they went to their hiding holes. The servants rummaged well, and did not find a thing. They returned and they told this.

"That is marvellous for me," said the king, "go you to lie down again, and if I notice it again I will go out myself."

When Conall and his sons perceived that the gillies were gone, they laid hands again on the horse, and one of them caught him, and if the noise that the horse made on the two former times was great, he made more this time.

"Be this from me," said the king, "it must be that someone is troubling my brown horse." He sounded the bell hastily, and when his waiting-man came to him, he said to him to let the stable gillies know that something was wrong with the horse. The gillies came, and the king went with them. When Conall and his sons perceived the company coming they went to the hiding holes.

The king was a wary man, and he saw where the horses were making a noise.

"Be wary," said the king, "there are men within the stable, let us get at them somehow."

The king followed the tracks of the men, and he found them. Everyone knew Conall, for he was a valued tenant of the king of Erin, and when the king brought them up out of the holes he said, "Oh, Conall, is it you that are here?"

"I am, Oh king, without question, and necessity made me come. I am under your pardon, and under your honour, and under your grace." He told how it happened to him, and that he had to get the brown horse for the king of Erin, or that his sons were to be put to death. "I knew that I should not get him by asking, and I was going to steal him."

"Yes, Conall, it is well enough, but come in," said the king. He desired his look-out men to set a watch on the sons of Conall, and to give them meat. And a double watch was set that night on the sons of Conall.

"Now, Oh, Conall," said the king, "were you ever in a harder place than to be seeing your lot of sons hanged tomorrow? But you set it to my goodness and to my grace, and say that it was necessity brought it on you, so I must not hang you. Tell me any case in which you were as hard as this, and if you tell that, you shall get the soul of your youngest son."

"I will tell a case as hard in which I was," said Conall. "I was once a young lad, and my father had much land, and he had parks of year-old cows, and one of them had just calved, and my father told me to bring her home. I found the cow, and took her with us. There fell a shower of snow. We went into the herd's bothy, and we took the cow and the calf in with us, and we were letting the shower pass from us. Who should come in but one cat and ten, and one great one-eyed fox-coloured cat as head bard over them. When they came in, in very deed I myself had no liking for their company. 'Strike up with you,' said the head bard, 'why should we be still? and sing a cronan to Conall Yellowclaw.' I was amazed that my name was known to the cats themselves. When they had sung the cronan, said the head bard, 'Now, Oh Conall, pay the reward of the cronan that the cats have sung to you.' 'Well then,' said I myself, 'I have no reward whatsoever for you, unless you should go down and take that calf.' No sooner said I the word than the two cats and ten went down to attack the calf, and in very deed, he did not last them long. 'Play up with you, why should you be silent? Make a cronan to Conall Yellowclaw,' said the head bard. Certainly I had no liking at all for the cronan, but up came the one cat and ten, and if they did not sing me a cronan then and there! 'Pay them now their reward,' said the great fox-coloured cat. 'I am tired myself of yourselves and your rewards,' said I. 'I have no reward for you unless you take that cow down there.'

They betook themselves to the cow, and indeed she did not last them long.

"Why will you be silent? Go up and sing a cronan to Conall Yellowclaw,' said the head bard. And surely, oh king, I had no care for them or for their cronan, for I began to see that they were not good comrades. When they had sung me the cronan they betook themselves down where the head bard was. 'Pay now their reward, said the head bard; and for sure, oh king, I had no reward for them; and I said to them, 'I have no reward for you.' And surely, oh king, there was caterwauling between them. So I leapt out at a turf window that was at the back of the house. I took myself off as hard as I might into the wood. I was swift enough and strong at that time; and when I felt the rustling toirm of the cats after me I climbed into as high a tree as I saw in the place, and one that was close in the top; and I hid myself as well as I might. The cats began to search for me through the wood, and they could not find me; and when they were tired, each one said to the other that they would turn back. 'But,' said the one-eyed fox-coloured cat that was commander-in-chief over them, 'you saw him not with your two eyes, and though I have but one eye, there's the rascal up in the tree.' When he had said that one of them went up in the tree, and as he was coming where I was, I drew a weapon that I had and I killed him. 'Be this from me!' said the one-eyed one—'I must not be losing my company thus; gather round the root of the tree and dig about it, and let down that villain to earth.' On this they gathered about the tree, and they dug about the root, and the first branching root that they cut, she gave a shiver to fall, and I myself gave a shout, and it was not to be wondered at.

"There was in the neighbourhood of the wood a priest, and he had ten men with him delving, and he said, 'There is a shout of a man in extremity and I must not be without replying to it.' And the wisest of the men said, 'Let it alone till we hear it again.' The cats began again digging wildly, and they broke the next root; and I myself gave the next shout, and in very deed it was not a weak one. 'Certainly,' said the priest, 'it is a man in extremity—let us move.' They set themselves in order for moving. And the cats arose on the tree, and they broke the third root, and the tree fell on her elbow. Then I gave the third shout. The stalwart men hastened, and when they saw how the cats served the tree, they began at them with the spades; and they themselves and the cats began at each other, till the cats ran away. And surely, oh king, I did not move till I saw the last one of them off. And then I came home. And there's the hardest case in which I ever was; and it seems to me that tearing by the cats were harder than hanging to-morrow by the king of Lochlann."

"Och! Conall," said the king, "you are full of words. You have freed the soul of your son with your tale; and if you tell me a harder case than that you will get your second youngest son, and then you will have two sons."

"Well then," said Conall, "on condition that you dost that, I will tell you how I was once in a harder case than to be in your power in prison to-night."

"Let's hear," said the king.

"I was then," said Conall, "quite a young lad, and I went out hunting, and my father's land was beside the sea, and it was rough with rocks, caves, and rifts. When I was going on the top of the shore, I saw as if there were a smoke coming up between two rocks, and I began to look what might be the meaning of the smoke coming up there. When I was looking, what should I do but fall; and the place was so full of heather, that neither bone nor skin was broken. I knew not how I should get out of this. I was not looking before me, but I kept looking overhead the way I came—and thinking that the day would never come that I could get up there. It was terrible for me to be there till I should die. I heard a great clattering coming, and what was there but a great giant and two dozen of goats with him, and a buck at their head. And when the giant had tied the goats, he came up and he said to me, 'Hao O! Conall, it's long since my knife has been rusting in my pouch waiting for your tender flesh.' 'Och!' said I, 'it's not much you will be bettered by me, though you should tear me asunder; I will make but one meal for you. But I see that you are one-eyed. I am a good leech, and I will give you the sight of the other eye.' The giant went and he drew the great caldron on the site of the fire. I myself was telling him how he should heat the water, so that I should give its sight to the other eye. I got heather and I made a rubber of it, and I set him upright in the caldron. I began at the eye that was well, pretending to him that I would give its sight to the other one, till I left them as bad as each other; and surely it was easier to spoil the one that was well than to give sight to the other.

"When he saw that he could not see a glimpse, and when I myself said to him that I would get out in spite of him, he gave a spring out of the water, and he stood in the mouth of the cave, and he said that he would have revenge for the sight of his eye. I had but to stay there crouched the length of the night, holding in my breath in such a way that he might not find out where I was.

"When he felt the birds calling in the morning, and knew that the day was, he said—'Art you sleeping? Awake and let out my lot of goats.' I killed the buck. He cried, 'I do believe that you are killing my buck.'

"I am not,' said I, 'but the ropes are so tight that I take long to loosen them.' I let out one of the goats, and there he was caressing her, and he said to her, 'There you are you shaggy, hairy white goat; and you see me, but I see you not.' I kept letting them out by the way of one and one, as I flayed the buck, and before the last one was out I had him flayed bag-wise. Then I went and I put my legs in place of his legs, and my hands in place of his forelegs, and my head in place of his head, and the horns on top of my head, so that the brute might think that it was the buck. I went out. When I was going out the giant laid his hand on me, and he said, 'There you are, you pretty buck; you see me, but I see you not.' When I myself got out, and I saw the world about me, surely, oh, king! joy was on me. When I was out and had shaken the skin off me, I said to the brute, 'I am out now in spite of you.'

"Aha!' said he, 'have you done this to me. Since you were so stalwart that you have got out, I will give you a ring that I have here; keep the ring, and it will do you good.'

"I will not take the ring from you,' said I, 'but throw it, and I will take it with me.' He threw the ring on the flat ground, I went myself and I lifted the ring, and I put it on my finger. When he said me then, 'Is the ring fitting you?' I said to him, 'It is.' Then he said, 'Where are you, ring?' And the ring said, 'I am here.' The brute went and went towards where the ring was speaking, and now I saw that I was in a harder case than ever I was. I drew a dirk. I cut the finger from off me, and I threw it from me as far as I could out on the loch, and there was a great depth in the place. He shouted, 'Where are you, ring?' And the ring said, 'I am here,' though it was on the bed of ocean. He gave a spring after the ring, and out he went in the sea. And I was as pleased then when I saw him drowning, as though you should grant my own life and the life of my two sons with me, and not lay any more trouble on me.

"When the giant was drowned I went in, and I took with me all he had of gold and silver, and I went home, and surely great joy was on my people when I arrived. And as a sign now look, the finger is off me."

"Yes, indeed, Conall, you are wordy and wise," said the king. "I see the finger is off you. You have freed your two sons, but tell me a case in which you ever were that is harder than to be looking on your son being hanged tomorrow, and you shall get the soul of your eldest son."

"Then went my father," said Conall, "and he got me a wife, and I was married. I went to hunt. I was going beside the sea, and I saw an island over in the midst of the loch, and I came there where a boat was with a rope before her, and a rope behind her, and many precious things within her. I looked myself on the boat to see how I might get part of them. I put in the one foot, and the other foot was on the ground, and when I raised my head what was it but the boat over in the middle of the loch, and she never stopped till she reached the island. When I went out of the boat the boat returned where she was before. I did not know now what I should do. The place was without meat or clothing, without the appearance of a house on it. I came out on the top of a hill. Then I came to a glen; I saw in it, at the bottom of a hollow, a woman with a child, and the child was naked on her knee, and she had a knife in her hand. She tried to put the knife to the throat of the babe, and the babe began to laugh in her face, and she began to cry, and she threw the knife behind her. I thought to myself that I was near my foe and far from my friends, and I called to the woman, 'What are you doing here?' And she said to me, 'What brought you here?' I told her myself word upon word how I came. 'Well then,' said she, 'it was so I came also.' She showed me to the place where I should come in where she was. I went in, and I said to her, 'What was the matter that you were putting the knife on the neck of the child?' 'It is that he must be cooked for the giant who is here, or else no more of my world will be before me.' Just then we could be hearing the footsteps of the giant, 'What shall I do? what shall I do?' cried the woman. I went to the caldron, and by luck it was not hot, so in it I got just as the brute came in. 'Hast you boiled that youngster for me?' he cried. 'He's not done yet,' said she, and I cried out from the caldron, 'Mammy, mammy, it's boiling I am.' Then the giant laughed out HAI, HAW, HOGARAICH, and heaped on wood under the caldron.

"And now I was sure I would scald before I could get out of that. As fortune favoured me, the brute slept beside the caldron. There I was scalded by the bottom of the caldron. When she perceived that he was asleep, she set her mouth quietly to the hole that was in the lid, and she said to me 'was I alive?' I said I was. I put up my head, and the hole in the lid was so large, that my head went through easily. Everything was coming easily with me till I began to bring up my hips. I left the skin of my hips behind me, but I came out. When I got out of the caldron I knew not what to do; and she said to me that there was no weapon that would kill him but his own weapon. I began to draw his spear and every breath that he drew I thought I would be down his throat, and when his breath came out I was back again just as far. But with every ill that befell me I got the spear loosed from him. Then I was as one under a bundle of straw in a great wind for I could not manage the spear. And it was fearful to look on the brute, who had but one eye in the midst of his face; and it was not agreeable for the like of me to attack him. I drew the dart as best I could, and I set it in his eye. When he felt this he gave his head a lift, and he struck the other end of the dart on the top of the cave, and it went through to the back of his head. And he fell cold dead where he was; and you may be sure, oh king, that joy was on me. I myself and the woman went out on clear ground, and we passed the night there. I went and got the boat with which I came, and she was no way lightened, and took the woman and the child over on dry land; and I returned home."

The king of Lochlann's mother was putting on a fire at this time, and listening to Conall telling the tale about the child.

"Is it you," said she, "that were there?"

"Well then," said he, "t'was I."

"Och! och!" said she, "t'was I that was there, and the king is the child whose life you saved; and it is to you that life thanks should be given." Then they took great joy.

The king said, "Oh, Conall, you came through great hardships. And now the brown horse is yours, and his sack full of the most precious things that are in my treasury."

They lay down that night, and if it was early that Conall rose, it was earlier than that that the queen was on foot making ready. He got the brown horse and his sack full of gold and silver and stones of great price, and then Conall and his three sons went away, and they returned home to the Erin realm of gladness. He left the gold and silver in his house, and he went with the horse to the king. They were good friends evermore. He returned home to his wife, and they set in order a feast; and that was a feast if ever there was one, oh son and brother.

Diarmid Bawn, The Piper

"Diarmid Bawn, the Piper" is a lively Irish folktale adapted from Fairy Legends and Traditions of the South of Ireland (1825–28) by Thomas Crofton Croker, one of the earliest collectors of Irish oral tradition in English. Set in County Cork, the tale follows Diarmid Bawn, a poor but gifted piper whose music has the power to charm listeners and unsettle the unseen world.

The story reflects Croker's recurring themes of music, enchantment, and the peril of crossing into the fairy realm. Like many Irish folk tales, it blends humour with warning: the piper's talent brings him honour among mortals but danger among spirits, reminding readers that the gift of art can draw one too close to the border between worlds.

One stormy night Patrick Burke was seated in the chimney corner smoking his pipe quite contentedly after his hard day's work; his two little boys were roasting potatoes in the ashes, while his rosy daughter held a splinter to her mother, who, seated on a siesteen, was mending a rent in Patrick's old coat; and Judy, the maid, was singing merrily to the sound of her wheel, that kept up a beautiful humming noise, just like the sweet drone of a bagpipe. Indeed they all seemed quite contented and happy; for the storm howled without, and they were warm and snug within, by the side of a blazing turf fire. "I was just thinking," said Patrick, taking the dudeen from his mouth and giving it a rap on his thumb-nail to shake out the ashes - "I was just thinking how thankful we ought to be to have a snug bit of a cabin this pelting night over our heads, for in all my born days I never heard the like of it."

"And that's no lie for you, Pat," said his wife, "but, whisht! what noise is that I hard?" and she dropped her work upon her knees, and looked fearfully towards the door. "The Virgin herself defend us all!" cried Judy, at the same time rapidly making a pious sign on her forehead, "if 'tis not the banshee!"

"Hold your tongue, you fool," said Patrick, "it's only the old gate swinging in the wind;" and he had scarcely spoken, when the door was assailed by a violent knocking. Molly began to mumble her prayers, and Judy proceeded to mutter over the muster-roll of saints; the youngsters scampered off to hide themselves behind the settle-bed; the storm howled louder and more fiercely than ever, and the rapping was renewed with redoubled violence.

"Whisht, whisht!" said Patrick - "what a noise ye're all making about nothing at all. Judy a-roon, can't you go and see who's at the door?" for, notwithstanding his assumed bravery, Pat Burke preferred that the maid should open the door.

"Why, then, is it me you're speaking to?" said Judy in the tone of astonishment, "and is it cracked mad you are, Mister Burke; or is it, may be, that you want me to be run away with, and made a horse of, like my grandfather was? - the sorrow a step will I stir to open the door, if you were as great a man again as you are, Pat Burke."

"Bother you, then! and hold your tongue, and I'll go myself." So saying, up got Patrick, and made the best of his way to the door. "Who's there?" said he, and his voice trembled mightily all the while. "In the name of Saint Patrick, who's there?"

"Tis I, Pat," answered a voice which he immediately knew to be the young squire's. In a moment the door was opened, and in walked a young man, with a gun in his hand, and a brace of dogs at his heels.

"Your honour's honour is quite welcome, entirely," said Patrick; who was a very civil sort of a fellow, especially to his betters. "Your honour's honour is quite welcome; and if ye'll be so condescending as to demean yourself by taking off your wet jacket, Molly can give you a brand-new blanket, and you can sit in front of the fire while the clothes are drying."

"Thank you, Pat," said the squire, as he wrapped himself, like Mr. Weld, in the proffered blanket.

"But what made you keep me so long at the door?"

"Why then, your honour, 'twas all along of Judy, there, being so much afraid of the good people; and a good right she has, after what happened to her grandfather - the Lord rest his soul!"

"And what was that, Pat?" said the squire.

"Why, then, your honour must know that Judy had a grandfather; and he was old Diarmid Bawn, the piper, as personable a looking man as any in the five parishes he was; and he could play the pipes so sweetly, and make them speak to such perfection, that it did one's heart good to hear him. We never had anyone, for that matter, in this side of the country like him, before or since, except James Gandsey, that is own piper to Lord Headley - his honour's lordship is the real good gentleman - and 'tis Mr. Gandsey's music that is the pride of Killarney lakes. Well, as I was saying, Diarmid was Judy's grandfather, and he rented a small mountain farm; and he was walking about the fields one moonlight night, quite melancholy-like in himself for want of the tobacco; because why, the river was flooded, and he could not get across to buy any, and Diarmid would rather go to bed without his supper than a whiff of the dudeen. Well, your honour, just as he came to the old fort in the far field, what should he see? - but a large army of the good people, clothed for all the world just like the dragoons! 'Are you all ready?' said a little fellow at their head dressed out like a general. 'No,' said a little curmudgeon of a chap all dressed in red, from the crown of his cocked hat to the sole of his boot. 'No, general,' said he, 'if you don't get the Fir Darrig a horse he must stay behind, and ye'll lose the battle."

"There's Diarmid Bawn,' said the general, pointing to Judy's grandfather, your honour, 'make a horse of him.'

"So with that master Fir Darrig comes up to Diarmid, who, you may be sure, was in a mighty great fright; but he determined, seeing there was no help for him, to put a bold face on the matter; and so he began to cross himself, and to say some blessed words, that nothing bad could stand before.

"Is that what you'd be after, you spalpeen?' said the little red imp, at the same time grinning a horrible grin, 'I'm not the man to care a straw for either your words or your crossings.' So, without more to do, he gives poor Diarmid a rap with the flat side of his sword, and in a moment he was changed into a horse, with little Fir Darrig stuck fast on his back.

"Away they all flew over the wide ocean, like so many wild geese, screaming and chattering all the time, till they came to Jamaica; and there they had a murdering fight with the good people of that country. Well, it was all very well with them, and they stuck to it manfully, and fought it out fairly, till one of the Jamaica men made a cut with his sword under Diarmid's left eye. And then, sir, you see, poor Diarmid lost his temper entirely, and he dashed into the very middle of them, with Fir Darrig mounted upon his back, and he threw out his heels, and whisked his tail about, and wheeled and turned round and round at such a rate, that he soon made a fair clearance of them, horse, foot, and dragoons. At last Diarmid's faction got the better, all through his means; and then they had such feasting and rejoicing, and gave Diarmid, who was the finest horse amongst them all, the best of everything.

"Let every man take a hand of tobacco for Diarmid Bawn,' said the general; and so they did; and away they flew, for 'twas getting near morning, to the old fort back again, and there they vanished like the mist from the mountain.

"When Diarmid looked about, the sun was rising, and he thought it was all a dream, till he saw a big rick of tobacco in the old fort, and felt the blood running from his left eye, for sure enough he was wounded in the battle, and would have been killed entirely, if it wasn't for a gospel composed by father Murphy that hung about his neck ever since he had the scarlet fever; and for certain, it was enough to have given him another scarlet fever to have had the little red man all night on his back, whip and spur for the bare life.

However, there was the tobacco heaped up in a great heap by his side; and he heard a voice, although he could see no one, telling him, 'That 'twas all his own, for his good behaviour in the battle; and that whenever Fir Darrig would want a horse again he'd know where to find a clever beast, as he never rode a better than Diarmid Bawn.' That's what he said, sir."

"Thank you, Pat," said the squire, "it certainly is a wonderful story, and I am not surprised at Judy's alarm. But now, as the storm is over, and the moon shining brightly, I'll make the best of my way home." So saying, he disrobed himself of the blanket, put on his coat, and whistling his dogs, set off across the mountain; while Patrick stood at the door, bawling after him, "May God and the blessed Virgin preserve your honour, and keep you from the good people; for 'twas of a moonlight night like this that Diarmid Bawn was made a horse of, for the Fir Darrig to ride."

Tales From The Land Of Saints & Scholars

Fair, Brown and Trembling

"Fair, Brown, and Trembling" is a traditional Irish fairy tale that first appeared in Celtic Fairy Tales (1892), collected and adapted by Joseph Jacobs from the oral tradition. The story is sometimes described as the Irish Cinderella, though it stands apart for its blend of Christian imagery, heroic courtship, and Celtic wonder.

Beneath its surface charm, the story reflects a uniquely Irish adaptation of the familiar Cinderella motif, rooted in local belief and landscape, and shaped by the rhythms of Irish oral storytelling.

King Hugh Curucha lived in Tir Conal, and he had three daughters, whose names were Fair, Brown, and Trembling. Fair and Brown had new dresses, and went to church every Sunday. Trembling was kept at home to do the cooking and work. They would not let her go out of the house at all; for she was more beautiful than the other two, and they were in dread she might marry before themselves.

They carried on in this way for seven years. At the end of seven years the son of the king of Emania fell in love with the eldest sister.

One Sunday morning, after the other two had gone to church, the old henwife came into the kitchen to Trembling, and said, "It's at church you ought to be this day, instead of working here at home."

"How could I go?" said Trembling. "I have no clothes good enough to wear at church; and if my sisters were to see me there, they'd kill me for going out of the house."

"I'll give you," said the henwife, "a finer dress than either of them has ever seen. And now tell me what dress you will have?"

"I'll have," said Trembling, "a dress as white as snow, and green shoes for my feet."

Then the henwife put on the cloak of darkness, clipped a piece from the old clothes the young woman had on, and asked for the whitest robes in the world and the most beautiful that could be found, and a pair of green shoes.

That moment she had the robe and the shoes, and she brought them to Trembling, who put them on. When Trembling was dressed and ready, the henwife said, "I have a honey-bird here to sit on your right shoulder, and a honey-finger to put on your left. At the door stands a milk-white mare, with a golden saddle for you to sit on, and a golden bridle to hold in your hand."

Trembling sat on the golden saddle; and when she was ready to start, the henwife said, "You must not go inside the door of the church, and the minute the people rise up at the end of Mass, do you make off, and ride home as fast as the mare will carry you."

When Trembling came to the door of the church there was no one inside who could get a glimpse of her but was striving to know who she was; and when they saw her hurrying away at the end of Mass, they ran out to overtake her. But no use in their running; she was away before any man could come near her. From the minute she left the church till she got home, she overtook the wind before her, and outstripped the wind behind.

She came down at the door, went in, and found the henwife had dinner ready. She put off the white robes, and had on her old dress in a twinkling.

When the two sisters came home the henwife asked, "Have you any news to-day from the church?"

"We have great news," said they. "We saw a wonderful grand lady at the church-door. The like of the robes she had we have never seen on woman before. It's little that was thought of our dresses beside what she had on; and there wasn't a man at the church, from the king to the beggar, but was trying to look at her and know who she was."

The sisters would give no peace till they had two dresses like the robes of the strange lady; but honey-birds and honey-fingers were not to be found.

Next Sunday the two sisters went to church again, and left the youngest at home to cook the dinner.

After they had gone, the henwife came in and asked, "Will you go to church to-day?"

"I would go," said Trembling, "if I could get the going."

"What robe will you wear?" asked the henwife.

"The finest black satin that can be found, and red shoes for my feet."

"What colour do you want the mare to be?"

"I want her to be so black and so glossy that I can see myself in her body."

The henwife put on the cloak of darkness, and asked for the robes and the mare. That moment she had them. When Trembling was dressed, the henwife put the honey-bird on her right shoulder and the honey-finger on her left. The saddle on the mare was silver, and so was the bridle.

When Trembling sat in the saddle and was going away, the henwife ordered her strictly not to go inside the door of the church, but to rush away as soon as the people rose at the end of Mass, and hurry home on the mare before any man could stop her.

That Sunday, the people were more astonished than ever, and gazed at her more than the first time; and all they were thinking of was to know who she was. But they had no chance; for the moment the people rose at the end of Mass she slipped from the church, was in the silver saddle, and home before a man could stop her or talk to her.

The henwife had the dinner ready. Trembling took off her satin robe, and had on her old clothes before her sisters got home.

"What news have you to-day?" asked the henwife of the sisters when they came from the church.

"Oh, we saw the grand strange lady again! And it's little that any man could think of our dresses after looking at the robes of satin that she had on! And all at church, from high to low, had their mouths open, gazing at her, and no man was looking at us."

The two sisters gave neither rest nor peace till they got dresses as nearly like the strange lady's robes as they could find. Of course they were not so good; for the like of those robes could not be found in Erin.

When the third Sunday came, Fair and Brown went to church dressed in black satin. They left Trembling at home to work in the kitchen, and told her to be sure and have dinner ready when they came back.

After they had gone and were out of sight, the henwife came to the kitchen and said, "Well, my dear, are you for church to-day?"

"I would go if I had a new dress to wear."

"I'll get you any dress you ask for. What dress would you like?" asked the henwife.

"A dress red as a rose from the waist down, and white as snow from the waist up; a cape of green on my shoulders; and a hat on my head with a red, a white, and a green feather in it; and shoes for my feet with the toes red, the middle white, and the backs and heels green."

The henwife put on the cloak of darkness, wished for all these things, and had them. When Trembling was dressed, the henwife put the honey-bird on her right shoulder and the honey-finger on her left, and, placing the hat on her head, clipped a few hairs from one lock and a few from another with her scissors, and that moment the most beautiful golden hair was flowing down over the girl's shoulders. Then the henwife asked what kind of a mare she would ride. She said white, with blue and gold-coloured diamond-shaped spots all over her body, on her back a saddle of gold, and on her head a golden bridle.

The mare stood there before the door, and a bird sitting between her ears, which began to sing as soon as Trembling was in the saddle, and never stopped till she came home from the church.

The fame of the beautiful, strange lady had gone out through the world, and all the princes and great men that were in it came to church that Sunday, each one hoping that it was himself would have her home with him after Mass.

The son of the king of Emania forgot all about the eldest sister, and remained outside the church, so as to catch the strange lady before she could hurry away.

The church was more crowded than ever before, and there were three times as many outside. There was such a throng before the church that Trembling could only come inside the gate.

As soon as the people were rising at the end of Mass, the lady slipped out through the gate, was in the golden saddle in an instant, and sweeping away ahead of the wind. But if she was, the prince of Emania was at her side, and, seizing her by the foot, he ran with the mare for thirty perches, and never let go of the beautiful lady till the shoe was pulled from her foot, and he was left behind with it in his hand. She came home as fast as the mare could carry her, and was thinking all the time that the henwife would kill her for losing the shoe.

Seeing her so vexed and so changed in the face, the old woman asked, "What's the trouble that's on you now?" "Oh! I've lost one of the shoes off my feet," said Trembling.

"Don't mind that; don't be vexed," said the henwife, "maybe it's the best thing that ever happened to you."

Then Trembling gave up all the things she had to the henwife, put on her old clothes, and went to work in the kitchen. When the sisters came home, the henwife asked, "Have you any news from the church?"

"We have indeed," said they, "for we saw the grandest sight to-day. The strange lady came again, in grander array than before. On herself and the horse she rode were the finest colours of the world, and between the ears of the horse was a bird which never stopped singing from the time she came till she went away. The lady herself is the most beautiful woman ever seen by man in Erin."

After Trembling had disappeared from the church, the son of the king of Emania said to the other kings' sons, "I will have that lady for my own."

They all said, "You didn't win her just by taking the shoe off her foot; you'll have to win her by the point of the sword; you'll have to fight for her with us before you can call her your own."

"Well," said the son of the king of Emania, "when I find the lady that shoe will fit, I'll fight for her, never fear, before I leave her to any of you."

Then all the king's sons were uneasy, and anxious to know who was she that lost the shoe; and they began to travel all over Erin to know could they find her. The prince of Emania and all the others went in a great company together, and made the round of Erin; they went everywhere, north, south, east, and west. They visited every place where a woman was to be found, and left not a house in the kingdom they did not search, to know could they find the woman the shoe would fit, not caring whether she was rich or poor, of high or low degree.

The prince of Emania always kept the shoe; and when the young women saw it, they had great hopes, for it was of proper size, neither large nor small, and it would beat any man to know of what material it was made. One thought it would fit her if she cut a little from her great toe; and another, with too short a foot, put something in the tip of her stocking. But no use; they only spoiled their feet, and were curing them for months afterwards.

The two sisters, Fair and Brown, heard that the princes of the world were looking all over Erin for the woman that could wear the shoe, and every day they were talking of trying it on; and one day Trembling spoke up and said, "Maybe it's my foot that the shoe will fit."

"Oh, the breaking of the dog's foot on you! Why say so when you were at home every Sunday?"

They were that way waiting, and scolding the younger sister, till the princes were near the place. The day they were to come, the sisters put Trembling in a closet, and locked the door on her. When the company came to the house, the prince of Emania gave the shoe to the sisters. But though they tried and tried, it would fit neither of them.

"Is there any other young woman in the house?" asked the prince.

"There is," said Trembling, speaking up in the closet, "I'm here."

"Oh! we have her for nothing but to put out the ashes," said the sisters.

But the prince and the others wouldn't leave the house till they had seen her; so the two sisters had to open the door. When Trembling came out, the shoe was given to her, and it fitted exactly.

The prince of Emania looked at her and said, "You are the woman the shoe fits, and you are the woman I took the shoe from."

Then Trembling spoke up, and said, "Do you stay here till I return."

Then she went to the henwife's house. The old woman put on the cloak of darkness, got everything for her she had the first Sunday at church, and put her on the white mare in the same fashion. Then Trembling rode along the highway to the front of the house. All who saw her the first time said, "This is the lady we saw at church."

Then she went away a second time, and a second time came back on the black mare in the second dress which the henwife gave her. All who saw her the second Sunday said, "That is the lady we saw at church."

A third time she asked for a short absence, and soon came back on the third mare and in the third dress. All who saw her the third time said, "That is the lady we saw at church." Every man was satisfied, and knew that she was the woman.

Then all the princes and great men spoke up, and said to the son of the king of Emania, "You'll have to fight now for her before we let her go with you."

"I'm here before you, ready for combat," answered the prince.

Then the son of the king of Lochlin stepped forth. The struggle began, and a terrible struggle it was. They fought for nine hours; and then the son of the king of Lochlin stopped, gave up his claim, and left the field. Next day the son of the king of Spain fought six hours, and yielded his claim. On the third day the son of the king of Nyerfói fought eight hours, and stopped. The fourth day the son of the king of Greece fought six hours, and stopped. On the fifth day no more strange princes wanted to fight; and all the sons of kings in Erin said they would not fight with a man of their own land, that the strangers had had their chance, and, as no others came to claim the woman, she belonged of right to the son of the king of Emania.

The marriage-day was fixed, and the invitations were sent out. The wedding lasted for a year and a day. When the wedding was over, the king's son brought home the bride, and when the time came a son was born. The young woman sent for her eldest sister, Fair, to be with her and care for her. One day, when Trembling was well, and when her husband was away hunting, the two sisters went out to walk; and when they came to the seaside, the eldest pushed the youngest sister in. A great whale came and swallowed her.

The eldest sister came home alone, and the husband asked, "Where is your sister?"

"She has gone home to her father in Ballyshannon; now that I am well, I don't need her."

"Well," said the husband, looking at her, "I'm in dread it's my wife that has gone."

"Oh! no," said she, "it's my sister Fair that's gone."

Since the sisters were very much alike, the prince was in doubt. That night he put his sword between them, and said, "If you are my wife, this sword will get warm; if not, it will stay cold."

In the morning when he rose up, the sword was as cold as when he put it there.

It happened, when the two sisters were walking by the seashore, that a little cowboy was down by the water minding cattle, and saw Fair push Trembling into the sea; and next day, when the tide came in, he saw the whale swim up and throw her out on the sand. When she was on the sand she said to the cowboy, "When you go home in the evening with the cows, tell the master that my sister Fair pushed me into the sea yesterday; that a whale swallowed me, and then threw me out, but will come again and swallow me with the coming of the next tide; then he'll go out with the tide, and come again with tomorrow's tide, and throw me again on the strand. The whale will cast me out three times. I'm under the enchantment of this whale, and cannot leave the beach or escape myself. Unless my husband saves me before I'm swallowed the fourth time, I shall be lost. He must come and shoot the whale with a silver bullet when he turns on the broad of his back. Under the breast-fin of the whale is a reddish-brown spot. My husband must hit him in that spot, for it is the only place in which he can be killed."

When the cowboy got home, the eldest sister gave him a draught of oblivion, and he did not tell.

Next day he went again to the sea. The whale came and cast Trembling on shore again. She asked the boy "Did you tell the master what I told you to tell him?"

"I did not," said he, "I forgot."

"How did you forget?" asked she.

"The woman of the house gave me a drink that made me forget."

"Well, don't forget telling him this night; and if she gives you a drink, don't take it from her."

As soon as the cowboy came home, the eldest sister offered him a drink. He refused to take it till he had delivered his message and told all to the master. The third day the prince went down with his gun and a silver bullet in it. He was not long down when the whale came and threw Trembling upon the beach as the two days before. She had no power to speak to her husband till he had killed the whale. Then the whale went out, turned over once on the broad of his back, and showed the spot for a moment only. That moment the prince fired. He had but the one chance, and a short one at that; but he took it, and hit the spot, and the whale, mad with pain, made the sea all around red with blood, and died.

That minute Trembling was able to speak, and went home with her husband, who sent word to her father what the eldest sister had done. The father came, and told him any death he chose to give her to give it. The prince told the father he would leave her life and death with himself. The father had her put out then on the sea in a barrel, with provisions in it for seven years.

In time Trembling had a second child, a daughter. The prince and she sent the cowboy to school, and trained him up as one of their own children, and said, "If the little girl that is born to us now lives, no other man in the world will get her but him."

The cowboy and the prince's daughter lived on till they were married. The mother said to her husband "You could not have saved me from the whale but for the little cowboy; on that account I don't grudge him my daughter."

The son of the king of Emania and Trembling had fourteen children, and they lived happily till the two died of old age.

Far Darrig in Donegal

"Far Darrig in Donegal" is a darkly comic Irish folktale, originally written by William Carleton and later adapted by W. B. Yeats in Fairy and Folk Tales of the Irish Peasantry *(1888). The story takes place in rural Donegal and centres on the Far Darrig, one of Ireland's mischievous "red men" of fairy lore, known for his fondness for cruel pranks and his unsettling laughter.*

Carleton's version, written in his vivid peasant idiom, captures the uneasy boundary between laughter and fear that runs through Irish supernatural lore. The Far Darrig, unlike the noble Sidhe or the tragic banshee, represents the low, mocking spirit of the fairy world, part jester, part tormentor.

Pat Diver, the tinker, was a man well-accustomed to a wandering life, and to strange shelters; he had shared the beggar's blanket in smoky cabins; he had crouched beside the still in many a nook and corner where poteen was made on the wild Innishowen mountains; he had even slept on the bare heather, or on the ditch, with no roof over him but the vault of heaven; yet were all his nights of adventure tame and commonplace when compared with one especial night.

During the day preceding that night, he had mended all the kettles and saucepans in Moville and Greencastle, and was on his way to Culdaff, when night overtook him on a lonely mountain road.

He knocked at one door after another asking for a night's lodging, while he jingled the halfpence in his pocket, but was everywhere refused.

Where was the boasted hospitality of Innishowen, which he had never before known to fail? It was of no use to be able to pay when the people seemed so churlish. Thus thinking, he made his way towards a light a little further on, and knocked at another cabin door.

An old man and woman were seated one at each side of the fire.

"Will you be pleased to give me a night's lodging, sir?" asked Pat respectfully.

"Can you tell a story?" returned the old man.

"No, then, sir, I canna say I'm good at storytelling," replied the puzzled tinker.

"Then you maun just gang further, for none but them that can tell a story will get in here."

This reply was made in so decided a tone that Pat did not attempt to repeat his appeal, but turned away reluctantly to resume his weary journey.

"A story, indeed," muttered he. "Auld wives fables to please the weans!"

As he took up his bundle of tinkering implements, he observed a barn standing rather behind the dwelling-house, and aided by the rising moon, he made his way towards it.

It was a clean, roomy barn, with a piled-up heap of straw in one corner. Here was a shelter not to be despised; so Pat crept under the straw, and was soon asleep.

He could not have slept very long when he was awakened by the tramp of feet, and, peeping cautiously through a crevice in his straw covering, he saw four immensely tall men enter the barn, dragging a body, which they threw roughly upon the floor.

They next lighted a fire in the middle of the barn, and fastened the corpse by the feet with a great rope to a beam in the roof. One of them then began to turn it slowly before the fire. "Come on," said he, addressing a gigantic fellow, the tallest of the four—"I'm tired; you take your turn now."

"Faix an' troth, I'll no turn him," replied the big man. "There's Pat Diver in under the straw, why wouldn't he take his turn?"

With hideous clamour the four men called the wretched Pat, who, seeing there was no escape, thought it was his wisest plan to come forth as he was bidden.

"Now, Pat," said they, "you'll turn the corpse, but if you let him burn you'll be tied up there and roasted in his place."

Pat's hair stood on end, and the cold perspiration poured from his forehead, but there was nothing for it but to perform his dreadful task.

Seeing him fairly embarked in it, the tall men went away.

Soon, however, the flames rose so high as to singe the rope, and the corpse fell with a great thud upon the fire, scattering the ashes and embers, and extracting a howl of anguish from the miserable cook, who rushed to the door, and ran for his life.

He ran on until he was ready to drop with fatigue, when, seeing a drain overgrown with tall, rank grass, he thought he would creep in there and lie hidden till morning.

But he was not many minutes in the drain before he heard the heavy tramping again, and the four men came up with their burthen, which they laid down on the edge of the drain.

"I'm tired," said one, to the giant, "it's your turn to carry him a piece now."

"Faix and troth, I'll no carry him," replied he, "but there's Pat Diver in the drain, why wouldn't he come out and take his turn?"

"Come out, Pat, come out," roared all the men, and Pat, almost dead with fright, crept out.

He staggered on under the weight of the corpse until he reached Kiltown Abbey, a ruin festooned with ivy, where the brown owl hooted all night long, and the forgotten dead slept around the walls under dense, matted tangles of brambles and ben-weed.

No one ever buried there now, but Pat's tall companions turned into the wild graveyard, and began digging a grave.

Pat, seeing them thus engaged, thought he might once more try to escape, and climbed up into a hawthorn tree in the fence, hoping to be hidden in the boughs.

"I'm tired," said the man who was digging the grave, "here, take the spade," addressing the big man, "it's your turn."

"Faix an' troth, it's not my turn," replied he, as before. "There's Pat Diver in the tree, why wouldn't he come down and take his turn?"

Pat came down to take the spade, but just then the cocks in the little farmyards and cabins round the abbey began to crow, and the men looked at one another.

"We must go," said they, "and well is it for you, Pat Diver, that the cocks crowed, for if they had not, you'd just ha' been bundled into that grave with the corpse."

Two months passed, and Pat had wandered far and wide over the county Donegal, when he chanced to arrive at Raphoe during a fair.

Among the crowd that filled the Diamond he came suddenly on the big man.

"How are you, Pat Diver?" said he, bending down to look into the tinker's face.

"You've the advantage of me, sir, for I haven't' the pleasure of knowing you," faltered Pat.

"Do you not know me, Pat?" Whisper -"When you go back to Innishowen, you'll have a story to tell!"

Tales From The Land Of Saints & Scholars

Fior Usga

The tale "Fior Usga" (literally "True Water") comes from Fairy Legends and Traditions of the South of Ireland (1825–28) by Thomas Crofton Croker, one of the earliest systematic collectors of Irish folklore. Set in the misty south-west of Ireland, it tells of a magical spring or well whose waters have miraculous properties.

In Croker's retelling, the story blends Christian and pre-Christian imagery, reflecting the transitional folklore of nineteenth-century Ireland. The enchanted well may echo the ancient reverence for holy springs, later absorbed into the cult of saints and pilgrimage. Yet the tone of the tale is earthy and comic rather than solemn, grounded in the language and humour of Irish peasant life.

A little way beyond the Gallows Green of Cork, and just outside the town, there is a great lough of water, where people in the winter go and skate for the sake of diversion; but the sport above the water is nothing to what is under it, for at the very bottom of this lough there are buildings and gardens, far more beautiful than any now to be seen, and how they came there was in this manner.

Long before Saxon foot pressed Irish ground, there was a great king called Core, whose palace stood where the lough now is, in a round green valley, that was just a mile about. In the middle of the courtyard was a spring of fair water, so pure, and so clear, that it was the wonder of all the world. Much did the king rejoice at having so great a curiosity within his palace; but as people came in crowds from far and near to draw the precious water of this spring, he was sorely afraid that in time it might become dry; so he caused a high wall to be built up round it, and would allow nobody to have the water, which was a very great loss to the poor people living about the palace. Whenever he wanted any for himself, he would send his daughter to get it, not liking to trust his servants with the key of the well-door, fearing that they might give some away.

One night the king gave a grand entertainment, and there were many great princes present, and lords and nobles without end; and there were wonderful doings throughout the palace. There were bonfires, whose blaze reached up to the very sky; and dancing was there, to such sweet music, that it ought to have waked up the dead out of their graves; and feasting was there in the greatest of plenty for all who came; nor was anyone turned away from the palace gates—but "you're welcome—you're welcome, heartily," was the porter's salute for all.

Now it happened at this grand entertainment there was one young prince above all the rest mighty comely to behold, and as tall and as straight as ever eye would wish to look on. Right merrily did he dance that night with the old king's daughter, wheeling here, and wheeling there, as light as a feather, and footing it away to the admiration of everyone. The musicians played the better for seeing their dancing; and they danced as if their lives depended upon it. After all this dancing came the supper; and the young prince was seated at table by the side of his beautiful partner, who smiled upon him as often as he spoke to her; and that was by no means so often as he wished, for he had constantly to turn to the company and thank them for the many compliments passed upon his fair partner and himself.

In the midst of this banquet, one of the great lords said to King Core, "May it please your majesty, here is everything in abundance that heart can wish for, both to eat and drink, except water."

"Water!" said the king, mightily pleased at someone calling for that of which purposely there was a want, "water shall you have, my lord, speedily, and that of such a delicious kind, that I challenge all the world to equal it. Daughter," said he, "go fetch some in the golden vessel which I caused to be made for the purpose."

The king's daughter, who was called Fior Usga, (which signifies, in English, Spring Water,) did not much like to be told to perform so menial a service before so many people, and though she did not venture to refuse the commands of her father, yet hesitated to obey him, and looked down upon the ground. The king, who loved his daughter very much, seeing this, was sorry for what he had desired her to do, but having said the word, he was never known to recall it; he therefore thought of a way to make his daughter go speedily and fetch the water, and it was by proposing that the young prince her partner should go along with her. Accordingly, with a loud voice, he said, "Daughter, I wonder not at your fearing to go alone so late at night; but I doubt not the young prince at your side will go with you." The prince was not displeased at hearing this; and taking the golden vessel in one hand, with the other led the king's daughter out of the hall so gracefully that all present gazed after them with delight.

When they came to the spring of water, in the courtyard of the palace, the fair Usga unlocked the door with the greatest care, and stooping down with the golden vessel to take some of the water out of the well, found the vessel so heavy that she lost her balance and fell in. The young prince tried in vain to save her, for the water rose and rose so fast, that the entire court-yard was speedily covered with it, and he hastened back almost in a state of distraction to the king.

The door of the well-being left open, the water, which had been so long confined, rejoiced at obtaining its liberty, rushed forth incessantly, every moment rising higher and higher, and was in the hall of the entertainment sooner than the young prince himself, so that when he attempted to speak to the king he was up to his neck in water. At length the water rose to such a height, that it filled the entire of the green valley in which the king's palace stood, and so the present lough of Cork was formed.

Yet the king and his guests were not drowned, as would now happen, if such an awful inundation were to take place; neither was his daughter, the fair Usga, who returned to the banquet-hall the very next night after this dreadful event; and every night since the same entertainment and dancing goes on in the palace at the bottom of the lough, and will last until someone has the luck to bring up out of it the golden vessel which was the cause of all this mischief.

Nobody can doubt that it was a judgment upon the king for his shutting up the well in the courtyard from the poor people, and if there are any who do not credit my story, they may go and see the lough of Cork, for there it is to be seen to this day; the road to Kinsale passes at one side of it; and when its waters are low and clear, the tops of towers and stately buildings may be plainly viewed in the bottom by those who have good eyesight, without the help of spectacles.

Tales From The Land Of Saints & Scholars

Hookedy-Crookedy

"Hookedy-Crookedy" is a lively Donegal folktale drawn from Donegal Fairy Stories by Seumas MacManus, first published in the early twentieth century. Like much of MacManus's work, it preserves the tone and rhythm of Irish oral storytelling, with its musical phrasing, humour, and sense of place.

The story belongs to the long Irish tradition of tales about the little people, spirits who exist on the margins of human life, guarding their own wealth and secrets. Hookedy-Crookedy, though comic and small, embodies the trickster's justice: he punishes arrogance and rewards wit.

Once on a time there was a King and Queen in Ireland, and they had one son named Jack, and when Jack grew up to be a big man, he rose up one day and said to his father and mother that he would go off and push his fortune.

All his father and mother could say to Jack, they could not keep him from going. So with his staff in his hand and his father's and mother's blessing on his head, off he started, and he travelled away far, farther than I could tell you, and twice as far as you could tell me. At length one day, coming up to a big wood, he met a grey-haired old man. The old man asked him, "Jack, where are you going?"

He says, "I am going to push my fortune."

"Well," says the old man, says he, "if 'tis looking for service you are, there is a Giant who lives at the other side of that wood that they call the Giant of the Hundred Hills, and I believe he wants a fine, strong, able, clever young fellow like you."

"Very well," says Jack, "I will push on to him."

Push on Jack did, away through the wood, until he got to the other side, and then he saw a big castle, and going up he knocked at the door, and a big Giant came out.

"Welcome, Jack," says he, "the King of Ireland's Son! Where are you going and what do you want?"

"I come," says Jack, "to push my fortune, and am looking for honest service. I have been told," he says to the Giant of the Hundred Hills, "that you wanted a clean, clever boy like me."

"Well," says the Giant, "I am the Giant of the Hundred Hills, and do want such a fine fellow as you. I have to go away every day," he says, "to battle with another giant at the other end of the world, and when I am away, I want somebody to look after my house and place. If you will be of good, faithful service to me, and do everything I tell you, I will give you a bag of gold at the end of the time."

Jack promised he would do all that. The Giant then gave him a hearty supper and a good bed, and well he slept that night. In the morning the Giant had him called up before the first lark was in the sky.

"Jack, my brave boy," says he, "I have got to be off to the other end of the world to-day to fight the Giant of the Four Winds, and it is time you were up and looking after your business. You have got to put this house in order, and look after everything in it until I come back tonight. To every room in the house and to every place about the house you can go, except the stable. My stable door is closed, and on the peril of your life, don't open it or go into the stable. Keep that in mind."

Jack he said certainly would. Then the Giant visited the stable, and started off; and as soon as he was gone, Jack went fixing and arranging the house and setting everything in order. And a wonderful house it was to Jack, so big and so great; and after that he went to the castle yard and into every house and building there, except the stable, and when he had visited all the rest of them, he stood before the stable and looked at it a long time. "And I wonder," says Jack, says he, "I wonder what can be in there, and what is the reason he wants me on the peril of my life not to go into it? I would like to go and peep in, and there certainly would be no harm."

Every door in and about the Giant's place was opened by a little ring turning on a pivot in the middle of the door. Forward to the stable door Jack then steps, turns the little ring, and the door flew open. Inside what does Jack see but a mare and a bear standing by the manger, and neither of them eating. There was hay before the bear and meat before the mare.

"Well," says Jack, "it is no wonder, poor creatures, you are not eating. That was a nice blunder of the Giant," and he stepped in and changed their food, putting hay before the mare and meat before the bear, and at once both of them fell to it and Jack went out and closed the stable door. As he did so his finger stuck in the ring, and he pulled and struggled to get it away, but he could not.

That was a fix for poor Jack, "And by this and by that," says he, "the Giant will be back and find me stuck here;" so he whips out his knife, and cuts off his finger, and leaves it there.

And when the Giant came home that night, says he to Jack, "Well, Jack, what sort of a day have you had this day, and how did you get along?

"I had a fine day," says Jack, "and got along very well indeed."

"Jack," says he, "show me your two hands;" and when Jack held out his two hands, the Giant saw one of his fingers gone. He got black in the face with rage when he saw this, and he said, "Jack, did I not warn you on the peril of your life not to go into that stable?"

Poor Jack pleaded all he could, and he said did not mean to, but curiosity got the best of him, and he thought he would open the door and peep in.

Says the Giant, "No man before ever opened that stable door and lived to tell it, and you, too, would be a dead man this minute only for one thing. Your father's father did my father a great service once. I am the man who never forgets a good thing, and for that service," says he, "I give you your life and pardon this time; but if you ever do the like again, you won't live."

Jack, he promised that surely and surely he would never do the like again. His supper he got that night, and to bed. And at early morning again the Giant had him up, and "Jack," says he, "I must be off to the other end of the world again and fight the Giant of the Four Winds. You know your duty is -- look after this house and place and set everything in order about it, and go everywhere you like, only don't open the stable door or go into the stable, on the peril of your life."

"I will mind all that," says Jack.

Then that morning again the Giant visited the stable before he went away. And after the Giant had gone, to his work went Jack, wandering through the house, cleaning and setting everything in order about it, and out into the yard he went, and fixed and arranged everything out there, except the stable. He stood before the stable door a good while this day, and says he to himself, "I wonder how the bear and the mare are doing, and what the Giant did when he went in to see them? I would give a great deal to know," says he. "I will take a peep in."

Into the ring of the door he put his finger, and turned it, and looked in, and there he saw the mare and the bear standing as on the day before and neither of them eating. In Jack steps. "And no wonder, poor creatures," says he. "You don't eat, when that is the way the Giant blundered," he says, after he saw the meat before the mare and the hay before the bear this time also.

Jack then changed the food, putting the hay before the mare and the meat before the bear as it should be, and very soon both the mare and the bear were eating heartily; and then Jack went out. He closed the door, and when he did so, his finger stuck in the ring; and pull and struggle though Jack did, he could not get it out.

"Och, och, och," says Jack, says he, "I am a dead man to-day surely."

He whips out his knife, and cuts off his finger, and leaves it there, and 'twas there when the Giant came home that night.

"Well, Jack, my fine boy," says he, "how have you got on to-day?"

"Oh, finely, finely," says Jack, says he, holding his hands behind his back all the same.

"Show me your hands, Jack," says the Giant, "till I see if you wash them and keep them clean always." And when Jack showed his hands, the Giant got black in the face with rage, and says he. "Didn't I forgive you your life yesterday for going into that stable, and you promised never to do it again, and here I find you out, once more?"

The Giant ranted and raged for a long time, and then says he, "Because your father's father did my father such a good turn, I suppose I will have to spare your life this second time; but, Jack," says he, "if you should live for a hundred years, and spend them all in my service, and it you should then again open that door and put your foot into my stable, that day," says he, you will be a dead man as sure as there is a head on you. Mind that!"

Jack, he thanked the Giant very much for sparing his life, and promised that he never, never would again disobey him.

The next morning the Giant had Jack up early, and told him he was going off this day to fight the Giant at the other end of the world, and gave Jack his directions, and warned him just as on the other days. Then he went into the stable before he went away. And when he was gone, Jack went through all the house, and through the whole yard, setting everything in order, and when everything was done, he stood before the stable door.

"I wonder," says Jack, "how the poor mare and the poor bear are getting along and what the Giant of the Hundred Hills was doing here to-day? I should very much like," says he, "to take one wee, wee peep in," and he opened the door.

Jack peeped in, and there the mare and the bear stood looking at each other again, and neither of them taking a morsel. And there was the meat before the mare and the hay before the bear, just as on the other days.

"Poor creatures," says Jack, "it is no wonder you are not eating, and hungry and hungry you must be." And forward he steps, and changes the food, putting it as it should be, the hay before the mare and the meat before the bear, and to it both of them fell.

And when he had done this, up speaks the mare, and "Poor Jack," says she, "I am sorry for you. This night you will be killed surely; and sorry for us, too, I am, for we will be killed as well as you."

"Oh, Oh, Oh!" says Jack, says he, "that is terrible. Is there nothing we can do?"

"Only one thing," says the mare.

"What is that?" says Jack.

"It's this," says the mare, "put that saddle and bridle on me, and let us start off and be away, far, far from this country, when the Giant comes back." And soon Jack had the saddle and bridle on the mare, and on her back he got to start off.

"Oh!" says the bear, speaking up, "both of you are going away to leave me in for all the trouble."

"No," says the mare, "we will not do that. Jack," says she, "take the chains and tie me to the bear."

Jack tied the mare to the bear with chains that were hanging by, and then the three of them, the mare and the bear and Jack, started, and on and on they went, as fast as they could gallop.

After a long time, says the mare, "Jack, look behind you, and see what you can see."

Jack looked behind him, and "Oh!" says he, "I see the Giant of the Hundred Hills coming like a raging storm. Very soon he will be on us, and we will all three be murdered."

Says the mare, says she, "We have a chance yet. Look in my left ear, and see what you can see;" and in her left ear Jack looked, and saw a little chestnut.

"Throw it over your left shoulder," says the mare.

Jack threw it over his left shoulder, and that minute there arose behind them a chestnut wood ten miles wide. On and on they went that day and that night; and till middle of the next day, "Jack," says the mare, "look behind you, and see what you can see."

Jack looked behind him, and "Oh!" says he, "I see the Giant of the Hundred Hills coming tearing after us like a harvest hurricane."

"Do you see anything strange about him, Jack?" says the mare.

"Yes," says Jack, says he, "there are as many bushes on the top of his head, and as much fowl stuck about his feet and legs as will keep him in fire-wood and flesh for years to come. We are done for this time, entirely," says poor Jack.

"Not yet," says the mare, "there is another chance. Look into my right ear, and see what you can see."

In the mare's right ear Jack looked, and found a drop of water.

"Throw it over your left shoulder, Jack," says the mare, "and see what will happen."

Over his left shoulder Jack threw it, and all at once a lough sprung up between them and the Giant that was one hundred miles wide every way and one hundred miles deep.

"Now," says the mare, "he cannot reach us until he drinks his way through the lough, and very likely he will drink until he bursts, and then we shall be rid of him altogether."

Jack thanked God, and on he went. It was not long now until he reached the borders of Scotland, and there he saw a great wood.

"Now," says the mare and the bear, "this wood must be our hiding-place."

"And what about me?" says Jack.

"For you, Jack," says the mare, "you must push on and look for employment. The castle of the King of Scotland is nearby, and I think you will be likely to get employment there; but first I must change you into an ugly little hookedy-crookedy fellow, because the King of Scotland has three beautiful daughters, and he won't take into his service a handsome fellow as you, for fear his daughters would fall in love with you."

Then the mare put her nostrils to Jack's breast and blew her breath over him, and Jack was turned into an ugly little hookedy-crookedy fellow.

"Jack," says the mare, "before you go, look into my left ear, and take what you see there."

Out of the mare's left ear Jack took a little cap.

"Jack," says she, "that is a wishing-cap, and every time you put it on and wish to have anything done, it will be done. Whenever you are in any trouble," the mare says, "come back to me, and I will do what I can for you, and now good-bye."

So Jack said good-bye to the mare and to the bear, and set off. When he got out of the wood, he soon saw a castle, and walked up to it and went in by the kitchen. A servant was employed scouring knives. He told her he wanted employment. She said the King of Scotland would employ no man in his house, so he might as well push on. But Jack insisted that the King would employ him, and at length the girl consented to go and let the King know.

When the girl had gone away, Jack put on his wishing-cap and wished the knives and forks scoured, and all at once the knives and forks, that were piled in a stack ten yards high, were scoured as brightly as new pins; and though the King of Scotland did not want to employ him, when he found how quickly Jack had scoured all the big stack of knives and forks, he agreed to keep him. But first he brought down his three daughters to see Jack, so that he could observe what impression Jack made upon them. When they came into the kitchen and saw the ugly little fellow, every one of the three fainted and had to be carried out.

"It is all right," says the King, "we will surely keep you," and Jack was employed, and sent out into the garden to work there.

Now at this time the King of the East declared war on the King of Scotland. The King of the East had a mighty army entirely, and he threatened to wipe the King of Scotland off the face of the earth.

The King of Scotland was very much troubled and he consulted with his Grand Adviser what was best to be done, and his Grand Adviser counselled that he should at once give his three daughters in marriage to sons of kings, and in that way get great help for the war. The King said this was a grand idea.

So he sent out messengers to all parts of the world to say that his three beautiful daughters were open for marriage. In a very short time the son of the King of Spain came and married the eldest daughter, and the son of the King of France came and married the second, and a whole lot of princes came looking for the youngest, who was the most beautiful of the three and whose name was Yellow Rose; but she would not take one of them, and for this the King ordered her never to come into his sight, nor into company, again.

Yellow Rose got very downhearted, and spent almost all her time now wandering in the garden, where the Hookedy-Crookedy was looking after the flowers, and she used to come around again and again, chatting to Hookedy-Crookedy. And so it was not long until Hookedy-Crookedy saw that the Yellow Rose was in love with him, and he got just as deeply in love with her, for she was a beautiful and charming girl.

The next thing the Grand Adviser counselled the King was that he should send his two new sons-in-law, the Prince of Spain and the Prince of France, to the Well of the World's End for bottles of loca to take to battle with them, that they might cure the wounded and dead men. Loca was a liquid that cured all wounds and restored the dead to life. So the King ordered his sons-in-law to go to the Well of the World's End and bring him back two bottles of loca.

The Yellow Rose told Hookedy-Crookedy all about this, and when he had turned it over in his mind, he said to himself, "I will go and have a chat with the mare and the bear about this."

So off to the woods he went, and right glad the mare and the bear were to see him. He told them all that had happened, and then he told them how the Kings two sons-in-law were to start to the Well of the World's End the next day, and asked the mare's advice about it.

"Well, Jack," says the mare, "I want you to go with them. Take an old hunter in the Kings stable, an old bony, skinny animal that is past all work, and put an old straw saddle on him, and dress yourself in the most ragged dress you can get, and join the two men on the road, and say that you are going with them. They will be heartily ashamed of you, Jack, and your old horse, and they will do everything to get rid of you. When you come to the cross-roads, one of them will propose to go in and have a drink; and while you are chatting over your drink, they will propose that the three of you separate and every one take a road by himself to go to the Well of the World's End, and that all three shall meet at the cross-roads again, and whoever is back first with the bottle of water is to be the greatest hero of them all. You agree to this. When they start on their roads, they will not go many miles till they fill their bottles from spring wells by the roadside and hurry back to the meeting-place, and then continue on home to the King of Scotland and give him these bottles as bottles of loca from the Well of the World's End. But you will be before them. After you have set out on the road, and when you have gone around the first bend, put on your wishing-cap and wish for two bottles of loca from the Well of the World's End, and at once you will have them." And then the mare directed Jack fully all that he was to do after.

Jack thanked the mare, and bade goodbye to her, and went away.

The next day, when the Kings two sons-in-law set out on their grand steeds to go to the Well of the World's End, they had not gone far when Jack, in a ragged old suit and sitting on a straw saddle on an old white skinny horse, joined them and told them he too was going with them for a bottle of loca. Right heartily ashamed were they of Jack and ready to do anything to get rid of him.

By and by, when they came to where the road divided into three, they proposed to have a drink, and as they set off to drink they proposed that each take a road for himself, and whoever got back first with a bottle of loca would be the greatest hero. All agreed, and each chose his own road and set out.

When Jack had got around the first bend, he put on his wishing-cap and wished for two bottles of loca from the Well of the World's End, and no sooner had he wished than he had them; and back again he came, and when the other two came riding up, surprised they were to find Jack there before them. They said that Jack had not been to the Well of the World's End and it was no loca he had with him, but some water from the roadside.

Said Jack, "Take care that is not your own story. Just test them; when the servant comes in, you cut off his head and then cure him with water from your bottles."

But both refused to do this, for they knew the water in their bottles could not cure anything, and they defied Jack to do it.

"Very soon I will do it," said Jack.

So when the servant came in with the bottles of loca, Jack drew his sword and whipped his head off him, and in a minute's time, with two drops from one of his bottles, he had the head on again.

Says they to Hookedy-Crookedy, "What will you take for your two bottles?"

Says Jack, "I will take the golden balls of your marriage pledge, and also you shall allow me to write something on your backs."

And they agreed to this. They handed over to Jack the two golden balls that were their marriage tokens, and they let Jack write on their bare backs; and what Jack wrote on each of them was, "This is an unlawfully married man." Then he gave them the bottles of loca, and they brought them to the King, and Jack returned to his garden again.

He did not tell the Yellow Rose where he had been and what doing, only he said was away on a message for her father. As soon as the King got the bottles of loca, he gave orders that his army should move to battle the next day.

The next morning early Jack was over to the wood to consult the mare. He told her what was going to happen that day. Says the mare, "Look in my left ear, Jack, and see what you will see."

Jack looked in the mare's left ear, and took out of it a grand soldier's dress. The mare told him to put it on and get on her back. On he put the dress, and at once Hookedy-Crookedy was transformed into a very handsome, dashing young fellow, and off went Jack and the mare and the bear, the three of them, away to the war. Everyone saw them, and they admired Jack very much, he was such a handsome, clever-looking fellow, and word was passed on to the King about the great Prince who was riding to the war -- himself, the mare, and the bear. The King came to see him, too, and asked him on which side he was going to fight.

"I will strike no stroke this day," says Jack, "except on the side of the King of Scotland."

The King thanked him very heartily, and he said was sure they would win. So they went into the battle with Jack at their head, and Jack struck east and west and in all directions, and at every blow of his sword the wind of his stroke tossed houses on the other side of the world, and in a very short time the King of the East ran off, with all his army that were still left alive. Then the King of Scotland invited Jack to come home with him, as he was going to give a great feast in his honour; but Jack said no, he could not go.

"They don't know at home," said Jack, "where I am at all",- and neither they did -- "so I must be off to them as quickly as possible."

"Then," says the King, "the least I can do is to give you a present. Here is a table-cloth," says he, "and every time you spread it out you will have it covered with eating and drinking of all sorts."

Jack took it, and thanked him, and rode away. He left the mare and the bear in their own wood, and became Hookedy-Crookedy again, and ran back to his garden. The Yellow Rose told him of the brave soldier that had won her father's battle that day.

"Well, well," says Jack, says he, "he must have been a grand fellow entirely. It is a pity I was not there, but I had to go on a message for the King."

"Poor Hookedy-Crookedy," says she, "what could you do if you were there yourself?"

Jack went to the wood again next morning, and consulted with the mare.

"Jack," said the mare, "look in the inside of my left ear, and see what you will see," and Jack took out of her left ear a soldier's suit, done off with silver, the grandest ever seen, and at the mare's advice he put the suit on, and mounted on her back, and the three of them went off to the battle. Everyone was admiring the beautiful, dashing fellow that was riding to the battle this day, and word came to the King, and the King came to speak to him and welcomed him heartily.

He said, "Your brother came with us the last day we went into the battle. Your brother is a very handsome, fine-looking fellow. What side are you going to fight on?"

Says Jack, "I will strike no stroke on any side but yours this day."

The King thanked him very heartily, and into the battle they went with Jack at their head, and Jack struck east and west and in all directions, and the wind of the strokes blew down forests in the other end of the world, and very soon the King of the East, with all his army that were still alive, drew off from the battle.

Then the King thanked Jack and invited him to his castle, where he would give a feast in his honour. But Jack he said could not go, for they did not know at home where he was, and they would be uneasy about him until he reached home again.

"Then," says the King, "the least I can do for you is to give you a present. Here is a purse, and no matter how often and how much you pay out of it, it will never be empty."

Jack took it, and thanked him, and rode away. In the wood he left the mare and the bear, and was again changed into Hookedy-Crookedy, and went home to his garden. The Yellow Rose came out, and told him about the great victory a brave and beautiful soldier, brother to the fine fellow of the day before, had won for her father.

"Well, well," says Jack, says he, "that was very wonderful entirely. I am sorry I was not there, but I had to be away on a message for your father."

"But my poor Hookedy-Crookedy," says she, "it was better so, for what could you do?"

Three days after that the King of the East took courage to come to battle again. The morning of the battle Jack went to the wood to consult the mare.

"Look into my left ear, Jack, and see what you will see," and from the mare's left ear Jack drew out a most gorgeous soldier's suit, done off with gold braiding and ornaments of every sort. By the mare's advice he put it on, and himself, the mare, and the bear went off to the war.

The King soon heard of the wonderfully grand fellow that was riding to the war to-day with the mare and the bear, and he came to Jack and welcomed him and told him how his two brothers had won the last two victories for him. He asked Jack on what side he was going to fight.

"I will strike no stroke this day," says Jack, only on the King of Scotland's side."

The King thanked him heartily, and said, "We will surely win the victory," and then into the battle they rode with Jack at their head, and Jack struck east and west and in all directions, and the wind of the strokes tumbled mountains at the other end of the world, and very soon the King of the East with all his army that were left alive took to their heels and never stopped running until they went as far as the world would let them.

Then the King came to Jack and thanked him over and over again, and he said would never be able to repay him. He then invited him to come to his castle, where he would give a little feast in his honour, but Jack said they didn't know at home where he was and they would be uneasy about him, and so he could not go with the King.

"But," says he, "I and my brothers will come to feast with you at any other time."

"What day will the three of you come?" said the King.

"Only one of us can leave home in one day," said Jack. "I will come to feast with you tomorrow, and my second brother the day after, and my third brother the day after that."

The King agreed to this and thanked him. "And now," said the King, "let me give you a present," and he gave him a comb, such that every time he combed his hair with it he would comb out of it bushels of gold and silver, and it would transform the ugliest man that ever was into the nicest and handsomest. Jack took it and thanked the King and rode away.

On this day, as on the other two days after the battle, they cured the dead and the wounded with the bottles of loca, and all were well again. When Jack went to the wood, he left the mare and the bear in it and became Hookedy-Crookedy again, and went home and to his garden. The Yellow Rose came to him and had wonderful news for him this day about the terrible grand fellow entirely, who had won the battle for her father that day; brother to the two brave fellows who had won the battles on the other two days.

"Well," says Jack, says he, "those must be wonderful chaps. I wish I had been there; but I had to be away on a message for your father all day."

"Oh, my poor Hookedy-Crookedy," says she, "it was better so, for what could you do?"

The next day, when it was near dinner time, he went off to the wood to the mare and the bear and got on the suit he had worn the day before in the battle, and mounted the mare and rode for the castle, and when he came there all the gates happened to be closed, but he put the mare at the walls, which were nine miles high, and leapt them.

The King scolded the gate-keepers, but Jack said a trifle like that didn't harm him or his mare. After dinner the King asked him what he thought of his two daughters and their husbands. Jack said they were very good and asked him if he had any more daughters in his family.

The King he said used to have another, the youngest, but she would not consent to marry as he wished, and he had banished her out of his sight.

Jack he said would like to see her.

The King he said never wished to let her enter company again, but he could not refuse Jack; so the Yellow Rose was sent for.

Jack fell a-chatting with her and used all his arts to win her, and of course, in this handsome Jack she did not recognize ugly little Hookedy-Crookedy. He told her he had heard that she had the very bad taste to fall in love with an ugly, crooked, wee fellow in her father's garden.

"I am a handsome fellow, and a rich prince," says Jack, "and I will give you myself and all I possess if you only say you will accept me."

She was highly insulted, and she showed him that very quickly. She said, "I won't sit here and hear the man I love abused;" and she got up to leave.

"Well," says Jack, "I admire your spirit; but before you go," says he," let me make you a little present," and he handed her a tablecloth. "There," says he, "if you marry Hookedy-Crookedy, as long as you have this tablecloth, you will never want eating and drinking of the best." The other two sisters grabbed to get the tablecloth from her, but Jack put out his hands and pushed them back.

At dinner-time the next day Jack came in the dress in which he had gone into the second battle, and with the mare he cleared the walls as on the day before.

The King was enraged at the gate-keepers and began to scold them, but Jack laughed at them and said a trifle like that was nothing to him or his mare.

After dinner was over the King asked what he thought of his two daughters and their husbands.

Jack said they were very good, and asked him if he had any more daughters in his family.

The King said, "I have no more except one who won't do as I wish and who has fallen in love with an ugly, crooked, wee fellow in my garden, and I ordered her never to come into my sight."

But Jack he said would very much like to see her.

The King said that on Jack's account he would break his vow and let her come in. So the Yellow Rose was brought in, and Jack fell to chatting with her. He did all he could to make her fall in love with him, and told her of all his great wealth and possessions and offered himself to her, and said if she only would marry him she should live in ease and luxury and happiness all the days of her life, as she never could do with Hookedy-Crookedy.

But Yellow Rose got very angry, and said, "I won't sit here and listen to such things," and she got up to leave the room.

"Well," says Jack, "I admire your spirit, and before you go let me make you a little present."

So he handed her a purse. "Here," says he, "is a purse, and all the days yourself and Hookedy-Crookedy live you will never want for money, for that purse will never be empty."

Her sisters made a grab to snatch it from her, but Jack shoved them back, and went out. And Jack rode away with the mare after dinner and left her in the wood.

When he came back to his garden he always came in the Hookedy-Crookedy shape and always pretended he had been off on a message for the King.

The third day he went to the wood again. He dressed in the suit in which he had gone to the first battle, and when he came back he went to the castle and cleared the walls, and when the King scolded the gate-keepers Jack told him never to mind, as that was a small trifle to him and his mare.

A very grand dinner indeed Jack had this day, and when they chatted after dinner the King asked him how he liked his two daughters and their husbands.

He said he liked them very well, and asked him if he had any more daughters in his family.

The King said no, except one foolish one who wouldn't do as he wished, and who had fallen in love with an ugly, crooked, wee fellow in his garden, and she was never to come within his sight again.

Says Jack, "I would like to see that girl."

The King he said could not refuse Jack any request he made, so he sent for the Yellow Rose. When she came in, Jack fell into chat with her, and did his very, very best to make her fall in love with him. But it was of no use. He told her of all his wealth and all his grand possessions, and said if she would marry him she should own all these, and all the days she should live she should be the happiest woman in the wide world, but if she married Hookedy-Crookedy, he said, she would never be free from want and hardships, besides having an ugly husband.

If the Yellow Rose was in a rage on the two days before, she was in a far greater rage now. She said she wouldn't sit there to listen. She told Jack that Hookedy-Crookedy was in her eyes a far more handsome and beautiful man than he or than any kings son she had ever seen. She said to Jack, that if he were ten times as handsome and a hundred times as wealthy, she wouldn't give Hookedy-Crookedy's little finger for himself, or for all his wealth and possessions, and then she got up to leave the room.

"Well," says Jack, says he, "I admire your spirit very much, and," says he, "I would like to make you a little present. Here is a comb," he said, "and it will comb out of your hair a bushel of gold and a bushel of silver every time you comb with it, and, besides," says he, "it will make handsome the ugliest man that ever was."

When the other sisters heard this they rushed to snatch the comb from her, but Jack threw them backwards so very roughly that their husbands sprang at him. With a back switch of his two hands Jack knocked the husbands down senseless. The King flew into a rage, and said, "How dare you do that to the two finest and bravest men of this world?"

"Fine and brave, indeed!" said Jack. "One and the other they are worthless creatures, and not even your lawful sons-in-law."

"How dare you say that?" says the King.

"Strip their backs where they lie and see for yourself." And there the King saw written, "An unlawfully married man."

"What is the meaning of this?" says the King. "They were lawfully married to my two daughters, and they have the golden tokens of the marriage."

Jack drew out from his pocket the golden balls and handed them to the King, and said, "It is I who have the tokens."

The Yellow Rose had gone off to the garden in the middle of all this. Jack made the King sit down, and told him all his story, and how he came by the golden balls. He told him how he was Hookedy-Crookedy, and that it reflected a great deal of honour on his youngest daughter that she whom the King thought so worthless should refuse to give up Hookedy-Crookedy for the one she thought a wealthy prince. The King, you may be sure, was now highly delighted to grant him all he desired. A couple of drops of loca brought the Kings two sons to their senses again, and at Jack's request, they were ordered to go and live elsewhere. Jack went off, left his mare in the wood, and came into the garden as Hookedy-Crookedy. He told the Yellow Rose he had been gathering bilberries.

"Oh," says she, "I have something grand for you. Let me comb your hair with this comb."

Hookedy-Crookedy put his head in her lap, and she combed out a bushel of gold and silver and when he stood up again, she saw Hookedy-Crookedy no more, but instead the beautiful prince that had been trying to win her in her father's drawing-room for the last three days; and then and there to her Jack told his whole story, and it's Yellow Rose who is the delighted girl.

With little delay they were married. The wedding lasted a year and a day, and there were five hundred fiddlers, five hundred fluters and a thousand fifers at it, and the last day was better than the first.

Shortly after the marriage, Jack and his bride were out walking one day. A beautiful young woman crossed their path. Jack addressed her, but she gave him a very curt reply.

"Your manners are not so handsome as your looks," said Jack to her.

"And bad as they are, they are better than your memory, Hookedy-Crookedy," says she.

"What do you mean?" says Jack.

She led Jack aside, and she told him, "I am the mare who was so good to you. I was condemned to that shape for a number of years, and now my enchantment is over. I had a brother who was enchanted into a bear, and whose enchantment is over now also. I had hopes," she says, "that someday you would be my husband, but I see," she says, "that you quickly forgot all about me. No matter now," she says, "I couldn't wish you a better and handsomer wife than you have got. Go home to your castle, and be happy and live prosperous. I shall never see you, and you will never see me again."

Tales From The Land Of Saints & Scholars

King Iubdan and King Fergus

"King Iubdan and King Fergus" is a whimsical Irish legend retold by Thomas William Hazen Rolleston in The High Deeds of Finn and Other Bardic Romances of Ancient Ireland (1910). The tale blends courtly comedy with mythic grandeur, recounting the meeting between Iubdan, the tiny king of the Leprechauns, and Fergus mac Léti, the mighty ruler of Ulster.

Rolleston's adaptation, based on medieval Irish sources, turns the ancient tale into a lyrical study of proportion and perspective. Through his polished Edwardian prose, he preserves the playful dignity of the original, its vision of a world where giants and tiny kings share the same moral stage. Beneath the humour lies a reflection on humility and the limits of power.

It happened on a day when Fergus son of Leda was King of Ulster, that Iubdan, King of the Leprechauns or Wee Folk, of the land of Faylinn, held a great banquet and assembly of the lords and princes of the Wee Folk. And all their captains and men of war came there, to show their feats before the King, among whom was the strong man, namely Glowar, whose might was such that with his battle-axe he could hew down a thistle at one stroke. There also came the Kings heir-apparent, Tiny, son of Tot, and the Queen Bebo with her maidens; and there were also the Kings harpers and singing-men, and the chief poet of the court, who was called Eisirt.

All these sat down to the feast in due order and precedence, with Bebo on the Kings right hand and the poet on his left, and Glowar kept the door. Soon the wine began to flow from the vats of dark-red yew-wood, and the carvers carved busily at great haunches of roast hares and ribs of field-mice; and they all ate and drank, and loudly the hall rang with gay talk and laughter, and the drinking of toasts, and clashing of silver goblets.

At last when they had put away desire of eating and drinking, Iubdan rose up, having in his hand the royal goblet of gold inlaid with precious many-coloured jewels, and the heir-apparent rose at the other end of the table, and they drank prosperity and victory to Faylinn. Then Iubdan's heart swelled with pride, and he asked of the company, "Come now, have any of you ever seen a king more glorious and powerful than I am?" "Never, in truth," cried they all. "Have you ever seen a stronger man than my giant, Glowar?" "Never, Oh King," said they. "Or battle-steeds and men-at-arms better than mine?" "By our words," they cried, "we never have." "Truly," went on Iubdan, "I deem that he who would assail our kingdom of Faylinn, and carry away captives and hostages from us, would have his work cut out for him, so fierce and mighty are our warriors; yea, any one of them have the stuff of kingship in him."

On hearing this, Eisirt, in whom the heady wine and ale had done their work, burst out laughing; and the King turned to him, saying, "Eisirt, what have moved you to this laughter?" "I know a province in Erinn," replied Eisirt, "one man of whom would harry Faylinn in the teeth of all four battalions of the Wee Folk." "Seize him," cried the King to his attendants, "Eisirt shall pay dearly in chains and in prison for that scornful speech against our glory."

Then Eisirt was put in bonds, and he repented him of his brag; but before they dragged him away he said, "Grant me, Oh mighty King, but three days' respite, that I may travel to Erinn to the court of Fergus mac Leda, and if I bring not back some clear token that I have uttered nought but the truth, then do with me as you will."

So Iubdan bade them release him, and he fared away to Erinn oversea.

They all trooped out, lords and ladies, to view the wee man

"They all trooped out, lords and ladies, to view the wee man"

After this, one day, as Fergus and his lords sat at the feast, the gatekeeper of the palace of Fergus in Emania heard outside a sound of ringing; he opened the gate, and there stood a wee man holding in his hand a rod of white bronze hung with little silver bells, by which poets are likely to procure silence for their recitations. Most noble and comely was the little man to look on, though the short grass of the lawn reached as high as to his knee. His hair was twisted in four-ply strands after the manner of poets and he wore a gold-embroidered tunic of silk and an ample scarlet cloak with a fringe of gold. On his feet he wore shoes of white bronze ornamented with gold, and a silken hood was on his head. The gatekeeper wondered at the sight of the wee man, and went to report the matter to King Fergus. "Is he less," asked Fergus, "than my dwarf and poet Æda?" "Verily," said the gatekeeper, "he could stand upon the palm of Æda's hand and have room to spare." Then with much laughter and wonder they all trooped out, lords and ladies, to the great gate to view the wee man and to speak with him. But Eisirt, when he saw them, waved them back in alarm, crying, "Avaunt, huge men; bring not your heavy breath so near me; but let yon man that is least among you approach me and bear me in". So the dwarf Æda put Eisirt on his palm and bore him into the banqueting hall.

Then they set him on the table, and Eisirt declared his name and calling. The King ordered that meat and drink should be given him, but Eisirt said, "I will neither eat of your meat nor drink of ale." "By our word," said Fergus, "tis a haughty wight; he ought to be dropped into a goblet that he might at least drink all round him." The cupbearer seized Eisirt and put him into a tankard of ale, and he swam on the surface of it. "Ye wise men of Ulster," he cried, "there is much knowledge and wisdom you might get from me, yet you will let me be drowned!" "What, then?" cried they. Then Eisirt, beginning with the King, set out to tell every hidden sin that each man or woman had done, and before he had gone far they with much laughter and chiding fetched him out of the ale-pot and dried him with fair satin napkins. "Now you have confessed that I know somewhat to the purpose," said Eisirt, "and I will even eat of your food, but do you give heed to my words, and do ill no more."

Fergus then said, "If you are a poet, Eisirt, give us now a taste of your delightful art." "That will I," said Eisirt, "and the poem that I shall recite to you shall be an ode in praise of my king, Iubdan the Great." Then he recited this lay:

"A monarch of might

Is Iubdan my king.

His brow is snow-white,

His hair black as night;

As a red copper bowl

When smitten will sing,

So rings the voice

Of Iubdan the king.

Tales From The Land Of Saints & Scholars

His eyes, they roll
Majestic and bland
On the lords of his land
Arrayed for the fight,
A spectacle grand!

Like a torrent they rush
With a waving of swords
And the bridles all ringing
And cheeks all aflush,
And the battle-steeds springing,
A beautiful, terrible, death-dealing band.

Like pines, straight and tall,
Where Iubdan is king,
Are the men one and all.
The maidens are fair -
Bright gold is their hair.

From silver we quaff
The dark, heady ale
That never shall fail;
We love and we laugh.

Gold frontlets we wear;
And aye through the air
Sweet music doth ring -

Tales From The Land Of Saints & Scholars

O Fergus, men say

That in all Inisfail

There is not a maiden so proud or so wise

But would give her two eyes

Your kisses to win -

But I tell you, that there

You can never compare

With the haughty, magnificent King of Faylinn!"

At this they all applauded, and Fergus said, "O youth and blameless bard, let us be friends henceforth." And they all heaped before him, as a poet's reward, gifts of rings and jewels and gold cups and weapons, as high as a tall man standing. Then Eisirt said, "Truly a generous and a worthy reward have you given me, Oh men of Ulster; yet take back these precious things I pray you, for every man in my king's household have an abundance of them." But the Ulster lords said, "Nothing that we have given may we take back." Eisirt then bade two-thirds of his reward be given to the bards and learned men of Ulster, and one-third to the horse-boys and jesters; and so it was done.

Three days and nights did Eisirt abide in Emania, and all the Kings court loved him and made much of him. Then he wished them blessing and victory, and prepared to depart to his own country. Now Æda, the Kings dwarf and minstrel, begged Eisirt to take him with him on a visit to the land of Faylinn; and Eisirt said, "I shall not bid you come, for then if kindness and hospitality be shown you, you will say it is only what I had undertaken; but if you come of your own motion, you will perchance be grateful."

So they went off together; but Eisirt could not keep up with Æda, and Æda said, "I perceive that Eisirt is but a poor walker." At this Eisirt ran off like a flash and was soon an arrow flight in front of Æda. When the latter at last came up with him, he said, "The right thing, Eisirt, is not too fast and not too slow." "Since I have been in Ulster," Eisirt replied, "I have never before heard you measure out the right."

By and by they reached the margin of the sea. "And what are we to do now?" asked Æda. "Be not troubled, Æda," said Eisirt, "the horse of Iubdan will bear us easily over this." They waited awhile on the beach, and before long they saw it coming toward them skimming over the surface of the waves. "Save and protect us!" cried Æda at that sight; and Eisirt asked him what he saw. "A red-maned hare," answered Æda. "Nay, but that is Iubdan's horse," said Eisirt, and with that the creature came prancing to land with flashing eyes and waving tail and a long russet-coloured mane; a bridle beset with gold it had. Eisirt mounted and bade Æda come up behind him. "Your boat is little enough for you alone," said Æda. "Cease fault-finding and grumbling," then said Eisirt, "for the weight of wisdom that is in you will not bear him down"

So Æda and Eisirt mounted on the fairy horse and away they sped over the tops of the waves and the deeps of the ocean till at last they reached the Kingdom of Faylinn, and there were a great concourse of the Wee Folk awaiting them. "Eisirt is coming! Eisirt is coming!" cried they all, "and a Fomorian giant along with him."

Then Iubdan went forth to meet Eisirt, and he kissed him, and said, "Why have you brought this Fomorian with you to slay us?" "He is no Fomor," said Eisirt, "but a learned man and a poet from Ulster.

He is moreover the King of Ulster's dwarf, and in all that realm he is the smallest man. He can lie in their great men's bosoms and stand upon their hands as though he were a child; yet for all that you would do well to be careful how you behave to him." "What is his name?" said they then. "He is the poet Æda." said Eisirt. "Uch," said they, "what a giant you have brought us!"

"And now, Oh King," said Eisirt to Iubdan, "I challenge you to go and see for yourself the region from which we have come, and make trial of the royal porridge which is made for Fergus King of Ulster this very night."

At this Iubdan was much dismayed, and he betook himself to Bebo his wife and told her how he was laid under bonds of chivalry by Eisirt to go to the land of the giants; and he bade her prepare to accompany him. "I will go," said she, "but you did an ill deed when you condemned Eisirt to prison."

So they mounted, both of them, on the fairy steed, and in no long time they reached Emania, and it was now past midnight. And they were greatly afraid, and said Bebo, "Let us search for that porridge and taste it, as we were bound, and make off again before the folk awake."

They made their way into the palace of Fergus, and soon they found a great porridge pot, but the rim was too high to be reached from the ground. "Get you up upon your horse," said Bebo, "and from there to the rim of this cauldron." And thus he did, but having gained the rim of the pot his arm was too short to reach the silver ladle that was in it. In straining downward to do so, however, he slipped and in he fell, and up to his middle in the thick porridge he stuck fast. And when Bebo heard what a plight he was in, she wept, and said, "Rash and hasty were you, Iubdan, to have got into this evil case, but surely there is no man under the sun that can make you hear reason." And he said, "Rash indeed it was, but you cannot help me, Bebo, now, and it is but folly to stay; take the horse and flee away before the daybreak." "Say not so," replied Bebo, "for surely I will not go till I see how things fall out with you."

At last the folk in the palace began to be stirring, and before long they found Iubdan in the porridge pot.

So they picked him out with great laughter bore him off to Fergus.

"By my conscience," said Fergus, "but this is not the little fellow that was here before, for he had yellow hair, but this one have a shock of the blackest; who are you at all, wee man?"

"I am of the Wee Folk," said Iubdan, "and am indeed king over them, and this woman is my wife and queen, Bebo."

"Take him away," then said Fergus to his varlets, "and guard him well"; for he misdoubted some mischief of Faery was on foot.

"Nay, nay," cried Iubdan, "but let me not be with these coarse fellows. I pledge you my word that I will not quit this place till you and Ulster give me leave."

"Could I believe that," said Fergus, "I would not put you in bonds."

"I have never broken my word," said Iubdan, "and I never will."

Then Fergus set him free and allotted him a fair chamber for himself, and a trusty serving man to wait upon him. Soon there came in a gillie whose business it was to see to the fires, and he kindled the fire for Iubdan, throwing on it a woodbine together with diverse other sorts of timber. Then Iubdan said, "Man of smoke, burn not the king of the trees, for it is not meet to burn him. Would you but take counsel from me you might go safely by sea or land."

Iubdan then chanted to him the following recital of the duties of his office, "O fire-gillie of Fergus of the Feasts, never by land or sea burn the King of the woods, High King of the forests of Inisfail, whom none may bind, but who like a strong monarch holds all the other trees in hard bondage. If you burn the twining one, misfortune will come of it, peril at the point of spear, or drowning in the waves.

"Burn not the sweet apple-tree of drooping branches, of the white blossoms, to whose gracious head each man puts forth his hand.

"The stubborn blackthorn wanders far and wide, the good craftsman burns not this timber; little though its bushes be, yet flocks of birds warble in them.

"Burn not the noble willow, the unfailing ornament of poems; bees drink from its blossoms, all delight in the graceful tent.

"The delicate, airy tree of the druids, the rowan with its berries, this burn; but avoid the weak tree, burn not the slender hazel.

"The ash-tree of the black buds burn not - timber that speeds the wheel, that yields the rider his switch; the ashen spear is the scale-beam of battle.

"The tangled, bitter bramble, burn him, the sharp and green; he flays and cuts the foot; he snares you and drags you back.

"Hottest of timber is the green oak; he will give you a pain in the head if you use him overmuch, a pain in the eyes will come from his biting fumes.

"Full-charged with witchcraft is the alder, the hottest tree in the fight; burn assuredly both the alder and the whitehorn at your will.

"Holly, burn it in the green and in the dry; of all trees in the world, holly is absolutely the best.

"The elder-tree of the rough brown bark, burn him to cinders, the steed of the Fairy Folk.

"The drooping birch, by all means burn him too, the tree of long-lasting bloom.

"And lay low, if it pleases you, the russet aspen; late or early, burn the tree with the quaking plumage.

"The yew is the venerable ancestor of the wood as the companion of feasts he is known; of him make goodly brown vats for ale and wine.

"Follow my counsel, Oh man of the smoke, and it shall go well with you, body and soul."

So Iubdan continued in Emania free to go and come as he pleased; and all the Ulstermen delighted to watch him and to hear his conversation.

One day it chanced that he was in the chamber of the Queen, and saw her putting on her feet a very dainty and richly embroidered pair of shoes. At this Iubdan gave a laugh. "Why dost you laugh?" said Fergus. "Me seems the healing is applied very far from the hurt," replied Iubdan. "What meanest you by that?" said Fergus. "Because the Queen is making her feet fine in order, Oh Fergus, that she may attract you to her lips," said Iubdan.

Another time it chanced that Iubdan overheard one of the Kings soldiers complaining of a pair of new brogues that had been served out to him, and grumbling that the soles were too thin. At this Iubdan laughed again, and being asked why, he said, "I must need laugh to hear yon fellow grumbling about his brogues, for the soles of these brogues, thin as they are, he will never wear out." And this was a true prophecy, for the same night this and another of the Kings men had a quarrel, and fought, and killed each the other.

At last the Wee Folk determined to go in search of their king, and seven battalions of them marched upon Emania and encamped upon the lawn over against the Kings Dún. Fergus and his nobles went out to confer with them. "Give us back our king," said the Wee Folk, "and we shall redeem him with a great ransom." "What ransom, then?" asked Fergus. "We shall," said they, "cause this great plain to stand thick with corn for you every year, and that without ploughing or sowing." "I will not give up Iubdan for that," said Fergus. "Then we shall do you a mischief," said the Wee Folk.

That night every calf in the Province of Ulster got access to its dam, and in the morn there was no milk to be had for man or child, for the cows were sucked dry.

Then said the Wee Folk to Fergus, "This night, unless we get Iubdan, we shall defile every well and lake and river in Ulster." "That is a trifle," said Fergus, "and you shall not get Iubdan."

The Wee Folk carried out this threat, and once more they came and demanded Iubdan, saying, "To-night we shall burn with fire the shaft of every mill in Ulster." "Yet not so shall you get Iubdan," said Fergus.

This being done, they came again, saying, "We shall have vengeance unless Iubdan be delivered to us" "What vengeance?" said Fergus. "We shall snip off every ear of corn in your kingdom," said they. "Even so," replied Fergus, "I shall not deliver Iubdan."

So the Wee Folk snipped off every ear of standing corn in Ulster, and once more they returned and demanded Iubdan. "What will you do next?" asked Fergus. "We shall shave the hair of every man and every woman in Ulster," said they, "so that you shall be shamed and disgraced for ever among the people of Erinn." "By my word," said

Fergus, "if you do that I shall slay Iubdan."

Then Iubdan said, "I have a better counsel than that, Oh King; let me have liberty to go and speak with them, and I shall bid them make good what mischief they have done, and they shall return home forthwith."

Fergus granted that; and when the Wee Folk saw Iubdan approaching them, they set up a shout of triumph that a man might have heard a bowshot off, for they believed they had prevailed and that Iubdan was released to them. But Iubdan said, "My faithful people, you must now be gone, and I may not go with you; make good also all the mischief that you have done, and know that if you do any more I must die."

Then the Wee Folk departed, very downcast and sorrowful, but they did as Iubdan had bidden them.

Iubdan, however, went to Fergus and said, "Take, Oh King, the choicest of my treasures, and let me go."

"What is your choicest treasure?" said Fergus.

Iubdan then began to recite to Fergus the list of his possessions, such as druidic weapons, and love-charms, and instruments of music that played without touch of human hand, and vats of ale that could never be emptied; and he named among other noble treasures a pair of shoes, wearing which a man could go over or under the sea as readily as on dry land.

At the same time Æda, the dwarf and poet of Ulster, returned hale and well from the land of Faylinn, and much did he entertain the King and all the court with tales of the smallness of the Wee Folk, and their marvel at his own size, and their bravery and beauty, and their marble palaces and matchless minstrelsy.

So the King, Fergus mac Leda, was well content to take a ransom, namely the magic shoes, which he desired above all the treasures of Faylinn, and to let Iubdan go. And he gave him rich gifts, as did also the nobles of Ulster, and wished him blessing and victory; and Iubdan he departed, with Bebo his wife, having first bestowed upon Fergus the magical shoes. And of him the tale have now no more to say.

But Fergus never tired of donning the shoes of Iubdan and traversing the secret depths of the lakes and rivers of Ulster. Thereby, too, in the end he got his death, for as the wise say that the gifts of Faery may not be enjoyed without peril by mortal men, so in this case too it proved. For, one day as Fergus was exploring the depths of Loch Rury he met the monster, namely the river-horse, which inhabited that lake. Horrible of form it was, swelling and contracting like a blacksmith's bellows, and with eyes like torches, and glittering tusks, and a mane of coarse hair on its crest and neck. When it saw Fergus it laid back its ears, and its neck arched like a rainbow over his head, and the vast mouth gaped to devour him. Then Fergus rose quickly to the surface and made for the land, and the beast after him, driving before it a huge wave of foam. Barely did he escape with his life; but with the horror of the sight his features were distorted and his mouth was twisted around to the side of his head, so that he was called Fergus Wry-mouth from that day forth. And the ghillie that was with him told the tale of the adventure.

Now there was a law in Ireland that no man might be king who was disfigured by any bodily blemish. His people, therefore, loving Fergus, kept from him all knowledge of his condition, and the Queen let all mirrors that were in the palace be put away. But one day it chanced that a bondmaid was negligent in preparing the bath, and Fergus being impatient, gave her a stroke with a switch which he had in his hand. The maid in anger turned upon him, and cried, "It would better become you to avenge yourself on the Riverhorse that have twisted your mouth, than to do brave deeds on women."

Fergus then bade a mirror be fetched, and when he saw his face in it, he said, "The woman spoke truth; the Riverhorse of Loch Rury has done this thing."

The next day Fergus put on the shoes of Iubdan and went forth to Loch Rury, and with him went the lords of Ulster. And when he reached the margin of the lake he drew his sword and went down into it, and soon the waters covered him.

After a while those that watched upon the bank saw a bubbling and a mighty commotion in the waters, now here, now there, and waves of bloody froth broke at their feet. At last, as they strained their eyes upon the tossing water, they saw Fergus rise to his middle from it, pale and bloody. In his right hand he waved aloft his sword, his left was twisted in the coarse hair of the monster's head, and they saw that his countenance was fair and kingly as of old. "Ulstermen, I have conquered," he cried; and as he did so he sank down again, dead with his dead foe, into their red grave in Loch Rury.

And the Ulster lords went back to Emania, sorrowful yet proud, for they knew that a seed of honour had been sown that day in their land from which should spring a breed of high-hearted fighting men for many a generation to come.

Tales From The Land Of Saints & Scholars

King O'Toole and St Kevin

"King O'Toole and St Kevin (A Legend of Glendalough)" is a humorous and characteristically Irish folktale that blends Christian legend with older, earthier storytelling. Originally written by Samuel Lover (1797–1868) and later retold by Alfred Perceval Graves in The Irish Fairy Book (1919), the tale centres on King O'Toole, an old, cantankerous monarch who rules a small glen near Glendalough in County Wicklow.

Beneath its comic charm and lively dialogue lies a wry allegory about greed, faith, and redemption, told in the teasing, conversational tone of the Irish storyteller. The tale reflects Ireland's blending of pagan humour and Christian piety: the holy man's miracles are earthy, the king's conversion reluctant, yet through wit and grace alike the valley of Glendalough becomes sanctified, a place where laughter and legend meet the divine.

There was once a king, called King O'Toole, who was a fine old king in the old ancient times, long ago; and it was him that owned the Churches in the early days.

"Surely," said I, "the Churches were not in King O'Toole's time?"

"Oh, by no means, your honour - truth, it's yourself that's right enough there; but you know the place is called 'The Churches' because they were built after by St. Kevin, and went by the name o' the Churches ever more; and, therefore, of course, the place being so called, I say that the King owned the Churches - and why not, sir, seeing t'was his birth right, time out o' mind, beyond the flood? Well, the King was the right sort - he was the real boy, and loved sport as he loved his life, and hunting in particular; and from the rising o' the sun up he got, and away he went over the mountains beyond after the deer, and the fine times them were; for the deer was as plenty thin, aye truth, far plentier than the sheep is now; and that's the way it was with the King, from the crow o' the cock to the song o' the redbreast. Well, it was all mighty good as long as the King had his health; but, you see, in course o' time, the King grew older, by raison he was stiff in his limbs, and when he got stricken in years, his heart failed him, and he was lost entirely for want o' diversion, because he couldn't go a hunting no longer; and, by dad, the poor King was obliged at last for to get a goose to divert him. You see, the goose used to swim across the lake, and go down diving for trout (and not finer trout in all Ireland than the same trout) and catch fish on a Friday for the King, and flew every other day round about the lake diverting the poor King that you'd think he'd break his sides laughing at the frolicsome tricks of his goose; so, in course o' time, the goose was the greatest pet in the country, and the biggest rogue, and diverted the King to no end, and the poor King was as happy as the day was long. So that's the way it was; and all went on mighty well until, by dad, the goose got stricken in years, as well as the King, and grew stiff in the limbs, like her master, and couldn't divert him no longer; and then it was that the poor King was lost complete, and didn't know what in the wide world to do, seeing he was gone out of all diversion by raison that the goose was no more in the flower of her bloom.

"Well, the King was nigh broken-hearted and melancholy entirely, and was walking one morning by the edge of the lake, lamenting his cruel fate, an' thinking o' drowning himself, that could get no diversion in life, when all of a sudden, turning round the corner beyond, who should he meet but a mighty decent young man coming up to him.

"God save you,' says the King (for the King was a civil-spoken gentleman, by all accounts), 'God save you,' says he to the young man.

"God save you kindly,' says the young man to him back again, 'God save you, King O'Toole.'

"True for you,' says the King, 'I am King O'Toole,' says he, 'prince and plennypennytinchery o' these parts,' says he, 'but how come you to know that?' says he.

"Oh, never mind,' says Saint Kevin (for 'twas he that was in it). 'And now, may I make bold to ask, how is your goose, King O'Toole?' says he.

"Blur-an-agers, how came you to know about my goose?' says the King.

Oh, no matter; I was given to understand it,' says Saint Kevin.

"Oh, that's a folly to talk,' says the King, 'because myself and my goose is private friends,' says he, 'and no one could tell you,' says he, 'barring the fairies.'

"Oh, thin, it wasn't the fairies,' says Saint Kevin, 'for I'd have you know,' says he, 'that I don't keep the likes of such company.'

"You might do worse, then, my gay fellow,' says the King, 'for its they could show you a crock o' money as aisy as kiss hand; and that's not to be sneezed at,' says the King, 'by a poor man,' says he.

"Maybe I've a better way of making money myself,' says the saint.

"By gor,' says the King, 'barring you're a coiner,' says he, 'that's impossible!'

"I'd scorn to be the like, my lord!' says Saint Kevin, mighty high, 'I'd scorn to be the like,' says he.

"Then, what are you?' says the King, 'that makes money so aisy, by your own account.'

"I'm an honest man,' says Saint Kevin.

"Well, honest man,' says the King, 'and how is it you make your money so aisy?'

"By making old things as good as new,' says Saint Kevin.

"Is it a tinker you are?' says the King.

No,' says the saint, 'I'm no tinker by trade, King O'Toole; I've a better trade than a tinker,' says he. 'What would you say,' says he, 'if I made your old goose as good as new?'

"My dear, at the word o' making his goose as good as new, you'd think the poor old Kings eyes was ready to jump out of his head, 'and,' says he - 'truth, thin, I'd give you more money nor you could count,' says he, 'if you did the like, and I'd be beholden to you in the bargain.'

"I scorn your dirty money,' says Saint Kevin.

"Faith, thin, I'm thinking a trifle o' change would do you no harm,' says the King, looking up sly at the old caubeen that Saint Kevin had on him.

"I have a vow against it,' says the saint, 'and I am book sworn,' says he, 'never to have gold, silver, or brass in my company.'

"Barring the trifle you can't help,' says the King, mighty cute, and looking him straight in the face.

"You just hot it,' says Saint Kevin, 'but though I can't take money,' says he, 'I could take a few acres o' land, if you'd give them to me.'

"With all the veins o' my heart,' says the King, 'if you can do what you say.'

"Try me!' says Saint Kevin. 'Call down your goose here,' says he, 'and I'll see what I can do for her.'

"With that the King whistled, and came the poor goose, all as one as a hound, waddling up to the poor old cripple, her master, and as like him as two pays. The minute the saint clapped his eyes on the goose, 'I'll do the job for you,' says he, 'King O'Toole!'

By Jaminee,' says King O'Toole, 'if you do, but I'll say you're the cleverest fellow in the seven parishes.'

"Oh, by dad,' says Saint Kevin, 'you must say more nor that - my horn isn't so soft all out,' says he, 'as to repair your old goose for nothing; what'll you give' me if I do the job for you? - that's the chat,' says Saint Kevin.

"I'll give you whatever you ask,' says the King, 'isn't that fair?'

"Devil a fairer,' says the saint, 'that's the way to do business. Now,' says he, 'this is the bargain I'll make with you, King O'Toole. Will you give me all the ground the goose flies over, the first offer, after I make her as good as new?'

"I will,' says the King.

"You won't go back o' your word?' says Saint Kevin.

"Honour bright!' says King O'Toole, holding out his fist.

"Honour bright,' says Saint Kevin back again, 'it's a bargain,' says he. 'Come here!' says he to the poor old goose - 'come here, you unfortunate old cripple,' says he, 'and it's I that'll make you the sporting bird.'

"With that, my dear, he took up the goose by the two wings - 'criss o' my crass an you,' says he, marking her to grace with the blessed sign at the same minute - and throwing her up in the air, 'whew!' says he, just given' her a blast to help her; and with that, my jewel, she took to her heels, flying like one o' the angels themselves, and cutting as many capers as a swallow before a shower of rain. Away she went down there, right in front of you, along the side o' the clift, and flew over Saint Kevin's bed (that is, where Saint Kevin's bed is now, but was not thin, by raison it wasn't made, but was contrived after by Saint Kevin himself, that the women might leave him alone), and on with her under Lugduff, and round the end of the lake there, far beyond where you see the waterfall - and on with her thin right over the lead mines o' Luganure (that is, where the lead mines is now, but was not thin, by raison they were not discovered, but was all gold in Saint Kevin's time). Well, over the end o' Luganure she flew, stout and sturdy, and round the other end of the little lake, by the Churches (that is, of course, where the Churches is now, but was not then, by reason they were not built, but afterwards by Saint Kevin), and over the big hill here over your head, where you see the big cleft - (and that cleft in the mountain was made by Finn Ma Cool, where he cut it across with a big sword that he got made on purpose by a blacksmith out o' Rathdrum, a cousin of his own, for to fight a joyant (giant) that dared him an' the Curragh o' Kildare; and he tried the sword first on the mountain, and cut it down into a gap, as is plain to this day; and faith, sure enough, it's the same sauce he served the joyant, soon and sudden, and chopped him in two like a pratie, for the glory of his soul and old Ireland) - well, down she flew over the cleft, and fluttering over the wood there at Poulanass. Well - as I said - after fluttering over the wood a little bit, to please herself, the goose flew down, and lit at the foot o' the King, as fresh as a daisy, after flying around his dominions, just as if she hadn't flown three perch.

Well, my dear, it was a beautiful sight to see the King standing with his mouth open, looking at his poor old goose flying as light as a lark, and better nor ever she was; and when she lit at his foot he patted her on the head, and 'ma vourneen,' says he, 'but you are the darling o' the world.'

"And what do you say to me,' says Saint Kevin, 'for making her the like?'

"By gor,' says the King, 'I say nothing beats the art o' men, 'barring the bees.'

"And do you say no more nor that?' says Saint Kevin.

"And that I'm beholden to you,' says the King.

"But will you give me all the ground the goose flew over?' says Saint Kevin.

"I will,' says King O'Toole, 'and you're welcome to it,' says he, 'though it's the last acre I have to give.'

"But you'll keep your word true?' says the saint.

"As true as the sun,' says the King.

"It's well for you,' says Saint Kevin, mighty sharp - 'it's well for you, King O'Toole, that you said that word,' says he, 'for if you didn't say that word, the devil receive the bit o' your goose as would ever fly again,' says Saint Kevin.

"Oh, you needn't laugh,' said old Joe, 'for its truth I'm telling you.'

"Well, when the King was as good as his word, Saint Kevin was pleased with him, and then it was that he made himself known to the King.

"Well, my dear, that's the way that the place came, all at once, into the hands of Saint Kevin; for the goose flew around every individual acre o' King O'Toole's property, you see, being let into the secret by Saint Kevin, who was mighty cute; and so, when he done the old King out of his property for the glory of God, he was pleased with him, and he and the King was the best o' friends ever more after (for the poor old King was doting, you see), and the King had his goose as good as new to divert him as long as he lived; and the saint supported him after he came into his property, as I told you, until the day of his death - and that was soon after; for the poor goose thought he was catching a trout one Friday; but, my jewel, it was a mistake he made - and instead of a trout, it was a thieving horse-eel! and, by gor, instead of the goose killing a trout for the Kings supper - by dad, the eel killed the Kings goose - and small blame to him; but he didn't eat her, because he didn't dare eat what Saint Kevin laid his blessed hands on."

Tales From The Land Of Saints & Scholars

Legend of Bottle Hill

"The Legend of Bottle Hill" is one of the best-known tales from Fairy Legends and Traditions of the South of Ireland (1825–1828) by Thomas Crofton Croker, whose work did much to preserve the wit and magic of southern Irish folklore.

The tale is humorous but cautionary: it mocks human weakness while evoking the playful cruelty of the fairy world. Croker's adaptation, written in the lively Anglo-Irish style of the early nineteenth century, captures the rhythms of oral storytelling and the sly wisdom of the peasantry.

It was in the good days, when the little people, most impudently called fairies, were more frequently seen than they are in these unbelieving times, that a farmer, named Mick Purcell, rented a few acres of barren ground in the neighbourhood of the once celebrated preceptory of Mourne, situated about three miles from Mallow, and thirteen from "the beautiful city called Cork." Mick had a wife and family and they all did what they could, and that was but little, for the poor man had no child grown up big enough to help him in his work, and all the poor woman could do was to mind the children, and to milk the one cow, and to boil the potatoes, and to carry the eggs to market to Mallow; but with all they could do, 'twas hard enough on them to pay the rent. Well, they did manage it for a good while; but at last came a bad year, and the little grain of oats was all spoiled, and the chickens died of the pip, and the pig got the measles, - she was sold in Mallow, and brought almost nothing; and poor Mick found that he hadn't enough to half pay his rent, and two gales were due.

"Why then, Molly," says he, "what'll we do?"

"Wisha, then, mavournene, what would you do but take the cow to the fair of Cork and sell her?" says she, "and Monday is fair day, and so you must go to-morrow, that the poor beast may be rested again the fair."

"And what'll we do when she's gone?" says Mick, sorrowfully.

"Never know I know, Mick; but sure God won't leave us without Him, Mick; and you know how good He was to us when poor little Billy was sick, and we had nothing at all for him to take, that good doctor gentleman at Ballydahin come riding and asking for a drink of milk; and how he gave us two shillings; and how he sent the things and bottles for the child, and gave me my breakfast when I went over to ask a question, so he did, and how he came to see Billy, and never left off his goodness till he was quite well?"

"Oh! you are always that way, Molly, and I believe you are right after all, so I won't be sorry for selling the cow; but I'll go to-morrow, and you must put a needle and thread through my coat, for you know 'tis ripped under the arm."

Molly told him he should have everything right; and about twelve o'clock next day he left her, getting a charge not to sell his cow except for the highest penny. Mick promised to mind it, and went his way along the road. He drove his cow slowly through the little stream which crosses it and runs by the old walls of Mourne. As he passed he glanced his eye upon the towers and one of the old elder trees which were only then little bits of switches.

"Oh, then, if I only had half the money that's buried in you, 'tisn't driving this poor cow I'd be now! Why, then, isn't it too bad that it should be there covered over with earth, and many a one besides me wanting? Well, if it is God's will, I'll have some money myself coming back."

So saying, he moved on after his beast, 'twas a fine day, and the sun shone brightly on the walls of the old abbey as he passed under them; he then crossed an extensive mountain tract, and after six long miles he came to the top of that hill - Bottle Hill 'tis called now, but that was not the name of it then, and just there a man overtook him.

"Good morrow," says he. "Good morrow," kindly, says Mick, looking at the stranger, who was a little man, you'd almost call him a dwarf, only he wasn't quite so little neither. He had a bit of an old, wrinkled, yellow face, for all the world like a dried cauliflower, only he had a sharp little nose, and red eyes, and white hair, and his lips were not red, but all his face was one colour, and his eyes never were quiet, but looking at everything, and although they were red, they made Mick feel quite cold when he looked at them. In truth he did not much like the little man's company; and he couldn't see one bit of his legs, nor his body; for, though the day was warm, he was all wrapped up in a big great-coat. Mick drove his cow something faster, but the little man kept up with him. Mick didn't know how he walked, for he was almost afraid to look at him, and to cross himself, for fear the old man would be angry. Yet he thought his fellow-traveller did not seem to walk like other men, nor to put one foot before the other, but to glide over the rough road, and rough enough it was, like a shadow, without noise and without effort. Mick's heart trembled within him, and he said a prayer to himself, wishing he hadn't come out that day, or that he was on fair hill, or that he hadn't the cow to mind, that he might run away from the bad thing - when, in the midst of his fears, he was again addressed by his companion.

"Where are you going with the cow, honest man?"

"To the fair of Cork then," says Mick, trembling at the shrill and piercing tones of the voice.

"Are you going to sell her?" said the stranger.

"Why, then, what else am I going for but to sell her?"

"Will you sell her to me?"

Mick started - he was afraid to have anything to do with the little man, and he was more afraid to say no.

"What'll you give for her?" at last says he.

"I'll tell you what, I'll give you this bottle," said the little one, pulling a bottle from under his coat.

Mick looked at him and the bottle, and, in spite of his terror, he could not help bursting into a loud fit of laughter.

"Laugh if you will," said the little man, "but I tell you this bottle is better for you than all the money you will get for the cow in Cork - ay, than ten thousand times as much."

Mick laughed again. "Why then," says he, "do you think I am such a fool as to give my good cow for a bottle - and an empty one, too? indeed, then, I won't."

"You had better give me the cow, and take the bottle - you'll not be sorry for it."

"Why, then, and what would Molly say? I'd never hear the end of it; and how would I pay the rent? and what would we all do without a penny of money?

"I tell you this bottle is better to you than money; take it, and give me the cow. I ask you for the last time, Mick Purcell."

Mick started.

"How does he know my name?" thought he.

The stranger proceeded, "Mick Purcell, I know you, and I have regard for you; therefore do as I warn you, or you may be sorry for it. How do you know but your cow will die before you get to Cork?"

Mick was going to say, "God forbid!" but the little man went on (and he was too attentive to say anything to stop him; for Mick was a very civil man, and he knew better than to interrupt a gentleman, and that's what many people, that hold their heads higher, don't mind now).

"And how do you know but there will be many cattle at the fair, and you will get a bad price, or maybe you might be robbed when you are coming home? but what need I talk more to you when you are determined to throw away your luck, Mick Purcell?

"Oh! no, I would not throw away my luck, sir," said Mick, "and if I was sure the bottle was as good as you say, though I never liked an empty bottle, although I had drunk what was in it, I'd give you the cow in the name... "

"Never mind names," said the stranger, "but give me the cow; I would not tell you a lie. Here, take the bottle, and when you go home do what I direct exactly."

Mick hesitated.

"Well then, goodbye, I can stay no longer. Once more, take it, and be rich; refuse it, and beg for your life, and see your children in poverty, and your wife dying for want. That will happen to you, Mick Purcell!" said the little man with a malicious grin, which made him look ten times uglier than ever.

"May be 'tis true," said Mick, still hesitating. He did not know what to do - he could hardly help believing the old man, and at length in a fit of desperation he seized the bottle - "Take the cow," said he, "and if you are telling a lie, the curse of the poor will be on you."

"I care neither for your curses nor your blessings, but I have spoken truth, Mick Purcell, and that you will find to-night, if you do what I tell you."

"And what's that?" says Mick.

"When you go home, never mind if your wife is angry, but be quiet yourself, and make her sweep the room clean, set the table out right, and spread a clean cloth over it; then put the bottle on the ground, saying these words, 'Bottle, do your duty,' and you will see the end of it."

"And is this all?" says Mick.

"No more," said the stranger. "Goodbye, Mick Purcell - you are a rich man."

"God grant it!" said Mick, as the old man moved after the cow, and Mick retraced the road towards his cabin; but he could not help turning back his head, to look after the purchaser of his cow, who was nowhere to be seen.

"Lord between us and harm!" said Mick, "He can't belong to this earth; but where is the cow?" She too was gone, and Mick went homeward muttering prayers, and holding fast the bottle.

"And what would I do if it broke?" thought he. "Oh! but I'll take care of that;" so he put it into his bosom, and went on anxious to prove his bottle, and doubting of the reception he should meet from his wife; balancing his anxieties with his expectations, his fears with his hopes, he reached home in the evening, and surprised his wife, sitting over the turf fire in the big chimney.

"Oh! Mick, are you come back! Sure you weren't at Cork all the way! What has happened to you? Where is the cow? Did you sell her? How much money did you get for her? What news have you? Tell us everything about it."

"Why then, Molly, if you'll give me time, I'll tell you all about it. If you want to know where the cow is, 'tisn't Mick can tell you, for how does he know where she is now?"

"Oh! then, you sold her; and where's the money?"

"Arrah! stop awhile, Molly, and I'll tell you all about it."

"But what is that bottle under your waistcoat?" said Molly, spying its neck sticking out.

"Why, then, be easy now, can't you," says Mick, "till I tell it to you?" and putting the bottle on the table, "That's all I got for the cow."

His poor wife was thunderstruck. "All you got! and what good is that, Mick? Oh! I never thought you were such a fool; and what'll we do for the rent, and what..."

"Now, Molly," says Mick, "can't you hearken to reason? Didn't I tell you how the old man, or whatsoever he was, met me, - no, he did not meet me neither, but he was there with me - on the big hill, and how he made me sell him the cow, and told me the bottle was the only thing for me?"

"Yes, indeed, the only thing for you, you fool!" said Molly, seizing the bottle to hurl it at her poor husband's head; but Mick caught it, and quietly (for he minded the old man's advice) loosened his wife's grasp, and placed the bottle again in his bosom. Poor Molly sat down crying, while Mick told his story, with many a crossing and blessing between him and harm. His wife could not help believing him, particularly as she had as much faith in fairies as she had in the priest, who indeed never discouraged her belief in the fairies; maybe, he didn't know she believed in them, and maybe, he believed in them himself. She got up, however, without saying one word, and began to sweep the earthen floor with a bunch of heather; then she tidied up everything, and put out the long table, and spread the clean cloth, for she had only one, upon it, and Mick, placing the bottle on the ground, looked at it and said, "Bottle, do your duty."

"Look there! look there, mammy!" said his chubby eldest son, a boy about five years old - "look there! look there!" and he sprang to his mother's side, as two tiny little fellows rose like light from the bottle, and in an instant covered the table with dishes and plates of gold and silver, full of the finest victuals that ever were seen, and when all was done went into the bottle again. Mick and his wife looked at everything with astonishment; they had never seen such plates and dishes before, and didn't think they could ever admire them enough; the very sight almost took away their appetites; but at length Molly said, "Come and sit down, Mick, and try and eat a bit. Sure you ought to be hungry after such a good day's work."

"Why, then, the man told no lie about the bottle."

Mick sat down, after putting the children to the table; and they made a hearty meal, though they couldn't taste half the dishes.

"Now," says Molly, "I wonder will those two good little gentlemen carry away these fine things again?" They waited, but no one came; so Molly put up the dishes and plates very carefully, saying, "Why, then, Mick, that was no lie sure enough; but you'll be a rich man yet, Mick Purcell."

Mick and his wife and children went to their bed, not to sleep, but to settle about selling the fine things they did not want, and to take more land. Mick went to Cork and sold his plate, and bought a horse and cart, and began to show that he was making money; and they did all they could to keep the bottle a secret; but for all that, their landlord found it out, for he came to Mick one day and asked him where he got all his money - sure it was not by the farm; and he bothered him so much, that at last Mick told him of the bottle. His landlord offered him a deal of money for it; but Mick would not give it, till at last he offered to give him all his farm for ever, so Mick, who was very rich, thought he'd never want any more money, and gave him the bottle, but Mick was mistaken - he and his family spent money as if there was no end of it; and, to make the story short, they became poorer and poorer, till at last they had nothing left but one cow; and Mick once more drove his cow before him to sell her at Cork fair, hoping to meet the old man and get another bottle. It was hardly day-break when he left home, and he walked on at a good pace till he reached the big hill. The mists were sleeping in the valleys and curling like smoke-wreaths upon the brown heath around him. The sun rose on his left, and just at his feet a lark sprang from its grassy couch and poured forth its joyous mating song, ascending into the clear blue sky,

"Till its form like a speck in the airiness blending

And thrilling with music, was melting in light."

Mick crossed himself, listening as he advanced to the sweet song of the lark, but thinking, notwithstanding, all the time of the little old man; when, just as he reached the summit of the hill, and cast his eyes over the extensive prospect before and around him, he was startled and rejoiced by the same well-known voice, "Well, Mick

Purcell, I told you, you would be a rich man."

"Indeed, then, sure enough I was, that's no lie for you, sir. Good morning to you, but it is not rich I am now - but have you another bottle, for I want it now as much as I did long ago; so if you have it, sir, here is the cow for it."

"And here is the bottle," said the old man, smiling, "you know what to do with it."

"Oh! then, sure I do, as good right I have."

"Well, farewell forever, Mick Purcell. I told you, you would be a rich man."

"And goodbye to you, sir," said Mick, as he turned back, "and good luck to you, and good luck to the big hill - it wants a name - Bottle Hill. - Goodbye, sir, goodbye;" so Mick walked back as fast as he could, never looking after the white-faced little gentleman and the cow, so anxious was he to bring home the bottle. Well, he arrived with it safely enough, and called out, as soon as he saw Molly, - "Oh! sure, I've another bottle!"

"Arrah! then have you? why, then, you're a lucky man, Mick Purcell, that's what you are."

In an instant she put everything right; and Mick, looking at his bottle, exultingly cried out, "Bottle, do your duty." In a twinkling, two great stout men with big cudgels issued from the bottle (I do not know how they got room in it), and belaboured poor Mick and his wife and all his family, till they lay on the floor, when in they went again. Mick, as soon as he recovered, got up and looked about him; he thought and thought, and at last he took up his wife and his children; and, leaving them to recover as well as they could, he took the bottle under his coat, and went to his landlord, who had a great company and he got a servant to tell him he wanted to speak to him, and at last he came out to Mick.

"Well, what do you want now?"

"Nothing, sir, only I have another bottle."

"Oh! ho! is it as good as the first?"

"Yes, sir, and better; if you like, I will show it to you before all the ladies and gentlemen."

"Come along, then." So saying, Mick was brought into the great hall, where he saw his old bottle standing high up on a shelf. "Ah! ha!" says he to himself, "maybe I won't have you by and by."

"Now," says his landlord, "show us your bottle." Mick set it on the floor, and uttered the words; in a moment the landlord was tumbled on the floor; ladies and gentlemen, servants and all, were running and roaring, and sprawling, and kicking and shrieking. Wine cups and salvers were knocked about in every direction, until the landlord called out, "Stop those two devils, Mick Purcell, or I'll have you hanged!"

"They never shall stop," said Mick, "till I get my own bottle that I see up there at top of that shelf."

"Give it down to him, give it down to him, before we are all killed!" says the landlord.

Mick put the bottle in his bosom; in jumped the two men into the new bottle, and he carried the bottles home. I need not lengthen my story by telling how he got richer than ever, how his son married his landlord's only daughter, how he and his wife died when they were very old, and how some of the servants, fighting at their wake, broke the bottles; but still the hill has the name upon it; aye, and so 'twill be always Bottle Hill to the end of the world, and so it ought, for it is a strange story.

Tales From The Land Of Saints & Scholars

Lough Leagh

"Lough Leagh" (often rendered Lough Neagh) is a legend originally written by William Carleton and later adapted by W. B. Yeats for his 1888 anthology Fairy and Folk Tales of the Irish Peasantry (The Walter Scott Publishing Company). The tale offers a mythic explanation for the creation of Lough Neagh, the vast inland lake in Northern Ireland.

In tone, the tale reflects the transition between oral folklore and literary romanticism. Yeats's adaptation smooths Carleton's dialect but retains the rhythm and charm of peasant speech, allowing the myth to breathe in simple, musical language. The story carries traces of pre-Christian cosmology, where the natural landscape was alive with spirit and consequence, yet it is told with the wry affection of a fireside anecdote.

"Do you see that bit of a lake," said my companion, turning his eyes towards the acclivity that overhung Lough Leagh. "Troth, and as little as you think of it, and as ugly as it looks with its weeds and its flags, it is the most famous one in all Ireland. Young and old, rich and poor, far and near, have come to that lake to get cured of all kinds of scurvy and sores. The Lord keep us our limbs whole and sound, for it's a sorrowful thing not to have the use o' them. 'Twas but last week we had a great grand Frenchman here; and, though he came upon crutches, faith he went home sound as a bell; and well he paid Billy Reily for curing him."

"And pray, how did Billy Reily cure him?"

"Oh, well enough. He took his long pole, dipped it down to the bottom of the lake, and brought up on the top of it as much plaster as would do for a thousand sores!"

"What kind of plaster?"

"What kind of plaster? why, black plaster to be sure; for isn't the bottom of the lake filled with a kind of black mud which cures all the world?"

"Then it ought to be a famous lake indeed."

"Famous, and so it is," replied my companion, "but it isn't for its cures neither that it is famous; for, sure, doesn't all the world know there is a fine beautiful city at the bottom of it, where the good people live just like Christians. Troth, it is the truth I tell you; for Shamus-a-sneidh saw it all when he followed his dun cow that was stolen."

"Who stole her?"

"I'll tell you all about it, "Shamus was a poor gossoon, who lived on the brow of the hill, in a cabin with his old mother. They lived by hook and by crook, one way and another, in the best way they could. They had a bit of ground that gave them the preaty, and a little dun cow that gave them the drop o' milk; and, considering how times go, they weren't badly off, for Shamus was a handy gossoon to boot; and, while minding the cow, cutting heather and making brooms, which his mother sold on a market-day, and brought home the bit o' tobacco, the grain of salt, and other nick-nacks, which a poor body can't well do without.

"Once upon a time, however, Shamus went farther than usual up the mountain, looking for long heather, for town's-people don't like to stoop, and so like long handles to their brooms. The little dun cow was almost as cunning as a Christian sinner, and followed Shamus like a lap-dog everywhere he'd go, so that she required little or no herding. On this day she found nice pickings on a round spot as green as a leek; and, as poor Shamus was weary, as a body would be on a fine summer's day, he lay down on the grass to rest himself, just as we're resting ourselves on the cairn here. Begad, he hadn't long lain there, sure enough, when, what should he see but whole loads of ganconers dancing about the place. Some o' them were hurling, some kicking a football, and others leaping a kick-step-and-a-leap. They were so supple and so active that Shamus was highly delighted with the sport, and a little tanned-skinned chap in a red cap pleased him better than any o' them, because he used to tumble the other fellows like mushrooms. At one time he had kept the ball up for as good as half-an-hour, when Shamus cried out, 'Well done, my hurler!' The word wasn't well out of his mouth when whap went the ball on his eye, and flash went the fire. Poor Shamus thought he was blind, and roared out, 'Mille murder!' but the only thing he heard was a loud laugh. 'Cross o' Christ about us,' says he to himself, 'what is this for?' and after rubbing his eyes they came to a little, and he could see the sun and the sky, and, by-and-by, he could see everything but his cow and the mischievous ganconers. They were gone to their rath or mote; but where was the little dun cow? He looked, and he looked, and he might have looked from that day to this, because she wasn't to be found, and good reason why - the ganconers took her away with them.

"Shamus-a-sneidh, however, didn't think so, but ran home to his mother.

"Where is the cow, Shamus?' asked the old woman.

"Och, Musha, bad luck to her,' said Shamus, 'I don't know where she is!'

"Is that an answer, you big blaggard, for the likes o' you to give your poor old mother?' said she.

"Och, Musha,' said Shamus, I don't kick up such a bollhous about nothing. The old cow is safe enough, I'll be bail, some place or other, though I could find her if I put my eyes upon kippeens, and, speaking of eyes, faith, I had very good luck o' my side, or I had never a one to look after her.'

"Why, what happened your eyes, agrah?' asked the old woman.

"Oh! didn't the ganconers - the Lord save us from all hurt and harm! - drive their hurling ball into them both! and sure I was stone blind for an hour.'

"And may be,' said the mother, 'the good people took our cow?'

"No, nor the devil a one of them,' said Shamus, 'for, by the powers, that same cow is as known as a lawyer, and wouldn't be such a fool as to go with the ganconers while she could get such grass as I found for her to-day."

In this way, continued my informant, they talked about the cow all that night, and next morning both o' them set off to look for her. After searching every place, high and low, what should Shamus see sticking out of a bog-hole but something very like the horns of his little beast!

"Oh, mother, mother," said he, "I've found her!"

"Where, Alanna?" asked the old woman.

"In the bog-hole, mother," answered Shamus.

At this the poor old creature set up such a pullallue that she brought the seven parishes about her; and the neighbours soon pulled the cow out of the bog-hole. You'd swear it was the same, and yet it wasn't, as you shall hear by-and-by.

Shamus and his mother brought the dead beast home with them; and, after skinning her, hung the meat up in the chimney. The loss of the drop o' milk was a sorrowful thing, and though they had a good deal of meat, that couldn't last always; besides, the whole parish chided them for eating the flesh of a beast that died without bleeding. But the pretty thing was, they couldn't eat the meat after all, for when it was boiled it was as tough as carrion, and as black as a turf. You might as well think of sinking your teeth in an oak plank as into a piece of it, and then you'd want to sit a great piece from the wall for fear of knocking your head against it when pulling it through your teeth. At last and at long run they were forced to throw it to the dogs, but the dogs wouldn't smell to it, and so it was thrown into the ditch, where it rotted. This misfortune cost poor Shamus many a salt tear, for he was now obliged to work twice as hard as before, and be out cutting heather on the mountain late and early. One day he was passing by this cairn with a load of brooms on his back, when what should he see but the little dun cow and two red-headed fellows herding her.

"That's my mother's cow," said Shamus-a-sneidh.

"No, it is not," said one of the chaps.

"But I say it is," said Shamus, throwing the brooms on the ground, and seizing the cow by the horns. At that the red fellows drove her as fast as they could to this steep place, and with one leap she bounced over, with Shamus stuck fast to her horns. They made only one splash in the lough, when the waters closed over them, and they sunk to the bottom. Just as Shamus-a-sneidh thought that all was over with him, he found himself before a most elegant palace built with jewels, and all manner of fine stones. Though his eyes were dazzled with the splendour of the place, faith he had gumption enough not to let go his hold, but in spite of all they could do, he held his little cow by the horns. He was asked into the palace, but wouldn't go.

The hubbub at last grew so great that the door flew open, and out walked a hundred ladies and gentlemen, as fine as any in the land.

"What does this boy want?" asked one o' them, who seemed to be the master.

"I want my mother's cow," said Shamus.

"That's not your mother's cow," said the gentleman.

"Bethershin!" cried Shamus-a-sneidh, "don't I know her as well as I know my right hand?"

"Where did you lose her?" asked the gentleman. And so Shamus up and told him all about it - how he was on the mountain - how he saw the good people hurling - how the ball was knocked in his eye, and his cow was lost.

"I believe you are right," said the gentleman, pulling out his purse, "and here is the price of twenty cows for you."

"No, no," said Shamus, "you'll not catch old birds with chaff. I'll have my cow and nothing else."

"You're a funny fellow," said the gentleman, "stop here and live in a palace."

"I'd rather live with my mother."

"Foolish boy!" said the gentleman, "stop here and live in a palace."

"I'd rather live in my mother's cabin."

"Here you can walk through gardens loaded with fruit and flowers."

"I'd rather," said Shamus, "be cutting heather on the mountain."

"Here you can eat and drink of the best."

"Since I've got my cow, I can have milk once more with the praties."

"Oh!" cried the ladies, gathering round him, "sure you wouldn't take away the cow that gives us milk for our tea?"

"Oh!" said Shamus, "my mother wants milk as bad as anyone, and she must have it; so there is no use in your palaver - I must have my cow."

At this they all gathered about him and offered him bushels of gold, but he wouldn't have anything but his cow. Seeing him as obstinate as a mule, they began to thump and beat him; but still he held fast by the horns, till at length a great blast of wind blew him out of the place, and in a moment he found himself and the cow standing on the side of the lake, the water of which looked as if it hadn't been disturbed since Adam was a boy - and that's a long time since.

Well, Shamus-a-sneidh drove home his cow, and right glad his mother was to see her; but the moment she said, "God bless the beast," she sunk down like the breesha of a turf rick. That was the end of Shamus-a-sneidh's dun cow.

"And, sure," continued my companion, standing up, "it is now time for me to look after my brown cow, and God send the ganconers haven't taken her!"

Of this I assured him there could be no fear; and so we parted.

Tales From The Land Of Saints & Scholars

Morraha

"Morraha" is one of the best-known tales collected by William Larminie in his West Irish Folk-Tales and Romances (1893), later adapted by Alfred Perceval Graves in The Irish Fairy Book (1909). The story belongs to the Irish wonder-tale tradition and combines the elements of myth, riddle, and transformation that characterise many Celtic narratives.

At its heart, the story of Morraha is a meditation on endurance and wisdom. The hero represents the old magical order of Ireland, the druidic, shape-changing world where intellect and cunning matter more than brute strength. Graves's adaptation softens Larminie's dialect and expands the tale's lyricism, giving it the tone of a myth retold for the drawing room rather than the hearth.

Morraha rose in the morning, and washed his hands and face, and said his prayers, and ate his food; and he asked God to prosper the day for him; and he went down to the brink of the sea, and he saw a currach, short and green, coming towards him; and in it there was but one youthful champion, and he playing hurly from prow to stern of the currach. He had a hurl of gold and a ball of silver; and he stopped not until the currach was in on the shore; and he drew her up on the green grass, and put fastening on her for a day and a year, whether he should be there all that time, or should only be on land for an hour by the clock. And Morraha saluted the young man in words intelligent, intelligible, such as were spoken at that time; and the other saluted him in the same fashion, and asked him would he play a game of cards with him; and Morraha he said had not the wherewithal; and the other answered that he was never without a candle or the making of it; and he put his hand in his pocket and drew out a table and two chairs and a pack of cards, and they sat down on the chairs and went to the card-playing. The first game Morraha won, and the slender red champion bade him make his claim; and he said that the land above him should be filled with stock of sheep in the morning. It was well, and he played no second game, but home he went.

The next day Morraha went to the brink of the sea, and the young man came in the currach and asked him would he play cards; and they played, and Morraha won. And the young man bade him make his claim; and he said that the land above should be filled with cattle in the morning. It was well, and he played no other game, but went home.

And on the third morning Morraha went to the brink of the sea, and he saw the young man coming. And he drew up his boat on the shore, and asked him would he play cards. And they played, and Morraha won the game; and the young man bade him give his claim. And he said he should have a castle, and of women the finest and fairest; and they were his. It was well, and the young man went away.

On the fourth day the woman asked him how he had found himself, and he told her. "And I am going out," said he, "to play again to-day."

"I cross (forbid) you go again to him. If you have won so much, you will lose more; and have no more to do with him."

But he went against her will, and he saw the currach coming, and the young man was driving his balls from end to end of the currach. He had balls of silver and a hurl of gold, and he stopped not till he drew his boat on the shore, and made her fast for a year and a day. And Morraha and he saluted each other; and he asked Morraha if he would play a game of cards, and they played and he won. And Morraha said to him, "Give your claim, now."

Said he, "You will hear it too soon. I lay on you the bonds of the art of the Druid not to sleep two nights in one house, nor finish a second meal at the one table, till you bring me the sword of light and news of the death of Anshgayliacht."

He went down to his wife, and sat down in a chair, and gave a groan, and the chair broke in pieces.

"It is the son of a king under spells you are," said his wife, "and you had better have taken my counsel than that the spells should be on you." He said to her to bring news of the death of Anshgayliacht and the sword of light to the slender red champion.

"Go out," said she, "in the morning of the morrow, and take the bridle in the window and shake it; and whatever beast, handsome or ugly, puts the head in it, take that one with you. Do not speak a word to her till she speaks to you; and take with you three pint bottles of ale and three sixpenny loaves, and do the thing she tells you; and when she runs to my father's land, on a height above the court, she will shake herself, and the bells will ring, and my father will say Brown Allree is in the land. And if the son of a king or queen is there, bring him to me on your shoulders; but if it is the son of a poor man, let him come no further."

He rose in the morning, and took the bridle that was in the window and went out and shook it, and Brown Allree came and put her head in it. And he took the three loaves and three bottles of ale, and went riding; and when he was riding, she bent her head down to take hold of her feet with her mouth, in hopes he would speak in ignorance; but he spoke not a word during the time, and the mare at last spoke to him, and said to him to dismount and give her dinner. He gave her the sixpenny loaf toasted and a bottle of ale to drink. "Sit up, now, riding and take good heed of yourself. There are three miles of fire I have to clear at a leap."

She cleared the three miles of fire at a leap, and asked if he were riding, and he said he was. They went on then, and she told him to dismount and give her a meal; and he did so, and gave her a sixpenny loaf and a bottle; and she consumed them, and said to him there were before them three miles of hill covered with steel thistles, and that she must clear it. And she cleared the hill with a leap, and she asked him if he were still riding, and he said he was. They went on, and she went not far before she told him to give her a meal, and he gave her the bread and the bottleful. And she went over three miles of sea with a leap, and she came then to the land of the King of France; and she went up on a height above the castle, and she shook herself and neighed, and the bells rang; and the King said that it was Brown Allree was in the land. "Go out," said he, "and if it is the son of a king or queen, carry him in on your shoulders; if it is not, leave him there."

They went out, and the stars of the son of a king were on his breast; and they lifted him high on their shoulders and bore him in to the King. And they passed the night cheerfully with playing and with drinking, with sport and with diversion, till the whiteness of the day came upon the morrow morning.

Then the young King told the cause of his journey, and he asked of the Queen her counsel and consent, and to give him counsel and good luck, and the woman told him everything she advised him to do. "Go now," said she, "and take with you the best mare in the stable, and go to the door of Rough Niall of the speckled rock, and knock, and call on him to give you news of the death of Anshgayliacht and the sword of light; and let the horse's back be to the door, and apply the spurs, and away with you!"

And in the morning he did so, and he took the best horse from the stable and rode to the door of Niall, and turned the horse's back to the door, and demanded news of the death of Anshgayliacht, and the sword of light; and he applied the spurs, and away with him. And Niall followed him, and as he was passing the gate cut the horse in two. And the mother was there with a dish of puddings and flesh, and she threw it in his eyes and blinded him, and said, "Fool, whatever kind of man it is that's mocking you, isn't that a fine condition you have got into on your father's horse?"

On the morning of the next day Morraha rose and took another horse from the stable, and went again to the door of Niall, and knocked and demanded news of the death of Anshgayliacht, and the sword of light, and applied the spurs to the horse, and away with him. And Niall followed, and as he was passing the gate cut the horse in two, and took half the saddle with him, and his mother met him, and threw the flesh in his eyes and blinded him.

And on the third day Morraha went also to the door of Niall; and Niall followed him, and as he was passing the gate cut away the saddle from under him and the clothes from his back.

Then his mother said to Niall, "Whatever fool it is that's mocking you, he is out yonder in the little currach, going home; and take good heed to yourself, and don't sleep one wink for three days."

And for three days the little currach was there before him, and then his mother came to him and said, "Sleep as much as you want now.

He is gone."

And he went to sleep, and there was heavy sleep on him, and Morraha went in and took hold of the sword that was on the bed at his head. And the sword thought to draw itself out of the hand of Morraha, but it failed. And then it gave a cry, and it wakened Niall, and Niall said it was a rude and rough thing to come into his house like that; and Morraha said to him, "Leave your much talking, or I will cut the head off you. Tell me the news of the death of Anshgayliacht."

"Oh, you can have my head."

"But your head is no good to me. Tell me the story."

"Oh," said Niall's wife, "you must get the story."

"Oh," said Morraha, "is the woman your wife?"

"Oh," said the man, "is it not you that have the story?"

"Oh," said she, "you will tell it to us."

"Well," said the man, "let us sit down together till I tell the story. I thought no one would ever get it, but now it will be heard by all."

When I was growing up my mother taught me the language of the birds, and when I got married I used to be listening to their conversation; and I would be laughing; and my wife would be asking me what the reason of my laughing was, but I did not like to tell her, as women are always asking questions. We went out walking one fine morning, and the birds were arguing with one another. One of them said to another, "Why should you be making comparison with me, when there is not a king nor knight that does not come to look at my tree?"

"Oh, what advantage has your tree over mine, on which there are three rods of magic and mastery growing?"

When I heard them arguing, and knew that the rods were there, I began to laugh.

"Oh," said my wife, "why are you always laughing? I believe it is at myself you are jesting, and I'll walk with you no more."

"Oh, it is not about you I am laughing. It is because I understand the language of the birds."

Then I had to tell her what the birds were saying to one another; and she was greatly delighted, and she asked me to go home, and she gave orders to the cook to have breakfast ready at six o'clock in the morning. I did not know why she was going out early, and breakfast was ready in the morning at the hour she appointed. She asked me to go out walking. I went with her. She went to the tree, and asked me to cut a rod for her.

"Oh, I will not cut it. Are we not better without it?"

"I will not leave this till I get the rod, to see if there is any good in it."

I cut the rod, and gave it to her. She turned from me, and struck a blow on a stone and changed it; and she struck a second blow on me, and made of me a black raven, and she went home, and left me after her. I thought she would come back; she did not come, and I had to go into a tree till morning. In the morning, at six o'clock, there was a bellman out, proclaiming that everyone who killed a raven would get a fourpenny bit. At last you would not find man or boy without a gun, nor, if you were to walk three miles, a raven that was not killed. I had to make a nest in the top of the parlour chimney, and hide myself all day till night came, and go out to pick up a bit to support me, till I spent a month. Here she is herself (to say) if it is a lie I am telling.

"It is not," said she.

Then I saw her out walking. I went up to her, and I thought she would turn me back to my own shape, and she struck me with the rod and made of me an old white horse, and she ordered me to be put to a cart with a man to draw stones from morning till night. I was worse off then. She spread abroad a report that I had died suddenly in my bed, and prepared a coffin, and waked me, and buried me. Then she had no trouble. But when I got tired, I began to kill everyone who came near me, and I used to go into the haggard every night and destroy the stacks of corn; and when a man came near me in the morning, I would follow him till I broke his bones. Everyone got afraid of me. When she saw I was doing mischief, she came to meet me, and I thought she would change me. And she did change me, and made a fox of me. When I saw she was doing me every sort of damage, I went away from her. I knew there was a badger's hole in the garden, and I went there till night came, and I made great slaughter among the ducks and geese. There she is herself to say if I am telling a lie.

"Oh, you are telling nothing but the truth, only less than the truth."

When she had enough of my killing the fowl, she came out into the garden, for she knew I was in the badger's hole. She came to me, and made me a wolf. I had to be off, and go to an island, where no one at all would see me, and now and then I used to be killing sheep, for there were not many of them, and I was afraid of being seen and hunted; and so I passed a year, till a shepherd saw me among the sheep, and a pursuit was made after me. And when the dogs came near me, there was no place for me to escape to from them; but I recognised the sign of the King among the men, and I made for him, and the King cried out to stop the hounds. I took a leap upon the front of the King's saddle, and the woman behind cried out, "My King and my lord, kill him, or he will kill you."

"Oh, he will not kill me. He knew me; and must be pardoned."

And the King took me home with him, and gave orders that I should be well cared for. I was so wise when I got food I would not eat one morsel until I got a knife and fork. The man told the King, and the King came to see if it was true, and I got a knife and fork, and I took the knife in one paw and the fork in the other, and I bowed to the King. The King gave orders to bring him drink, and it came; and the King filled a glass of wine, and gave it to me.

I took hold of it in my paw, and drank it, and thanked the King.

"Oh, on my honour, it is some king that has lost him when he came on the island; and I will keep him, as he is trained; and perhaps he will serve us yet."

And this is the sort of King he was—a King who had not a child living. Eight sons were born to him and three daughters, and they were stolen the same night they were born. No matter what guard was placed over them, the child would be gone in the morning. The Queen was now carrying the twelfth child, and when she was lying-in, the King took me with him to watch the baby. The women were not satisfied with me. "Oh," said the King, "what was all your watching ever? One that was born to me I have not; and I will leave this one in the dog's care, and he will not let it go."

A coupling was put between me and the cradle, and when everyone went to sleep I was watching till the person woke who attended in the daytime; but I was there only two nights when, it was near the day, I saw the hand coming down through the chimney, and the hand was so big that it took round the child altogether, and thought to take him away. I caught hold of the hand above the wrist, and, as I was fastened to the cradle, I did not let go my hold till I cut the hand from the wrist, and there was a howl from the person without. I laid the hand in the cradle with the child, and, as I was tired, I fell asleep; and when I awoke I had neither child nor hand; and I began to howl, and the King heard me, and he cried out that something was wrong with me, and he sent servants to see what was the matter with me, and when the messenger came he saw me covered with blood, and he could not see the child; and he went to the King, and told him the child was not to be got. The King came, and saw the cradle coloured with the blood, and he cried out, "Where was the child gone?" and everyone said it was the dog had eaten it.

The King said, "It is not. Loose him, and he will get the pursuit himself."

When I was loosed, I found the scent of the blood till I came to a door of the room in which the child was. I went to the King, and took hold of him, and went back again, and began to tear at the door. The King followed me, and asked for the key. The servant said it was in the room of the stranger woman. The King caused search to be made for her, and she was not to be found. "I will break the door," said the King, "as I can't get the key." The King broke the door, and I went in, and went to the trunk, and the King asked for a key to unlock it. He got no key, and he broke the lock. When he opened the trunk the child and the hand were stretched side by side, and the child was asleep. The King took the hand, and ordered a woman to come for the child, and he showed the hand to everyone in the house. But the stranger woman was gone, and she did not see the King; and here she is herself to say if I am telling lies of her.

"Oh, it's nothing but the truth you have."

The King did not allow me to be tied any more. He said there was nothing so much to wonder at as that I cut the hand off, and I tied.

The child was growing till he was a year old, and he was beginning to walk, and there was no one caring for him more than I was. He was growing till he was three, and he was running out every minute; so the King ordered a silver chain to be put between me and the child, so that he might not go away from me. I was out with him in the garden every day, and the King was as proud as the world of the child. He would be watching him every place we went, till the child grew so wise that he would loosen the chain and get off. But one day that he loosed it I failed to find him; and I ran into the house and searched the house, but there was no getting him for me. The King cried to go out and find the child, that he had got loose from the dog. They went searching for him, but they could not find him. When they failed altogether to find him, there remained no more favour with the King towards me, and everyone disliked me, and I grew weak, for I did not get a morsel to eat half the time. When summer came I said I would try and go home to my own country. I went away one fine morning, and I went swimming, and God helped me till I came home. I went into the garden, for I knew there was a place in the garden where I could hide myself, for fear she should see me. In the morning I saw my wife out walking, and my child with her, held by the hand. I pushed out to see the child, and, as he was looking about him everywhere, he saw me, and called out, "I see my shaggy papa. Oh," said he, "oh, my heart's love, my shaggy papa, come here till I see you."

I was afraid the woman would see me, as she was asking the child where he saw me, and he said I was up in a tree; and the more the child called me, the more I hid myself. The woman took the child home with her, but I knew he would be up early in the morning.

I went to the parlour window, and the child was within, and he playing. When he saw me, he cried out, "Oh, my heart's love, come here till I see you, shaggy papa." I broke the window, and went in, and he began to kiss me. I saw the rod in front of the chimney, and I jumped up at the rod and knocked it down. "Oh, my heart's love, no one would give me the pretty rod." I thought he would strike me with the rod, but he did not. When I saw the time was short, I raised my paw, and I gave him a scratch below the knee. "Oh, you naughty, dirty, shaggy papa; you have hurt me so much—I'll give yourself a blow of the rod." He struck me a light blow, and as there was no sin on him, I came back to my own shape again. When he saw a man standing before him he gave a cry, and I took him up in my arms. The servants heard the child. A maid came in to see what the matter with him was. When she saw me she gave a cry out of her, and she said, "Oh, my soul to God, if the master isn't come to life again."

Another came in, and said it was he, really. And when the mistress heard of it, she came to see with her own eyes, for she would not believe I was there; and when she saw me she said she'd drown herself. And I said to her, "If you yourself will keep the secret, no living man will ever get the story from me until I lose my head."

Many's the man has come asking for the story, and I never let one return; but now everyone will know it, but she is as much to blame as I. I gave you my head on the spot, and a thousand welcomes, and she cannot say I have been telling anything but the truth.

"Oh, surely, nor are you now."

When I saw I was in a man's shape I said I would take the child back to his father and mother, as I knew the grief they were in after him. I got a ship, and took the child with me; and when I was journeying I came to land on an island, and I saw not a living soul on it, only a court, dark and gloomy. I went in to see was there anyone in it. There was no one but an old hag, tall and frightful, and she asked me, "What sort of person are you?" I heard someone groaning in another room, and I said I was a doctor, and I asked her what ailed the person who was groaning.

"Oh," said she, "it is my son, whose hand has been bitten from his wrist by a dog."

I knew then it was the boy who was taking the child from me, and I said I would cure him if I got a good reward.

I have nothing, but there are eight young lads and three young women, as handsome as anyone laid eyes on, and if you cure him I will give you them."

"But tell me in what place his hand was cut from."

"Oh, it was out in another country twelve years ago."

"Show me the way, that I may see him."

She brought me into a room, so that I saw him, and his arm was swelled up to the shoulder. He asked if I would cure him; and I said I could cure him if he would give me the reward his mother promised.

"Oh, I will give it, but cure me."

"Well, bring them out to me."

The hag brought them out of the room. I said I would burn the flesh that was on his arm. When I looked on him he was howling with pain. I said that I would not leave him in pain long. The thief had only one eye in his forehead. I took a bar of iron, and put it in the fire till it was red, and I said to the hag, "He will be howling at first, but will fall asleep presently, and do not wake him until he has slept as much as he wants. I will close the door when I am going out." I took the bar with me, and I stood over him, and I turned it across through his eye as far as I could. He began to bellow, and tried to catch me, but I was out and away, having closed the door. The hag asked me, "Why is he bellowing?"

"Oh, he will be quiet presently, and will sleep for a good while, and I'll come again to have a look at him; but bring me out the young men and the young women."

I took them with me, and I said to her, "Tell me where you got them."

Oh, my son brought them with him, and they are the offspring of the one King."

I was well satisfied, and I had no liking for delay to get myself free from the hag, and I took them on board the ship, and the child I had myself. I thought the King might leave me the child I nursed myself; but when I came to land, and all those young people with me, the King and Queen were out walking. The King was very aged, and the Queen aged likewise. When I came to converse with them, and the twelve with me, the King and Queen began to cry. I asked, "Why are you crying?"

"Oh, it is for good cause I am crying. As many children as these I should have, and now I am withered, grey, at the end of my life, and I have not one at all."

"Oh, belike, you will yet have plenty."

I told him all I went through, and I gave him the child in his hand, and "These are your other children who were stolen from you, whom I am giving to you safe. They are gently reared."

When the King heard who they were, he smothered them with kisses and drowned them with tears, and dried them with fine cloths, silken, and the hairs of his own head, and so also did their mother, and great was his welcome for me, as it was I who found them all. And the King said to me, "I will give you your own child, as it is you who have earned him best; but you must come to my court every year, and the child with you, and I will share with you my possessions."

"Oh, I have enough of my own, and after my death I will leave it to the child."

I spent a time till my visit was over, and I told the King all the troubles I went through, only I said nothing about my wife. And now you have the story of the death of Anshgayliacht, the hag's son.

And Morraha thanked Rough Niall for the story, and he struck the ground with the Sword of Light, and Brown Allree was beside of him and she said to him, "Sit up, now, riding, and take good heed of yourself," and at one leap she cleared the sea and at the next the three miles of hill covered with steel thistles and at the third the three miles of fire, and then he was home and he told the tale of the death of Anshgayliacht to the Slender Red Champion and gave him the Sword of Light, and he was well pleased to get them, and he took the spells of Morraha, and he had his wife and his castle back again, and by-and-by the five children; but he never put his hand to card-playing with strangers again.

Tales From The Land Of Saints & Scholars

Munachar and Manachar

"Munachar and Manachar" is a short, rhythmic Irish folktale of comic absurdity and circular logic, first collected by Douglas Hyde and later adapted by W. B. Yeats in Fairy and Folk Tales of the Irish Peasantry (1888, The Walter Scott Publishing Company). It tells of two companions, Munachar and Manachar, whose friendship breaks down when Manachar eats all the berries from a tree they had found together.

The tale's humour lies in its rhythm and repetition, echoing oral performance and the storyteller's delight in absurd persistence. It belongs to a class of "chain tales" found across Europe and beyond, where meaning comes as much from the pattern as from the plot.

There once lived a Munachar and a Manachar, a long time ago, and it is a long time since it was, and if they were alive then they would not be alive now. They went out together to pick raspberries, and as many as Munachar used to pick Manachar used to eat. Munachar he said must go look for a rod to make a gad (a withy band) to hang Manachar, who ate his raspberries, each and every one.

When he came to the rod, "God save you," said the rod. "God and Mary save you." "How far are you going?"

"Going looking for a rod, a rod to make a gad, a gad to hang Manachar, who ate my raspberries, every one of them."

"You will not get me," said the rod, "until you get an axe to cut me."
Munachar found the axe.

"God save you," said the axe. "God and Mary save you." "How far are you going?"

"Going looking for an axe, an axe to cut a rod, a rod to make a gad, a gad to hang Manachar, who ate my raspberries, every one of them."

"You will not get me," said the axe, "until you get a flag to edge me."
Munachar found the flag.

"God save you," says the flag. "God and Mary save you." "How far are you going?"

"Going looking for an axe, an axe to cut a rod, a rod to make a gad, a gad to hang Manachar, who ate my raspberries, every one of them."

"You will not get me," says the flag, "till you get water to wet me."
Munachar found the water.

"God save you," says the water. "God and Mary save you." "How far are you going?"

"Going looking for water, water to wet flag to edge an axe, an axe to cut a rod, a rod to make a gad, a gad to hang Manachar, who ate my raspberries, every one of them."

"You will not get me," said the water, "until you get a deer who will swim me."

Munachar found the deer.

"God save you," says the deer. "God and Mary save you." "How far are you going?"

"Going looking for a deer, deer to swim water, water to wet flag, flag to edge an axe, an axe to cut a rod, a rod to make a gad, a gad to hang Manachar, who ate my raspberries, every one of them."

"You will not get me," said the deer, "until you get a hound who will hunt me."

Munachar found the hound. "God save you," says the hound. "God and Mary save you." "How far are you going?"

"Going looking for a hound, hound to hunt deer, deer to swim water, water to wet flag, flag to edge axe, axe to cut a rod, a rod to make a gad, a gad to hang Manachar, who ate my raspberries, every one of them."

"You will not get me," said the hound, "until you get a bit of butter to put in my claw."

Munachar found the butter. "God save you," says the butter. "God and Mary save you." "How far are you going?"

"Going looking for butter, butter to go in claw of hound, hound to hunt deer, deer to swim water, water to wet flag, flag to edge axe, axe to cut a rod, a rod to make a gad, a gad to hang Manachar, who ate my raspberries, every one of them."

"You will not get me," said the butter, "until you get a cat who shall scrape me."

Munachar found the cat.

"God save you," said the cat. "God and Mary save you." "How far are you going?"

"Going looking for a cat, cat to scrape butter, butter to go in claw of hound, hound to hunt deer, deer to swim water, water to wet flag, flag to edge axe, axe to cut a rod, a rod to make a gad, gad to hang Manachar, who ate my raspberries, every one of them."

"You will not get me," said the cat, "until you will get milk which you will give me."

Munachar found the cow.

"God save you," said the cow. "God and Mary save you." "How far are you going?" "Going looking for a cow, cow to give me milk, milk I will give to the cat, cat to scrape butter, butter to go in claw of hound, hound to hunt deer, deer to swim water, water to wet flag, flag to edge axe, axe to cut a rod, a rod to make a gad, a gad to hang Manachar, who ate my raspberries, every one of them."

"You will not get any milk from me," said the cow, "until you bring me a wisp of straw from those threshers yonder."

Munachar found the threshers.

"God save you," said the threshers. "God and Mary save ye." "How far are you going?"

"Going looking for a wisp of straw from you to give to the cow, the cow to give me milk, milk I will give to the cat, cat to scrape butter, butter to go in claw of hound, hound to hunt deer, deer to swim water, water to wet flag, flag to edge axe, axe to cut a rod, a rod to make a gad, a gad to hang Manachar, who ate my raspberries, every one of them."

"You will not get any wisp of straw from us," said the threshers, "until you bring us the makings of a cake from the miller over yonder."

Munachar found the miller.

"God save you." "God and Mary save you." "How far are you going?"

"Going looking for the makings of a cake, which I will give to the threshers, the threshers to give me a wisp of straw, the wisp of straw I will give to the cow, the cow to give me milk, milk I will give to the cat, cat to scrape butter, butter to go in claw of hound, hound to hunt deer, deer to swim water, water to wet flag, flag to edge axe, axe to cut a rod, a rod to make a gad, a gad to hang Manachar, who ate my raspberries, every one of them."

"You will not get any makings of a cake from me," said the miller, "till you bring me a full sieve of water from the river over there."

Munachar took the sieve in his hand and went over to the river, but as often as ever he would stoop and fill it with water, the moment he raised it the water would run out of it again, and sure, if he had been there from that day till this, he never could have filled it.

A crow went flying by him, over his head. "Daub! daub!" said the crow.

"My soul to God, then," said Munachar, "but it's the good advice you have," and he took the red clay and the daub that was by the brink, and he rubbed it to the bottom of the sieve, until all the holes were filled, and then the sieve held the water, and he brought the water to the miller, and the miller gave him the makings of a cake, and he gave the makings of the cake to the threshers, and the threshers gave him a wisp of straw, and he gave the wisp of straw to the cow, and the cow gave him milk, the milk he gave to the cat, the cat scraped the butter, the butter went into the claw of the hound, the hound hunted the deer, the deer swam the water, the water wet the flag, the flag sharpened the axe, the axe cut the rod, and the rod made a gad, and when he had it ready… well, I'll stand bail that Manachar was, by then, a long way away from him.

Tales From The Land Of Saints & Scholars

Ned Sheehy's Excuse

"Ned Sheehy's Excuse" is a humorous Irish folktale first recorded by Thomas Crofton Croker in his influential collection Fairy Legends and Traditions of the South of Ireland (1825–28). Like much of Croker's work, the story blends local superstition, rural wit, and the light mockery of peasant life that fascinated nineteenth-century readers.

The piece captures the comic folklore tradition of the Irish south, where encounters with the "Good People" or the supernatural often serve as metaphors for human folly and cunning. Croker presents Ned not as a fool but as an improviser, using myth to excuse mischief, a reminder of how deeply the fairy world had rooted itself in everyday thought.

Ned Sheehy was servant-man to Richard Gumbleton, Esquire, of Mountbally, Gumbletonmore, in the north of the county of Cork; and a better servant than Ned was not to be found in that honest county, from Cape Clear to the Kilworth Mountains; for nobody - no, not his worst enemy - could say a word against him, only that he was rather given to drinking, idling, lying, and loitering, especially the last; for send Ned of a five-minute message at nine o'clock in the morning, and you were a lucky man if you saw him before dinner. If there happened to be a public-house in the way, or even a little out of it, Ned was sure to mark it as dead as a pointer; and, knowing everybody, and everybody liking him, it is not to be wondered at he had so much to say and to hear, that the time slipped away as if the sun somehow or other had knocked two hours into one.

But when he came home, he never was short of an excuse. He had, for that matter, five hundred ready upon the tip of his tongue; so much so, that I doubt if even the very reverend doctor Swift, for many years Dean of St. Patrick's, in Dublin, could match him in that particular, though his reverence had a pretty way of his own of writing things which brought him into very decent company. In fact, Ned would fret a saint, but then he was so good-humoured a fellow, and really so handy about a house, - for, as he said himself, he was as good as a lady's maid, - that his master could not find it in his heart to part with him.

In your grand houses - not that I am saying that Richard Gumbleton, esquire of Mountbally, Gumbletonmore, did not keep a good house, but a plain country gentleman, although he is second-cousin to the last high-sheriff of the county, cannot have all the army of servants that the lord-lieutenant has in the castle of Dublin - I say, in your grand houses, you can have a servant for every kind of thing, but in Mountbally, Gumbletonmore, Ned was expected to please master and mistress; or, as counsellor Curran said, - by the same token the counsellor was a little dark man - one day that he dined there, on his way to the Clonmel assizes - Ned was minister for the home and foreign departments.

But to make a long story short, Ned Sheehy was a good butler, and a right good one too, and as for a groom, let him alone with a horse and he could dress it, or ride it, or shoe it, or physic it, or do anything with it but make it speak - he was a second whisperer! - there was not his match in the barony, or the next one neither. A pack of hounds he could manage well, ay, and ride after them with the boldest man in the land. It was Ned who leaped the old bounds' ditch at the turn of the boreen of the lands of Reenascreena, after the English captain pulled up on looking at it, and cried out it was "No go." Ned rode that day Brian Boro, Mr. Gumbleton's famous chestnut, and people call it Ned Sheehy's Leap to this hour.

So, you see, it was hard to do without him, however, many a scolding he got; and although his master often said of an evening, "I'll turn off Ned," he always forgot to do so in the morning. These threats mended Ned not a bit; indeed, he was mending the other way, like bad fish in hot weather.

One cold winter's day, about three o'clock in the afternoon, Mr. Gumbleton said to him, "Ned," said he, "go take Modderaroo down to black Falvey, the horse-doctor, and bid him look at her knees; for Doctor Jenkinson, who rode her home last night, has hurt her somehow. I suppose he thought a parson's horse ought to go upon its knees; but, indeed, it was I was the fool to give her to him at all, for he sits twenty stone if he sits a pound, and knows no more of riding, particularly after his third bottle, than I do of preaching. Now mind and be back in an hour at farthest, for I want to have the plate cleaned up properly for dinner, as Sir Augustus O'Toole, you know, is to dine here to-day. - Don't loiter, for your life."

"Is it I, sir?" says Ned. "Well, that beats anything; as if I'd stop out a minute!" So, mounting Modderaroo, off he set.

Four, five, six o'clock came, and so did Sir Augustus and lady O'Toole, and the four misses O'Toole, and Mr. O'Toole, and Mr. Edward O'Toole, and Mr. James O'Toole, which were all the young O'Tooles that were at home, but no Ned Sheehy appeared to clean the plate, or to lay the table-cloth, or even to put dinner on. It is needless to say how Mr. and Mrs. Dick Gumbleton fretted and fumed; but it was all to no use. They did their best, however, only it was a disgrace to see long Jem the stable boy, and Bill the gossoon that used to go of errands, waiting, without any body to direct them, when there was a real baronet and his lady at table; for Sir Augustus was none of your knights. But a good bottle of claret makes up for much, and it was not one only they had that night. However, it is not to be concealed that Mr. Dick Gumbleton went to bed very cross, and he awoke still crosser.

He heard that Ned had not made his appearance for the whole night; so he dressed himself in a great fret, and, taking his horse whip in his hand, he said,

"There is no farther use in tolerating this scoundrel; I'll go look for him, and if I find him, I'll cut the soul out of his vagabond body! so I will."

"Don't say so, Dick, dear," said Mrs. Gumbleton (for she was always a mild woman, being daughter of fighting Tom Crofts, who shot a couple of gentlemen, friends of his, in the cool of the evening, after the Mallow races, one after the other,) "don't swear, Dick, dear," said she, "but do, my dear, oblige me by cutting the flesh off his bones, for he richly deserves it. I was quite ashamed of Lady O'Toole, yesterday, I was, 'pon honour."

Out sallied Mr. Gumbleton; and he had not far to walk, for, not more than two hundred yards from the house, he found Ned lying fast asleep under a ditch (a hedge,) and Modderaroo standing by him, poor beast, shaking every limb. The loud snoring of Ned, who was lying with his head upon a stone as easy and as comfortable as if it had been a bed of down or a hop-bag, drew him to the spot, and Mr. Gumbleton at once perceived, from the disarray of Ned's face and person, that he had been engaged in some perilous adventure during the night. Ned appeared not to have descended in the most regular manner; for one of his shoes remained sticking in the stirrup, and his hat, having rolled down a little slope, was imbedded in green mud. Mr. Gumbleton, however, did not give himself much trouble to make a curious survey, but with a vigorous application of his thong, soon banished sleep from the eyes of Ned Sheehy.

"Ned!" thundered his master in great indignation, - and on this occasion it was not a word and blow, for with that one word came half a dozen, "Get up, you scoundrel," said he.

Ned roared lustily, and no wonder, for his master's hand was not one of the lightest; and he cried out, between sleeping and waking - "O, sir! - don't be angry, sir! - don't be angry, and I'll roast you easier - easy as a lamb!"

"Roast me easier, you vagabond!" said Mr. Gumbleton, "what do you mean? - I'll roast you, my lad. Where were you all night? - Modderaroo will never get over it. - Pack out of my service, you worthless villain, this moment; and, indeed, you may be thankful that I don't get you transported."

"Thank God, master dear," said Ned, who was now perfectly awakened - "it's yourself, anyhow. There never was a gentleman in the whole country ever did so good a turn to a poor man as your honour has been after doing to me. The Lord reward you for that same. Oh! but strike me again, and let me feel that it is yourself, master dear; - may whisky be my poison - "

"It will be your poison, you good-for-nothing scoundrel," said Mr. Gumbleton.

"Well, then, may whiskey be my poison," said Ned, "if 'twas not I was - in the blackest of misfortunes, and they were before me, whichever way I turned 'twas no matter. Your honour sent me last night, sure enough, with Modderaroo to mister Falvey's - I don't deny it - why should I? for reason enough I have to remember what happened."

"Ned, my man," said Mr. Gumbleton, "I'll listen to none of your excuses. Just take the mare into the stable and yourself off, for I vow - "

"Begging your honour's pardon," said Ned, earnestly, "for interrupting your honour; but, master, master! make no vows - they are bad things. I never made but one in all my life, which was, to drink nothing at all for a year and a day, and 'tis myself repented of it for the clean twelvemonth after. But if your honour would only listen to reason. I'll just take in the poor beast, and if your honour don't pardon me this one time may I never see another day's luck or grace."

"I know you, Ned," said Mr. Gumbleton. "Whatever your luck has been, you never had any grace to lose, but I don't intend discussing the matter with you. Take in the mare, sir."

Ned obeyed, and his master saw him to the stables. Here he reiterated his commands to quit, and Ned Sheehy's excuse for himself began. That it was heard uninterruptedly is more than I can affirm; but as interruptions, like explanations, spoil a story, we must let Ned tell it his own way.

"No wonder your honour," said he, "should be a bit angry - grand company coming to the house and all, and no regular serving-man to wait, only long Jem; so I don't blame your honour the least for being fretted like; but when all's heard, you will see that no poor man is more to be pitied for last night than myself. Fin Mac Coul never went through more in his born days than I did, though he was a great joint (giant,) and I only a man.

"I had not ridden half a mile from the house, when it came on, as your honour must have perceived clearly, mighty dark all of a sudden, for all the world as if the sun had tumbled down plump out of the fine clear blue sky. It was not so late, being only four o'clock at the most, but it was as black as your honour's hat. Well, I didn't care much, seeing I knew the road as well as I knew the way to my mouth, whether I saw it or not, and I put the mare into a smart canter; but just as I turned down by the corner of Terence Leahy's field - sure your honour ought to know the place well - just at the very spot the fox was killed when your honour came in first out of a whole field of a hundred and fifty gentlemen, and may be more, all of them brave riders."

"Just then, there, I heard the low cry of the good people wafting upon the wind. 'How early you are at your work, my little fellows!' says I to myself; and, dark as it was, having no wish for such company, I thought it best to get out of their way; so I turned the horse a little up to the left, thinking to get down by the boreen, that is that way, and so round to Falvey's; but there I heard the voice plainer and plainer close behind, and I could hear these words:

'Ned! Ned!
By my cap so red!
You're as good, Ned,
As a man that is dead.'

'A clean pair of spurs is all that's for it now,' said I; so off I set, as hard as I could lick, and in my hurry knew no more where I was going than I do the road to the hill of Tarah. Away I galloped on for some time, until I came to the noise of a stream, roaring away by itself in the darkness. 'What river is this?' said I to myself - for there was nobody else to ask - 'I thought,' says I, 'I knew every inch of ground, and of water too, within twenty miles, and never the river surely is there in this direction.' So I stopped to look about; but I might have spared myself that trouble, for I could not see as much as my hand. I didn't know what to do; but I thought in myself, it's a queer river, surely, if somebody does not live near it; and I shouted out as loud as I could, Murder! murder! - fire! - robbery! - anything that would be natural in such a place - but not a sound did I hear except my own voice echoed back to me, like a hundred packs of hounds in full cry above and below, right and left. This didn't do at all; so I dismounted, and guided myself along the stream, directed by the noise of the water, as cautious as if I was treading upon eggs, holding poor Modderaroo by the bridle, who shook, the poor brute, all over in a tremble, like my old grandmother, rest her soul any how! in the ague. Well, sir, the heart was sinking in me, and I was giving myself up, when, as good luck would have it, I saw a light. 'May be,' said I, 'my good fellow, you are only a Jacky Lantern, and want to bog me and Modderaroo.' But I looked at the light hard, and I thought it was too study (steady) for a Jacky Lantern. 'I'll try you,' says I - 'so here goes; and, walking as quick as a thief, I came towards it, being very near plumping into the river once or twice, and being stuck up to my middle, as your honour may perceive cleanly the marks of, two or three times in the slob. At last I made the light out, and it coming from a bit of a house by the roadside; so I went to the door and gave three kicks at it, as strong as I could.

"Open the door for Ned Sheehy,' said a voice inside. Now, besides that I could not, for the life of me, make out how anyone inside should know me before I spoke a word at all, I did not like the sound of that voice, 'twas so hoarse and so hollow, just like a dead man's! - so I said nothing immediately. The same voice spoke again, and said, 'Why don't you open the door to Ned Sheehy?' 'How pat my name is to you,' said I, without speaking out, 'on tip of your tongue, like butter;' and I was between two minds about staying or going, when what should the door do but open, and out came a man holding a candle in his hand, and he had upon him a face as white as a sheet.

"Why, then, Ned Sheehy,' says he, 'how grand you're grown, that you won't come in and see a friend, as you're passing by?'

"Pray, sir,' says I, looking at him - though that face of his was enough to dumbfound any honest man like me - 'Pray, sir,' says I, 'may I make so bold as to ask if you are not Jack Myers that was drowned seven years ago, next Martinmas, in the ford of Ah-na-fourish?'

"Suppose I was,' says he, 'has not a man a right to be drowned in the ford facing his own cabin-door any day of the week that he likes, from Sunday morning to Saturday night?'

"I'm not denying that same, Mr. Myers, sir,' says I, 'if 'tis yourself is to the fore speaking to me.'

"Well,' says he, 'no more words about that matter now. Sure you and I, Ned, were friends of old; come in, and take a glass; and here's a good fire before you, and nobody shall hurt or harm you, and I to the fore, and myself able to do it.'

"Now, your honour, though 'twas much to drink with a man that was drowned seven years before, in the ford of Ah-na-fourish, facing his own door, yet the glass was hard to be withstood - to say nothing of the fire that was blazing within - for the night was mortal cold. So tying Modderaroo to the hasp of the door - if I don't love the creature as I love my own life - I went in with Jack Myers.

"Civil enough he was - I'll never say otherwise to my dying hour - for he handed me a stool by the fire, and bid me sit down and make myself comfortable. But his face, as I said before, was as white as the snow on the hills, and his two eyes fell dead on me, like the eyes of a cod without any life in them. Just as I was going to put the glass to my lips, a voice - 'twas the same that I heard bidding the door be opened - spoke out of a cupboard that was convenient to the left-hand side of the chimney, and said, 'Have you any news for me, Ned Sheehy?'

"The never a word, sir,' says I, making answer before I tasted the whisky, all out of civility; and, to speak the truth, never the least could I remember at that moment of what had happened to me, or how I got there; for I was quite bothered with the fright.

"Have you no news,' says the voice, 'Ned, to tell me, from Mountbally Gumbletonmore; or from the Mill; or about Moll Trantum that was married last week to Bryan Oge, and you at the wedding?'

"No, sir,' says I, 'never the word.'

"What brought you in here, Ned, then?' says the voice. I could say nothing; for, whatever other people might do, I never could frame an excuse; and I was loath to say it was on account of the glass and the fire, for that would be to speak the truth.

"Turn the scoundrel out,' says the voice; and at the sound of it, who would I see but Jack Myers making over to me with a lump of a stick in his hand, and it clenched on the stick so wicked. For certain, I did not stop to feel the weight of the blow; so, dropping the glass, and it full of the stuff too, I bolted out of the door, and never rested from running away, for as good, I believe, as twenty miles, till I found myself in a big wood.

"The Lord preserve me! what will become of me now!' says I. 'Oh, Ned Sheehy!' says I, speaking to myself, 'my man, you're in a pretty hobble; and to leave poor Modderaroo after you!' But the words were not well out of my mouth, when I heard the most dismal ullagoane in the world, enough to break anyone's heart that was not broke before, with the grief entirely; and it was not long till I could plainly see four men coming towards me, with a great black coffin on their shoulders. 'I'd better get up in a tree,' says I, 'for they say 'tis not lucky to meet a corpse. I'm in the way of misfortune to-night, if ever man was.'

"I could not help wondering how a berrin (funeral) should come there in the lone wood at that time of night, seeing it could not be far from the dead hour. But it was little good for me thinking, for they soon came under the very tree I was roosting in, and down they put the coffin, and began to make a fine fire under me. I'll be smothered alive now, thinks I, and that will be the end of me; but I was afraid to stir for the life, or to speak out to bid them just make their fire under some other tree, if it would be all the same thing to them. Presently they opened the coffin, and out they dragged as fine-looking a man as you'd meet with in a day's walk.

"Where's the spit?' says one.

"Here 'tis,' says another, handing it over; and for certain they spitted him, and began to turn him before the fire.

"If they are not going to eat him, thinks I, like the Hannibals father Quinlan told us about in his sermon last Sunday.

"Who'll turn the spit while we go for the other ingredients?' says one of them that brought the coffin, and a big ugly-looking blackguard he was.

"Who'd turn the spit but Ned Sheehy?' says another.

"Burn you! thinks I, how should you know that I was here so handy to you up in the tree?

"Come down, Ned Sheehy, and turn the spit,' says he.

"I'm not here at all, sir,' says I, putting my hand over my face that he might not see me.

"That won't do for you, my man,' says he, 'you'd better come down, or maybe I'd make you.'

"I'm coming, sir,' says I; for 'tis always right to make a virtue of necessity. So down I came, and there they left me turning the spit in the middle of the wide wood.

"Don't scorch me, Ned Sheehy, you vagabond,' says the man on the spit.

"And my lord, sir, and aren't you dead, sir,' says I, 'and your honour taken out of the coffin and all?'

"I aren't,' says he.

"But surely you are, sir,' says I, 'for 'tis to no use now for me denying that I saw your honour, and I up in the tree.'

"I aren't,' says he again, speaking quite short and snappish.

"So I said no more, until presently he called out to me to turn him easy, or that may be 'twould be the worse turn for myself.

"Will that do, sir?' says I, turning him as easy as I could.

"That's too easy,' says he, so I turned him faster.

"That's too fast,' says he; so finding that, turn him which way I would, I could not please him, I got into a bit of a fret at last, and desired him to turn himself, for a grumbling spalpeen as he was, if he liked it better.

"Away I ran, and away he came hopping, spit and all, after me, and he but half-roasted. 'Murder!' says I, shouting out, 'I'm done for at long last - now or never!', when all of a sudden, and 'twas really wonderful, not knowing where I was rightly, I found myself at the door of the very little cabin by the roadside that I had bolted out of from Jack Myers; and there was Modderaroo standing hard by.

"Open the door for Ned Sheehy,' says the voice, - for 'twas shut against me, - and the door flew open in an instant. In I ran without stop or stay, thinking it better to be beat by Jack Myers, he being an old friend of mine, than to be spitted like a Michaelmas goose by a man that I knew nothing about, either of him or his family, one or the other.

"Have you any news for me?' says the voice, putting just the same question to me that it did before.

"Yes, sir,' says I, 'and plenty.' So I mentioned all that had happened to me in the big wood, and how I got up in the tree, and how I was made come down again, and put to turning the spit, roasting the gentleman, and how I could not please him, turn him fast or easy, although I tried my best, and how he ran after me at last, spit and all.

"If you had told me this before, you would not have been turned out in the cold,' said the voice.

"And how could I tell it to you, sir,' says I, 'before it happened?'

"No matter,' says he, 'you may sleep now till morning on that bundle of hay in the corner there, and only I was your friend, you'd have been killed entirely.' So down I lay, but I was dreaming, dreaming all the rest of the night; and when you, master dear, woke me with that blessed blow, I thought 'twas the man on the spit had hold of me, and could hardly believe my eyes, when I found myself in your honour's presence, and poor Modderaroo safe and sound by my side;

but how I came there is more than I can say, if 'twas not Jack Myers, although he did make the offer to strike me, or someone among the good people that befriended me."

"It is all a drunken dream, you scoundrel," said Mr. Gumbleton, "have I not had fifty such excuses from you?"

"But never one, your honour, that really happened before," said Ned, with unblushing front. "Howsoever, since your honour fancies 'tis drinking I was, I'd rather never drink again to the world's end, than lose so good a master as yourself, and if I'm forgiven this once, and get another trial - - "

"Well," said Mr. Gumbleton, "you may, for this once, go into Mountbally Gumbletonmore again; let me see that you keep your promise as to not drinking, or mind the consequences; and, above all, let me hear no more of the good people, for I don't believe a single word about them, whatever I may do of bad ones."

So saying, Mr. Gumbleton turned on his heel, and Ned's countenance relaxed into its usual expression.

"Now I would not be after saying about the good people what the master said last," exclaimed Peggy, the maid, who was within hearing, and who, by the way, had an eye after Ned. "I would not be after saying such a thing; the good people, may be, will make him feel the differ (difference) to his cost."

Nor was Peggy wrong; for whether Ned Sheehy dreamt of the Fir Darrig or not, within a fortnight after, two of Mr. Gumbleton's cows, the best milkers in the parish, ran dry, and before the week was out, Modderaroo was lying dead in the stone quarry.

Tales From The Land Of Saints & Scholars

Rent-Day

"Rent-Day", as adapted by W. B. Yeats in Fairy and Folk Tales of the Irish Peasantry (1888), is a moral tale drawn from the Irish oral and literary tradition of the nineteenth century, portraying the hardships and small redemptions of rural tenant life.

Yeats included Rent-Day for the way it captures both the earthy realism and the spiritual imagination of the Irish peasantry. It belongs to that borderland between social parable and folk vision, where poverty and humour, endurance and faith intertwine.

"Oh, Ullagone! Ullagone! This is a wide world, but what will we do in it, or where will we go?" muttered Bill Doody, as he sat on a rock by the Lake of Killarney. "What will we do? To-morrow's rent-day, and Tim the Driver swears if we don't pay our rent, he'll count every ha'porth we have; and then, sure enough, there's Judy and myself, and the poor grawls, will be turned out to starve on the high-road, for the never a halfpenny of rent have I! - Oh my, that ever I should live to see this day!"

Thus did Bill Doody bemoan his hard fate, pouring his sorrows to the reckless waves of the most beautiful of lakes, which seemed to mock his misery as they rejoiced beneath the cloudless sky of a May morning. That lake, glittering in sunshine, sprinkled with fairy isles of rock and verdure, and bounded by giant hills of ever-varying hues, might, with its magic beauty, charm all sadness but despair; for alas,

"How ill the scene that offers rest
And heart that cannot rest agree!"

Yet Bill Doody was not so desolate as he supposed; there was one listening to him he little thought of, and help was at hand from a quarter he could not have expected.

"What's the matter with you, my poor man?" said a tall, portly-looking gentleman, at the same time stepping out of a furze-brake. Now Bill was seated on a rock that commanded the view of a large field. Nothing in the field could be concealed from him, except this furze-brake, which grew in a hollow near the margin of the lake. He was, therefore, not a little surprised at the gentleman's sudden appearance, and began to question whether the personage before him belonged to this world or not. He, however, soon mustered courage sufficient to tell him how his crops had failed, how some bad member had charmed away his butter, and how Tim the Driver threatened to turn him out of the farm if he didn't pay up every penny of the rent by twelve o'clock next day.

"A sad story, indeed," said the stranger, "but surely, if you represented the case to your landlord's agent, he won't have the heart to turn you out."

"Heart, your honour; where would an agent get a heart!" exclaimed Bill. "I see your honour does not know him; besides, he has an eye on the farm this long time for a fosterer of his own; so I expect no mercy at all at all, only to be turned out."

"Take this, my poor fellow, take this," said the stranger, pouring a purse full of gold into Bill's old hat, which in his grief he had flung on the ground. "Pay the fellow your rent, but I'll take care it shall do him no good. I remember the time when things went otherwise in this country, when I would have hung up such a fellow in the twinkling of an eye!"

These words were lost upon Bill, who was insensible to everything but the sight of the gold, and before he could unfix his gaze, and lift up his head to pour out his hundred thousand blessings, the stranger was gone. The bewildered peasant looked around in search of his benefactor, and at last he thought he saw him riding on a white horse a long way off on the lake.

"O'Donoghue!" shouted Bill, "the good, the blessed O'Donoghue!" and he ran capering like a madman to show Judy the gold, and to please her with the prospect of wealth and happiness.

The next day Bill proceeded to the agent's; not sneakingly, with his hat in his hand, his eyes fixed on the ground, and his knees bending under him; but bold and upright, like a man conscious of his independence.

"Why don't you take off your hat, fellow? don't you know you are speaking to a magistrate?" said the agent.

"I know I'm not speaking to the king, sir," said Bill, "and I never takes off my hat but to them I can respect and love. The Eye that sees all knows I've no right either to respect or love an agent!"

"You scoundrel!" retorted the man in office, biting his lips with rage at such an unusual and unexpected opposition, "I'll teach you how to be insolent again; I have the power, remember."

"To the cost of the country, I know you have," said Bill, who still remained with his head as firmly covered as if he was the Lord Kingsale himself.

"But, come," said the magistrate, "have you got the money for me? this is rent-day. If there's one penny of it wanting, or the running gale that's due, prepare to turn out before night, for you shall not remain another hour in possession."

"There is your rent," said Bill, with an unmoved expression of tone and countenance, "you'd better count it, and give me a receipt in full for the running gale and all."

The agent gave a look of amazement at the gold; for it was gold - real guineas! and not bits of dirty ragged small notes, that are only fit to light one's pipe with. However willing the agent may have been to ruin, as he thought, the unfortunate tenant, he took up the gold, and handed the receipt to Bill, who strutted off with it as proud as a cat of her whiskers.

The agent going to his desk shortly after, was confounded at beholding a heap of gingerbread cakes instead of the money he had deposited there. He raved and swore, but all to no purpose; the gold had become gingerbread cakes, just marked like the guineas, with the king's head; and Bill had the receipt in his pocket; so he saw there was no use in saying anything about the affair, as he would only get laughed at for his pains.

From that hour Bill Doody grew rich; all his undertakings prospered; and he often blesses the day that he met with O'Donoghue, the great prince that lives down under the lake of Killarney.

Tales From The Land Of Saints & Scholars

The Amadan of the Dough

"The Amadan of the Dough" is a Donegal folktale collected and retold by Seumas MacManus in his Donegal Fairy Stories (first published 1900), and later adapted in various anthologies of Irish folklore. The word Amadan, meaning a fool or simpleton, sets the tone for a tale that sits somewhere between farce and fable.

Beneath the humour, however, lies a recognisably Irish moral about luck, wit, and the thin line between foolishness and grace. The Amadan's blunders often lead, through accident or sheer good heart, to a surprisingly fortunate end, an inversion common in rural Irish storytelling, where cleverness is less prized than a certain innocent resilience.

There was a king once on a time that had a son that was an Amadan. The Amadan's mother died, and the king married again.

The Amadan's step-mother was always afraid of him beating her children, he was growing so big and strong. So to keep him from growing and to weaken him, she had him fed on dough made of raw meal and water, and for that he was called "The Amadan of the Dough." But instead of getting weaker, it was getting stronger the Amadan was on this fare, and he was able to thrash all of his step-brothers together.

At length his step-mother told his father that he would have to drive the Amadan away. The father consented to put him away; but the Amadan refused to go till his father would give him a sword so sharp that it would cut a pack of wool falling on it.

After a great deal of time and trouble the father got such a sword and gave it to the Amadan; and when the Amadan had tried it and found it what he wanted, he bade them all goodbye and set off.

For seven days and seven nights he travelled away before him without meeting anything wonderful, but on the seventh night he came up to a great castle. He went in and found no one there, but he found a great dinner spread on the table in the hall. So to be making the most of his time, down the Amadan sat at the table and whacked away.

When he had finished with his dinner, up to the castle came three young princes, stout, strong, able fellows, but very, very tired, and bleeding from wounds all over them.

They struck the castle with a flint, and all at once the whole castle shone as if it were on fire. The Amadan sprang at the three of them to kill them. He said, "What do you mean by putting the castle on fire?"

"O Amadan," they said, "don't interfere with us, for we are nearly killed as it is. The castle isn't on fire. Every day we have to go out to fight three giants -- Slat Mor, Slat Marr and Slat Beag. We fight them all day long, and just as night is falling we have them killed. But however it comes, in the night they always come to life again, and if they didn't see this castle lit up, they'd come in on top of us and murder us while we slept. So every night, when we come back from the fight, we light up the castle. Then we can sleep in peace until morning, and in the morning go off and fight the giants again.

When the Amadan heard this, he wondered; and he said he would very much like to help them kill the giants. They said they would be very glad to have such a fine fellow's help; and so it was agreed that the Amadan should go with them to the fight next day.

Then the three princes washed themselves and took their supper, and they and the Amadan went to bed.

In the morning all four of them set off, and travelled to the Glen of the Echoes, where they met the three giants.

"Now," says the Amadan, "if you three will engage the two smaller giants, Slat Marr and Slat Beag, I'll engage Slat Mor myself and kill him."

They agreed to this.

Now the smallest of the giants was far bigger and more terrible than anything ever the Amadan had seen or heard of in his life before, so you can fancy what Slat Mor must have been like.

But the Amadan was little concerned at this. He went to meet Slat Mor, and the two of them fell to the fight, and a great, great fight they had. They made the hard ground into soft, and the soft into spring wells; they made the rocks into pebbles, and the pebbles into gravel, and the gravel fell over the country like hailstones. All the birds of the air from the lower end of the world to the upper end of the world, and all the wild beasts and tame from the four ends of the earth, came flocking to see the fight; and in the end the Amadan ran Slat Mor through with his sword and laid him down dead.

Then he turned to help the three princes, and very soon he laid the other two giants down dead for them also.

Then the three princes said they would all go home. The Amadan told them to go, but warned them not to light up the castle this night, and he said would sit by the giants' corpses and watch if they came to life again.

The three princes begged of him not to do this, for the three giants would come to life, and then he, having no help, would be killed.

The Amadan was angry with them, and ordered them off instantly. Then he sat down by the giants' corpses to watch. But he was so tired from his great day's fighting that by and by he fell asleep.

About twelve o'clock at night, when the Amadan was sleeping soundly, up comes a cailliach [old hag] and four badachs [unwieldy big fellows], and the cailliach carried with her a feather and a bottle of iocshlainte [ointment of health], with which she began to rub the giants' wounds. Two of the giants were already alive when the Amadan awoke, and the third was just opening his eyes. Up sprang the Amadan, and at him leaped them all -- Slat Mor, Slat Marr, Slat Beag, the cailliach, and the four badachs.

If the Amadan had had a hard fight during the day, this one was surely ten times harder. But a brave and a bold fellow he was, and not to be daunted by numbers or showers of blows. They fought for long and long. They made the hard ground into soft, and the soft into spring wells; they made the rocks into pebbles, and the pebbles into gravel, and the gravel fell over the country like hailstones. All the birds of the air from the lower end of the world to the upper end of the world, and all the wild beasts and tame from the four ends of the earth, came flocking to see the fight; and one after the other of them the Amadan ran his sword through, until he had every one of them stretched on the ground, dying or dead.

And when the old cailliach was dying, she called the Amadan to her and put him under geasa [an obligation that he could not shirk] to lose the power of his feet, of his strength, of his sight, and of his memory if he did not go to meet and fight the Black Bull of the Brown Wood.

When the old hag died outright, the Amadan rubbed some of the iocshlainte to his wounds with the feather, and at once he was as hale and as fresh as when the fight began. Then he took the feather and the bottle of iocshlainte, buckled on his sword, and started away before him to fulfil his geasa.

He travelled for the length of all that lee-long day, and when night was falling, he came to a little hut on the edge of a wood; and the hut had no shelter inside or out but one feather over it, and there was a rough, red woman standing in the door.

"You're welcome," says she, "Amadan of the Dough, the King of Ireland's son. What have you been doing or where are you going?"

"Last night," says the Amadan, "I fought a great fight, and killed Slat Mor, Slat Marr, Slat Beag, the Cailliach of the Rocks, and four badachs. Now I'm under geasa to meet and to fight the Black Bull of the Brown Wood. Can you tell me where to find him?"

"I can that," says she, "but it's now night. Come in and eat and sleep."

So she spread for the Amadan a fine supper, and made a soft bed, and he ate heartily and slept heartily that night.

In the morning she called him early, and she directed him on his way to meet the Black Bull of the Brown Wood. "But my poor Amadan," she said, "no one has ever yet met that bull and come back alive."

She told him that when he reached the place of meeting, the bull would come tearing down the hill like a hurricane. "Here's a cloak," says she, "to throw upon the rock that is standing there. You hide yourself behind the rock, and when the bull comes tearing down, he will dash at the cloak, and blind himself with the crash against the rock. Then you jump on the bull's back and fight for life. If, after the fight, you are living, come back and see me; and if you are dead, I'll go and see you."

The Amadan took the cloak, thanked her, and set off, and travelled on and on until he came to the place of meeting.

When the Amadan came there, he saw the Bull of the Brown Wood come tearing down the hill like a hurricane, and he threw the cloak on the rock and hid behind it, and with the fury of his dash against the cloak the bull blinded himself, and the roar of his fury split the rock.

The Amadan lost no time jumping on his back, and with his sword began hacking and slashing him; but he was no easy bull to conquer, and a great fight the Amadan had. They made the hard ground into soft, and the soft into spring wells; they made the rocks into pebbles, and the pebbles into gravel, and the gravel fell over the country like hailstones. All the birds of the air from the lower end of the world to the upper end of the world, and all the wild beasts and tame from the four ends of the earth, came flocking to see the fight; at length, after a long time, the Amadan ran his sword right through the bull's heart, and the bull fell down dead. But before he died he put the Amadan under geasa to meet and to fight the White Wether of the Hill of the Waterfalls.

Then the Amadan rubbed his own wounds with the iocshlainte, and he was as fresh and hale as when he went into the fight. Then he set out and travelled back again to the little hut that had no shelter without or within, only one feather over it, and the rough, red woman was standing in the door, and she welcomed the Amadan and asked him the news.

He told her all about the fight, and that the Black Bull of the Wood had put him under geasa to meet and to fight the White Wether of the Hill of the Waterfalls.

"I'm sorry for you, my poor Amadan," says she, "for no one ever before met that White Wether and came back alive. But come in and eat and rest anyhow, for you must be both hungry and sleepy."

So she spread him a hearty meal and made him a soft bed, and the Amadan ate and slept heartily; and in the morning she directed him to where he would meet the White Wether of the Hill of the Waterfalls. And she told him that no steel was tougher than the hide of the White Wether, that a sword was never yet made that could go through it, and that there was only one place -- a little white spot just over the Wether's heart -- where he could be killed or sword could cut through. And she told the Amadan that his only chance was to hit this spot.

The Amadan thanked her, and set out. He travelled away and away before him until he came to the Hill of the Waterfalls, and as soon as he reached it he saw the White Wether coming tearing toward him in a furious rage, and the earth he was throwing up with his horns was shutting out the sun.

And when the Wether came up and asked the Amadan what great feats he had done that made him impudent enough to dare to come there, the Amadan said, "With this sword I have killed Slat Mor, Slatt Marr, Slatt Beag, the Cailliach of the Rocks and her four badachs, and likewise the Black Bull of the Brown Wood."

"Then," said the White Wether, "you'll never kill any other." And at the Amadan he sprang.

The Amadan struck at him with his sword, and the sword glanced off as it might off steel. Both of them fell to the fight with all their hearts, and such a fight never was before or since. They made the hard ground into soft, and the soft into spring wells; they made the rocks into pebbles, and the pebbles into gravel, and the gravel fell over the country like hailstones. All the birds of the air from the lower end of the world to the upper end of the world, and all the wild beasts and tame from the four ends of the earth, came flocking to see the fight. But at length and at last, after a long and terrible fight, the Amadan seeing the little spot above the heart that the red woman had told him of, struck for it and hit it, and drove his sword through the White Wether's heart, and he fell down. And when he was dying, he called the Amadan and put him under a geasa to meet and fight the Beggarman of the King of Sweden.

The Amadan took out his bottle of iocshlainte and rubbed himself with the iocshlainte, and he was as fresh and hale as when he began the fight. Then he set out again, and when night was falling, he reached the hut that had no shelter within or without, only one feather over it, and the rough, red woman was standing in the door.

Right glad she was to see the Amadan coming back alive, and she welcomed him heartily and asked him the news.

He told her of the wonderful fight he had had, and that he was now under geasa to meet and fight the Beggarman of the King of Sweden.

She made him come in and eat and sleep, for he was tired and hungry. And heartily the Amadan ate and heartily he slept; and in the morning she called him early, and directed him on his way to meet the Beggarman of the King of Sweden.

She told him that when he reached a certain hill, the Beggarman would come down from the sky in a cloud; and that he would see the whole world between the Beggarman's legs and nothing above his head. "If ever he finds himself beaten," she said, "he goes up into the sky in a mist, and stays there to refresh himself. You may let him go up once; but if you let him go up the second time, he will surely kill you when he comes down. Remember that. If you are alive when the fight is over, come to see me. If you are dead, I will go to see you."

The Amadan thanked her, parted with her, and travelled away and away before him until he reached the hill which she had told him of. And when he came there, he saw a great cloud that shot out of the sky, descending on the hill, and when it came down on the hill and melted away, there it left the Beggarman of the King of Sweden standing, and between his legs the Amadan saw the whole world and nothing over his head.

And with a roar and a run the Beggarman made for the Amadan, and the roar of him rattled the stars in the sky. He asked the Amadan who he was, and what he had done to have the impudence to come there and meet him.

The Amadan said, "They call me the Amadan of the Dough, and I have killed Slat Mor, Slat Marr, Slat Beag, the Cailliach of the Rocks and her four badachs, the Black Bull of the Brown Wood, and the White Wether of the Hill of the Waterfalls, and before night I'll have killed the Beggarman of the King of Sweden."

"That you never will, you miserable object," says the Beggarman. "You're going to die now, and I'll give you your choice to die either by a hard squeeze of wrestling or a stroke of the sword."

"Well," says the Amadan, "if I have to die, I'd sooner die by a stroke of the sword."

"All right," says the Beggarman, and drew his sword.

But the Amadan drew his sword at the same time, and both went to it. And if his fights before had been hard, this one was harder and greater and more terrible than the others put together. They made the hard ground into soft, and the soft into spring wells; they made the rocks into pebbles, and the pebbles into gravel, and the gravel fell over the country like hailstones. All the birds of the air from the lower end of the world to the upper end of the world, and, all the wild beasts and tame from the four ends of the earth, came flocking to see the fight. And at length the fight was putting so hard upon the Beggarman, and he was getting so weak, that he whistled, and the mist came around him, and he went up into the sky before the Amadan knew. He remained there until he refreshed himself and then came down again, and at it again he went for the Amadan, and fought harder and harder than before, and again it was putting too hard on him, and he whistled as before for the mist to come down and take him up.

But the Amadan remembered what the red woman had warned him; he gave one leap into the air, and coming down, drove the sword through the Beggarman's heart, and the Beggarman fell dead. But before he died he put geasa on the Amadan to meet and fight the Silver Cat of the Seven Glens.

The Amadan rubbed his wounds with the iocshlainte, and he was as fresh and hale as when he began the fight; and then he set out, and when night was falling, he reached the hut that had no shelter within or without, only one feather over it, and the rough, red woman was standing in the door.

Right glad she was to see the Amadan coming back alive, and she welcomed him right heartily, and asked him the news.

He told her that he had killed the Beggarman, and he said was now under geasa to meet and fight the Silver Cat of the Seven Glens.

"Well," she said, "I'm sorry for you, for no one ever before went to meet the Silver Cat and came back alive. But," she says, "you're both tired and hungry; come in and rest and sleep."

So in the Amadan went, and had a hearty supper and a soft bed; and in the morning she called him up early, and she gave him directions where to meet the cat and how to find it, and she told him there was only one vital spot on that cat, and it was a black speck on the bottom of the cat's stomach, and unless he could happen to run his sword right through this, the cat would surely kill him.

She said, "My poor Amadan, I'm very much afraid you'll not come back alive. I cannot go to help you myself or I would; but there is a well in my garden, and by watching that well I will know how the fight goes with you. While there is honey on top of the well, I will know you are getting the better of the cat; but if the blood comes on top, then the cat is getting the better of you; and if the blood stays there, I will know, my poor Amadan, that you are dead."

The Amadan bade her good-by, and set out to travel to where the Seven Glens met at the sea. Here there was a precipice, and under the precipice a cave. In this cave the Silver Cat lived, and once a day she came out to sun herself on the rocks.

The Amadan let himself down over the precipice by a rope, and he waited until the cat came out to sun herself.

When the cat came out at twelve o'clock and saw the Amadan, she let a roar out of her that drove back the waters of the sea and piled them up a quarter of a mile high, and she asked him who he was and how he had the impudence to come there to meet her.

The Amadan said, "They call me the Amadan of the Dough, and I have killed Slat Mor, Slat Marr, Slat Beag, the Cailliach of the Rocks and her four badachs, the Black Bull of the Brown Woods, the White

Wether of the Hill of the Waterfalls, and the Beggarman of the King of Sweden, and before night I will have killed the Silver Cat of the Seven Glens."

"That you never will," says she, "for a dead man you will be yourself." And at him she sprang.

But the Amadan raised his sword and struck at her, and both of them fell to the fight, and a great, great fight they had. They made the hard ground into soft, and the soft into spring wells; they made the rocks into pebbles, and the pebbles into gravel, and the gravel fell over the country like hailstones. All the birds of the air from the lower end of the world to the upper end of the world, and all the wild beasts and tame from the four ends of the earth, came flocking to see the fight; and if the fights that the Amadan had had on the other days were great and terrible, this one was far greater and far more terrible than all the others put together, and the poor Amadan sorely feared that before night fell he would be a dead man.

The red woman was watching at the well in her garden, and she was sorely distressed, for though at one time the honey was uppermost, at another time it was all blood, and again the blood and the honey would be mixed; so she felt bad for the poor Amadan.

At length the blood and the honey got mixed again, and it remained that way until night; so she cried, for she believed the Amadan himself was dead as well as the Silver Cat.

And so he was. For when the fight had gone on for long and long, the cat, with a great long nail which she had in the end of her tail, tore him open from his mouth to his toes; and as she tore the Amadan open and he was about to fall, she opened her mouth so wide that the Amadan saw down to the very bottom of her stomach, and there he saw the black speck that the red woman had told him of. And just before he dropped he drove his sword through this spot, and the Silver Cat, too, fell over dead.

It was not long now till the red woman arrived at the place and found both the Amadan and the cat lying side by side dead. At this the poor woman was frantic with sorrow, but suddenly she saw by the Amadan's side the bottle of iocshlainte and the feather. She took them up and rubbed the Amadan with the iocshlainte, and he jumped to his feet alive and well, and fresh as when he began the fight.

He smothered her with kisses and drowned her with tears. He took the red woman with him, and set out on his journey back, and travelled and travelled on and on till he came to the Castle of Fire.

Here he met the three young princes, who were now living happily with no giants to molest them. They had one sister, the most beautiful young maiden that the Amadan had ever beheld. They gave her to the Amadan in marriage, and gave her half of all they owned for fortune.

The marriage lasted nine days and nine nights. There were nine hundred fiddlers, nine hundred fluters, and nine hundred pipers, and the last day and night of the wedding were better than the first.

Tales From The Land Of Saints & Scholars

The Banshee of the Mac Carthys

"The Banshee of the Mac Carthys" is one of the classic Irish ghost legends collected by Thomas Crofton Croker in the early nineteenth century and later adapted by W. B. Yeats in Fairy and Folk Tales of the Irish Peasantry (1888, The Walter Scott Publishing Company). The tale centres on the ancient Mac Carthy family of Munster, whose ancestral castle becomes the setting for a spectral visitation.

Croker's version, which Yeats preserved in simpler and more rhythmic prose, captures the eerie stillness of the Irish night and the solemn beauty of the banshee's lament. Yeats included the story to illustrate how the banshee myth bridges pagan and Christian Ireland, turning death into ritual, mourning into song.

Charles Mac Carthy was, in the year 1749, the only surviving son of a very numerous family. His father died when he was little more than twenty, leaving him the Mac Carthy estate, not much encumbered, considering that it was an Irish one. Charles was gay, handsome, unfettered either by poverty, a father, or guardians, and therefore was not, at the age of one-and-twenty, a pattern of regularity and virtue. In plain terms, he was an exceedingly dissipated - I fear I may say debauched, young man.

His companions were, as may be supposed, of the higher classes of the youth in his neighbourhood, and, in general, of those whose fortunes were larger than his own, whose dispositions to pleasure were, therefore, under still less restrictions, and in whose example he found at once an incentive and an apology for his irregularities. Besides, Ireland, a place to this day not very remarkable for the coolness and steadiness of its youth, was then one of the cheapest countries in the world in most of those articles which money supplies for the indulgence of the passions. The odious exciseman, - with his portentous book in one hand, his unrelenting pen held in the other, or stuck beneath his hat-band, and the ink-bottle ('black emblem of the informer') dangling from his waistcoat-button - went not then from ale-house to ale-house, denouncing all those patriotic dealers in spirits, who preferred selling whiskey, which had nothing to do with English laws (but to elude them), to retailing that poisonous liquor, which derived its name from the British "Parliament" that compelled its circulation among a reluctant people. Or if the gauger - recording angel of the law - wrote down the peccadillo of a publican, he dropped a tear upon the word, and blotted it out forever! For, welcome to the tables of their hospitable neighbours, the guardians of the excise, where they existed at all, scrupled to abridge those luxuries which they freely shared; and thus the competition in the market between the smuggler, who incurred little hazard, and the personage ycleped fair trader, who enjoyed little protection, made Ireland a land flowing, not merely with milk and honey, but with whiskey and wine.

In the enjoyments supplied by these, and in the many kindred pleasures to which frail youth is but too prone, Charles Mac Carthy indulged to such a degree, that just about the time when he had completed his four-and-twentieth year, after a week of great excesses, he was seized with a violent fever, which, from its malignity, and the weakness of his frame, left scarcely a hope of his recovery. His mother, who had at first made many efforts to check his vices, and at last had been obliged to look on at his rapid progress to ruin in silent despair, watched day and night at his pillow. The anguish of parental feeling was blended with that still deeper misery which those only know who have striven hard to rear in virtue and piety a beloved and favourite child; have found him grow up all that their hearts could desire, until he reached manhood; and then, when their pride was highest, and their hopes almost ended in the fulfilment of their fondest expectations, have seen this idol of their affections plunge headlong into a course of reckless profligacy, and, after a rapid career of vice, hang upon the verge of eternity, without the leisure or the power of repentance.

Fervently she prayed that, if his life could not be spared, at least the delirium, which continued with increasing violence from the first few hours of his disorder, might vanish before death, and leave enough of light and of calm for making his peace with offended Heaven. After several days, however, nature seemed quite exhausted, and he sunk into a state too like death to be mistaken for the repose of sleep. His face had that pale, glossy, marble look, which is in general so sure a symptom that life has left its tenement of clay. His eyes were closed and sunk; the lids having that compressed and stiffened appearance which seemed to indicate that some friendly hand had done its last office. The lips, half closed and perfectly ashy, discovered just so much of the teeth as to give to the features of death their most ghastly, but most impressive look.

He lay upon his back, with his hands stretched beside him, quite motionless; and his distracted mother, after repeated trials, could discover not the least symptom of animation. The medical man who attended, having tried the usual modes for ascertaining the presence of life, declared at last his opinion that it was flown, and prepared to depart from the house of mourning. His horse was seen to come to the door. A crowd of people who were collected before the windows, or scattered in groups on the lawn in front, gathered around when the door opened. These were tenants, fosterers, and poor relations of the family, with others attracted by affection, or by that interest which partakes of curiosity, but is something more, and which collects the lower ranks round a house where a human being is in his passage to another world.

They saw the professional man come out from the hall door and approach his horse; and while slowly, and with a melancholy air, he prepared to mount, they clustered round him with inquiring and wistful looks. Not a word was spoken, but their meaning could not be misunderstood; and the physician, when he had got into his saddle, and while the servant was still holding the bridle as if to delay him, and was looking anxiously at his face as if expecting that he would relieve the general suspense, shook his head, and said in a low voice, "It's all over, James;" and moved slowly away.

The moment he had spoken, the women present, who were very numerous, uttered a shrill cry, which, having been sustained for about half a minute, fell suddenly into a full, loud, continued, and discordant but plaintive wailing, above which occasionally were heard the deep sounds of a man's voice, sometimes in deep sobs, sometimes in more distinct exclamations of sorrow. This was Charles's foster-brother, who moved about the crowd, now clapping his hands, now rubbing them together in an agony of grief. The poor fellow had been Charles's playmate and companion when a boy, and afterwards his servant; had always been distinguished by his peculiar regard, and loved his young master as much, at least, as he did his own life.

When Mrs. Mac Carthy became convinced that the blow was indeed struck, and that her beloved son was sent to his last account, even in the blossoms of his sin, she remained for some time gazing with fixedness upon his cold features; then, as if something had suddenly touched the string of her tenderest affections, tear after tear trickled down her cheeks, pale with anxiety and watching. Still she continued looking at her son, apparently unconscious that she was weeping, without once lifting her handkerchief to her eyes, until reminded of the sad duties which the custom of the country imposed upon her, by the crowd of females belonging to the better class of the peasantry, who now, crying audibly, nearly filled the apartment. She then withdrew, to give directions for the ceremony of waking, and for supplying the numerous visitors of all ranks with the refreshments usual on these melancholy occasions. Though her voice was scarcely heard, and though no one saw her but the servants and one or two old followers of the family, who assisted her in the necessary arrangements, everything was conducted with the greatest regularity; and though she made no effort to check her sorrows they never once suspended her attention, now more than ever required to preserve order in her household, which, in this season of calamity, but for her would have been all confusion.

The night was pretty far advanced; the boisterous lamentations which had prevailed during part of the day in and about the house had given place to a solemn and mournful stillness; and Mrs. Mac Carthy, whose heart, notwithstanding her long fatigue and watching, was yet too sore for sleep, was kneeling in fervent prayer in a chamber adjoining that of her son. Suddenly her devotions were disturbed by an unusual noise, proceeding from the persons who were watching round the body. First there was a low murmur, then all was silent, as if the movements of those in the chamber were checked by a sudden panic, and then a loud cry of terror burst from all within. The door of the chamber was thrown open, and all who were not overturned in the press rushed wildly into the passage which led to the stairs, and into which Mrs. Mac Carthy's room opened. Mrs. Mac Carthy made her way through the crowd into her son's chamber, where she found him sitting up in the bed, and looking vacantly around, like one risen from the grave. The glare thrown upon his sunk features and thin lathy frame gave an unearthly horror to his whole aspect. Mrs. Mac Carthy was a woman of some firmness; but she was a woman, and not quite free from the superstitions of her country. She dropped on her knees, and, clasping her hands, began to pray aloud. The form before her moved only its lips, and barely uttered "Mother"; but though the pale lips moved, as if there was a design to finish the sentence, the tongue refused its office. Mrs. Mac Carthy sprung forward, and catching the arm of her son, exclaimed, "Speak! in the name of God and His saints, speak! are you alive?"

He turned to her slowly, and said, speaking still with apparent difficulty, "Yes, my mother, alive, and - but sit down and collect yourself; I have that to tell which will astonish you still more than what you have seen." He leaned back upon his pillow, and while his mother remained kneeling by the bedside, holding one of his hands clasped in hers, and gazing on him with the look of one who distrusted all her senses, he proceeded, "Do not interrupt me until I have done. I wish to speak while the excitement of returning life is upon me, as I know I shall soon need much repose. Of the commencement of my illness I have only a confused recollection; but within the last twelve hours I have been before the judgment-seat of God. Do not stare incredulously on me - 'tis as true as have been my crimes, and as, I trust, shall be repentance. I saw the awful Judge arrayed in all the terrors which invest him when mercy gives place to justice. The dreadful pomp of offended omnipotence, I saw - I remember. It is fixed here; printed on my brain in characters indelible; but it passes human language. What I can describe I will - I may speak it briefly. It is enough to say, I was weighed in the balance, and found wanting. The irrevocable sentence was upon the point of being pronounced; the eye of my Almighty Judge, which had already glanced upon me, half spoke my doom; when I observed the guardian saint, to whom you so often directed my prayers when I was a child, looking at me with an expression of benevolence and compassion. I stretched forth my hands to him, and begged his intercession. I implored that one year, one month, might be given to me on earth to do penance and atonement for my transgressions. He threw himself at the feet of my Judge, and supplicated for mercy. Oh! never - not if I should pass through ten thousand successive states of being - never, for eternity, shall I forget the horrors of that moment, when my fate hung suspended - when an instant was to decide whether torments unutterable were to be my portion for endless ages! But Justice suspended its decree, and Mercy spoke in accents of firmness, but mildness, 'Return to that world in which you have lived but to outrage the laws of Him who made that world and you. Three years are given you for repentance; when these are ended, you shalt again stand here, to be saved or lost forever.' I heard no more; I saw no more, until I awoke to life, the moment before you entered."

Charles's strength continued just long enough to finish these last words, and on uttering them he closed his eyes, and lay quite exhausted. His mother, though, as was before said, somewhat disposed to give credit to supernatural visitations, yet hesitated whether or not she should believe that, although awakened from a swoon which might have been the crisis of his disease, he was still under the influence of delirium. Repose, however, was at all events necessary, and she took immediate measures that he should enjoy it undisturbed. After some hours' sleep, he awoke refreshed, and thenceforward gradually but steadily recovered.

Still he persisted in his account of the vision, as he had at first related it; and his persuasion of its reality had an obvious and decided influence on his habits and conduct. He did not altogether abandon the society of his former associates, for his temper was not soured by his reformation; but he never joined in their excesses, and often endeavoured to reclaim them. How his pious exertions succeeded, I have never learnt; but of himself it is recorded that he was religious without ostentation, and temperate without austerity; giving a practical proof that vice may be exchanged for virtue, without the loss of respectability, popularity, or happiness.

Time rolled on, and long before the three years were ended the story of his vision was forgotten, or, when spoken of, was usually mentioned as an instance proving the folly of believing in such things. Charles's health, from the temperance and regularity of his habits, became more robust than ever. His friends, indeed, had often occasion to rally him upon a seriousness and abstractedness of demeanour, which grew upon him as he approached the completion of his seven-and-twentieth year, but for the most part his manner exhibited the same animation and cheerfulness for which he had always been remarkable. In company he evaded every endeavour to draw from him a distinct opinion on the subject of the supposed prediction; but among his own family it was well known that he still firmly believed it. However, when the day had nearly arrived on which the prophecy was, if at all, to be fulfilled, his whole appearance gave such promise of a long and healthy life, that he was persuaded by his friends to ask a large party to an entertainment at Spring House, to celebrate his birthday. But the occasion of this party, and the circumstances which attended it, will be best learned from a perusal of the following letters, which have been carefully preserved by some relations of his family. The first is from Mrs. Mac Carthy to a lady, a very near connection and valued friend of hers, who lived in the county of Cork, at about fifty miles' distance from Spring House.

"TO MRS. BARRY, CASTLE BARRY.

"Spring House, Tuesday morning, October 15th, 1752.

"My dearest Mary, "I am afraid I am going to put your affection for your old friend and kinswoman to a severe trial. A two days' journey at this season, over bad roads and through a troubled country, it will indeed require friendship such as yours to persuade a sober woman to encounter. But the truth is, I have, or fancy I have, more than usual cause for wishing you near me. You know my son's story. I can't tell you how it is, but as next Sunday approaches, when the prediction of his dream, or vision, will be proved false or true, I feel a sickening of the heart, which I cannot suppress, but which your presence, my dear Mary, will soften, as it has done so many of my sorrows. My nephew, James Ryan, is to be married to Jane Osborne (who, you know, is my son's ward), and the bridal entertainment will take place here on Sunday next, though Charles pleaded hard to have it postponed for a day or two longer. Would to God - but no more of this till we meet. Do prevail upon yourself to leave your good man for one week, if his farming concerns will not admit of his accompanying you; and come to us, with the girls, as soon before Sunday as you can.

"Ever my dear Mary's attached cousin and friend, "Ann Mac Carthy."

Although this letter reached Castle Barry early on Wednesday, the messenger having travelled on foot over bog and moor, by paths impassable to horse or carriage, Mrs. Barry, who at once determined on going, had so many arrangements to make for the regulation of her domestic affairs (which, in Ireland, among the middle orders of the gentry, fall soon into confusion when the mistress of the family is away), that she and her two young daughters were unable to leave until late on the morning of Friday. The eldest daughter remained to keep her father company, and superintend the concerns of the household. As the travellers were to journey in an open one-horse vehicle, called a jaunting-car (still used in Ireland), and as the roads, bad at all times, were rendered still worse by the heavy rains, it was their design to make two easy stages - to stop about midway the first night, and reach Spring House early on Saturday evening. This arrangement was now altered, as they found that from the lateness of their departure they could proceed, at the utmost, no farther than twenty miles on the first day; and they, therefore, purposed sleeping at the house of a Mr. Bourke, a friend of theirs, who lived at somewhat less than that distance from Castle Barry. They reached Mr. Bourke's in safety after a rather disagreeable ride. What befell them on their journey the next day to Spring House, and after their arrival there, is fully recounted in a letter from the second Miss Barry to her eldest sister.

"Spring House, Sunday evening, 20th October 1752.

"Dear Ellen, "As my mother's letter, which encloses this, will announce to you briefly the sad intelligence which I shall here relate more fully, I think it better to go regularly through the recital of the extraordinary events of the last two days.

"The Bourkes kept us up so late on Friday night that yesterday was pretty far advanced before we could begin our journey, and the day closed when we were nearly fifteen miles distant from this place. The roads were excessively deep, from the heavy rains of the last week, and we proceeded so slowly that, at last, my mother resolved on passing the night at the house of Mr. Bourke's brother (who lives about a quarter-of-a-mile off the road), and coming here to breakfast in the morning. The day had been windy and showery, and the sky looked fitful, gloomy, and uncertain. The moon was full, and at times shone clear and bright; at others it was wholly concealed behind the thick, black, and rugged masses of clouds that rolled rapidly along, and were every moment becoming larger, and collecting together as if gathering strength for a coming storm. The wind, which blew in our faces, whistled bleakly along the low hedges of the narrow road, on which we proceeded with difficulty from the number of deep sloughs, and which afforded not the least shelter, no plantation being within some miles of us. My mother, therefore, asked Leary, who drove the jaunting-car, how far we were from Mr. Bourke's? "Tis about ten spades from this to the cross, and we have then only to turn to the left into the avenue, ma'am.' 'Very well, Leary; turn up to Mr. Bourke's as soon as you reach the crossroads.' My mother had scarcely spoken these words, when a shriek, that made us thrill as if our very hearts were pierced by it, burst from the hedge to the right of our way. If it resembled anything earthly it seemed the cry of a female, struck by a sudden and mortal blow, and giving out her life in one long deep pang of expiring agony. 'Heaven defend us!' exclaimed my mother. 'Go you over the hedge, Leary, and save that woman, if she is not yet dead, while we run back to the hut we have just passed, and alarm the village near it.' 'Woman!' said Leary, beating the horse violently, while his voice trembled, 'that's no woman; the sooner we get on, ma'am, the better;' and he continued his efforts to quicken the horse's pace. We saw nothing. The moon was hiding. It was quite dark, and we had been for some time expecting a heavy fall of rain. But just as Leary had spoken, and had succeeded in making the horse trot briskly forward, we distinctly heard a loud clapping of hands, followed by a succession of screams, that seemed to denote the last excess of despair and anguish, and to issue from a person running forward inside the hedge, to keep pace with our progress. Still we saw nothing; until, when we were within about ten yards of the place where an avenue branched off to Mr. Bourke's to the left, and the road turned to Spring House on the right, the moon started suddenly from behind a cloud, and enabled us to see, as plainly as I now see this paper, the figure of a tall, thin woman, with uncovered head, and long hair that floated around her shoulders, attired in something which seemed either a loose white cloak or a sheet thrown hastily about her. She stood on the corner hedge, where the road on which we were met that which leads to Spring House, with her face towards us, her left hand pointing to this place, and her right arm waving rapidly and violently as if to draw us on in that direction. The horse had stopped, apparently frightened at the sudden presence of the figure, which stood in the manner I have described, still uttering the same piercing cries, for about half a minute. It then leaped upon the road, disappeared from our view for one instant, and the next was seen standing upon a high wall a little way up the avenue on which we purposed going, still pointing towards the road to Spring House, but in an attitude of defiance and command, as if prepared to oppose our passage up the avenue. The figure was now quite silent, and its garments, which had before flown loosely in the wind, were closely wrapped around it 'Go on, Leary, to Spring House, in God's name!'

said my mother, 'whatever world it belongs to, we will provoke it no longer.' "Tis the Banshee, ma'am,' said Leary, 'and I would not, for what my life is worth, go anywhere this blessed night but to Spring House. But I'm afraid there's something bad going forward, or she would not send us there.' So saying, he drove forward; and as we turned on the road to the right, the moon suddenly withdrew its light, and we saw the apparition no more; but we heard plainly a prolonged clapping of hands, gradually dying away, as if it issued from a person rapidly retreating. We proceeded as quickly as the badness of the roads and the fatigue of the poor animal that drew us would allow, and arrived here about eleven o'clock last night. The scene which awaited us you have learned from my mother's letter. To explain it fully, I must recount to you some of the transactions which took place here during the last week.

"You are aware that Jane Osborne was to have been married this day to James Ryan, and that they and their friends have been here for the last week. On Tuesday last, the very day on the morning of which cousin Mac Carthy despatched the letter inviting us here, the whole of the company were walking about the grounds a little before dinner. It seems that an unfortunate creature, who had been seduced by James Ryan, was seen prowling in the neighbourhood in a moody, melancholy state for some days previous. He had separated from her for several months, and, they say, had provided for her rather handsomely; but she had been seduced by the promise of his marrying her; and the shame of her unhappy condition, uniting with disappointment and jealousy, had disordered her intellects. During the whole forenoon of this Tuesday she had been walking in the plantations near Spring House, with her cloak folded tight round her, the hood nearly covering her face; and she had avoided conversing with or even meeting any of the family.

"Charles Mac Carthy, at the time I mentioned, was walking between James Ryan and another, at a little distance from the rest, on a gravel path, skirting a shrubbery. The whole party was thrown into the utmost consternation by the report of a pistol, fired from a thickly planted part of the shrubbery which Charles and his companions had just passed. He fell instantly, and it was found that he had been wounded in the leg. One of the party was a medical man. His assistance was immediately given, and, on examining, he declared that the injury was very slight, that no bone was broken, it was merely a flesh wound, and that it would certainly be well in a few days. 'We shall know more by Sunday,' said Charles, as he was carried to his chamber. His wound was immediately dressed, and so slight was the inconvenience which it gave that several of his friends spent a portion of the evening in his apartment.

"On inquiry, it was found that the unlucky shot was fired by the poor girl I just mentioned. It was also manifest that she had aimed, not at Charles, but at the destroyer of her innocence and happiness, who was walking beside him. After a fruitless search for her through the grounds, she walked into the house of her own accord, laughing and dancing, and singing wildly, and every moment exclaiming that she had at last killed Mr. Ryan. When she heard that it was Charles, and not Mr. Ryan, who was shot, she fell into a violent fit, out of which, after working convulsively for some time, she sprung to the door, escaped from the crowd that pursued her, and could never be taken until last night, when she was brought here, perfectly frantic, a little before our arrival.

"Charles's wound was thought of such little consequence that the preparations went forward, as usual, for the wedding entertainment on Sunday. But on Friday night he grew restless and feverish, and on Saturday (yesterday) morning felt so ill that it was deemed necessary to obtain additional medical advice. Two physicians and a surgeon met in consultation about twelve o'clock in the day, and the dreadful intelligence was announced, that unless a change, hardly hoped for, took place before night, death must happen within twenty-four hours after. The wound, it seems, had been too tightly bandaged, and otherwise injudiciously treated. The physicians were right in their anticipations. No favourable symptom appeared, and long before we reached Spring House every ray of hope had vanished. The scene we witnessed on our arrival would have wrung the heart of a demon. We heard briefly at the gate that Mr. Charles was upon his death-bed. When we reached the house, the information was confirmed by the servant who opened the door. But just as we entered we were horrified by the most appalling screams issuing from the staircase. My mother thought she heard the voice of poor Mrs. Mac Carthy, and sprung forward. We followed, and on ascending a few steps of the stairs, we found a young woman, in a state of frantic passion, struggling furiously with two men-servants, whose united strength was hardly sufficient to prevent her rushing upstairs over the body of Mrs. Mac Carthy, who was lying in strong hysterics upon the steps. This, I afterwards discovered, was the unhappy girl I before described, who was attempting to gain access to Charles's room, to 'get his forgiveness,' as she said, 'before he went away to accuse her for having killed him.' This wild idea was mingled with another, which seemed to dispute with the former possession of her mind. In one sentence she called on Charles to forgive her, in the next she would denounce James Ryan as the murderer, both of Charles and her. At length she was torn away; and the last words I heard her scream were, 'James Ryan, 'twas you killed him, and not I - 'twas you killed him, and not I.'

"Mrs. Mac Carthy, on recovering, fell into the arms of my mother, whose presence seemed a great relief to her. She wept - the first tears,

I was told, that she had shed since the fatal accident. She conducted us to Charles's room, who, she said, had desired to see us the moment of our arrival, as he found his end approaching, and wished to devote the last hours of his existence to uninterrupted prayer and meditation. We found him perfectly calm, resigned, and even cheerful. He spoke of the awful event, which was at hand with courage and confidence, and treated it as a doom for which he had been preparing ever since his former remarkable illness, and which he never once doubted was truly foretold to him. He bade us farewell with the air of one who was about to travel a short and easy journey; and we left him with impressions which, notwithstanding all their anguish, will, I trust, never entirely forsake us.

"Poor Mrs. Mac Carthy - but I am just called away. There seems a slight stir in the family; perhaps - "

The above letter was never finished. The enclosure to which it more than once alludes told the sequel briefly, and it is all that I have further learned of the family of Mac Carthy. Before the sun had gone down upon Charles's seven-and-twentieth birthday, his soul had gone to render its last account to its Creator.

Tales From The Land Of Saints & Scholars

The Birth of Bran

"The Birth of Bran", as retold by James Stephens in Irish Fairy Tales (1920), draws from the ancient Fenian Cycle of Irish mythology, in which Fionn mac Cumhaill's origins and adventures are celebrated. In this tale, Stephens reimagines the mysterious beginnings of Bran, Fionn's beloved hound, weaving myth, transformation, and destiny into a lyrical fable.

Stephens's version is both poetic and playful, written in his distinctive, musical prose that captures the rhythm of oral storytelling. Beneath its humour and tenderness lies a deep sense of connection between the human and the otherworldly, a theme that runs throughout Irish myth.

Chapter I

There are people who do not like dogs a bit and in this story there is a man who did not like dogs. In fact, he hated them. When he saw one he used to go black in the face, and he threw rocks at it until it got out of sight. But the Power that protects all creatures had put a squint into this man's eye, so that he always threw crooked.

This gentleman's name was Fergus Fionnliath, and his stronghold was near the harbour of Galway. Whenever a dog barked he would leap out of his seat, and he would throw everything that he owned out of the window in the direction of the bark. He gave prizes to servants who disliked dogs, and when he heard that a man had drowned a litter of pups he used to visit that person and try to marry his daughter.

Now Fionn, the son of Uail, was the reverse of Fergus Fionnliath in this matter, for he delighted in dogs, and he knew everything about them from the setting of the first little white tooth to the rocking of the last long yellow one. He knew the affections and antipathies which are proper in a dog; the degree of obedience to which dogs may be trained without losing their honourable qualities or becoming servile and suspicious; he knew the hopes that animate them, the apprehensions which tingle in their blood, and all that is to be demanded from, or forgiven in, a paw, an ear, a nose, an eye, or a tooth; and he understood these things because he loved dogs, for it is by love alone that we understand anything.

Among the three hundred dogs which Fionn owned there were two to whom he gave an especial tenderness, and who were his daily and nightly companions. These two were Bran and Sceo'lan, but if a person were to guess for twenty years he would not find out why Fionn loved these two dogs and why he would never be separated from them.

Fionn's mother, Muirne, went to wide Allen of Leinster to visit her son, and she brought her young sister Tuiren with her. The mother and aunt of the great captain were well treated among the Fianna, first, because they were parents to Fionn, and second, because they were beautiful and noblewomen.

No words can describe how delightful Muirne was - she took the branch; and as to Tuiren, a man could not look at her without becoming angry or dejected. Her face was fresh as a spring morning; her voice more cheerful than the cuckoo calling from the branch that is highest in the hedge; and her form swayed like a reed and flowed like a river, so that each person thought she would surely flow to him.

Men who had wives of their own grew moody and downcast because they could not hope to marry her, while the bachelors of the Fianna stared at each other with truculent, bloodshot eyes, and then they gazed on Tuiren so gently that she may have imagined she was being beamed on by the mild eyes of the dawn.

It was to an Ulster gentleman, Iollan Eachtach, that she gave her love, and this chief stated his rights and qualities and asked for her in marriage.

Now Fionn did not dislike the man of Ulster, but either he did not know them well or else he knew them too well, for he made a curious stipulation before consenting to the marriage. He bound Iollan to return the lady if there should be occasion to think her unhappy, and Iollan agreed to do so. The sureties to this bargain were Caelte mac Ronan, Goll mac Morna, and Lugaidh. Lugaidh himself gave the bride away, but it was not a pleasant ceremony for him, because he also was in love with the lady, and he would have preferred keeping her to giving her away. When she had gone he made a poem about her, beginning, "There is no more light in the sky…"

And hundreds of sad people learned the poem by heart.

Chapter II

When Iollan and Tuiren were married they went to Ulster, and they lived together very happily. But the law of life is change; nothing continues in the same way for any length of time; happiness must become unhappiness, and will be succeeded again by the joy it had displaced. The past also must be reckoned with; it is seldom as far behind us as we could wish, it is more often in front, blocking the way, and the future trips over it just when we think that the road is clear and joy our own.

Iollan had a past. He was not ashamed of it; he merely thought it was finished, although in truth it was only beginning, for it is that perpetual beginning of the past that we call the future.

Before he joined the Fianna he had been in love with a lady of the Shi', named Uct Dealv (Fair Breast), and they had been sweethearts for years. How often he had visited his sweetheart in Faery! With what eagerness and anticipation he had gone there; the lover's whistle that he used to give was known to every person in that Shi', and he had been discussed by more than one of the delicate sweet ladies of Faery. "That is your whistle, Fair Breast," her sister of the Shi' would say.

And Uct Dealv would reply, "Yes, that is my mortal, my lover, my pulse, and my one treasure."

She laid her spinning aside, or her embroidery if she was at that, or if she were baking a cake of fine wheaten bread mixed with honey she would leave the cake to bake itself and fly to Iollan. Then they went hand in hand in the country that smells of apple-blossom and honey, looking on heavy-boughed trees and on dancing and beaming clouds. Or they stood dreaming together, locked in a clasping of arms and eyes, gazing up and down on each other, Iollan staring down into sweet grey wells that peeped and flickered under thin brows, and Uct Dealv looking up into great black ones that went dreamy and went hot in endless alternation.

Then Iollan would go back to the world of men, and Uct Dealv would return to her occupations in the Land of the Ever Young.

"What did he say?" her sister of the Shi' would ask.

"He said I was the Berry of the Mountain, the Star of Knowledge, and the Blossom of the Raspberry."

"They always say the same thing," her sister pouted.

"But they look other things," Uct Dealv insisted. "They feel other things," she murmured; and an endless conversation recommenced.

Then for some time Iollan did not come to Faery, and Uct Dealv marvelled at that, while her sister made a hundred surmises, each one worse than the last.

"He is not dead or he would be here," she said. "He has forgotten you, my darling."

News was brought to Tlr na n-Og of the marriage of Iollan and Tuiren, and when Uct Dealv heard that news her heart ceased to beat for a moment, and she closed her eyes.

"Now!" said her sister of the Shi'. "That is how long the love of a mortal lasts," she added, in the voice of sad triumph which is proper to sisters.

But on Uct Dealv there came a rage of jealousy and despair such as no person in the Shi' had ever heard of, and from that moment she became capable of every ill deed; for there are two things not easily controlled, and they are hunger and jealousy. She determined that the woman who had supplanted her in Iollan's affections should rue the day she did it. She pondered and brooded revenge in her heart, sitting in thoughtful solitude and bitter collectedness until at last she had a plan.

She understood the arts of magic and shape-changing, so she changed her shape into that of Fionn's female runner, the best-known woman in Ireland; then she set out from Faery and appeared in the world. She travelled in the direction of Iollan's stronghold.

Iollan knew the appearance of Fionn's messenger, but he was surprised to see her.

She saluted him.

"Health and long life, my master.".

"Health and good days," he replied. "What brings you here, dear heart?"

"I come from Fionn."

"And your message?" said he.

"The royal captain intends to visit you."

"He will be welcome," said Iollan. "We shall give him an Ulster feast."

"The world knows what that is," said the messenger courteously. "And now," she continued, "I have messages for your queen."

Tuiren then walked from the house with the messenger, but when they had gone a short distance Uct Dealv drew a hazel rod from beneath her cloak and struck it on the queen's shoulder, and on the instant Tuiren's figure trembled and quivered, and it began to whirl inwards and downwards, and she changed into the appearance of a hound.

It was sad to see the beautiful, slender dog standing shivering and astonished, and sad to see the lovely eyes that looked out pitifully in terror and amazement. But Uct Dealv did not feel sad. She clasped a chain about the hound's neck, and they set off westward towards the house of Fergus Fionnliath, who was reputed to be the unfriendliest man in the world to a dog. It was because of his reputation that Uct Dealv was bringing the hound to him. She did not want a good home for this dog. She wanted the worst home that could be found in the world, and she thought that Fergus would revenge for her the rage and jealousy which she felt towards Tuiren.

Chapter III

As they paced along Uct Dealv railed bitterly against the hound, and shook and jerked her chain. Many a sharp cry the hound gave in that journey, many a mild lament.

"Ah, supplanter! Ah, taker of another girl's sweetheart!" said Uct Dealv fiercely. "How would your lover take it if he could see you now? How would he look if he saw your pointy ears, your long thin snout, your shivering, skinny legs, and your long grey tail? He would not love you now, bad girl!"

"Have you heard of Fergus Fionnliath," she said again, "the man who does not like dogs?"

Tuiren had indeed heard of him.

"It is to Fergus I shall bring you," cried Uct Dealv. "He will throw stones at you. You have never had a stone thrown at you. Ah, bad girl! You do not know how a stone sounds as it nips the ear with a whirling buzz, nor how jagged and heavy it feels as it thumps against a skinny leg. Robber! Mortal! Bad girl! You have never been whipped, but you will be whipped now. You shall hear the song of a lash as it curls forward and bites inward and drags backward. You shall dig up old bones stealthily at night, and chew them against famine. You shall whine and squeal at the moon, and shiver in the cold, and you will never take another girl's sweetheart again."

And it was in those terms and in that tone that she spoke to Tuiren as they journeyed forward, so that the hound trembled and shrank, and whined pitifully and in despair.

They came to Fergus Fionnliath's stronghold, and Uct Dealv

demanded admittance.

"Leave that dog outside," said the servant.

"I will not do so," said the pretended messenger.

"You can come in without the dog, or you can stay out with the dog," said the surly guardian.

"By my hand," cried Uct Dealv, "I will come in with this dog, or your master shall answer for it to Fionn."

At the name of Fionn the servant almost fell out of his standing. He flew to acquaint his master, and Fergus himself came to the great door of the stronghold.

"By my faith," he cried in amazement, "it is a dog."

"A dog it is," growled the glum servant.

"Go you away," said Fergus to Uct Dealv, "and when you have killed the dog come back to me and I will give you a present."

"Life and health, my good master, from Fionn, the son of Uail, the son of Baiscne," she said to Fergus.

"Life and health back to Fionn," he replied. "Come into the house and give your message, but leave the dog outside, for I don't like dogs."

"The dog comes in," the messenger replied.

"How is that?" cried Fergus angrily.

"Fionn sends you this hound to take care of until he comes for her," said the messenger.

"I wonder at that," Fergus growled, "for Fionn knows well that there is not a man in the world has less of a liking for dogs than I have."

"However that may be, master, I have given Fionn's message, and here at my heel is the dog. Do you take her or refuse her?"

"If I could refuse anything to Fionn it would be a dog," said Fergus, "but I could not refuse anything to Fionn, so give me the hound."

Uct Dealv put the chain in his hand.

"Ah, bad dog!" said she.

And then she went away well satisfied with her revenge, and returned to her own people in the Shi.

Chapter IV

On the following day Fergus called his servant.

"Has that dog stopped shivering yet?" he asked.

"It has not, sir," said the servant.

"Bring the beast here," said his master, "for whoever else is dissatisfied Fionn must be satisfied."

The dog was brought, and he examined it with a jaundiced and bitter eye.

"It has the shivers indeed," he said.

"The shivers it has," said the servant.

"How do you cure the shivers?" his master demanded, for he thought that if the animal's legs dropped off Fionn would not be satisfied.

"There is a way," said the servant doubtfully.

"If there is a way, tell it to me," cried his master angrily.

"If you were to take the beast up in your arms and hug it and kiss it, the shivers would stop," said the man.

"Do you mean?" his master thundered, and he stretched his hand for a club.

"I heard that," said the servant humbly.

"Take that dog up," Fergus commanded, "and hug it and kiss it, and if I find a single shiver left in the beast I'll break your head."

The man bent to the hound, but it snapped a piece out of his hand, and nearly bit his nose off as well.

"That dog doesn't like me," said the man.

"Nor do I," roared Fergus, "get out of my sight."

The man went away and Fergus was left alone with the hound, but the poor creature was so terrified that it began to tremble ten times worse than before.

"Its legs will drop off," said Fergus. "Fionn will blame me," he cried in despair.

He walked to the hound.

"If you snap at my nose, or if you put as much as the start of a tooth into the beginning of a finger!" he growled.

He picked up the dog, but it did not snap, it only trembled. He held it gingerly for a few moments.

"If it has to be hugged," he said, "I'll hug it. I'd do more than that for Fionn."

He tucked and tightened the animal into his breast, and marched moodily up and down the room. The dog's nose lay along his breast under his chin, and as he gave it dutiful hugs, one hug to every five paces, the dog put out its tongue and licked him timidly under the chin.

"Stop," roared Fergus, "stop that forever," and he grew very red in the face, and stared truculently down along his nose. A soft brown eye looked up at him and the shy tongue touched again on his chin.

"If it has to be kissed," said Fergus gloomily, "I'll kiss it; I'd do more than that for Fionn," he groaned.

He bent his head, shut his eyes, and brought the dog's jaw against his lips. And at that the dog gave little wriggles in his arms, and little barks, and little licks, so that he could scarcely hold her. He put the hound down at last.

"There is not a single shiver left in her," he said.

And that was true.

Everywhere he walked the dog followed him, giving little prances and little pats against him, and keeping her eyes fixed on his with such eagerness and intelligence that he marvelled.

"That dog likes me," he murmured in amazement.

"By my hand," he cried next day, "I like that dog."

The day after that he was calling her "My One Treasure, My Little Branch." And within a week he could not bear her to be out of his sight for an instant.

He was tormented by the idea that some evil person might throw a stone at the hound, so he assembled his servants and retainers and addressed them.

He told them that the hound was the Queen of Creatures, the Pulse of his Heart, and the Apple of his Eye, and he warned them that the person who as much as looked sideways on her, or knocked one shiver out of her, would answer for the deed with pains and indignities. He recited a list of calamities which would befall such a miscreant, and these woes began with flaying and ended with dismemberment, and had inside bits of such complicated and ingenious torment that the blood of the men who heard it ran chill in their veins, and the women of the household fainted where they stood.

Chapter V

In course of time the news came to Fionn that his mother's sister was not living with Iollan. He at once sent a messenger calling for fulfilment of the pledge that had been given to the Fianna, and demanding the instant return of Tuiren. Iollan was in a sad condition when this demand was made. He guessed that Uct Dealv had a hand in the disappearance of his queen, and he begged that time should be given him in which to find the lost girl. He promised if he could not discover her within a certain period that he would deliver his body into Fionn's hands, and would abide by whatever judgement Fionn might pronounce. The great captain agreed to that.

"Tell the wife-loser that I will have the girl or I will have his head," said Fionn.

Iollan set out then for Faery. He knew the way, and in no great time he came to the hill where Uct Dealv was.

It was hard to get Uct Dealv to meet him, but at last she consented, and they met under the apple boughs of Faery.

"Well!" said Uct Dealv. "Ah! Breaker of Vows and Traitor to Love," said she.

"Hail and a blessing," said Iollan humbly.

"By my hand," she cried, "I will give you no blessing, for it was no blessing you left with me when we parted."

"I am in danger," said Iollan.

"What is that to me?" she replied fiercely.

"Fionn may claim my head," he murmured.

"Let him claim what he can take," said she.

"No," said Iollan proudly, "he will claim what I can give."

"Tell me your tale," she said coldly.

Iollan told his story then, and, he concluded, "I am certain that you have hidden the girl."

"If I save your head from Fionn," the woman of the Shi' replied, "then your head will belong to me."

"That is true," said Iollan.

"And if your head is mine, the body that goes under it is mine. Do you agree to that?"

"I do," said Iollan.

"Give me your pledge," said Uct Dealv, "that if I save you from this danger you will keep me as your sweetheart until the end of life and time."

"I give that pledge," said Iollan.

Uct Dealv went then to the house of Fergus Fionnliath, and she broke the enchantment that was on the hound, so that Tuiren's own shape came back to her; but in the matter of two small whelps, to which the hound had given birth, the enchantment could not be broken, so they had to remain as they were. These two whelps were Bran and Sceo'lan. They were sent to Fionn, and he loved them for ever after, for they were loyal and affectionate, as only dogs can be, and they were as intelligent as human beings. Besides that, they were Fionn's own cousins.

Tuiren was then asked in marriage by Lugaidh who had loved her so long. He had to prove to her that he was not any other woman's sweetheart, and when he proved that they were married, and they lived happily ever after, which is the proper way to live. He wrote a poem beginning, "Lovely the day. Dear is the eye of the dawn…"

And a thousand merry people learned it after him.

But as to Fergus Fionnliath, he took to his bed, and he stayed there for a year and a day suffering from blighted affection, and he would have died in the bed only that Fionn sent him a special pup, and in a week that young hound became the Star of Fortune and the very Pulse of his Heart, so that he got well again, and he also lived happily ever after.

The Boyhood of Fion

"The Boyhood of Fion" (or Fionn mac Cumhaill) is one of the central tales in James Stephens's Irish Fairy Tales (1920), his lyrical retelling of stories from the Fenian Cycle of Irish mythology. It recounts the early life of the great hero Fionn, born of noble but outlawed lineage, and raised in secret after his father Cumhal's death.

Stephens renders Fionn's tale not as dry legend but as living myth, half wonder, half melancholy. The world he builds is one of enchanted landscapes and ancient wisdom, where the boy's awakening mirrors that of Ireland itself: untamed, poetic, and perilous.

He was a king, a seer and a poet. He was a lord with a manifold and great train. He was our magician, our knowledgeable one, our soothsayer. All that he did was sweet with him. And, however you deem my testimony of Fionn excessive, and, although you hold my praising overstrained, nevertheless, and by the King that is above me, he was three times better than all I say. *Saint Patrick.*

Chapter I

Fionn [pronounce Fewn to rhyme with "tune"] got his first training among women. There is no wonder in that, for it is the pup's mother teaches it to fight, and women know that fighting is a necessary art although men pretend there are others that are better. These were the women druids, Bovmall and Lia Luachra. It will be wondered why his own mother did not train him in the first natural savageries of existence, but she could not do it. She could not keep him with her for dread of the clan-Morna. The sons of Morna had been fighting and intriguing for a long time to oust her husband, Uail, from the captaincy of the Fianna of Ireland, and they had ousted him at last by killing him. It was the only way they could get rid of such a man; but it was not an easy way, for what Fionn's father did not know in arms could not be taught to him even by Morna. Still, the hound that can wait will catch a hare at last, and even Manana'nn sleeps. Fionn's mother was beautiful, long-haired Muirne. so she is always referred to. She was the daughter of Teigue, the son of Nuada from Faery, and her mother was Ethlinn. That is, her brother was Lugh of the Long Hand himself, and with a god, and such a god, for brother we may marvel that she could have been in dread of Morna or his sons, or of anyone. But women have strange loves, strange fears, and these are so bound up with one another that the thing which is presented to us is not often the thing that is to be seen.

However it may be, when Uall died Muirne got married again to the King of Kerry. She gave the child to Bovmall and Lia Luachra to rear, and we may be sure that she gave injunctions with him, and many of them. The youngster was brought to the woods of Slieve Bloom and was nursed there in secret.

It is likely the women were fond of him, for other than Fionn there was no life about them. He would be their life; and their eyes may have seemed like twin benedictions resting on the small fair head. He was fair-haired, and it was for his fairness that he was afterwards called Fionn; but at this period he was known as Deimne. They saw the food they put into his little frame reproduce itself lengthways and sideways in tough inches, and in springs and energies that crawled at first, and then toddled, and then ran. He had birds for playmates, but all the creatures that live in a wood must have been his comrades. There would have been for little Fionn long hours of lonely sunshine when the world seemed just sunshine and a sky. There would have been hours as long, when existence passed like a shade among shadows, in the multitudinous tappings of rain that dripped from leaf to leaf in the wood, and slipped so to the ground. He would have known little snaky paths, narrow enough to be filled by his own small feet, or a goat's; and he would have wondered where they went, and have marvelled again to find that, wherever they went, they came at last, through loops and twists of the branchy wood, to his own door. He may have thought of his own door as the beginning and end of the world, from where all things went, and where all things came.

Perhaps he did not see the lark for a long time, but he would have heard him, far out of sight in the endless sky, thrilling and thrilling until the world seemed to have no other sound but that clear sweetness; and what a world it was to make that sound! Whistles and chirps, coos and caws and croaks, would have grown familiar to him. And he could at last have told which brother of the great brotherhood was making the noise he heard at any moment. The wind too. He would have listened to its thousand voices as it moved in all seasons and in all moods. Perhaps a horse would stray into the thick screen about his home, and would look as solemnly on Fionn as Fionn did on it. Or, coming suddenly on him, the horse might stare, all a-cock with eyes and ears and nose, one long-drawn facial extension, before he turned and bounded away with manes all over him and hoofs all under him and tails all round him. A solemn-nosed, stern-eyed cow would amble and stamp in his wood to find a flyless shadow; or a strayed sheep would poke its gentle muzzle through leaves.

"A boy," he might think, as he stared on a staring horse, "a boy cannot wag his tail to keep the flies off," and that lack may have saddened him. He may have thought that a cow can snort and be dignified at the one moment, and that timidity is comely in a sheep. He would have scolded the jackdaw, and tried to out-whistle the throstle, and wondered why his pipe got tired when the blackbird's didn't. There would be flies to be watched, slender atoms in yellow gauze that flew, and filmy specks that flitted, and sturdy, thick-ribbed brutes that pounced like cats and bit like dogs and flew like lightning. He may have mourned for the spider in bad luck who caught that fly. There would be much to see and remember and compare, and there would be, always, his two guardians. The flies change from second to second; one cannot tell if this bird is a visitor or an inhabitant, and a sheep is just sister to a sheep; but the women were as rooted as the house itself.

Chapter II

Were his nurses comely or harsh-looking? Fionn would not know. This was the one who picked him up when he fell, and that was the one who patted the bruise. This one said, "Mind you do not tumble in the well!"

And that one, "Mind the little knees among the nettles."

But he did tumble and record that the only notable thing about a well is that it is wet. And as for nettles, if they hit him he hit back. He slashed into them with a stick and brought them low. There was nothing in wells or nettles, only women dreaded them. One patronised women and instructed them and comforted them, for they were afraid about one.

They thought that one should not climb a tree!

"Next week," they said at last, "you may climb this one," and "next week" lived at the end of the world!

But the tree that was climbed was not worthwhile when it had been climbed twice. There was a bigger one nearby. There were trees that no one could climb, with vast shadow on one side and vaster sunshine on the other. It took a long time to walk around them, and you could not see their tops.

It was pleasant to stand on a branch that swayed and sprung, and it was good to stare at an impenetrable roof of leaves and then climb into it. How wonderful the loneliness was up there! When he looked down there was an undulating floor of leaves, green and green and greener to a very blackness of greenness; and when he looked up there were leaves again, green and less green and not green at all, up to a very snow and blindness of greenness; and above and below and around there was sway and motion, the whisper of leaf on leaf, and the eternal silence to which one listened and at which one tried to look.

When he was six years of age his mother, beautiful, long-haired Muirne, came to see him. She came secretly, for she feared the sons of Morna, and she had paced through lonely places in many counties before she reached the hut in the wood, and the cot where he lay with his fists shut and sleep gripped in them.

He awakened to be sure. He would have one ear that would catch an unusual voice, one eye that would open, however sleepy the other one was. She took him in her arms and kissed him, and she sang a sleepy song until the small boy slept again.

We may be sure that the eye that could stay open stayed open that night as long as it could, and that the one ear listened to the sleepy song until the song got too low to be heard, until it was too tender to be felt vibrating along those soft arms, until Fionn was asleep again, with a new picture in his little head and a new notion to ponder on.

The mother of himself! His own mother!

But when he awakened she was gone.

She was going back secretly, in dread of the sons of Morna, slipping through gloomy woods, keeping away from habitations, getting by desolate and lonely ways to her lord in Kerry.

Perhaps it was he that was afraid of the sons of Morna, and perhaps she loved him.

Chapter III

The women Druids, his guardians, belonged to his father's people. Bovmall was Uail's sister, and, consequently, Fionn's aunt. Only such a blood-tie could have bound them to the clan-Baiscne, for it is not easy, having moved in the world of court and camp, to go hide with a baby in a wood; and to live, as they must have lived, in terror.

What stories they would have told the child of the sons of Morna. Of Morna himself, the huge-shouldered, stern-eyed, violent Connachtman; and of his sons - young Goll Mor mac Morna in particular, as huge-shouldered as his father, as fierce in the onset, but merry-eyed when the other was grim, and bubbling with a laughter that made men forgive even his butcheries. Of Cona'n Mael mac Morna his brother, gruff as a badger, bearded like a boar, bald as a crow, and with a tongue that could manage an insult where another man would not find even a stammer. His boast was that when he saw an open door he went into it, and when he saw a closed door he went into it. When he saw a peaceful man he insulted him, and when he met a man who was not peaceful he insulted him. There was Garra Duv mac Morna, and savage Art Og, who cared as little for their own skins as they did for the next man's, and Garra must have been rough indeed to have earned in that clan the name of the Rough mac Morna. There were others, wild Connachtmen all, as untameable, as unaccountable as their own wonderful countryside.

Fionn would have heard much of them, and it is likely that he practised on a nettle at taking the head off Goll, and that he hunted a sheep from cover in the implacable manner he intended later on for Cona'n the Swearer.

But it is of Uail mac Baiscne he would have heard most. With what a dilation of spirit the ladies would have told tales of him, Fionn's father. How their voices would have become a chant as feat was added to feat, glory piled on glory. The most famous of men and the most beautiful; the hardest fighter; the easiest giver; the kingly champion; the chief of the Fianna na h-Eirinn. Tales of how he had been waylaid and got free; of how he had been generous and got free; of how he had been angry and went marching with the speed of an eagle and the direct approach of a storm; while in front and at the sides, angled from the prow of his terrific advance, were fleeing multitudes who did not dare to wait and scarce had time to run. And of how at last, when the time came to quell him, nothing less than the whole might of Ireland was sufficient for that great downfall.

We may be sure that on these adventures Fionn was with his father, going step for step with the long-striding hero, and heartening him mightily.

Chapter IV

He was given good training by the women in running and leaping and swimming.

One of them would take a thorn switch in her hand, and Fionn would take a thorn switch in his hand, and each would try to strike the other running round a tree.

You had to go fast to keep away from the switch behind, and a small boy feels a switch. Fionn would run his best to get away from that prickly stinger, but how he would run when it was his turn to deal the strokes!

With reason too, for his nurses had suddenly grown implacable. They pursued him with a savagery which he could not distinguish from hatred, and they swished him well whenever they got the chance.

Fionn learned to run. After a while he could buzz around a tree like a maddened fly, and oh, the joy, when he felt himself drawing from the switch and gaining from behind on its bearer! How he strained and panted to catch on that pursuing person and pursue her and get his own switch into action.

He learned to jump by chasing hares in a bumpy field. Up went the hare and up went Fionn, and away with the two of them, hopping and popping across the field. If the hare turned while Fionn was after her it was switch for Fionn; so that in a while it did not matter to Fionn which way the hare jumped for he could jump that way too. Long-ways, sideways or bow-ways, Fionn hopped where the hare hopped, and at last he was the owner of a hop that any hare would give an ear for.

He was taught to swim, and it may be that his heart sank when he fronted the lesson. The water was cold. It was deep. One could see the bottom, leagues below, millions of miles below. A small boy might shiver as he stared into that wink and blink and twink of brown pebbles and murder. And these implacable women threw him in!

Perhaps he would not go in at first. He may have smiled at them, and coaxed, and hung back. It was a leg and an arm gripped then; a swing for Fionn, and out and away with him; plop and flop for him; down into chill deep death for him, and up with a splutter; with a sob; with a grasp at everything that caught nothing; with a wild flurry; with a raging despair; with a bubble and snort as he was hauled again down, and down, and down, and found as suddenly that he had been hauled out.

Fionn learned to swim until he could pop into the water like an otter and slide through it like an eel.

He used to try to chase a fish the way he chased hares in the bumpy field - but there are terrible spurts in a fish. It may be that a fish cannot hop, but he gets there in a flash, and he isn't there in another. Up or down, sideways or endways, it is all one to a fish. He goes and is gone. He twists this way and disappears the other way. He is over you when he ought to be under you, and he is biting your toe when you thought you were biting his tail.

You cannot catch a fish by swimming, but you can try, and Fionn tried. He got a grudging commendation from the terrible women when he was able to slip noiselessly in the tide, swim under water to where a wild duck was floating and grip it by the leg.

"Qu..." said the duck, and he disappeared before he had time to get the "...ack" out of him.

So the time went, and Fionn grew long and straight and tough like a sapling; limber as a willow, and with the flirt and spring of a young bird. One of the ladies may have said, "He is shaping very well, my dear," and the other replied, as is the morose privilege of an aunt, "He will never be as good as his father," but their hearts must have overflowed in the night, in the silence, in the darkness, when they thought of the living swiftness they had fashioned, and that dear fair head.

Chapter V

ONE day his guardians were agitated. They held confabulations at which Fionn was not permitted to assist. A man who passed by in the morning had spoken to them. They fed the man, and during his feeding Fionn had been shooed from the door as if he were a chicken. When the stranger took his road the women went with him a short distance. As they passed the man lifted a hand and bent a knee to Fionn.

"My soul to you, young master," he said, and as he said it, Fionn knew that he could have the man's soul, or his boots, or his feet, or anything that belonged to him.

When the women returned they were mysterious and whispery. They chased Fionn into the house, and when they got him in they chased him out again. They chased each other around the house for another whisper. They calculated things by the shape of clouds, by lengths of shadows, by the flight of birds, by two flies racing on a flat stone, by throwing bones over their left shoulders, and by every kind of trick and game and chance that you could put a mind to.

They told Fionn he must sleep in a tree that night, and they put him under bonds not to sing or whistle or cough or sneeze until the morning.

Fionn did sneeze. He never sneezed so much in his life. He sat up in his tree and nearly sneezed himself out of it. Flies got up his nose, two at a time, one up each nose, and his head nearly fell off the way he sneezed.

"You are doing that on purpose," said a savage whisper from the foot of the tree.

But Fionn was not doing it on purpose. He tucked himself into a fork the way he had been taught, and he passed the crawliest, tickliest night he had ever known. After a while he did not want to sneeze, he wanted to scream, and in particular he wanted to come down from the tree. But he did not scream, nor did he leave the tree. His word was passed, and he stayed in his tree as silent as a mouse and as watchful, until he fell out of it.

In the morning a band of travelling poets were passing, and the women handed Fionn over to them. This time they could not prevent him overhearing.

"The sons of Morna!" they said.

And Fionn's heart might have swelled with rage, but that it was already swollen with adventure. And also the expected was happening. Behind every hour of their day and every moment of their lives lay the sons of Morna. Fionn had run after them as deer. He jumped after them as hares. He dived after them as fish. They lived in the house with him. They sat at the table and ate his meat. One dreamed of them, and they were expected in the morning as the sun is. They knew only too well that the son of Uail was living, and they knew that their own sons would know no ease while that son lived; for they believed in those days that like breeds like, and that the son of Uail would be Uail with additions.

His guardians knew that their hiding-place must at last be discovered, and that, when it was found, the sons of Morna would come. They had no doubt of that, and every action of their lives was based on that certainty. For no secret can remain secret. Some broken soldier tramping home to his people will find it out; a herd seeking his strayed cattle or a band of travelling musicians will get the wind of it. How many people will move through even the remotest wood in a year! The crows will tell a secret if no one else does; and under a bush, behind a clump of bracken, what eyes may there not be! But if your secret is legged like a young goat! If it is tongued like a wolf! One can hide a baby, but you cannot hide a boy. He will rove unless you tie him to a post, and he will whistle then.

The sons of Morna came, but there were only two grim women living in a lonely hut to greet them. We may be sure they were well greeted. One can imagine Goll's merry stare taking in all that could be seen; Cona'n's grim eye raking the women's faces while his tongue raked them again; the Rough mac Morna shouldering here and there in the house and about it, with maybe a hatchet in his hand, and Art Og coursing further afield and vowing that if the cub was there he would find him.

Chapter VI

But Fionn was gone. He was away, bound with his band of poets for the Galtees.

It is likely they were junior poets come to the end of a year's training, and returning to their own province to see again the people at home, and to be wondered at and exclaimed at as they exhibited bits of the knowledge which they had brought from the great schools. They would know tags of rhyme and tricks about learning which Fionn would hear of; and now and again, as they rested in a glade or by the brink of a river, they might try their lessons over. They might even refer to the ogham wands on which the first words of their tasks and the opening lines of poems were cut; and it is likely that, being new to these things, they would talk of them to a youngster, and, thinking that his wits could be no better than their own, they might have explained to him how ogham was written. But it is far more likely that his women guardians had already started him at those lessons.

Still this band of young bards would have been of infinite interest to

Fionn, not on account of what they had learned, but because of what they knew. All the things that he should have known as by nature; the look, the movement, the feeling of crowds; the shouldering and intercourse of man with man; the clustering of houses and how people bore themselves in and about them; the movement of armed men, and the homecoming look of wounds; tales of births, and marriages and deaths; the chase with its multitudes of men and dogs; all the noise, the dust, the excitement of mere living. These, to Fionn, new come from leaves and shadows and the dipple and dapple of a wood, would have seemed wonderful; and the tales they would have told of their masters, their looks, fads, severities, sillinesses, would have been wonderful also.

That band should have chattered like a rookery.

They must have been young, for one time a Leinsterman came on them, a great robber named Fiacuil mac Cona, and he killed the poets. He chopped them up and chopped them down. He did not leave one poteen of them all. He put them out of the world and out of life, so that they stopped being, and no one could tell where they went or what had really happened to them; and it is a wonder indeed that one can do that to anything let alone a band. If they were not youngsters, the bold Fiacuil could not have managed them all. Or, perhaps, he too had a band, although the record does not say so; but kill them he did, and they died that way.

Fionn saw that deed, and his blood may have been cold enough as he watched the great robber coursing the poets as a wild dog rages in a flock. And when his turn came, when they were all dead, and the grim, red-handed man trod at him, Fionn may have shivered, but he would have shown his teeth and laid roundly on the monster with his hands. Perhaps he did that, and perhaps for that he was spared.

"Who are you?" roared the staring black-mouth with the red tongue squirming in it like a frisky fish.

"The son of Uail, son of Baiscne," said hardy Fionn. And at that the robber ceased to be a robber, the murderer disappeared, the black-rimmed chasm packed with red fish and precipices changed to something else, and the round eyes that had been popping out of their sockets and trying to bite, changed also. There remained a laughing and crying and loving servant who wanted to tie himself into knots if that would please the son of his great captain. Fionn went home on the robber's shoulder, and the robber gave great snorts and made great jumps and behaved like a first-rate horse. For this same Fiacuil was the husband of Bovmall, Fionn's aunt. He had taken to the wilds when clan-Baiscne was broken, and he was at war with a world that had dared to kill his Chief.

Chapter VII

A new life for Fionn in the robber's den that was hidden in a vast cold marsh.

A tricky place that would be, with sudden exits and even more sudden entrances, and with damp, winding, spidery places to hoard treasure in, or to hide oneself in.

If the robber was a solitary he would, for lack of someone else, have talked greatly to Fionn. He would have shown his weapons and demonstrated how he used them, and with what slash he chipped his victim, and with what slice he chopped him. He would have told why a slash was enough for this man and why that man should be sliced. All men are masters when one is young, and Fionn would have found knowledge here also. He would have seen Fiacuil's great spear that had thirty rivets of Arabian gold in its socket, and that had to be kept wrapped up and tied down so that it would not kill people out of mere spitefulness. It had come from Faery, out of the Shi' of Aillen mac Midna, and it would be brought back again later on between the same man's shoulder-blades.

What tales that man could tell a boy, and what questions a boy could ask him. He would have known a thousand tricks, and because our instinct is to teach, and because no man can keep a trick from a boy, he would show them to Fionn.

There was the marsh too; a whole new life to be learned; a complicated, mysterious, dank, slippery, reedy, treacherous life, but with its own beauty and an allurement that could grow on one, so that you could forget the solid world and love only that which quaked and gurgled.

In this place you may swim. By this sign and this you will know if it is safe to do so, said Fiacuil mac Cona; but in this place, with this sign on it and that, you must not venture a toe.

But where Fionn would venture his toes his ears would follow.

There are coiling weeds down there, the robber counselled him; there are thin, tough, snaky binders that will trip you and grip you, that will pull you and will not let you go again until you are drowned; until you are swaying and swinging away below, with outstretched arms, with outstretched legs, with a face all stares and smiles and jockeyings, gripped in those leathery arms, until there is no more to be gripped of you even by them.

"Watch these and this and that," Fionn would have been told, "and always swim with a knife in your teeth."

He lived there until his guardians found out where he was and came after him. Fiacuil gave him up to them, and he was brought home again to the woods of Slieve Bloom, but he had gathered great knowledge and new suppleness.

The sons of Morna left him alone for a long time. Having made their essay they grew careless.

"Let him be," they said. "He will come to us when the time comes."

But it is likely too that they had had their own means of getting information about him. How he shaped? what muscles he had? and did he spring clean from the mark or had he to get off with a push? Fionn stayed with his guardians and hunted for them. He could run a deer down and haul it home by the reluctant skull. "Come on, Goll," he would say to his stag, or, lifting it over a tussock with a tough grip on the snout, "Are you coming, bald Cona'n, or shall I kick you in the neck?"

The time must have been nigh when he would think of taking the world itself by the nose, to haul it over tussocks and drag it into his pen; for he was of the breed in whom mastery is born, and who are good masters.

But reports of his prowess were getting abroad. Clann-Morna began to stretch itself uneasily, and, one day, his guardians sent him on his travels.

"It is best for you to leave us now," they said to the tall stripling, "for the sons of Morna are watching again to kill you."

The woods at that may have seemed haunted. A stone might sling at one from a tree-top; but from which tree of a thousand trees did it come? An arrow buzzing by one's ear would slide into the ground and quiver there silently, menacingly, hinting of the brothers it had left in the quiver behind; to the right? to the left? how many brothers? in how many quivers...? Fionn was a woodsman, but he had only two eyes to look with, one set of feet to carry him in one sole direction.

But when he was looking to the front what, or how many what's, could be staring at him from the back? He might face in this direction, away from, or towards a smile on a hidden face and a finger on a string. A lance might slide at him from this bush or from the one yonder.. In the night he might have fought them; his ears against theirs; his noiseless feet against their lurking ones; his knowledge of the wood against their legion, but during the day he had no chance.

Fionn went to seek his fortune, to match himself against all that might happen, and to carve a name for himself that will live while Time has an ear and knows an Irishman.

Chapter VIII

Fionn went away, and now he was alone. But he was as fitted for loneliness as the crane is that haunts the solitudes and bleak wastes of the sea; for the man with a thought has a comrade, and Fionn's mind worked as featly as his body did. To be alone was no trouble to him who, however surrounded, was to be lonely his lifelong; for this will be said of Fionn when all is said, that all that came to him went from him, and that happiness was never his companion for more than a moment.

But he was not now looking for loneliness. He was seeking the instruction of a crowd, and therefore when he met a crowd he went into it. His eyes were skilled to observe in the moving dusk and dapple of green woods. They were trained to pick out of shadows birds that were themselves dun-coloured shades, and to see among trees the animals that are coloured like the bark of trees. The hare crouching in the fronds was visible to him, and the fish that swayed in-visibly in the sway and flicker of a green bank. He would see all that was to be seen, and he would see all that is passed by the eye that is half blind from use and wont.

At Moy Life' he came on lads swimming in a pool; and, as he looked on them sporting in the flush tide, he thought that the tricks they performed were not hard for him, and that he could have shown them new ones.

Boys must know what another boy can do, and they will match themselves against everything. They did their best under these observing eyes, and it was not long until he was invited to compete with them and show his mettle. Such an invitation is a challenge; it is almost, among boys, a declaration of war. But Fionn was so far beyond them in swimming that even the word master did not apply to that superiority.

While he was swimming one remarked, "He is fair and well-shaped," and thereafter he was called "Fionn" or the Fair One. His name came from boys, and will, perhaps, be preserved by them.

He stayed with these lads for some time, and it may be that they idolised him at first, for it is the way with boys to be astounded and enraptured by feats; but in the end, and that was inevitable, they grew jealous of the stranger. Those who had been the champions before he came would marshal each other, and, by social pressure, would muster all the others against him; so that in the end not a friendly eye was turned on Fionn in that assembly. For not only did he beat them at swimming, but he also beat their best at running and jumping, and when the sport degenerated into violence, as it was bound to, the roughness of Fionn would be ten times as rough as the roughness of the roughest rough they could put forward. Bravery is pride when one is young, and Fionn was proud.

There must have been anger in his mind as he went away leaving that lake behind him, and those snarling and scowling boys, but there would have been disappointment also, for his desire at this time should have been towards friendliness.

He went there to Lock Le'in and took service with the King of Finntraigh. That kingdom may have been thus called from Fionn himself and would have been known by another name when he arrived there.

He hunted for the King of Finntraigh, and it soon grew evident that there was no hunter in his service to equal Fionn. More, there was no hunter of them all who even distantly approached him in excellence. The others ran after deer, using the speed of their legs, the noses of their dogs and a thousand well-worn tricks to bring them within reach, and, often enough, the animal escaped them. But the deer that Fionn got the track of did not get away, and it seemed even that the animals sought him so many did he catch.

The king marvelled at the stories that were told of this new hunter, but as kings are greater than other people so they are more curious; and, being on the plane of excellence, they must see all that is excellently told of.

The king wished to see him, and Fionn must have wondered what the king thought as that gracious lord looked on him. Whatever was thought, what the king said was as direct in utterance as it was in observation.

"If Uail the son of Baiscne has a son," said the king, "you would surely be that son."

We are not told if the King of Finntraigh said anything more, but we know that Fionn left his service soon afterwards.

He went southwards and was next in the employment of the King of Kerry, the same lord who had married his own mother. In that service he came to such consideration that we hear of him as playing a match of chess with the king, and by this game we know that he was still a boy in his mind however mightily his limbs were spreading. Able as he was in sports and huntings, he was yet too young to be politic, but he remained impolitic to the end of his days, for whatever he was able to do he would do, no matter who was offended thereat; and whatever he was not able to do he would do also. That was Fionn.

Once, as they rested on a chase, a debate arose among the Fianna-Finn as to what was the finest music in the world.

"Tell us that," said Fionn turning to Oisi'n [pronounced Usheen]

"The cuckoo calling from the tree that is highest in the hedge," cried his merry son.

"A good sound," said Fionn. "And you, Oscar," he asked, "what is to your mind the finest of music?"

"The top of music is the ring of a spear on a shield," cried the stout lad.

"It is a good sound," said Fionn. And the other champions told their delight; the belling of a stag across water, the baying of a tuneful pack heard in the distance, the song of a lark, the laugh of a gleeful girl, or the whisper of a moved one.

"They are good sounds all," said Fionn.

"Tell us, chief," one ventured, "what you think?"

"The music of what happens," said great Fionn, "that is the finest music in the world."

He loved "what happened," and would not evade it by the swerve of a hair; so on this occasion what was occurring he would have occur, although a king was his rival and his master. It may be that his mother was watching the match and that he could not but exhibit his skill before her. He committed the enormity of winning seven games in succession from the king himself!!!

It is seldom indeed that a subject can beat a king at chess, and this monarch was properly amazed.

"Who are you at all?" he cried, starting back from the chessboard and staring on Fionn.

"I am the son of a countryman of the Luigne of Tara," said Fionn.

He may have blushed as he said it, for the king, possibly for the first time, was really looking at him, and was looking back through twenty years of time as he did so. The observation of a king is faultless - it is proved a thousand times over in the tales, and this king's equipment was as royal as the next.

"You are no such son," said the indignant monarch, "but you are the son that Muirne my wife bore to Uall mac Balscne."

And at that Fionn had no more to say; but his eyes may have flown to his mother and stayed there.

"You cannot remain here," his step-father continued. "I do not want you killed under my protection," he explained, or complained.

Perhaps it was on Fionn's account he dreaded the sons of Morna, but no one knows what Fionn thought of him for he never thereafter spoke of his step-father. As for Muirne she must have loved her lord; or she may have been terrified in truth of the sons of Morna and for Fionn; but it is so also, that if a woman loves her second husband she can dislike all that reminds her of the first one. Fionn went on his travels again.

Chapter IX

All desires save one are fleeting, but that one lasts forever. Fionn, with all desires, had the lasting one, for he would go anywhere and forsake anything for wisdom; and it was in search of this that he went to the place where Finegas lived on a bank of the Boyne Water. But for dread of the clan-Morna he did not go as Fionn. He called himself Deimne on that journey.

We get wise by asking questions, and even if these are not answered we get wise, for a well-packed question carries its answer on its back as a snail carries its shell. Fionn asked every question he could think of, and his master, who was a poet, and so an honourable man, answered them all, not to the limit of his patience, for it was limitless, but to the limit of his ability.

"Why do you live on the bank of a river?" was one of these questions. "Because a poem is a revelation, and it is by the brink of running water that poetry is revealed to the mind."

"How long have you been here?" was the next query. "Seven years," the poet answered.

"It is a long time," said wondering Fionn.

"I would wait twice as long for a poem," said the inveterate bard.

"Have you caught good poems?" Fionn asked him.

"The poems I am fit for," said the mild master. "No person can get more than that, for a man's readiness is his limit."

"Would you have got as good poems by the Shannon or the Suir or by sweet Ana Life'?"

"They are good rivers," was the answer. "They all belong to good gods."

"But why did you choose this river out of all the rivers?"

Finegas beamed on his pupil.

"I would tell you anything," said he, "and I will tell you that."

Fionn sat at the kindly man's feet, his hands absent among tall grasses, and listening with all his ears. "A prophecy was made to me," Finegas began. "A man of knowledge foretold that I should catch the Salmon of Knowledge in the Boyne Water."

"And then?" said Fionn eagerly.

"Then I would have All Knowledge."

"And after that?" the boy insisted.

"What should there be after that?" the poet retorted.

"I mean, what would you do with All Knowledge?"

"A weighty question," said Finegas smilingly. "I could answer it if I had All Knowledge, but not until then. What would you do, my dear?"

"I would make a poem," Fionn cried.

"I think too," said the poet, "that that is what would be done."

In return for instruction Fionn had taken over the service of his master's hut, and as he went about the household duties, drawing the water, lighting the fire, and carrying rushes for the floor and the beds, he thought over all the poet had taught him, and his mind dwelt on the rules of metre, the cunningness of words, and the need for a clean, brave mind. But in his thousand thoughts he yet remembered the Salmon of Knowledge as eagerly as his master did. He already venerated Finegas for his great learning, his poetic skill, for a hundred reasons; but, looking on him as the ordained eater of the

Salmon of Knowledge, he venerated him to the edge of measure. Indeed, he loved as well as venerated this master because of his unfailing kindness, his patience, his readiness to teach, and his skill in teaching.

"I have learned much from you, dear master," said Fionn gratefully.

"All that I have is yours if you can take it," the poet answered, "for you are entitled to all that you can take, but to no more than that. Take, so, with both hands."

"You may catch the salmon while I am with you," the hopeful boy mused. "Would not that be a great happening!" and he stared in ecstasy across the grass at those visions which a boy's mind knows.

"Let us pray for that," said Finegas fervently.

"Here is a question," Fionn continued. "How does this salmon get wisdom into his flesh?"

"There is a hazel bush overhanging a secret pool in a secret place. The Nuts of Knowledge drop from the Sacred Bush into the pool, and as they float, a salmon takes them in his mouth and eats them."

"It would be almost as easy," the boy submitted, "if one were to set on the track of the Sacred Hazel and eat the nuts straight from the bush."

"That would not be very easy," said the poet, "and yet it is not as easy as that, for the bush can only be found by its own knowledge, and that knowledge can only be got by eating the nuts, and the nuts can only be got by eating the salmon."

"We must wait for the salmon," said Fionn in a rage of resignation.

Chapter X

Life continued for him in a round of timeless time, wherein days and nights were uneventful and were yet filled with interest. As the day packed its load of strength into his frame, so it added its store of knowledge to his mind, and each night sealed the twain, for it is in the night that we make secure what we have gathered in the day.

If he had told of these days he would have told of a succession of meals and sleeps, and of an endless conversation, from which his mind would now and again slip away to a solitude of its own, where, in large hazy atmospheres, it swung and drifted and reposed. Then he would be back again, and it was a pleasure for him to catch up on the thought that was forward and re-create for it all the matter he had missed. But he could not often make these sleepy sallies; his master was too experienced a teacher to allow any such bright-faced, eager-eyed abstractions, and as the druid women had switched his legs around a tree, so Finegas chased his mind, demanding sense in his questions and understanding in his replies.

To ask questions can become the laziest and wobbliest occupation of a mind, but when you must yourself answer the problem that you have posed, you will meditate your question with care and frame it with precision. Fionn's mind learned to jump in a bumpier field than that in which he had chased rabbits. And when he had asked his question, and given his own answer to it, Finegas would take the matter up and make clear to him where the query was badly formed or at what point the answer had begun to go astray, so that Fionn came to understand by what successions a good question grows at last to a good answer.

One day, not long after the conversation told of, Finegas came to the place where Fionn was. The poet had a shallow osier basket on his arm, and on his face there was a look that was at once triumphant and gloomy. He was excited certainly, but he was sad also, and as he stood gazing on Fionn his eyes were so kind that the boy was touched, and they were yet so melancholy that it almost made Fionn weep. "What is it, my master?" said the alarmed boy.

The poet placed his osier basket on the grass.

"Look in the basket, dear son," he said. Fionn looked.

"There is a salmon in the basket."

"It is The Salmon," said Finegas with a great sigh. Fionn leaped for delight.

"I am glad for you, master," he cried. "Indeed I am glad for you."

"And I am glad, my dear soul," the master re-joined.

But, having said it, he bent his brow to his hand and for a long time he was silent and gathered into himself.

"What should be done now?" Fionn demanded, as he stared on the beautiful fish.

Finegas rose from where he sat by the osier basket.

"I will be back in a short time," he said heavily. "While I am away you may roast the salmon, so that it will be ready against my return."

"I will roast it indeed," said Fionn.

The poet gazed long and earnestly on him.

"You will not eat any of my salmon while I am away?" he asked.

"I will not eat the littlest piece," said Fionn.

"I am sure you will not," the other murmured, as he turned and walked slowly across the grass and behind the sheltering bushes on the ridge.

Fionn cooked the salmon. It was beautiful and tempting and savoury as it smoked on a wooden platter among cool green leaves; and it looked all these to Finegas when he came from behind the fringing bushes and sat in the grass outside his door. He gazed on the fish with more than his eyes. He looked on it with his heart, with his soul in his eyes, and when he turned to look on Fionn the boy did not know whether the love that was in his eyes was for the fish or for himself. Yet he did know that a great moment had arrived for the poet.

"So," said Finegas, "you did not eat it on me after all?" "Did I not promise?" Fionn replied.

"And yet," his master continued, "I went away so that you might eat the fish if you felt you had to."

"Why should I want another man's fish?" said proud Fionn.

"Because young people have strong desires. I thought you might have tasted it, and then you would have eaten it on me."

"I did taste it by chance," Fionn laughed, "for while the fish was roasting a great blister rose on its skin. I did not like the look of that blister, and I pressed it down with my thumb. That burned my thumb, so I popped it in my mouth to heal the smart. If your salmon tastes as nice as my thumb did," he laughed, "it will taste very nice."

"What did you say your name was, dear heart?" the poet asked.

"I said my name was Deimne."

"Your name is not Deimne," said the mild man, "your name is Fionn."

"That is true," the boy answered, "but I do not know how you know it."

"Even if I have not eaten the Salmon of Knowledge I have some small science of my own."

"It is very clever to know things as you know them," Fionn replied wonderingly. "What more do you know of me, dear master?"

"I know that I did not tell you the truth," said the heavy-hearted man.

"What did you tell me instead of it?"

"I told you a lie."

"It is not a good thing to do," Fionn admitted. "What sort of a lie was the lie, master?" "I told you that the Salmon of Knowledge was to be caught by me, according to the prophecy."

"Yes."

"That was true indeed, and I have caught the fish. But I did not tell you that the salmon was not to be eaten by me, although that also was in the prophecy, and that omission was the lie."

"It is not a great lie," said Fionn soothingly.

"It must not become a greater one," the poet replied sternly.

"Who was the fish given to?" his companion wondered.

"It was given to you," Finegas answered. "It was given to Fionn, the son of Uail, the son of Baiscne, and it will be given to him."

"You shall have a half of the fish," cried Fionn.

"I will not eat a piece of its skin that is as small as the point of its smallest bone," said the resolute and trembling bard. "Let you now eat up the fish, and I shall watch you and give praise to the gods of the Underworld and of the Elements."

Fionn then ate the Salmon of Knowledge, and when it had disappeared a great jollity and tranquillity and exuberance returned to the poet.

"Ah," said he, "I had a great combat with that fish."

"Did it fight for its life?" Fionn inquired.

"It did, but that was not the fight I meant."

"You shall eat a Salmon of Knowledge too," Fionn assured him.

"You have eaten one," cried the blithe poet, "and if you make such a promise it will be because you know."

"I promise it and know it," said Fionn, "you shall eat a Salmon of Knowledge yet."

Chapter XI

He had received all that he could get from Finegas. His education was finished and the time had come to test it, and to try all else that he had of mind and body. He bade farewell to the gentle poet, and set out for Tara of the Kings.

It was Samhain-tide, and the feast of Tara was being held, at which all that was wise or skilful or well-born in Ireland were gathered together.

This is how Tara was when Tara was. There was the High King's palace with its fortification; without it was another fortification enclosing the four minor palaces, each of which was maintained by one of the four provincial kings; without that again was the great banqueting hall, and around it and enclosing all of the sacred hill in its gigantic bound ran the main outer ramparts of Tara. From it, the centre of Ireland, four great roads went, north, south, east, and west, and along these roads, from the top and the bottom and the two sides of Ireland, there moved for weeks before Samhain an endless stream of passengers.

Here a gay band went carrying rich treasure to decorate the pavilion of a Munster lord. On another road a vat of seasoned yew, monstrous as a house on wheels and drawn by a hundred laborious oxen, came bumping and joggling the ale that thirsty Connaught princes would drink. On a road again the learned men of Leinster, each with an idea in his head that would discomfit a northern ollave and make a southern one gape and fidget, would be marching solemnly, each by a horse that was piled high on the back and widely at the sides with clean-peeled willow or oaken wands, that were carved from the top to the bottom with the ogham signs; the first lines of poems (for it was an offence against wisdom to commit more than initial lines to writing), the names and dates of kings, the procession of laws of Tara and of the sub-kingdoms, the names of places and their meanings. On the brown stallion ambling peacefully yonder there might go the warring of the gods for two or ten thousand years; this mare with the dainty pace and the vicious eye might be sidling under a load of oaken odes in honour of her owner's family, with a few bundles of tales of wonder added in case they might be useful; and perhaps the restive piebald was backing the history of Ireland into a ditch.

On such a journey all people spoke together, for all were friends, and no person regarded the weapon in another man's hand other than as an implement to poke a reluctant cow with, or to pacify with loud wallops some hoof-proud colt.

Into this teem and profusion of jolly humanity Fionn slipped, and if his mood had been as bellicose as a wounded boar he would yet have found no man to quarrel with, and if his eye had been as sharp as a jealous husband's he would have found no eye to meet it with calculation or menace or fear; for the Peace of Ireland was in being, and for six weeks man was neighbour to man, and the nation was the guest of the High King. Fionn went in with the notables.

His arrival had been timed for the opening day and the great feast of welcome. He may have marvelled, looking on the bright city, with its pillars of gleaming bronze and the roofs that were painted in many colours, so that each house seemed to be covered by the spreading wings of some gigantic and gorgeous bird. And the palaces themselves, mellow with red oak, polished within and without by the wear and the care of a thousand years, and carved with the patient skill of unending generations of the most famous artists of the most artistic country of the western world, would have given him much to marvel at also. It must have seemed like a city of dream, a city to catch the heart, when, coming over the great plain, Fionn saw Tara of the Kings held on its hill as in a hand to gather all the gold of the falling sun, and to restore a brightness as mellow and tender as that universal largess.

In the great banqueting hall everything was in order for the feast. The nobles of Ireland with their winsome consorts, the learned and artistic professions represented by the pick of their time were in place. The Ard-Ri, Corm of the Hundred Battles, had taken his place on the raised dais which commanded the whole of that vast hall. At his Right hand his son Art, to be afterwards as famous as his famous father, took his seat, and on his left Goll mor mac Morna, chief of the Fianna of Ireland, had the seat of honour. As the High King took his place he could see every person who was noted in the land for any reason. He would know everyone who was present, for the fame of all men is sealed at Tara, and behind his chair a herald stood to tell anything the king might not know or had forgotten.

Conn gave the signal and his guests seated themselves.

The time had come for the squires to take their stations behind their masters and mistresses. But, for the moment, the great room was seated, and the doors were held to allow a moment of respect to pass before the servers and squires came in.

Looking over his guests, Conn observed that a young man was yet standing.

"There is a gentleman," he murmured, "for whom no seat has been found."

We may be sure that the Master of the Banquet blushed at that.

"And" the king continued, "I do not seem to know the young man."

Nor did his herald, nor did the unfortunate Master, nor did anybody; for the eyes of all were now turned where the king went.

"Give me my horn," said the gracious monarch.

The horn of state was put to his hand.

"Young gentleman," he called to the stranger, "I wish to drink to your health and to welcome you to Tara."

The young man came forward then, greater-shouldered than any mighty man of that gathering, longer and cleaner limbed, with his fair curls dancing about his beardless face. The king put the great horn into his hand.

"Tell me your name," he commanded gently.

"I am Fionn, the son of Uail, the son of Baiscne," said the youth.

And at that saying a touch as of lightning went through the gathering so that each person quivered, and the son of the great, murdered captain looked by the king's shoulder into the twinkling eye of Goll. But no word was uttered, no movement made except the movement and the utterance of the Ard-Ri'.

"You are the son of a friend," said the great-hearted monarch. "You shall have the seat of a friend."

He placed Fionn at the right hand of his own son Art.

Chapter XII

It is to be known that on the night of the Feast of Samhain the doors separating this world and the next one are opened, and the inhabitants of either world can leave their respective spheres and appear in the world of the other beings.

Now there was a grandson to the Dagda Mor, the Lord of the Underworld, and he was named Aillen mac Midna, out of Shi' Finnachy, and this Aillen bore an implacable enmity to Tara and the Ard-Ri'.

As well as being monarch of Ireland her High King was chief of the people learned in magic, and it is possible that at some time Conn had adventured into Tir na n-Og, the Land of the Young, and had done some deed or misdeed in Aillen's lordship or in his family. It must have been an ill deed in truth, for it was in a very rage of revenge that Aillen came yearly at the permitted time to ravage Tara.

Nine times he had come on this mission of revenge, but it is not to be supposed that he could actually destroy the holy city. The Ard-Ri' and magicians could prevent that, but he could yet do a damage so considerable that it was worth Conn's while to take special extra precautions against him, including the precaution of chance.

Therefore, when the feast was over and the banquet had commenced, the Hundred Fighter stood from his throne and looked over his assembled people.

The Chain of Silence was shaken by the attendant whose duty and honour was the Silver Chain, and at that delicate chime the halt went silent, and a general wonder ensued as to what matter the High King would submit to his people.

"Friends and heroes," said Conn, "Aillen, the son of Midna, will come to-night from Slieve Fuaid with occult, terrible fire against our city. Is there among you one who loves Tara and the king, and who will undertake our defence against that being?"

He spoke in silence, and when he had finished he listened to the same silence, but it was now deep, ominous, agonized. Each man glanced uneasily on his neighbour and then stared at his wine-cup or his fingers. The hearts of young men went hot for a gallant moment and were chilled in the succeeding one, for they had all heard of Aillen out of Shl Finnachy in the north. The lesser gentlemen looked under their brows at the greater champions, and these peered furtively at the greatest of all. Art og mac Morna of the Hard Strokes fell to biting his fingers, Cona'n the Swearer and Garra mac Morna grumbled irritably to each other and at their neighbours, even Caelte, the son of Rona'n, looked down into his own lap, and Goll Mor sipped at his wine without any twinkle in his eye. A horrid embarrassment came into the great hall, and as the High King stood in that palpitating silence his noble face changed from kindly to grave and from that to a terrible sternness. In another moment, to the undying shame of every person present, he would have been compelled to lift his own challenge and declare himself the champion of Tara for that night, but the shame that was on the faces of his people would remain in the heart of their king. Goll's merry mind would help him to forget, but even his heart would be wrung by a memory that he would not dare to face. It was at that terrible moment that Fionn stood up.

"What," said he, "will be given to the man who undertakes this defence?"

"All that can be rightly asked will be royally bestowed," was the king's answer.

"Who are the sureties?" said Fionn.

"The kings of Ireland, and Red Cith with his magicians."

"I will undertake the defence," said Fionn. And on that, the kings and magicians who were present bound themselves to the fulfilment of the bargain.

Fionn marched from the banqueting hall, and as he went, all who were present of nobles and retainers and servants acclaimed him and wished him luck. But in their hearts they were bidding him goodbye, for all were assured that the lad was marching to a death so inescapable that he might already be counted as a dead man.

It is likely that Fionn looked for help to the people of the Shi' themselves, for, through his mother, he belonged to the tribes of Dana, although, on the father's side, his blood was well compounded with mortal clay. It may be, too, that he knew how events would turn, for he had eaten the Salmon of Knowledge. Yet it is not recorded that on this occasion he invoked any magical art as he did on other adventures.

Fionn's way of discovering whatever was happening and hidden was always the same and is many times referred to. A shallow, oblong dish of pure, pale gold was brought to him. This dish was filled with clear water. Then Fionn would bend his head and stare into the water, and as he stared he would place his thumb in his mouth under his "Tooth of Knowledge," his "wisdom tooth."

Knowledge, may it be said, is higher than magic and is more to be sought. It is quite possible to see what is happening and yet not know what is forward, for while seeing is believing it does not follow that either seeing or believing is knowing. Many a person can see a thing and believe a thing and know just as little about it as the person who does neither. But Fionn would see and know, or he would understand a decent ratio of his visions. That he was versed in magic is true, for he was ever known as the Knowledgeable man, and later he had two magicians in his household named Dirim and mac-Reith to do the rough work of knowledge for their busy master.

It was not from the Shi', however, that assistance came to Fionn.

Chapter XIII

He marched through the successive fortifications until he came to the outer, great wall, the boundary of the city, and when he had passed this he was on the wide plain of Tara.

Other than himself no person was abroad, for on the night of the Feast of Samhain none but a madman would quit the shelter of a house even if it were on fire; for whatever disasters might be within a house would be as nothing to the calamities without it.

The noise of the banquet was not now audible to Fionn - it is possible, however, that there was a shamefaced silence in the great hall - and the lights of the city were hidden by the successive great ramparts. The sky was over him; the earth under him; and then these there was nothing, or there was but the darkness and the wind.

But darkness was not a thing to terrify him, bred in the nightness of a wood and the very fosterling of gloom; nor could the wind afflict his ear or his heart. There was no note in its orchestra that he had not brooded on and become, which becoming is magic. The long-drawn moan of it; the thrilling whisper and hush; the shrill, sweet whistle, so thin it can scarcely be heard, and is taken more by the nerves than by the ear; the screech, sudden as a devil's yell and loud as ten thunders; the cry as of one who flies with backward look to the shelter of leaves and darkness; and the sob as of one stricken with an age-long misery, only at times remembered, but remembered then with what a pang! His ear knew by what successions they arrived, and by what stages they grew and diminished. Listening in the dark to the bundle of noises which make a noise he could disentangle them and assign a place and a reason to each gradation of sound that formed the chorus. There was the patter of a rabbit, and there the scurrying of a hare; a bush rustled yonder, but that brief rustle was a bird; that pressure was a wolf, and this hesitation a fox; the scraping yonder was but a rough leaf against bark, and the scratching beyond it was a ferret's claw.

Fear cannot be where knowledge is, and Fionn was not fearful.

His mind, quietly busy on all sides, picked up one sound and dwelt on it. "A man," said Fionn, and he listened in that direction, back towards the city.

A man it was, almost as skilled in darkness as Fionn himself "This is no enemy," Fionn thought, "his walking is open."

"Who comes?" he called.

"A friend," said the newcomer.

"Give a friend's name," said Fionn.

"Fiacuil mac Cona," was the answer.

"Ah, my pulse and heart!" cried Fionn, and he strode a few paces to meet the great robber who had fostered him among the marshes.

"So you are not afraid," he said joyfully.

"I am afraid in good truth," Fiacuil whispered, "and the minute my business with you is finished I will trot back as quick as legs will carry me. May the gods protect my going as they protected my coming," said the robber piously.

"Amen," said Fionn, "and now, tell me what you have come for?"

"Have you any plan against this lord of the Shl?" Fiacuil whispered.

"I will attack him," said Fionn.

"That is not a plan," the other groaned, "we do not plan to deliver an attack but to win a victory."

"Is this a very terrible person?" Fionn asked.

"Terrible indeed. No one can get near him or away from him. He comes out of the Shi' playing sweet, low music on a bodhran and a pipe, and all who hear this music fall asleep."

"I will not fall asleep," said Fionn.

"You will indeed, for everybody does."

"What happens then?" Fionn asked.

"When all are asleep Aillen mac Midna blows a dart of fire out of his mouth, and everything that is touched by that fire is destroyed, and he can blow his fire to an incredible distance and to any direction."

"You are very brave to come to help me," Fionn murmured, "especially when you are not able to help me at all."

"I can help," Fiacuil replied, "but I must be paid."

"What payment?"

"A third of all you earn and a seat at your council."

"I grant that," said Fionn, "and now, tell me your plan?"

"You remember my spear with the thirty rivets of Arabian gold in its socket?"

"The one," Fionn queried, "that had its head wrapped in a blanket and was stuck in a bucket of water and was chained to a wall as well

- the venomous Birgha?" "That one," Fiacuil replied.

"It is Aillen mac Midna's own spear," he continued, "and it was taken out of his Shi' by your father."

"Well?" said Fionn, wondering nevertheless where Fiacuil got the spear, but too generous to ask.

"When you hear the great man of the Shi' coming, take the wrappings off the head of the spear and bend your face over it; the heat of the spear, the stench of it, all its pernicious and acrid qualities will prevent you from going to sleep."

"Are you sure of that?" said Fionn.

"You couldn't go to sleep close to that stench; nobody could," Fiacuil replied decidedly.

He continued, "Aillen mac Midna will be off his guard when he stops playing and begins to blow his fire; he will think everybody is asleep; then you can deliver the attack you were speaking of, and all good luck go with it."

"I will give him back his spear," said Fionn.

"Here it is," said Fiacuil, taking the Birgha from under his cloak. "But be as careful of it, my pulse, be as frightened of it as you are of the man of Dana."

"I will be frightened of nothing," said Fionn, "and the only person I will be sorry for is that Aillen mac Midna, who is going to get his own spear back."

"I will go away now," his companion whispered, "for it is growing darker where you would have thought there was no more room for darkness, and there is an eerie feeling abroad which I do not like. That man from the Shi' may come any minute, and if I catch one sound of his music I am done for."

The robber went away and again Fionn was alone.

Chapter XIV

He listened to the retreating footsteps until they could be heard no more, and the one sound that came to his tense ears was the beating of his own heart.

Even the wind had ceased, and there seemed to be nothing in the world but the darkness and himself. In that gigantic blackness, in that unseen quietude and vacancy, the mind could cease to be personal to itself. It could be overwhelmed and merged in space, so that consciousness would be transferred or dissipated, and one might sleep standing; for the mind fears loneliness more than all else, and will escape to the moon rather than be driven inwards on its own being.

But Fionn was not lonely, and he was not afraid when the son of Midna came.

A long stretch of the silent night had gone by, minute following minute in a slow sequence, wherein as there was no change there was no time; wherein there was no past and no future, but a stupefying, endless present which is almost the annihilation of consciousness. A change came then, for the clouds had also been moving and the moon at last was sensed behind them - not as a radiance, but as a percolation of light, a gleam that was strained through matter after matter and was less than the very wraith or remembrance of itself; a thing seen so narrowly, so sparsely, that the eye could doubt if it was or was not seeing, and might conceive that its own memory was re-creating that which was still absent.

But Fionn's eye was the eye of a wild creature that spies on darkness and moves there wittingly. He saw, then, not a thing but a movement; something that was darker than the darkness it loomed on; not a being but a presence, and, as it were, impending pressure. And in a little he heard the deliberate pace of that great being.

Fionn bent to his spear and unloosed its coverings.

Then from the darkness there came another sound; a low, sweet sound; thrillingly joyous, thrillingly low; so low the ear could scarcely note it, so sweet the ear wished to catch nothing else and would strive to hear it rather than all sounds that may be heard by man - the music of another world! The unearthly, dear melody of the Shi'! So sweet it was that the sense strained to it, and having reached must follow drowsily in its wake, and would merge in it, and could not return again to its own place until that strange harmony was finished and the ear restored to freedom.

But Fionn had taken the covering from his spear, and with his brow pressed close to it he kept his mind and all his senses engaged on that sizzling, murderous point.

The music ceased and Aillen hissed a fierce blue flame from his mouth, and it was as though he hissed lightning.

Here it would seem that Fionn used magic, for spreading out his fringed mantle he caught the flame. Rather he stopped it, for it slid from the mantle and sped down into the earth to the depth of twenty-six spans; from which that slope is still called the Glen of the Mantle, and the rise on which Aillen stood is known as the Ard of Fire.

One can imagine the surprise of Aillen mac Midna, seeing his fire caught and quenched by an invisible hand. And one can imagine that at this check he might be frightened, for who would be more terrified than a magician who sees his magic fail, and who, knowing of power, will guess at powers of which he has no conception and may well dread.

Everything had been done by him as it should be done. His pipe had been played and his bodhran, all who heard that music should be asleep, and yet his fire was caught in full course and was quenched.

Aillen, with all the terrific strength of which he was master, blew again, and the great jet of blue flame came roaring and whistling from him and was caught and disappeared.

Panic swirled into the man from Faery; he turned from that terrible spot and fled, not knowing what might be behind, but dreading it as he had never before dreaded anything, and the unknown pursued him; that terrible defence became offence and hung to his heel as a wolf pads by the flank of a bull.

And Aillen was not in his own world! He was in the world of men, where movement is not easy and the very air a burden. In his own sphere, in his own element, he might have outrun Fionn, but this was Fionn's world, Fionn's element, and the flying god was not gross enough to outstrip him. Yet what a race he gave, for it was but at the entrance to his own Shi' that the pursuer got close enough. Fionn put a finger into the thong of the great spear, and at that cast night fell on Aillen mac Midna. His eyes went black, his mind whirled and ceased, there came nothingness where he had been, and as the Birgha whistled into his shoulder-blades he withered away, he tumbled emptily and was dead. Fionn took his lovely head from its shoulders and went back through the night to Tara.

Triumphant Fionn, who had dealt death to a god, and to whom death would be dealt, and who is now dead!

He reached the palace at sunrise.

On that morning all were astir early. They wished to see what destruction had been wrought by the great being, but it was young Fionn they saw and that redoubtable head swinging by its hair. "What is your demand?" said the Ard-Ri'. "The thing that it is right I should ask," said Fionn, "the command of the Fianna of Ireland."

"Make your choice," said Conn to Goll Mor, "you will leave Ireland, or you will place your hand in the hand of this champion and be his man."

Goll could do a thing that would be hard for another person, and he could do it so beautifully that he was not diminished by any action.

"Here is my hand," said Goll. And he twinkled at the stern, young eyes that gazed on him as he made his submission.

Tales From The Land Of Saints & Scholars

The Brewery of Eggshells

"The Brewery of Eggshells" is one of the best-known Irish changeling tales, originally collected by Thomas Crofton Croker in the early nineteenth century and later adapted by W. B. Yeats in Fairy and Folk Tales of the Irish Peasantry (1888, The Walter Scott Publishing Company). The story tells of a mother in a rural cottage whose baby has been stolen by the fairies and replaced with a wizened, ill-tempered changeling.

The tale's power lies in its blend of domestic unease and supernatural folklore, reflecting the deep fear among Irish country people of fairy interference in family life. It captures the way folklore often worked as both moral warning and psychological allegory, commenting on motherhood, loss, and the fragile boundary between reason and belief.

Mrs. Sullivan fancied that her youngest child had been exchanged by "fairies' theft," and certainly appearances warranted such a conclusion; for in one night her healthy, blue-eyed boy had become shrivelled up into almost nothing, and never ceased squalling and crying. This naturally made poor Mrs. Sullivan very unhappy; and all the neighbours, by way of comforting her, said that her own child was, beyond any kind of doubt, with the good people, and that one of themselves was put in his place.

Mrs. Sullivan of course could not disbelieve what everyone told her, but she did not wish to hurt the thing; for although its face was so withered, and its body wasted away to a mere skeleton, it had still a strong resemblance to her own boy. She, therefore, could not find it in her heart to roast it alive on the griddle, or to burn its nose off with the red-hot tongs, or to throw it out in the snow on the road-side, notwithstanding these, and several like proceedings, were strongly recommended to her for the recovery of her child.

One day who should Mrs. Sullivan meet but a cunning woman, well known about the country by the name of Ellen Leah (or Grey Ellen). She had the gift, however she got it, of telling where the dead were, and what was good for the rest of their souls; and could charm away warts and wens, and do a great many wonderful things of the same nature.

"You're in grief this morning, Mrs. Sullivan," were the first words of Ellen Leah to her.

"You may say that, Ellen," said Mrs. Sullivan, "and good cause I have to be in grief, for there was my own fine child whipped of from me out of his cradle, without as much as 'by your leave' or 'ask your pardon,' and an ugly dony bit of a shrivelled-up fairy put in his place; no wonder, then, that you see me in grief, Ellen."

"Small blame to you, Mrs. Sullivan," said Ellen Leah, "but are you sure 'tis a fairy?"

"Sure!" echoed Mrs. Sullivan, "sure enough I am to my sorrow, and can I doubt my own two eyes? Every mother's soul must feel for me!"

"Will you take an old woman's advice?" said Ellen Leah, fixing her wild and mysterious gaze upon the unhappy mother; and, after a pause, she added, "but maybe you'll call it foolish?"

"Can you get me back my child, my own child, Ellen?" said Mrs. Sullivan with great energy.

"If you do as I bid you," returned Ellen Leah, "you'll know." Mrs. Sullivan was silent in expectation, and Ellen continued, "Put down the big pot, full of water, on the fire, and make it boil like mad; then get a dozen new-laid eggs, break them, and keep the shells, but throw away the rest; when that is done, put the shells in the pot of boiling water, and you will soon know whether it is your own boy or a fairy. If you find that it is a fairy in the cradle, take the red-hot poker and cram it down his ugly throat, and you will not have much trouble with him after that, I promise you."

Home went Mrs. Sullivan, and did as Ellen Leah desired. She put the pot on the fire, and plenty of turf under it, and set the water boiling at such a rate, that if ever water was red-hot, it surely was.

The child was lying, for a wonder, quite easy and quiet in the cradle, every now and then cocking his eye, that would twinkle as keen as a star in a frosty night, over at the great fire, and the big pot upon it; and he looked on with great attention at Mrs. Sullivan breaking the eggs and putting down the eggshells to boil. At last he asked, with the voice of a very old man, "What are you doing, mammy?"

Mrs. Sullivan's heart, as she said herself, was up in her mouth ready to choke her, at hearing the child speak. But she contrived to put the poker in the fire, and to answer, without making any wonder at the words, "I'm brewing, a vick" (my son).

"And what are you brewing, mammy?" said the little imp, whose supernatural gift of speech now proved beyond question that he was a fairy substitute.

"I wish the poker was red," thought Mrs. Sullivan; but it was a large one, and took a long-time heating; so she determined to keep him in talk until the poker was in a proper state to thrust down his throat, and therefore repeated the question.

"Is it what I'm brewing, a vick," said she, "you want to know?"

"Yes, mammy, what are you brewing?" returned the fairy.

"Eggshells, a vick," said Mrs. Sullivan.

"Oh!" shrieked the imp, starting up in the cradle, and clapping his hands together, "I'm fifteen hundred years in the world, and I never saw a brewery of eggshells before!" The poker was by this time quite red, and Mrs. Sullivan, seizing it, ran furiously towards the cradle; but somehow or other her foot slipped, and she fell flat on the floor, and the poker flew out of her hand to the other end of the house. However, she got up without much loss of time and went to the cradle, intending to pitch the wicked thing that was in it into the pot of boiling water, when there she saw her own child in a sweet sleep, one of his soft round arms rested upon the pillow—his features were as placid as if their repose had never been disturbed, save the rosy mouth, which moved with a gentle and regular breathing.

Tales From The Land Of Saints & Scholars

The Carving of Mac Datho's Boar

"The Carving of Mac Dathó's Boar" is an ancient Irish saga drawn from the Ulster Cycle, retold in modern form by T. W. Rolleston in The High Deeds of Finn and Other Bardic Romances of Ancient Ireland (1910). Set in the heroic age of Ireland's mythic kingdoms, it tells of Mac Dathó, a chieftain famed for possessing two treasures: a hound of extraordinary prowess and a gigantic boar.

The tale combines satire and savagery, exposing the vanity and competitiveness that underlie the warrior code. In Rolleston's retelling, as in the original, the story captures both the grandeur and absurdity of heroic honour, balancing dark humour with the stark violence of mythic Ireland.

Once upon a time there dwelt in the province of Leinster a wealthy hospitable lord named Mesroda, son of Datho. Two possessions had he; namely, a hound which could outrun every other hound and every wild beast in Erinn, and a boar which was the finest and greatest in size that man had ever beheld.

Now the fame of this hound was noised all about the land, and many were the princes and lords who longed to possess it. And it came to pass that Conor, King of Ulster, and Maev, Queen of Connacht, sent messengers to mac Datho to ask him to sell them the hound for a price, and both the messengers arrived at the Dún of mac Datho on the same day. Said the Connacht messenger, "We will give you in exchange for the hound six hundred milk cows, and a chariot with two horses, the best that are to be found in Connacht, and at the end of a year you shalt have as much again." And the messenger of King Conor said, "We will give no less than Connacht, and the friendship and alliance of Ulster, and that will be better for you than the friendship of Connacht."

Then Mesroda mac Datho fell silent, and for three days he would not eat nor drink, nor could he sleep o' nights, but tossed restlessly on his bed. His wife observed his condition, and said to him, "Your fast have been long, Mesroda, though good food is by you in plenty; and at night you turn your face to the wall, and well I know you dost not sleep. What is the cause of your trouble?"

"There is a saying," replied mac Datho, "Trust not a thrall with money, nor a woman with a secret."

"When should a man talk to a woman," said his wife, "but when something were amiss? What your mind cannot solve perchance another's may."

Then mac Datho told his wife of the request for his hound both from Ulster and from Connacht at one and the same time, "and whichever of them I deny," he said, "they will harry my cattle and slay my people."

"Then hear my counsel," said the woman. "Give it to both of them, and bid them come and fetch it; and if there be any harrying to be done, let them even harry each other; but in no way may you keep the hound."

On that, mac Datho rose up and shook himself, and called for food and drink, and made merry with himself and his guests. Then he sent privately for the messenger of Queen Maev, and said to him, "Long have I doubted what to do, but now I am resolved to give the hound to Connacht. Let you send for it on such a day with a train of your nobles or warriors and bear him forth nobly and proudly, for he is worth it; and you shall all have drink and food and royal entertainment in my Dún." So the messenger departed, well pleased.

To the Ulster messenger mac Datho said, "After much perplexity I have resolved to give my hound to Conor. Let the best of the Ulstermen come to fetch him, and they shall be welcomed and entertained as is fitting." And for these he named the same day as he had done for the embassy from Connacht.

When the appointed day came round, the flower of the fighting men of two provinces of Ireland were assembled before the Dún of the son of Datho, and there were also Conor, King of Ulster, and Ailill, the husband of Maev, Queen of Connacht. Mac Datho went forth to meet them. "Welcome, warriors," he said to them, "albeit for two armies at once we were not prepared." Then he bade them into the Dún, and in the great hall they sat down. Now in this hall there were seven doors, and between every two doors were benches for fifty men. Not as friends bidden to a feast did the men of Ulster and of Connacht look upon one another, since for three hundred years the provinces had ever been at war.

"Let the great boar be killed," said mac Datho, and it was done. For seven years had that boar been nourished on the milk of fifty cows; yet rather on venom should it have been nourished, such was the mischief that was to come from the carving of it.

When the boar was roasted it was brought in, and many other kinds of food as side dishes, "and if more be wanting to the feast," said mac Datho, "it shall be slain for you before the morning."

"The boar is good," said Conor.

"It is a fine boar," said Ailill, "and now, Oh mac Datho, how shall it be divided among us?"

There was among the Ulster company one Bricru, son of Carbad, whose delight was in biting speeches and in fomenting strife, though he himself was never known to draw sword in any quarrel. He now spoke from his couch in answer to Ailill, "How should the boar be divided, Oh son of Datho, except by appointing to carve it him who is best in deeds of arms? Here be all the valiant men of Ireland assembled; have none of us hit each other a blow on the nose before now?"

"Good," said Ailill, "so let it be done."

"We also agree," said Conor, "there are plenty of our lads in the house that have many a time gone round the border of the Provinces."

"You will want them to-night, Conor," said an old warrior from Conlad in the West. "They have often been seen on their backs on the roads of rushy Dedah, and many a fat steer have they left with me."

"It was a fat bullock you did have with you once upon a day," replied Moonremar of Ulster, "even your own brother, and by the rushy road of Conlad he came and went not back."

"Twas a better man than he, even Irloth, son of Fergus mac Leda, who fell by the hand of Echbael in Tara Luachra," replied Lugad of Munster.

"Echbael?" cried Keltchar, son of Uthecar Hornskin of Ulster. "Is it of him you boast, whom I myself slew and cut off his head?"

And thus the heroes bandied about the tales and taunts of their victories, until at length Ket, son of Maga of the Connachtmen, arose and stood over the boar and took the knife into his hand. "Now," he cried, "let one man in Ulster match his deeds with mine, or else hold you your peace and let me carve the boar!"

For a while there was silence, and then Conor King of Ulster, said to Logary the Triumphant, "Stay that for me." So Logary arose and said, "Ket shall never carve the boar for all of us."

"Not so fast, Logary," said Ket. "It is the custom among you Ulstermen that when a youth first takes arms he comes to prove himself on us. So did you, Logary, and we met you at the border. From that meeting I have your chariot and horses, and you had a spear through your ribs Not thus will you get the boar from me." Then Logary sat down on his bench.

"Ket shall never divide that pig," spoke then a tall fair-haired warrior from Ulster, coming down the hall. "Whom have we here?" asked Ket. "A better man than you," shouted the Ulstermen, "even Angus, son of Lama Gabad." "Indeed?" said Ket, "and why is his father called Lama Gabad [wanting a hand]?" "We know not," said they. "But I know it," said Ket. "Once I went on a foray to the East, and was attacked by a troop, Lama Gabad among them. He flung a lance at me. I seized the same lance and flung it back, and it shore off his hand, and it lay there on the field before him. Shall that man's son measure himself with me?" And Angus went to his bench and sat down.

"Keep up the contest," then cried Ket tauntingly, "or let me divide the boar." "That you shalt not," cried another Ulster warrior of great stature. "And who is this?" said Ket. "Owen Mór, King of Fermag," said the Ulstermen. "I have seen him before now," said Ket. "I took a drove of cattle from him before his own house. He put a spear through my shield and I flung it back and it tore out one of his eyes, and one-eyed he is to this day." Then Owen Mór sat down.

"Have you any more to contest the pig with me?" then said Ket. "You have not won it yet," said Moonremar, son of Gerrkind, rising up. "Is that Moonremar?" said Ket, "It is," they cried.

"It is but three days," said Ket, "since I was the last man who won renown of you. Three heads of your fighting men did I carry off from Dún Moonremar, and one of the three was the head of your eldest son." Moonremar then sat down.

"Still the contest," said Ket, "or I shall carve the boar." "Contest you shalt have," said Mend, son of Sword-heel. "Who is this?" said Ket. "'Tis Mend," cried all the Ulstermen.

"Shall the sons of fellows with nicknames come here to contend with me?" cried Ket. "I was the priest who christened your father that name. 'Twas I who cut the heel off him, so that off he went with only one. What brings the son of that man to contend with me?" Mend then sat down in his seat.

"Come to the contest," said Ket, "or I shall begin to carve." Then arose from the Ulstermen a huge grey and terrible warrior. "Who is this?" asked Ket. "'Tis Keltcar, son of Uthecar," cried they all.

"Wait a while, Keltcar," said Ket, "do not pound me to pieces just yet. Once, Oh Keltcar, I made a foray on you and came in front of Dún. All your folk attacked me, and you amongst them. In a narrow pass we fought, and you did fling a spear at me and I at you, but my spear went through your loins and you have never been the better of it since." Then Keltcar sat down in his seat.

"Who else comes to the contest," cried Ket "or shall I at last divide the pig?" Up rose then the son of King Conor, named Cuscrid the Stammerer "Whom have we here?" said Ket. "'Tis Cuscrid son of Conor," cried they all. "He has the stuff of a king in him," said Ket. "No thanks to you for that," said the youth.

"Well, then," said Ket, "thou made your first foray against us Connachtmen, and on the border of the Provinces we met you. A third of your people, you did leave behind you, and came away with my spear through your throat, so that you cannot speak rightly ever since, for the sinews of your throat were severed. And so is Cuscrid the Stammerer your byname ever since."

So thus Ket laid shame and defeat on the whole Province of Ulster, nor was there any other warrior in the hall found to contend with him.

Then Ket stood up triumphing, and took the knife in his hand and prepared to carve the boar when a noise and trampling were heard at the great door of the hall, and a mighty shout of exultation arose from the Ulstermen. When the press parted, Ket saw coming up the centre of the hall Conall of the Victories, and Conor the King dashed the helmet from his head and sprang up for joy.

"Glad we are," cried Conall, "that all is ready for feast; and who is carving the boar for us?"

"Ket, son of Maga," replied they, "for none could contest the place of honour with him."

"Is that so, Ket?" says Conall Cearnach.

"Even so," replied Ket. "And now welcome to you, Oh Conall, you of the iron heart and fiery blood; keen as the glitter of ice, ever-victorious chieftain; hail mighty son of Finnchoom!"

And Conall said, "Hail to you, Ket, flower of heroes, lord of chariots, a raging sea in battle; a strong, majestic bull; hail, son of Maga!"

"And now," went on Conall, "rise up from the boar and give me place."

"Why so?" replied Ket.

"Dost you seek a contest from me?" said Conall, "verily you shalt have it. By the gods of my nation I swear that since I first took weapons in my hand I have never passed one day that I did not slay a Connachtman, nor one night that I did not make a foray on them, nor have I ever slept but I had the head of a Connachtman under my knee."

"I confess," then, said Ket, "that you are a better man than I, and I yield you the boar. But if Anluan my brother were here, he would match you deed for deed, and sorrow and shame it is that he is not."

"Anluan is here," shouted Conall, and with that he drew from his girdle the head of Anluan and dashed it in the face of Ket.

Then all sprang to their feet and a wild shouting and tumult arose, and the swords flew out of themselves, and battle raged in the hall of mac Datho. Soon the hosts burst out through the doors of the Dún and smote and slew each other in the open field, until the Connacht host were put to flight. The hound of mac Datho pursued them along with the Ulstermen, and it came up with the chariot in which King Ailill was driving, and seized the pole of the chariot, but the charioteer dealt it a blow that cut off its head. When Ailill drew rein they found the hound's head still clinging to the pole, which is why that place is called Ibar Cinn Chon, or the Yew Tree of the Hound's Head.

Now when Conor pursued hard upon King Ailill, Ferloga, the charioteer of Ailill, lit down and hid in the heather; and as Conor drove past, Ferloga leapt up and gripped him by the throat.

"What will you have of me?" said Conor.

"Give over the pursuit," said Ferloga, "and take me with you to Emania, and let the maidens of Emania so long as I am there sing a serenade before my dwelling every night."

"Granted," said Conor. So he took Ferloga with him to Emania, and at the end of a year sent him back to Connacht, escorting him as far as to Athlone; and Ferloga had from the King of Ulster two noble horses with golden bridles, but the serenade from the maidens of Ulster he did not get, though he got the horses instead. And thus ends the tale of the contention between Ulster and Connacht over the Carving of mac Datho's Boar.

Tales From The Land Of Saints & Scholars

The Countess Kathleen O'Shea

"The Countess Kathleen O'Shea" is one of the more solemn and symbolic tales in Fairy and Folk Tales of the Irish Peasantry (1888), edited by W. B. Yeats. Set during a time of famine and despair, it tells of a noblewoman, the Countess Kathleen, whose compassion for her starving people leads her to make a profound sacrifice.

Yeats adapted the story from older Irish folk sources, but he reshaped it to reflect his preoccupation with spiritual beauty, redemption, and Ireland's moral identity. The tale's mingling of Christian imagery and Celtic supernaturalism captures the mood of the late nineteenth-century Irish Revival, where folklore served both as cultural inheritance and as moral allegory.

A very long time ago, there suddenly appeared in old Ireland two unknown merchants of whom nobody had ever heard, and who nevertheless spoke the language of the country with the greatest perfection. Their locks were black, and bound round with gold, and their garments were of rare magnificence.

Both seemed of like age; they appeared to be men of fifty, for their foreheads were wrinkled and their beards tinged with grey.

In the hostelry where the pompous traders alighted it was sought to penetrate their designs; but in vain - they led a silent and retired life. And whilst they stopped there, they did nothing but count over and again out of their money-bags pieces of gold, whose yellow brightness could be seen through the windows of their lodging.

"Gentlemen," said the landlady one day, "how is it that you are so rich, and that, being able to succour the public misery, you do no good works?"

"Fair hostess," replied one of them, "we didn't like to present alms to the honest poor, in dread we might be deceived by make-believe paupers. Let want knock at our door, we shall open it."

The following day, when the rumour spread that two rich strangers had come, ready to lavish their gold, a crowd besieged their dwelling; but the figures of those who came out were widely different. Some carried pride in their mien; others were shame-faced.

The two chapmen traded in souls for the demon. The souls of the aged was worth twenty pieces of gold, not a penny more; for Satan had had time to make his valuation. The soul of a matron was valued at fifty, when she was handsome, and a hundred when she was ugly. The soul of a young maiden fetched an extravagant sum; the freshest and purest flowers are the dearest.

At that time there lived in the city an angel of beauty, the Countess Kathleen O'Shea. She was the idol of the people and the providence of the indigent. As soon as she learned that these miscreants profited to the public misery to steal away hearts from God, she called to her butler.

"Patrick," she said to him, "how many pieces of gold in my coffers?"

"A hundred thousand."

"How many jewels?"

"The money's worth of the gold."

"How much property in castles, forests, and lands?"

"Double the rest."

"Very well, Patrick; sell all that is not gold; and bring me the account. I only wish to keep this mansion and the demesne that surrounds it."

Two days afterwards the orders of the pious Kathleen were executed, and the treasure was distributed to the poor in proportion to their wants. This, says the tradition, did not suit the purposes of the Evil Spirit, who found no more souls to purchase. Aided by an infamous servant, they penetrated into the retreat of the noble dame, and purloined from her the rest of her treasure. In vain she struggled with all her strength to save the contents of her coffers; the diabolical thieves were the stronger. If Kathleen had been able to make the sign of the Cross, adds the legend, she would have put them to flight, but her hands were captive. The larceny was effected.

Then the poor called for aid to the plundered Kathleen, alas, to no good. She was able to succour their misery no longer; she had to abandon them to the temptation.

Meanwhile, but eight days had to pass before the grain and provender would arrive in abundance from the western lands. Eight such days were an age. Eight days required an immense sum to relieve the exigencies of the dearth, and the poor should either perish in the agonies of hunger, or, denying the holy maxims of the Gospel, vend, for base lucre, their souls, the richest gift from the bounteous hand of the Almighty. And Kathleen hadn't anything, for she had given up her mansion to the unhappy. She passed twelve hours in tears and mourning, rending her sun-tinted hair, and bruising her breast, of the whiteness of the lily; afterwards she stood up, resolute, animated by a vivid sentiment of despair.

She went to the traders in souls.

"What do you want?" they said.

"You buy souls?"

"Yes, a few still, in spite of you. Isn't that so, saint, with the eyes of sapphire?"

"To-day I am come to offer you a bargain," replied she.

"What?"

"I have a soul to sell, but it is costly."

"What does that signify if it is precious? The soul, like the diamond, is appraised by its transparency."

"It is mine."

The two emissaries of Satan started. Their claws were clutched under their gloves of leather; their grey eyes sparkled; the soul, pure, spotless, virginal of Kathleen—it was a priceless acquisition!

"Beauteous lady, how much do you ask?"

"A hundred and fifty thousand pieces of gold."

"It's at your service," replied the traders, and they tendered Kathleen a parchment sealed with black, which she signed with a shudder.

The sum was counted out to her.

As soon as she got home she said to the butler, "Here, distribute this - with this money that I give you the poor can tide over the eight days that remain, and not one of their souls will be delivered to the demon."

Afterwards she shut herself up in her room, and gave orders that none should disturb her.

Three days passed; she called nobody, she did not come out.

When the door was opened, they found her cold and stiff; she was dead of grief.

But the sale of this soul, so adorable in its charity, was declared null by the Lord; for she had saved her fellow-citizens from eternal death.

After the eight days had passed, numerous vessels brought into famished Ireland immense provisions in grain. Hunger was no longer possible. As to the traders, they disappeared from their hotel without anyone knowing what became of them. But the fishermen of the Blackwater pretend that they are enchained in a subterranean prison by order of Lucifer, until they shall be able to render up the soul of Kathleen, which escaped from them.

Tales From The Land Of Saints & Scholars

The Demon Cat

"The Demon Cat" is a dark, atmospheric Irish folktale collected by Lady Wilde (Speranza) and later adapted by W. B. Yeats in Fairy and Folk Tales of the Irish Peasantry (1888, The Walter Scott Publishing Company). The story unfolds in a remote Irish household haunted by a monstrous black cat that seems more spirit than beast.

The tale belongs to the Irish tradition of supernatural domestic hauntings, where the uncanny intrudes into the ordinary world without explanation or resolution. Beneath its simple plot runs a current of moral and spiritual warning, consistent with Lady Wilde's fascination with occult folklore and Catholic demonology.

There was a woman in Connemara, the wife of a fisherman; as he had always good luck, she had plenty of fish at all times stored away in the house ready for market. But, to her great annoyance, she found that a great cat used to come in at night and devour all the best and finest fish. So she kept a big stick by her, and determined to watch.

One day, as she and a woman were spinning together, the house suddenly became quite dark; and the door was burst open as if by the blast of the tempest, when in walked a huge black cat, who went straight up to the fire, then turned round and growled at them.

"Why, surely this is the devil," said a young girl, who was by, sorting fish.

"I'll teach you how to call me names," said the cat; and, jumping at her, he scratched her arm till the blood came. "There, now," he said, "you will be more civil another time when a gentleman comes to see you." And with that he walked over to the door and shut it close, to prevent any of them going out, for the poor young girl, while crying loudly from fright and pain, had made a desperate rush to get away.

Just then a man was going by, and hearing the cries, he pushed open the door and tried to get in; but the cat stood on the threshold, and would let no one pass. On this the man attacked him with his stick, and gave him a sound blow; the cat, however, was more than a match in the fight, for it flew at him and tore his face and hands so badly that the man at last took to his heels and ran away as fast as he could.

"Now, it's time for my dinner," said the cat, going up to examine the fish that was laid out on the tables. "I hope the fish is good to-day. Now, don't disturb me, nor make a fuss; I can help myself." With that he jumped up, and began to devour all the best fish, while he growled at the woman.

"Away, out of this, you wicked beast," she cried, giving it a blow with the tongs that would have broken its back, only it was a devil, "out of this; no fish shall you have to-day."

But the cat only grinned at her, and went on tearing and spoiling and devouring the fish, evidently not a bit the worse for the blow. On this, both the women attacked it with sticks, and struck hard blows enough to kill it, on which the cat glared at them, and spit fire; then, making a leap, it tore their heads and arms till the blood came, and the frightened women rushed shrieking from the house.

But presently the mistress returned, carrying with her a bottle of holy water; and, looking in, she saw the cat still devouring the fish, and not minding. So she crept over quietly and threw holy water on it without a word. No sooner was this done than a dense black smoke filled the place, through which nothing was seen but the two red eyes of the cat, burning like coals of fire. Then the smoke gradually cleared away, and she saw the body of the creature burning slowly till it became shrivelled and black like a cinder, and finally disappeared. And from that time the fish remained untouched and safe from harm, for the power of the evil one was broken, and the demon cat was seen no more.

Tales From The Land Of Saints & Scholars

The Enchanted Cave of Cesh Corran

"The Enchanted Cave of Cesh Corran" is one of the mythic tales retold by James Stephens in his Irish Fairy Tales (1920), drawn from the ancient Fenian Cycle of Irish mythology. The story centres on Finn mac Cumhaill (Fionn mac Cumhaill), leader of the Fianna, and his miraculous son Oisín, whose birth is surrounded by magic and danger.

Stephens's version transforms this myth into a lyrical meditation on destiny, transformation, and the mingling of mythic time with human experience. His prose, rich in rhythm and irony, fuses oral tradition with modern narrative artistry, giving the ancient legend the tone of a living dream rather than a relic of the past.

Chapter I

FIONN MAC UAIL WAS THE MOST prudent chief of an army in the world, but he was not always prudent on his own account. Discipline sometimes irked him, and he would then take any opportunity that presented for an adventure; for he was not only a soldier, he was a poet also, that is, a man of science, and whatever was strange or unusual had an irresistible attraction for him. Such a soldier was he that, single-handed, he could take the Fianna out of any hole they got into, but such an inveterate poet was he that all the Fianna together could scarcely retrieve him from the abysses into which he tumbled. It took him to keep the Fianna safe, but it took all the Fianna to keep their captain out of danger. They did not complain of this, for they loved every hair of Fionn's head more than they loved their wives and children, and that was reasonable for there was never in the world a person worthier of love than Fionn was.

Goll mac Morna did not admit so much in words, but he admitted it in all his actions, for although he never lost an opportunity of killing a member of Fionn's family (there was deadly feud between clan-Baiscne and clan-Morna), yet a call from Fionn brought Goll raging to his assistance like a lion that rages tenderly by his mate. Not even a call was necessary, for Goll felt in his heart when Fionn was threatened, and he would leave Fionn's own brother only half-killed to fly where his arm was wanted. He was never thanked, of course, for although Fionn loved Goll he did not like him, and that was how Goll felt towards Fionn.

Fionn, with Cona'n the Swearer and the dogs Bran and Sceo'lan, was sitting on the hunting-mound at the top of Cesh Corran. Below and around on every side the Fianna were beating the coverts in Legney and Brefny, ranging the fastnesses of Glen Dallan, creeping in the nut and beech forests of Carbury, spying among the woods of Kyle Conor, and ranging the wide plain of Moy Conal.

The great captain was happy. His eyes were resting on the sights he liked best - the sunlight of a clear day, the waving trees, the pure sky, and the lovely movement of the earth; and his ears were filled with delectable sounds - the baying of eager dogs, the clear calling of young men, the shrill whistling that came from every side, and each sound of which told a definite thing about the hunt. There was also the plunge and scurry of the deer, the yapping of badgers, and the whirr of birds driven into reluctant flight.

Chapter II

Now the king of the Shi' of Cesh Corran, Conaran, son of Imidel, was also watching the hunt, but Fionn did not see him, for we cannot see the people of Faery until we enter their realm, and Fionn was not thinking of Faery at that moment. Conaran did not like Fionn, and, seeing that the great champion was alone, save for Cona'n and the two hounds Bran and Sceo'lan, he thought the time had come to get Fionn into his power. We do not know what Fionn had done to Conaran, but it must have been bad enough, for the king of the Shi' of Cesh Cotran was filled with joy at the sight of Fionn thus close to him, thus unprotected, thus unsuspicious.

This Conaran had four daughters. He was fond of them and proud of them, but if one were to search the Shi's of Ireland or the land of Ireland, the equal of these four would not be found for ugliness and bad humour and twisted temperaments.

Their hair was black as ink and tough as wire, and it stuck up and poked out and hung down about their heads in bushes and spikes and tangles. Their eyes were bleary and red. Their mouths were black and twisted, and in each of these mouths there was a hedge of curved yellow fangs. They had long scraggy necks that could turn all the way round like the neck of a hen. Their arms were long and skinny and muscular, and at the end of each finger they had a spiked nail that was as hard as horn and as sharp as a briar. Their bodies were covered with a bristle of hair and fur and fluff, so that they looked like dogs in some parts and like cats in others, and in other parts again they looked like chickens. They had moustaches poking under their noses and woolly wads growing out of their ears, so that when you looked at them the first time you never wanted to look at them again, and if you had to look at them a second time you were likely to die of the sight.

They were called Caevo'g, Cuillen, and Iaran. The fourth daughter, Iarnach, was not present at that moment, so nothing need be said of her yet.

Conaran called these three to him.

"Fionn is alone," said he. "Fionn is alone, my treasures."

"Ah!" said Caevo'g, and her jaw crunched upwards and stuck outwards, as was usual with her when she was satisfied.

"When the chance comes take it," Conaran continued, and he smiled a black, beetle-browed, unbenevolent smile.

"It's a good word," said Cuillen, and she swung her jaw loose and made it waggle up and down, for that was the way she smiled.

"And here is the chance," her father added.

"The chance is here," Iaran echoed, with a smile that was very like her sister's, only that it was worse, and the wen that grew on her nose joggled to and fro and did not get its balance again for a long time.

Then they smiled a smile that was agreeable to their own eyes, but which would have been a deadly thing for anybody else to see.

"But Fionn cannot see us," Caevo'g objected, and her brow set downwards and her chin set upwards and her mouth squeezed sideways, so that her face looked like a badly disappointed nut.

"And we are worth seeing," Cuillen continued, and the disappointment that was set in her sister's face got carved and twisted into hers, but it was worse in her case.

"That is the truth," said Iaran in a voice of lamentation, and her face took on a gnarl and a writhe and a solidity of ugly woe that beat the other two and made even her father marvel.

"He cannot see us now," Conaran replied, "but he will see us in a minute."

"Won't Fionn be glad when he sees us!" said the three sisters.

And then they joined hands and danced joyfully around their father, and they sang a song, the first line of which is, "Fionn thinks he is safe. But who knows when the sky will fall?"

Lots of the people in the Shi' learned that song by heart, and they applied it to every kind of circumstance.

Chapter III

By his arts Conaran changed the sight of Fionn's eyes, and he did the same for Cona'n.

In a few minutes Fionn stood up from his place on the mound. Everything was about him as before, and he did not know that he had gone into Faery. He walked for a minute up and down the hillock. Then, as by chance, he stepped down the sloping end of the mound and stood with his mouth open, staring. He cried out, "Come down here, Cona'n, my darling."

Cona'n stepped down to him.

"Am I dreaming?" Fionn demanded, and he stretched out his finger before him.

"If you are dreaming," said Congn, "I'm dreaming too. They weren't here a minute ago," he stammered.

Fionn looked up at the sky and found that it was still there. He stared to one side and saw the trees of Kyle Conor waving in the distance. He bent his ear to the wind and heard the shouting of hunters, the yapping of dogs, and the clear whistles, which told how the hunt was going.

"Well!" said Fionn to himself.

"By my hand!" said Cona'n to his own soul.

And the two men stared into the hillside as though what they were looking at was too wonderful to be looked away from.

"Who are they?" said Fionn.

"What are they?" Cona'n gasped. And they stared again.

For there was a great hole like a doorway in the side of the mound, and in that doorway the daughters of Conaran sat spinning. They had three crooked sticks of holly set up before the cave, and they were reeling yarn off these. But it was enchantment they were weaving.

"One could not call them handsome," said Cona'n.

"One could," Fionn replied, "but it would not be true."

"I cannot see them properly," Fionn complained. "They are hiding behind the holly."

"I would be contented if I could not see them at all," his companion grumbled.

But the Chief insisted.

"I want to make sure that it is whiskers they are wearing."

"Let them wear whiskers or not wear them," Cona'n counselled. "But let us have nothing to do with them."

"One must not be frightened of anything," Fionn stated.

"I am not frightened," Cona'n explained. "I only want to keep my good opinion of women, and if the three yonder are women, then I feel sure I shall begin to dislike females from this minute out."

"Come on, my love," said Fionn, "for I must find out if these whiskers are true."

He strode resolutely into the cave. He pushed the branches of holly aside and marched up to Conaran's daughters, with Cona'n behind him.

Chapter IV

The instant they passed the holly a strange weakness came over the heroes. Their fists seemed to grow heavy as lead, and went dingle-dangle at the ends of their arms; their legs became as light as straws and began to bend in and out; their necks became too delicate to hold anything up, so that their heads wibbled and wobbled from side to side.

"What's wrong at all?" said Cona'n, as he tumbled to the ground.

"Everything is," Fionn replied, and he tumbled beside him.

The three sisters then tied the heroes with every kind of loop and twist and knot that could be thought of.

"Those are whiskers!" said Fionn.

"Alas!" said Conan.

"What a place you must hunt whiskers in?" he mumbled savagely. "Who wants whiskers?" he groaned.

But Fionn was thinking of other things.

"If there was any way of warning the Fianna not to come here," Fionn murmured.

"There is no way, my darling," said Caevo'g, and she smiled a smile that would have killed Fionn, only that he shut his eyes in time.

After a moment he murmured again, "Conan, my dear love, give the warning whistle so that the Fianna will keep out of this place."

A little woof, like the sound that would be made by a baby and it asleep, came from Cona'n.

"Fionn," said he, "there isn't a whistle in me. We are done for," said he.

"You are done for, indeed," said Cuillen, and she smiled a hairy and twisty and fangy smile that almost finished Cona'n.

By that time some of the Fianna had returned to the mound to see why Bran and Sceo'lan were barking so outrageously. They saw the cave and went into it, but no sooner had they passed the holly branches than their strength went from them, and they were seized and bound by the vicious hags. Little by little all the members of the Fianna returned to the hill, and each of them was drawn into the cave, and each was bound by the sisters.

Oisi'n and Oscar and mac Lugac came, with the nobles of clan-Baiscne, and with those of clan-Corcoran and clan-Smo'l; they all came, and they were all bound.

It was a wonderful sight and a great deed this binding of the Fianna, and the three sisters laughed with a joy that was terrible to hear and was almost death to see. As the men were captured they were carried by the hags into dark mysterious holes and black perplexing labyrinths.

"Here is another one," cried Caevo'g as she bundled a trussed champion along.

"This one is fat," said Cuillen, and she rolled a bulky Fenian along like a wheel.

"Here," said Iaran, "is a love of a man. One could eat this kind of man," she murmured, and she licked a lip that had whiskers growing inside as well as out.

And the corded champion whimpered in her arms, for he did not know but eating might indeed be his fate, and he would have preferred to be coffined anywhere in the world rather than to be coffined inside of that face. So far for them.

Chapter V

Within the cave there was silence except for the voices of the hags and the scarcely audible moaning of the Fianna-Finn, but without there was a dreadful uproar, for as each man returned from the chase his dogs came with him, and although the men went into the cave the dogs did not.

They were too wise.

They stood outside, filled with savagery and terror, for they could scent their masters and their masters' danger, and perhaps they could get from the cave smells till then unknown and full of alarm.

From the troop of dogs there arose a baying and barking, a snarling and howling and growling, a yelping and squealing and bawling for which no words can be found. Now and again a dog nosed among a thousand smells and scented his master; the ruff of his neck stood up like a hog's bristles and a netty ridge prickled along his spine. Then with red eyes, with bared fangs, with a hoarse, deep snort and growl he rushed at the cave, and then he halted and sneaked back again with all his ruffles smoothed, his tail between his legs, his eyes screwed sideways in miserable apology and alarm, and a long thin whine of woe dribbling out of his nose.

The three sisters took their wide-channelled, hard-tempered swords in their hands, and prepared to slay the Fianna, but before doing so they gave one more look from the door of the cave to see if there might be a straggler of the Fianna who was escaping death by straggling, and they saw one coming towards them with Bran and

Sceo'lan leaping beside him, while all the other dogs began to burst their throats with barks and split their noses with snorts and wag their tails off at sight of the tall, valiant, white-toothed champion, Goll mor mac Morna. "We will kill that one first," said Caevo'g.

"There is only one of him," said Cuillen.

"And each of us three is the match for a hundred," said Iaran.

The uncanny, misbehaved, and outrageous harridans advanced then to meet the son of Morna, and when he saw these three Goll whipped the sword from his thigh, swung his buckler round, and got to them in ten great leaps.

Silence fell on the world during that conflict. The wind went down; the clouds stood still; the old hill itself held its breath; the warriors within ceased to be men and became each an ear; and the dogs sat in a vast circle round the combatants, with their heads all to one side, their noses poked forward, their mouths half open, and their tails forgotten. Now and again a dog whined in a whisper and snapped a little snap on the air, but except for that there was neither sound nor movement.

It was a long fight. It was a hard and a tricky fight, and Goll won it by bravery and strategy and great good luck; for with one shrewd slice of his blade he carved two of these mighty termagants into equal halves, so that there were noses and whiskers to his right hand and knees and toes to his left, and that stroke was known afterwards as one of the three great sword-strokes of Ireland. The third hag, however, had managed to get behind Goll, and she leaped onto his back with the bound of a panther, and hung here with the skilful, many-legged, tight-twisted clutching of a spider. But the great champion gave a twist of his hips and a swing of his shoulders that whirled her around him like a sack. He got her on the ground and tied her hands with the straps of a shield, and he was going to give her the last blow when she appealed to his honour and bravery.

"I put my life under your protection," said she. "And if you let me go free I will lift the enchantment from the Fianna-Finn and will give them all back to you again."

"I agree to that," said Goll, and he untied her straps. The harridan did as she had promised, and in a short time Fionn and Oisi'n and Oscar and Cona'n were released, and after that all the Fianna were released.

Chapter VI

As each man came out of the cave he gave a jump and a shout; the courage of the world went into him and he felt that he could fight twenty. But while they were talking over the adventure and explaining how it had happened, a vast figure strode over the side of the hill and descended among them. It was Conaran's fourth daughter.

If the other three had been terrible to look on, this one was more terrible than the three together. She was clad in iron plate, and she had a wicked sword by her side and a knobby club in her hand She halted by the bodies of her sisters, and bitter tears streamed down into her beard.

"Alas, my sweet ones," said she, "I am too late."

And then she stared fiercely at Fionn.

"I demand a combat," she roared.

"It is your right," said Fionn. He turned to his son.

"Oisi'n, my heart, kill me this honourable hag." But for the only time in his life Oisi'n shrank from a combat.

"I cannot do it," he said, "I feel too weak."

Fionn was astounded. "Oscar," he said, "will you kill me this great hag?"

Oscar stammered miserably. "I would not be able to," he said.

Cona'n also refused, and so did Caelte mac Rona'n and mac Lugac, for there was no man there but was terrified by the sight of that mighty and valiant harridan.

Fionn rose to his feet. "I will take this combat myself," he said sternly.

And he swung his buckler forward and stretched his right hand to the sword. But at that terrible sight Goll mac Morna blushed deeply and leaped from the ground.

"No, no," he cried, "no, my soul, Fionn, this would not be a proper combat for you. I take this fight."

"You have done your share, Goll," said the captain.

"I should finish the fight I began," Goll continued, "for it was I who killed the two sisters of this valiant hag, and it is against me the feud lies."

"That will do for me," said the horrible daughter of Conaran. "I will kill Goll mor mac Morna first, and after that I will kill Fionn, and after that I will kill every Fenian of the Fianna-Finn."

"You may begin, Goll," said Fionn, "and I give you my blessing."

Goll then strode forward to the fight, and the hag moved against him with equal alacrity. In a moment the heavens rang to the clash of swords on bucklers. It was hard to withstand the terrific blows of that mighty female, for her sword played with the quickness of lightning and smote like the heavy crashing of a storm. But into that din and encirclement Goll pressed and ventured, steady as a rock in water, agile as a creature of the sea, and when one of the combatants retreated it was the hag that gave backwards. As her foot moved a great shout of joy rose from the Fianna. A snarl went over the huge face of the monster and she leaped forward again, but she met Goll's point in the road; it went through her, and in another moment Goll took her head from its shoulders and swung it on high before Fionn.

As the Fianna turned homewards Fionn spoke to his great champion and enemy.

"Goll," he said, "I have a daughter."

"A lovely girl, a blossom of the dawn," said Goll.

"Would she please you as a wife?" the chief demanded.

"She would please me," said Goll.

"She is your wife," said Fionn.

But that did not prevent Goll from killing Fionn's brother Cairell later on, nor did it prevent Fionn from killing Goll later on again, and the last did not prevent Goll from rescuing Fionn out of hell when the Fianna-Finn were sent there under the new God. Nor is there any reason to complain or to be astonished at these things, for it is a mutual world we live in, a give-and-take world, and there is no great harm in it.

Tales From The Land Of Saints & Scholars

The Enchantment of Gearoidh Iarla

"The Enchantment of Gearoidh Iarla" is a legend rooted in the folklore of Gerald Fitzgerald, the Earl of Kildare, one of the most storied figures of late medieval Ireland. The tale, first recorded by the folklorist Patrick Kennedy and later adapted by W. B. Yeats in Fairy and Folk Tales of the Irish Peasantry (1888, The Walter Scott Publishing Company), tells how the Earl, known in Irish as Gearóid Iarla, was a man of great wisdom, poetry, and magic.

The story blends chivalric legend with Celtic myth, turning a historical nobleman into a sleeping hero of the Otherworld. Yeats presents it as one of Ireland's "Arthurian" echoes, where a leader's spirit is not lost but preserved, ready to awaken and restore justice.

In old times in Ireland there was a great man of the Fitzgeralds. The name on him was Gerald, but the Irish, that always had a great liking for the family, called him Gearoidh Iarla (Earl Gerald). He had a great castle or rath at Mullymast (Mullaghmast); and whenever the English Government were striving to put some wrong on the country, he was always the man that stood up for it. Along with being a great leader in a fight, and very skilful at all weapons, he was deep in the black art, and could change himself into whatever shape he pleased. His lady knew that he had this power, and often asked him to let her into some of his secrets, but he never would gratify her.

She wanted particularly to see him in some strange shape, but he put her off and off on one pretence or other. But she wouldn't be a woman if she hadn't perseverance; and so at last he let her know that if she took the least fright while he'd be out of his natural form, he would never recover it till many generations of men would be under the mould. "Oh! she wouldn't be a fit wife for Gearoidh Iarla if she could be easily frightened. Let him but gratify her in this whim, and he'd see what a hero she was!" So one beautiful summer evening, as they were sitting in their grand drawing-room, he turned his face away from her and muttered some words, and while you'd wink he was clever and clean out of sight, and a lovely goldfinch was flying about the room.

The lady, as courageous as she thought herself, was a little startled, but she held her own pretty well, especially when he came and perched on her shoulder, and shook his wings, and put his little beak to her lips, and whistled the most delightful tune you ever heard. Well, he flew in circles round the room, and played hide and go seek with his lady, and flew out into the garden, and flew back again, and lay down in her lap as if he was asleep, and jumped up again.

Well, when the thing had lasted long enough to satisfy both, he took one flight more into the open air; but by my word he was soon on his return. He flew right into his lady's bosom, and the next moment a fierce hawk was after him. The wife gave one loud scream, though there was no need, for the wild bird came in like an arrow, and struck against a table with such force that the life was dashed out of him. She turned her eyes from his quivering body to where she saw the goldfinch an instant before, but neither goldfinch nor Earl Gerald did she ever lay eyes on again.

Once every seven years the Earl rides round the Curragh of Kildare on a steed, whose silver shoes were half an inch thick the time he disappeared; and when these shoes are worn as thin as a cat's ear, he will be restored to the society of living men, fight a great battle with the English, and reign king of Ireland for two-score years.

Himself and his warriors are now sleeping in a long cavern under the Rath of Mullaghmast. There is a table running along through the middle of the cave. The Earl is sitting at the head, and his troopers down along in complete armour both sides of the table, and their heads resting on it. Their horses, saddled and bridled, are standing behind their masters in their stalls at each side; and when the day comes, the miller's son that's to be born with six fingers on each hand, will blow his trumpet, and the horses will stamp and whinny, and the knights awake and mount their steeds, and go forth to battle.

Some night that happens once in every seven years, while the Earl is riding round the Curragh, the entrance may be seen by anyone chancing to pass by. About a hundred years ago, a horse-dealer that was late abroad and a little drunk, saw the lighted cavern, and went in. The lights, and the stillness, and the sight of the men in armour, cowed him a good deal, and he became sober. His hands began to tremble, and he let a bridle fall on the pavement. The sound of the bit echoed through the long cave, and one of the warriors that was next him lifted his head a little, and said, in a deep hoarse voice, "Is it time yet?" He had the wit to say, "Not yet, but soon will," and the heavy helmet sunk down on the table. The horse-dealer made the best of his way out, and I never heard of any other one having got the same opportunity.

Tales From The Land Of Saints & Scholars

The Fairy Greyhound

"The Fairy Greyhound", as adapted by W. B. Yeats in Irish Fairy Tales, draws on the deep-rooted Irish belief in the Otherworld and the uncanny presence of fairies within the natural landscape. The tale centres on a beautiful greyhound that appears to a young man, often in a lonely or liminal place, a crossroads, a moor, or a misted glen, and lures him into pursuit.

Yeats's version preserves the eerie simplicity of the old oral telling, using the greyhound as a symbol of beauty, danger, and desire, qualities that recur throughout Irish folklore. The story warns of curiosity and pride, of the peril in following what gleams too brightly on the horizon.

Paddy M'dermid was one of the most rollicking boys in the whole county of Kildare. Fair or pattern wouldn't be held barring he was in the midst of it. He was in every place, like bad luck, and his poor little farm was seldom sowed in season; and where he expected barley, there grew nothing but weeds. Money became scarce in poor Paddy's pocket; and the cow went after the pig, until nearly all he had was gone. Lucky however for him, if he had gomch (sense) enough to mind it, he had a most beautiful dream one night as he lay tossicated (drunk) in the Rath of Monogue, because he wasn't able to come home. He dreamt that, under the place where he lay, a pot of money was buried since long before the memory of man.

Paddy kept the dream to himself until the next night, when, taking a spade and pickaxe, with a bottle of holy water, he went to the Rath, and, having made a circle round the place, commenced digging sure enough, for the bare life and soul of him thinking that he was made up for ever and ever. He had sunk about twice the depth of his knees, when whack the pickaxe struck against a flag, and at the same time Paddy heard something breathe quite near him. He looked up, and just in front of him there sat on his haunches a comely-looking greyhound.

'God save you,' said Paddy, every hair in his head standing up as straight as a sally twig.

'Save you kindly,' answered the greyhound—leaving out God, the beast, because he was the devil. Christ defend us from ever seeing the likes o' him.

'Musha, Paddy M'Dermid,' said he, 'what would you be looking after in that grave of a hole you're digging there?'

'Faith, nothing at all, at all,' answered Paddy; because you see he didn't like the stranger.

'Arrah, be easy now, Paddy M'Dermid,' said the greyhound, 'don't I know very well what you are looking for?'

'Why then in truth, if you do, I may as well tell you at once, particularly as you seem a civil-looking gentleman, that's not above speaking to a poor gossoon like me.' (Paddy wanted to butter him up a bit.)

'Well then,' said the greyhound, 'come out here and sit down on this bank,' and Paddy, like a gomulagh (fool), did as he was desired, but had hardly put his brogue outside of the circle made by the holy water, when the beast of a hound set upon him, and drove him out of the Rath; for Paddy was frightened, as well he might, at the fire that flamed from his mouth. But next night he returned, full sure the money was there. As before, he made a circle, and touched the flag, when my gentleman, the greyhound, appeared in the old place.

'Oh ho,' said Paddy, 'you are there, are you? but it will be a long day, I promise you, before you trick me again'; and he made another stroke at the flag.

'Well, Paddy M'Dermid,' said the hound, 'since you will have money, you must; but say, how much will satisfy you?'

Paddy scratched his conlaan, and after a while said, 'How much will your honour give me?' for he thought it better to be civil.

'Just as much as you consider reasonable, Paddy M'Dermid.'

'Egad,' says Paddy to himself, 'there's nothing like asking enough.'

'Say fifty thousand pounds,' said he. (He might as well have said a hundred thousand, for I'll be bail the beast had money galore.)

'You shall have it,' said the hound; and then, after trotting away a little bit, he came back with a crock full of guineas between his paws.

'Come here and reckon them,' said he; but Paddy was up to him, and refused to stir, so the crock was shoved alongside the blessed and holy circle, and Paddy pulled it in, right glad to have it in his clutches, and never stood still until he reached his own home, where his guineas turned into little bones, and his old mother laughed at him. Paddy now swore vengeance against the deceitful beast of a greyhound, and went next night to the Rath again, where, as before, he met Mr. Hound.

'So you are here again, Paddy?' said he.

'Yes, you big blaggard,' said Paddy, 'and I'll never leave this place until I pull out the pot of money that's buried here.'

'Oh, you won't,' said he. 'Well, Paddy M'Dermid, since I see you are such a brave venturesome fellow I'll be after making you up if you walk downstairs with me out of the cold'; and sure enough it was snowing like murder.

'Oh may I never see Athy if I do,' returned Paddy, 'for you only want to be loading me with old bones, or perhaps breaking my own, which would be just as bad.'

"On my honour,' said the hound, 'I am your friend, and so don't stand in your own light; come with me and your fortune is made. Remain where you are and you'll die a beggar-man.' So bedad, with one palaver and another, Paddy consented; and in the middle of the Rath opened up a beautiful staircase, down which they walked; and after winding they came to a house much finer than the Duke of Leinster's, in which all the tables and chairs were solid gold. Paddy was delighted; and after sitting down, a fine lady handed him a glass of something to drink; but he had hardly swallowed a spoonful when all around set up a horrid yell, and those who before appeared beautiful now looked like what they were - enraged 'good people'.

Before Paddy could bless himself, they seized him, legs and arms, carried him out to a great high hill that stood like a wall over a river, and flung him down. 'Murder!' cried Paddy; but it was no use, no use; he fell upon a rock, and lay there as dead until next morning, where some people found him in the trench that surrounds the mote of Coulhall, the 'good people' having carried him there; and from that hour to the day of his death he was the greatest object in the world. He walked double, and had his mouth (God bless us) where his ear should be.

Tales From The Land Of Saints & Scholars

The Fate of Frank M'Kenna

"The Fate of Frank M'Kenna" is a dark moral tale drawn from the folklore of rural Ulster, first told by William Carleton and later adapted by W. B. Yeats in Fairy and Folk Tales of the Irish Peasantry (1888, The Walter Scott Publishing Company). It follows Frank M'Kenna, a lively but irreverent young man whose fondness for mockery and blasphemy leads him into the supernatural.

Carleton's version, while told with the colour and cadence of rural Irish speech, carries a distinctly moral undertone. It warns against impiety, arrogance, and disbelief in the unseen world. Yeats's adaptation preserves the folk realism and eerie atmosphere, presenting the story as an example of the Irish peasantry's belief that the supernatural is not distant, but perilously near.

There lived a man named M'Kenna at the hip of one of the mountainous hills which divide the county of Tyrone from that of Monaghan. This M'Kenna had two sons, one of whom was in the habit of tracing hares of a Sunday whenever there happened to be a fall of snow. His father, it seems, had frequently remonstrated with him upon what he considered to be a violation of the Lord's day, as well as for his general neglect of mass. The young man, however, though otherwise harmless and inoffensive, was in this matter quite insensible to paternal reproof, and continued to trace whenever the avocations of labour would allow him.

It so happened that upon a Christmas morning, I think in the year 1814, there was a deep fall of snow, and young M'Kenna, instead of going to mass, got down his cock-stick - which is a staff much thicker and heavier at one end than at the other - and prepared to set out on his favourite amusement. His father, seeing this, reproved him seriously, and insisted that he should attend prayers. His enthusiasm for the sport, however, was stronger than his love of religion, and he refused to be guided by his father's advice.

The old man during the altercation got warm; and on finding that the son obstinately scorned his authority, he knelt down and prayed that if the boy persisted in following his own will, he might never return from the mountains unless as a corpse. The imprecation, which was certainly as harsh as it was impious and senseless, might have startled many a mind from a purpose that was, to say the least of it, at variance with religion and the respect due to a father. It had no effect, however, upon the son, who is said to have replied, that whether he ever returned or not, he was determined on going; and go accordingly he did.

He was not, however, alone, for it appears that three or four of the neighbouring young men accompanied him. Whether their sport was good or otherwise, is not to the purpose, neither am I able to say; but the story goes that towards the latter part of the day they started a larger and darker hare than any they had ever seen, and that she kept dodging on before them bit by bit, leading them to suppose that every succeeding cast of the cock-stick would bring her down. It was observed afterwards that she also led them into the recesses of the mountains, and that although they tried to turn her course homewards, they could not succeed in doing so.

As evening advanced, the companions of M'Kenna began to feel the folly of pursuing her further, and to perceive the danger of losing their way in the mountains should night or a snow-storm come upon them. They therefore proposed to give over the chase and return home; but M'Kenna would not hear of it.

"If you wish to go home, you may," said he, "as for me, I'll never leave the hills till I have her with me."

They begged and entreated of him to desist and return, but all to no purpose. He appeared to be what the Scotch call fey - that is, to act as if he were moved by some impulse that leads to death, and from the influence of which a man cannot withdraw himself. At length, on finding him invincibly obstinate, they left him pursuing the hare directly into the heart of the mountains, and returned to their respective homes.

In the meantime one of the most terrible snow-storms ever remembered in that part of the country came on, and the consequence was, that the self-willed young man, who had equally trampled on the sanctities of religion and parental authority, was given over for lost.

As soon as the tempest became still, the neighbours assembled in a body and proceeded to look for him. The snow, however, had fallen so heavily that not a single mark of a footstep could be seen. Nothing but one wide waste of white undulating hills met the eye wherever it turned, and of M'Kenna no trace whatever was visible or could be found.

His father, now remembering the unnatural character of his imprecation, was nearly distracted; for although the body had not yet been found, still by everyone who witnessed the sudden rage of the storm and who knew the mountains, escape or survival was felt to be impossible. Every day for about a week large parties were out among the hill-ranges seeking him, but to no purpose. At length there came a thaw, and his body was found on a snow-wreath, lying in a supine posture within a circle which he had drawn around him with his cock-stick. His prayer-book lay opened upon his mouth, and his hat was pulled down so as to cover it and his face.

It is unnecessary to say that the rumour of his death, and of the circumstances under which he left home, created a most extraordinary sensation in the country - a sensation that was the greater in proportion to the uncertainty occasioned by his not having been found either alive or dead. Some affirmed that he had crossed the mountains, and was seen in Monaghan; others, that he had been seen in Clones, in Emyvale, in Five-mile-town; but despite of all these agreeable reports, the melancholy truth was at length made clear by the appearance of the body as just stated.

Now, it so happened that the house nearest the spot where he lay was inhabited by a man named Daly, who was a herd or care-taker to Dr. Porter, then Bishop of Clogher. The situation of this house was the most lonely and desolate-looking that could be imagined. It was at least two miles distant from any human habitation, being surrounded by one wide and dreary waste of dark moor. By this house lay the route of those who had found the corpse, and I believe the door of it was borrowed for the purpose of conveying it home. Be this as it may, the family witnessed the melancholy procession as it passed slowly through the mountains, and when the place and circumstances are all considered, we may admit that to ignorant and superstitious people, whose minds, even upon ordinary occasions, were strongly affected by such matters, it was a sight calculated to leave behind it a deep, if not a terrible impression. Time soon proved that it did so.

An incident is said to have occurred at the funeral in fine keeping with the wild spirit of the whole melancholy event. When the procession had advanced to a place called Mullaghtinny, a large dark-coloured hare, which was instantly recognised, by those who had been out with him on the hills, as the identical one that led him to his fate, is said to have crossed the roads about twenty yards or so before the coffin. The story goes, that a man struck it on the side with a stone, and that the blow, which would have killed any ordinary hare, not only did it no injury, but occasioned a sound to proceed from the body resembling the hollow one emitted by an empty barrel when struck.

In the meantime the interment took place, and the sensation began, like every other, to die away in the natural progress of time, when, behold, a report ran abroad like wildfire that, to use the language of the people, "Frank M'Kenna was appearing!"

One night, about a fortnight after his funeral, the daughter of Daly, the herd, a girl about fourteen, while lying in bed saw what appeared to be the likeness of M'Kenna, who had been lost. She screamed out, and covering her head with the bed-clothes, told her father and mother that Frank M'Kenna was in the house. This alarming intelligence naturally produced great terror; still, Daly, who, notwithstanding his belief in such matters, possessed a good deal of moral courage, was cool enough to rise and examine the house, which consisted of only one apartment. This gave the daughter some courage, who, on finding that her father could not see him, ventured to look out, and she then could see nothing of him herself. She very soon fell asleep, and her father attributed what she saw to fear, or some accidental combination of shadows proceeding from the furniture, for it was a clear moonlight night.

The light of the following day dispelled a great deal of their apprehensions, and comparatively little was thought of it until evening again advanced, when the fears of the daughter began to return. They appeared to be prophetic, for she said when night came that she knew he would appear again; and accordingly at the same hour he did so. This was repeated for several successive nights, until the girl, from the very hardihood of terror, began to become so far familiarised to the spectre as to venture to address it.

"In the name of God!" she asked, "what is troubling you, or why do you appear to me instead of to some of your own family or relations?"

The ghost's answer alone might settle the question involved in the authenticity of its appearance, being, as it was, an account of one of the most ludicrous missions that ever a spirit was despatched upon.

"I'm not allowed," said he, "to speak to any of my friends, for I parted with them in anger; but I'm come to tell you that they are quarrelling about my breeches - a new pair that I got made for Christmas day; an' as I was coming up to thrash in the mountains, I thought the old one would do better, an' of course I didn't put the new pair on me. My reason for appearing," he added, "is, that you may tell my friends that none of them is to wear them - they must be given in charity."

This serious and solemn intimation from the ghost was duly communicated to the family, and it was found that the circumstances were exactly as it had represented them. This, of course, was considered as sufficient proof of the truth of its mission. Their conversations now became not only frequent, but quite friendly and familiar. The girl became a favourite with the spectre, and the spectre, on the other hand, soon lost all his terrors in her eyes. He told her that whilst his friends were bearing home his body, the handspikes or poles on which they carried him had cut his back, and occasioned him great pain! The cutting of the back also was known to be true, and strengthened, of course, the truth and authenticity of their dialogues.

The whole neighbourhood was now in a commotion with this story of the apparition, and persons incited by curiosity began to visit the girl in order to satisfy themselves of the truth of what they had heard. Everything, however, was corroborated, and the child herself, without any symptoms of anxiety or terror, artlessly related her conversations with the spirit. Hitherto their interviews had been all nocturnal, but now that the ghost found his footing made good, he put a hardy face on, and ventured to appear by daylight. The girl also fell into states of syncope, and while the fits lasted, long conversations with him upon the subject of God, the blessed Virgin, and Heaven, took place between them.

He was certainly an excellent moralist, and gave the best advice. Swearing, drunkenness, theft, and every evil propensity of our nature, were declaimed against with a degree of spectral eloquence quite surprising. Common fame had now a topic dear to her heart, and never was a ghost made more of by his best friends than she made of him. The whole country was in a tumult, and I well remember the crowds which flocked to the lonely little cabin in the mountains, now the scene of matters so interesting and important. Not a single day passed in which I should think from ten to twenty, thirty, or fifty persons, were not present at these singular interviews. Nothing else was talked of, thought of, and, as I can well testify, dreamt of.

I would myself have gone to Daly's were it not for a confounded misgiving I had, that perhaps the ghost might take such a fancy of appearing to me, as he had taken to cultivate an intimacy with the girl; and it so happens, that when I see the face of an individual nailed down in the coffin - chilling and gloomy operation! - I experience no particular wish to look upon it again.

The spot where the body of M'Kenna was found is now marked by a little heap of stones, which has been collected since the melancholy event of his death. Every person who passes it throws a stone upon the heap; but why this old custom is practised, or what it means, I do not know, unless it be simply to mark the spot as a visible means of preserving the memory of the occurrence.

Daly's house, the scene of the supposed apparition, is now a shapeless ruin, which could scarcely be seen were it not for the green spot that once was a garden, and which now shines at a distance like an emerald, but with no agreeable or pleasing associations. It is a spot which no solitary schoolboy will ever visit, nor indeed would the unflinching believer in the popular nonsense of ghosts wish to pass it without a companion. It is, under any circumstances, a gloomy and barren place; but when looked upon in connection with what we have just recited, it is lonely, desolate, and awful.

Tales From The Land Of Saints & Scholars

The Field of Boliauns

"The Field of Boliauns", adapted by Joseph Jacobs in Celtic Fairy Tales (1892), is one of the classic Irish leprechaun stories, mixing sly humour with a moral warning about greed and impatience.

Jacobs's version, drawn from oral tradition, captures the mischievous charm of Irish fairy lore. The story reflects the deep rural sense of humour that underpins much of Ireland's folklore, where mortals who try to outwit the fairies usually end up tricked themselves.

One fine day in harvest - it was indeed Lady-day in harvest, that everybody knows to be one of the greatest holidays in the year - Tom Fitzpatrick was taking a ramble through the ground, and went along the sunny side of a hedge; when all of a sudden he heard a clacking sort of noise a little before him in the hedge.

"Dear me," said Tom, "but isn't it surprising to hear the stonechatters singing so late in the season?"

So Tom stole on, going on the tops of his toes to try if he could get a sight of what was making the noise, to see if he was right in his guess. The noise stopped; but as Tom looked sharply through the bushes, what should he see in a nook of the hedge but a brown pitcher, that might hold about a gallon and a half of liquor; and by-and-by a little wee teeny tiny bit of an old man, with a little motty of a cocked hat stuck upon the top of his head, a deeshy daushy leather apron hanging before him, pulled out a little wooden stool, and stood up upon it, and dipped a little piggin into the pitcher, and took out the full of it, and put it beside the stool, and then sat down under the pitcher, and began to work at putting a heel-piece on a bit of a brogue just fit for himself.

"Well, by the powers," said Tom to himself, "I often heard tell of the Leprechauns, and to tell God's truth I never rightly believed in them - but here's one of them in real earnest. If I go knowingly to work, I'm a made man. They say a body must never take their eyes off them, or they'll escape."

Tom stole on a little further, with his eye fixed on the little man just as a cat does with a mouse. So when he got up quite close to him, "God bless your work, neighbour," said Tom.

The little man raised up his head, and "Thank you kindly," said he.

"I wonder you'd be working on the holiday!" said Tom.

"That's my own business, not yours," was the reply.

"Well, maybe you'd be civil enough to tell us what you've got in the pitcher there?" said Tom.

"That I will, with pleasure," said he, "it's good beer."

"Beer!" said Tom. "Thunder and fire! where did you get it?"

"Where did I get it, is it? Why, I made it. And what do you think I made it of?"

"Devil a one of me knows," said Tom, "but of malt, I suppose, what else?"

"There you're out. I made it of heath."

"Of heath!" said Tom, bursting out laughing, "sure you don't think me to be such a fool as to believe that?"

"Do as you please," said he, "but what I tell you is the truth. Did you never hear tell of the Danes?"

"Well, what about them?" said Tom.

"Why, all the about them there is, is that when they were here they taught us to make beer out of the heath, and the secret's in my family ever since."

"Will you give a body a taste of your beer?" said Tom.

"I'll tell you what it is, young man, it would be fitter for you to be looking after your father's property than to be bothering decent quiet people with your foolish questions. There now, while you're idling away your time here, there's the cows have broken into the oats, and are knocking the corn all about."

Tom was taken so by surprise with this that he was just on the very point of turning round when he recollected himself; so, afraid that the like might happen again, he made a grab at the Leprechaun, and caught him up in his hand; but in his hurry he overset the pitcher, and spilt all the beer, so that he could not get a taste of it to tell what sort it was. He then swore that he would kill him if he did not show him where his money was. Tom looked so wicked and so bloody-minded that the little man was quite frightened; so says he, "Come along with me a couple of fields off, and I'll show you a crock of gold."

So they went, and Tom held the Leprechaun fast in his hand, and never took his eyes from off him, though they had to cross hedges and ditches, and a crooked bit of bog, till at last they came to a great field all full of boliauns, and the Leprechaun pointed to a big boliaun, and says he, "Dig under that boliaun, and you'll get the great crock all full of guineas."

Tom in his hurry had never thought of bringing a spade with him, so he made up his mind to run home and fetch one; and that he might know the place again he took off one of his red garters, and tied it round the boliaun.

Then he said to the Leprechaun, "Swear ye'll not take that garter away from that boliaun." And the Leprechaun swore right away not to touch it.

"I suppose," said the Leprechaun, very civilly, "you have no further occasion for me?"

"No," says Tom, "you may go away now, if you please, and God speed you, and may good luck attend you wherever you go."

"Well, goodbye to you, Tom Fitzpatrick," said the Leprechaun, "and much good may it do you when you get it."

So Tom ran for dear life, till he came home and got a spade, and then away with him, as hard as he could go, back to the field of boliauns; but when he got there, lo and behold! not a boliaun in the field but had a red garter, the very model of his own, tied about it; and as to digging up the whole field, that was all nonsense, for there were more than forty good Irish acres in it. So Tom came home again with his spade on his shoulder, a little cooler than he went, and many's the hearty curse he gave the Leprechaun every time he thought of the neat turn he had served him.

Tales From The Land Of Saints & Scholars

The Good Woman

"The Good Woman" is one of the more delicate and morally reflective tales drawn from Thomas Crofton Croker's Fairy Legends and Traditions of the South of Ireland (1825–1828). It tells of a mortal woman who encounters one of the Good People, a euphemism for the fairies, under circumstances that test her compassion and caution.

Croker's retelling blends the supernatural with the moral realism of rural Ireland. The "good woman" represents the ideal of quiet virtue amid mystery, embodying the folk belief that fairies mirror human society but live by sterner laws.

In a pleasant and not unpicturesque valley of the White Knight's country, at the foot of the Galtee mountains, lived Larry Dodd and his wife Nancy. They rented a cabin and a few acres of land, which they cultivated with great care, and its crops rewarded their industry. They were independent and respected by their neighbours; they loved each other in a marriageable sort of way, and few couples had altogether more the appearance of comfort about them.

Larry was a hardworking, and, occasionally, a hard drinking, Dutch-built, little man, with a fiddle head and a round stern; a steady-going straight-forward fellow, barring when he carried too much whisky, which, it must be confessed, might occasionally prevent his walking the chalked line with perfect philomathical accuracy. He had a moist, ruddy countenance, rather inclined to an expression of gravity, and particularly so in the morning; but, taken all together he was generally looked upon as a marvellously proper person, notwithstanding he had, every day in the year, a sort of unholy dew upon his face, even in the coldest weather, which gave rise to a supposition (amongst censorious persons, of course,) that Larry was apt to indulge in strong and frequent potations. However, all men of talents have their faults, - indeed, who is without them? - and as Larry, setting aside his domestic virtues and skill in farming, was decidedly the most distinguished breaker of horses for forty miles round, he must be in some degree excused, considering the inducements of "the stirrup cup," and the fox-hunting society in which he mixed, if he had also been the greatest drunkard in the county, but, in truth, this was not the case.

Larry was a man of mixed habits, as well in his mode of life and his drink, as in his costume. His dress accorded well with his character - a sort of half-and-half between farmer and horse-jockey. He wore a blue coat of coarse cloth, with short skirts, and a stand-up collar; his waistcoat was red, and his lower habiliments were made of leather, which in course of time had shrunk so much, that they fitted like a second skin; and long use had absorbed their moisture to such a degree, that they made a strange sort of crackling noise as he walked along. A hat covered with oilskin; a cutting-whip, all worn and jagged at the end; a pair of second-hand, or, to speak more correctly second-footed, greasy top boots, that seemed never to have imbibed a refreshing draught of Warren's blacking of matchless lustre! - and one spur without a rowel, completed the every-day dress of Larry Dodd.

Thus equipped was Larry returning from Cashel, mounted on a rough-coated and wall-eyed nag, though, notwithstanding these and a few other trifling blemishes, a well-built animal; having just purchased the said nag, with a fancy that he could make his own money again of his bargain, and may be, turn an odd penny more by it at the ensuing Kildorrery fair. Well pleased with himself, he trotted fair and easy along the road in the delicious and lingering twilight of a lovely June evening, thinking of nothing at all, only whistling, and wondering would horses always be so low.

"If they go at this rate," he said to himself, "for half nothing, and that paid in butter buyer's notes, who would be the fool to walk?"

This very thought, indeed, was passing in his mind, when his attention was roused by a woman pacing quickly by the side of his horse and hurrying on as if endeavouring to reach her destination before the night closed in. Her figure, considering the long strides she took, appeared to be under the common size - rather of the dumpy order; but farther, as to whether the damsel was young or old, fair or brown, pretty or ugly, Larry could form no precise notion, from her wearing a large cloak (the usual garb of the female Irish peasant,) the hood of which was turned up, and completely concealed every feature.

Enveloped in this mass of dark and concealing drapery, the strange woman, without much exertion, contrived to keep up with Larry Dodd's steed for some time, when his master very civilly offered her a lift behind him, as far as he was going her way. "Civility begets civility," they say; however he received no answer; and thinking that the lady's silence proceeded only from bashfulness, like a man of true gallantry, not a word more said Larry until he pulled up by the side of a gap, and then says he, "Ma colleen beg, just jump up behind me, without a word more, though never a one have you spoke, and I'll take you safe and sound through the lonesome bit of road that is before us."

She jumped at the offer, sure enough, and up with her on the back of the horse as light as a feather. In an instant there she was seated up behind Larry, with her hand and arm buckled round his waist holding on.

"I hope you're comfortable there, my dear," said Larry, in his own good-humoured way; but there was no answer; and on they went - trot, trot, trot - along the road; and all was so still and so quiet, that you might have heard the sound of the hoofs on the limestone a mile off; for that matter there was nothing else to hear except the moaning of a distant stream, that kept up a continued cronane, like a nurse hushoing.

Larry, who had a keen ear, did not, however, require so profound a silence to detect the click of one of the shoes. "Tis only loose the shoe is," he said to his companion, as they were just entering on the lonesome bit of road of which he had before spoken. Some old trees, with huge trunks, all covered, and irregular branches festooned with ivy, grew over a dark pool of water, which had been formed as a drinking-place for cattle; and in the distance was seen the majestic head of Gaultee-more. Here the horse, as if in grateful recognition, made a dead halt; and Larry, not knowing what vicious tricks his new purchase might have, and unwilling that through any odd chance the young woman should get spilt in the water, dismounted, thinking to lead the horse quietly by the pool.

"By the piper's luck, that always found what he wanted," said Larry, recollecting himself, "I've a nail in my pocket. 'Tis not the first time I've put on a shoe, and maybe it won't be the last; for here is no want of paving-stones to make hammers in plenty."

No sooner was Larry off, than off with a spring came the young woman just at his side. Her feet touched the ground without making the least noise in life, and away she bounded like an ill-mannered wench, as she was, without saying, "by your leave," or no matter what else. She seemed to glide rather than run, not along the road, but across a field, up towards the old ivy-covered walls of Kilnaslattery church - and a pretty church it was.

"Not so fast, if you please, young woman - not so fast," cried Larry, calling after her, but away she ran, and Larry followed, his leathern garment, already described, crack, crick, crackling at every step he took.

"Where's my wages?" said Larry, "Thorum pog, ma colleen oge, - sure I've earned a kiss from your pair of pretty lips - and I'll have it too!"

But she went on faster and faster, regardless of these and other flattering speeches from her pursuer; at last she came to the church-yard wall, and then over with her in an instant.

"Well, she's a mighty smart creature anyhow. To be sure, how neat she steps upon her pasterns! Did anyone ever see the like of that before; - but I'll not be baulked by any woman that ever wore a head, or any ditch either," exclaimed Larry, as with a desperate bound he vaulted, scrambled, and tumbled over the wall into the church-yard.

Up he got from the elastic sod of a newly-made grave in which Tade Leary that morning was buried - rest his soul! - and on went Larry, stumbling over headstones, and footstones, over old graves and new graves, pieces of coffins, and the skulls and bones of dead men - the Lord save us! - that were scattered about there as plenty as paving-stones; floundering amidst great overgrown dock-leaves and brambles that, with their long prickly arms, tangled round his limbs, and held him back with a fearful grasp. Mean time the merry wench in the cloak moved through all these obstructions as evenly and as gaily as if the church-yard, crowded up as it was with graves and gravestones (for people came to be buried there from far and near,) had been the floor of a dancing-room. Round and round the walls of the old church she went.

"I'll just wait," said Larry, seeing this, and thinking it all nothing but a trick to frighten him, "when she comes round again, if I don't take the kiss, I won't, that's all, - and here she is!"

Larry Dodd sprang forward with open arms, and clasped in them - a woman, it is true - but a woman without any lips to kiss, by reason of her having no head.

"Murder!" cried he. "Well, that accounts for her not speaking."

Having uttered these words, Larry himself became dumb with fear and astonishment; his blood seemed turned to ice, and a dizziness came over him; and, staggering like a drunken man, he rolled against the broken window of the ruin, horrified at the conviction that he had actually held a Dullahan in his embrace!

When he recovered to something like a feeling of consciousness, he slowly opened his eyes, and then, indeed, a scene of wonder burst upon him. In the midst of the ruin stood an old wheel of torture, ornamented with heads, like Cork gaol, when the heads of Murty Sullivan and other gentlemen were stuck upon it. This was plainly visible in the strange light which spread itself around. It was fearful to behold, but Larry could not choose but look, for his limbs were powerless through the wonder and the fear. Useless as it was, he would have called for help, but his tongue cleaved to the roof of his mouth, and not one word could he say. In short, there was Larry, gazing through a shattered window of the old church, with eyes bleared and almost starting from their sockets; his breast resting on the thickness of the wall, over which, on one side, his head and outstretched neck projected, and on the other, although one toe touched the ground, it derived no support from there. Terror, as it were, kept him balanced. Strange noises assailed his ears, until at last they tingled painfully to the sharp clatter of little bells, which kept up a continued ding - ding - ding – ding. Marrowless bones rattled and clanked, and the deep and solemn sound of a great bell came booming on the night wind.

'Twas a spectre rung

That bell when it swung -

Swing-swang!

And the chain it squeaked,

And the pulley creaked,

Swing-swang!

And with every roll

Of the deep death toll

Ding-dong!

The hollow vault rang

As the clapper went bang,

Ding-dong!'

It was strange music to dance by; nevertheless, moving to it, round and round the wheel set with skulls, were well-dressed ladies and gentlemen, and soldiers and sailors, and priests and publicans, and jockeys and jennys, but all without their heads. Some poor skeletons, whose bleached bones were ill covered by moth-eaten palls, and who were not admitted into the ring, amused themselves by bowling their brainless noddles at one another, which seemed to enjoy the sport beyond measure.

Larry did not know what to think; his brains were all in a mist; and losing the balance which he had so long maintained, he fell head foremost into the midst of the company of Dullahans.

"I'm done for and lost for ever," roared Larry, with his heels turned towards the stars, and souse down he came.

"Welcome, Larry Dodd, welcome," cried every head, bobbing up and down in the air.

"A drink for Larry Dodd," shouted they, as with one voice, that quavered like a shake on the bagpipes.

No sooner said than done, for a player at heads, catching his own as it was bowled at him, for fear of its going astray, jumped up, put the head, without a word, under his left arm, and, with the right stretched out, presented a brimming cup to Larry, who, to show his manners, drank it off like a man.

"Tis capital stuff," he would have said, which surely it was, but he got no farther than cap, when decapitated was he, and his head began dancing over his shoulders like those of the rest of the party. Larry, however, was not the first man who lost his head through the temptation of looking at the bottom of a brimming cup. Nothing more did he remember clearly, - for it seems body and head being parted is not very favourable to thought - but a great hurry scurry with the noise of carriages and the cracking of whips.

When his senses returned, his first act was to put up his hand to where his head formerly grew, and to his great joy there he found it still. He then shook it gently, but his head remained firm enough, and somewhat assured at this, he proceeded to open his eyes and look around him. It was broad daylight, and in the old church of Kilnaslattery he found himself lying, with that head, the loss of which he had anticipated, quietly resting, poor youth, "upon the lap of earth." Could it have been an ugly dream?

"Oh no," said Larry, "a dream could never have brought me here, stretched on the flat of my back, with that death's head and cross marrow bones in front of me on the fine old tombstone there that was faced by Pat Kearney of Kilcrea - but where is the horse?"

He got up slowly, every joint aching with pain from the bruises he had received, and went to the pool of water, but no horse was there.

"Tis home I must go," said Larry, with a rueful countenance, "but how will I face Nancy? - what will I tell her about the horse, and the seven I. O. U.'s that he cost me? - 'Tis them Dullahans that have made their own of him from me - the horse-stealing robbers of the world, that have no fear of the gallows! - but what's gone is gone, that's a clear case!"

So saying, he turned his steps homewards, and arrived at his cabin about noon without encountering any further adventures. There he found Nancy, who, as he expected, looked as black as a thundercloud at him for being out all night. She listened to the marvellous relation which he gave with exclamations of astonishment, and, when he had concluded, of grief, at the loss of the horse that he had paid for like an honest man with seven I. O. U.'s, three of which she knew to be as good as gold.

"But what took you up to the old church at all, out of the road, and at that time of the night, Larry?" inquired his wife.

Larry looked like a criminal for whom there was no reprieve; he scratched his head for an excuse, but not one could he muster up, so he knew not what to say.

"Oh! Larry, Larry," muttered Nancy, after waiting some time for his answer, her jealous fears during the pause rising like barm, "tis the very same way with you as with any other man - you are all alike for that matter - I've no pity for you - but confess the truth."

Larry shuddered at the tempest which he perceived was about to break upon his devoted head.

"Nancy," said he, "I do confess, - it was a young woman without any head that..."

His wife heard no more. "A woman I knew it was," cried she, "but a woman without a head, Larry!"

Well, it is long before Nancy Gollagher ever thought it would come to that with her! - that she would be left dissolute and alone here by her baste of a husband, for a woman without a head! - Oh father, father! and Oh mother, mother! it is well you are low to-day! - that you don't see this affliction and disgrace to your daughter that you reared decent and tender.

"O Larry, you villain, you'll be the death of your lawful wife going after such Oh - Oh - O"

"Well," says Larry, putting his hands in his coat pockets, "least said is soonest mended. Of the young woman I know no more than I do of Moll Flanders, but this I know, that a woman without a head may well be called a Good Woman, because she has no tongue!"

How this remark operated on the matrimonial dispute history does not inform us. It is, however, reported that the lady had the last word.

Tales From The Land Of Saints & Scholars

The Haughty Princess

"The Haughty Princess" is a lively Irish folktale first collected by Patrick Kennedy in the mid-nineteenth century and later adapted by W. B. Yeats in Fairy and Folk Tales of the Irish Peasantry (1888). The story follows a proud and wilful princess who refuses to marry any suitor, scorning them all as beneath her.

The story's roots lie in a broad European folk motif, the taming of the proud princess or "shrew", but Kennedy's Irish version gives it a distinctly local voice, full of sharp dialogue, rustic idiom, and moral irony.

There was once a very worthy king, whose daughter was the greatest beauty that could be seen far or near, but she was as proud as Lucifer, and no king or prince would she agree to marry. Her father was tired out at last, and invited every king, and prince, and duke, and earl that he knew or didn't know to come to his court to give her one trial more. They all came, and next day after breakfast they stood in a row in the lawn, and the princess walked along in the front of them to make her choice.

One was fat, and says she, "I won't have you, Beer-barrel!" One was tall and thin, and to him she said, "I won't have you, Ramrod!" To a white-faced man she said, "I won't have you, Pale Death;" and to a red-cheeked man she said, "I won't have you, Cockscomb!"

She stopped a little before the last of all, for he was a fine man in face and form. She wanted to find some defect in him, but he had nothing remarkable but a ring of brown curling hair under his chin. She admired him a little, and then carried it off with, "I won't have you, Whiskers!"

So all went away, and the king was so vexed, he said to her, "Now to punish your impudence, I'll give you to the first Beggarman or singing sthronshuch that calls;" and, as sure as the hearth-money, a fellow all over-rags, and hair that came to his shoulders, and a bushy red beard all over his face, came next morning, and began to sing before the parlour window.

When the song was over, the hall-door was opened, the singer asked in, the priest brought, and the princess married to Beardy. She roared and she bawled, but her father didn't mind her.

"There," says he to the bridegroom, "is five guineas for you. Take your wife out of my sight, and never let me lay eyes on you or her again."

Off he led her, and dismal enough she was. The only thing that gave her relief was the tones of her husband's voice and his genteel manners.

"Whose wood is this?" said she, as they were going through one.

"It belongs to the king you called Whiskers yesterday."

He gave her the same answer about meadows and corn-fields, and at last a fine city. "Ah, what a fool I was!" she said to herself.

"He was a fine man, and I might have him for a husband."

At last they were coming up to a poor cabin.

"Why are you bringing me here?" says the poor lady.

"This was my house," said he, "and now it's yours."

She began to cry, but she was tired and hungry, and she went in with him. There was neither a table laid out, nor a fire burning, and she was obliged to help her husband to light it, and boil their dinner, and clean up the place after; and next day he made her put on a stuff gown and a cotton handkerchief.

When she had her house readied up, and no business to keep her employed, he brought home sallies [willows], peeled them, and showed her how to make baskets. But the hard twigs bruised her delicate fingers, and she began to cry. Well, then he asked her to mend their clothes, but the needle drew blood from her fingers, and she cried again. He couldn't bear to see her tears, so he bought a creel of earthenware, and sent her to the market to sell them. This was the hardest trial of all, but she looked so handsome and sorrowful, and had such a nice air about her, that all her pans, and jugs, and plates, and dishes were gone before noon, and the only mark of her old pride she showed was a slap she gave a buckeen across the face when he axed her to go in an' take share of a quart.

Well, her husband was so glad, he sent her with another creel the next day; but faith! her luck was after deserting her. A drunken huntsman came up riding, and his beast got in among her ware, and made brishe of every mother's son of them. She went home crying, and her husband wasn't at all pleased.

"I see," said he, "you're not fit for business. Come along, I'll get you a kitchen-maid's place in the palace. I know the cook."

So the poor thing was obliged to stifle her pride once more. She was kept very busy, and the footman and the butler would be very impudent about looking for a kiss, but she let a screech out of her the first attempt was made, and the cook gave the fellow such a lambasting with the besom that he made no second offer. She went home to her husband every night, and she carried broken victuals wrapped in papers in her side pockets.

A week after she got service there was great bustle in the kitchen. The king was going to be married, but no one knew who the bride was to be. Well, in the evening the cook filled the princess's pockets with cold meat and puddings, and, says she, "Before you go, let us have a look at the great doings in the big parlour."

So they came near the door to get a peep, and who should come out but the king himself, as handsome as you please, and no other but King Whiskers himself. "Your handsome helper must pay for her peeping," he said to the cook, "and dance a jig with me."

Whether she would or no, he held her hand and brought her into the parlour. The fiddlers struck up, and away went him with her. But they hadn't danced two steps when the meat and the puddings flew out of her pockets. Everyone roared out, and she flew to the door, crying piteously. But she was soon caught by the king, and taken into the back parlour.

"Don't you know me, my darling?" said he. "I'm both King Whiskers, your husband the ballad-singer, and the drunken huntsman. Your father knew me well enough when he gave you to me, and all was to drive your pride out of you."

Well, she didn't know how she was with fright, and shame, and joy. Love was uppermost anyhow, for she laid her head on her husband's breast and cried like a child. The maids-of-honour soon had her away and dressed her as fine as hands and pins could do it; and there were her mother and father, too; and while the company were wondering what end of the handsome girl and the king, he and his queen, who they didn't know in her fine clothes, and the other king and queen, came in, and such rejoicings and fine doings as there was, none of us will ever see, anyway.

Tales From The Land Of Saints & Scholars

The Headless Horseman

"The Headless Horseman" is one of the most striking supernatural tales from Fairy Legends and Traditions of the South of Ireland (1825–28) by Thomas Crofton Croker, whose work helped preserve many oral traditions of southern Ireland. The story concerns a spectral rider, known in Irish as the Dullahan, a terrifying figure who gallops through the night on a black horse, carrying his own head under one arm.

In Croker's retelling, the tale is rooted in the rural landscapes of Munster, where travellers whisper of seeing the headless rider on lonely roads near graveyards or crossways. His severed head glows faintly, lighting his path and revealing the faces of those who cross him.

"God speed you, and a safe journey this night to you, Charley," ejaculated the master of the little sheebeen house at Ballyhooley after his old friend and good customer, Charley Culnane, who at length had turned his face homewards, with the prospect of as dreary a ride and as dark a night as ever fell upon the Blackwater, along the banks of which he was about to journey.

Charley Culnane knew the country well, and, moreover, was as bold a rider as any Mallow-boy that ever rattled a four-year-old upon Drumrue race-course. He had gone to Fermoy in the morning, as well for the purpose of purchasing some ingredients required for the

Christmas dinner by his wife, as to gratify his own vanity by having new reins fitted to his snaffle, in which he intended showing off the old mare at the approaching St. Stephen's Day hunt.

Charley did not get out of Fermoy until late; for although he was not one of your "nasty particular sort of fellows" in any thing that related to the common occurrences of life, yet in all the appointments connected with hunting, riding, leaping, in short, in whatever was connected with the old mare, "Charley," the saddlers said, "was the devil to please." An illustration of this fastidiousness was afforded by his going such a distance for his snaffle bridle. Mallow was full twelve miles nearer "Charley's farm" (which lay just three quarters of a mile below Carrick) than Fermoy; but Charley had quarrelled with all the Mallow saddlers, from hard-working and hard-drinking Tim Clancey, up to Mr. Ryan, who wrote himself "Saddler to the Duhallow Hunt;" and no one could content him in all particulars but honest Michael Twomey of Fermoy, who used to assert - and who will doubt it - that he could stitch a saddle better than the lord-lieutenant, although they made him all as one as king over Ireland.

This delay in the arrangement of the snaffle bridle did not allow Charley Culnane to pay so long a visit as he had at first intended to his old friend and gossip, Con Buckley, of the "Harp of Erin." Con, however, knew the value of time, and insisted upon Charley making good use of what he had to spare. "I won't bother you waiting for water, Charley, because I think you'll have enough of that same before you get home; so drink off your liquor, man. It's as good parliament as ever a gentleman tasted, ay, and holy church too, for it will bear 'x waters,' and carry the bead after that, may be."

Charley, it must be confessed, nothing loath, drank success to Con, and success to the jolly "Harp of Erin," with its head of beauty and its strings of the hair of gold, and to their better acquaintance, and so on, from the bottom of his soul, until the bottom of the bottle reminded him that Carrick was at the bottom of the hill on the other side of Castletown Roche, and that he had got no further on his journey than his gossip's at Ballyhooley, close to the big gate of Convamore. Catching hold of his oil-skin hat, therefore, whilst Con Buckley went to the cupboard for another bottle of the "real stuff," he regularly, as it is termed, bolted from his friend's hospitality, darted to the stable, tightened his girths, and put the old mare into a canter towards home.

The road from Ballyhooley to Carrick follows pretty nearly the course of the Blackwater, occasionally diverging from the river and passing through rather wild scenery, when contrasted with the beautiful seats that adorn its banks. Charley cantered gaily, regardless of the rain, which, as his friend Con had anticipated, fell in torrents. The good woman's currants and raisins were carefully packed between the folds of his yeomanry cloak, which Charley, who was proud of showing that he belonged to the "Royal Mallow Light Horse Volunteers," always strapped to the saddle before him, and took care never to destroy the military effect of by putting it on. - Away he went singing like a thrush -

"Sporting, belling, dancing, drinking,
Breaking windows - (hiccup!) - sinking,
Ever raking - never thinking,
Live the rakes of Mallow.

"Spending faster than it comes,
Beating - (hiccup, hic,) and duns,

Duhallow's true-begotten sons,
Live the rakes of Mallow."

Notwithstanding that the visit to the jolly "Harp of Erin" had a little increased the natural complacency of his mind, the drenching of the new snaffle reins began to disturb him; and then followed a train of more anxious thoughts than even were occasioned by the dreaded defeat of the pride of his long-anticipated turnout on St. Stephen's Day. In an hour of good fellowship, when his heart was warm, and his head not over cool, Charley had backed the old mare against Mr. Jephson's bay filly Desdemona for a neat hundred, and he now felt sore misgivings as to the prudence of the match. In a less gay tone he continued -

"Living short, but merry lives,
Going where the devil drives,
Keeping..."

"Keeping" he muttered, as the old mare had reduced her canter to a trot at the bottom of Kilcummer Hill. Charley's eye fell on the old walls that belonged, in former times, to the Templars, but the silent gloom of the ruin was broken only by the heavy rain which splashed and pattered on the gravestones. He then looked up at the sky, to see if there was, among the clouds, any hopes for mercy on his new snaffle reins; and no sooner were his eyes lowered, than his attention was arrested by an object so extraordinary as almost led him to doubt the evidence of his senses. The head, apparently, of a white horse, with short, cropped ears, large open nostrils and immense eyes, seemed rapidly to follow him. No connexion with body, legs, or rider, could possibly be traced - the head advanced - Charley's old mare, too, was moved at this unnatural sight, and snorting violently, increased her trot up the hill. The head moved forward, and passed on, Charley, pursuing it with astonished gaze, and wondering by what means, and for what purpose, this detached head thus proceeded through the air, did not perceive the corresponding body until he was suddenly startled by finding it close at his side. Charley turned to examine what was thus so sociably jogging on with him, when a most unexampled apparition presented itself to his view. A figure, whose height (judging as well as the obscurity of the night would permit him) he computed to be at least eight feet, was seated on the body and legs of a white horse full eighteen hands and a half high. In this measurement Charley could not be mistaken, for his own mare was exactly fifteen hands, and the body that thus jogged alongside he could at once determine, from his practice in horseflesh, was at least three hands and a half higher.

After the first feeling of astonishment, which found vent in the exclamation "I'm sold now forever!" was over, the attention of Charley, being a keen sportsman, was naturally directed to this extraordinary body; and having examined it with the eye of a connoisseur, he proceeded to reconnoitre the figure so unusually mounted, who had hitherto remained perfectly mute. Wishing to see whether his companion's silence proceeded from bad temper, want of conversational powers, or from a distaste to water, and the fear that the opening of his mouth might subject him to have it filled by the rain, which was then drifting in violent gusts against them, Charley endeavoured to catch a sight of his companion's face, in order to form an opinion on that point. But his vision failed in carrying him farther than the top of the collar of the figure's coat, which was a scarlet single-breasted hunting frock, having a waist of a very old-fashioned cut reaching to the saddle, with two huge shining buttons at about a yard distance behind. "I ought to see farther than this, too," thought Charley, "although he is mounted on his high horse, like my cousin Darby, who was made barony constable last week, unless 'tis Con's whiskey that has blinded me entirely." However, see farther he could not, and after straining his eyes for a considerable time to no purpose, he exclaimed, with pure vexation, "By the big bridge of Mallow, it is no head at all he has!"

"Look again, Charley Culnane," said a hoarse voice, that seemed to proceed from under the right arm of the figure.

Charley did look again, and now in the proper place, for he clearly saw, under the aforesaid right arm, that head from which the voice had proceeded, and such a head no mortal ever saw before. It looked like a large cream cheese hung round with black puddings; no speck of colour enlivened the ashy paleness of the depressed features; the skin lay stretched over the unearthly surface, almost like the parchment head of a drum. Two fiery eyes of prodigious circumference, with a strange and irregular motion, flashed like meteors upon Charley, and to complete all, a mouth reached from either extremity of two ears, which peeped forth from under a profusion of matted locks of lustreless blackness. This head, which the figure had evidently hitherto concealed from Charley's eyes, now burst upon his view in all its hideousness. Charley, although a lad of proverbial courage in the county of Cork, yet could not but feel his nerves a little shaken by this unexpected visit from the headless horseman, whom he considered his fellow-traveller must be. The cropped-eared head of the gigantic horse moved steadily forward, always keeping from six to eight yards in advance. The horseman, unaided by whip or spur, and disdaining the use of stirrups, which dangled uselessly from the saddle, followed at a trot by Charley's side, his hideous head now lost behind the lappet of his coat, now starting forth in all its horror, as the motion of the horse caused his arm to move to and fro. The ground shook under the weight of its supernatural burden, and the water in the pools became agitated into waves as he trotted by them.

On they went - heads without bodies, and bodies without heads. - The deadly silence of night was broken only by the fearful clattering of hoofs, and the distant sound of thunder, which rumbled above the mystic hill of Cecaune a Mona Finnea. Charley, who was naturally a merry-hearted, and rather a talkative fellow, had hitherto felt tongue-tied by apprehension, but finding his companion showed no evil disposition towards him, and having become somewhat more reconciled to the Patagonian dimensions of the horseman and his headless steed, plucked up all his courage, and thus addressed the stranger, "Why, then, your honour rides mighty well without the stirrups!"

"Humph," growled the head from under the horseman's right arm.

"'Tis not an over civil answer," thought Charley, "but no matter, he was taught in one of them riding-houses, may be, and thinks nothing at all about bumping his leather breeches at the rate of ten miles an hour. I'll try him on the other track. Ahem!" said Charley, clearing his throat, and feeling at the same time rather daunted at this second attempt to establish a conversation. "Ahem! that's a mighty neat coat of your honour's, although 'tis a little too long in the waist for the present cut."

"Humph," growled again the head.

This second humph was a terrible thump in the face to poor Charley, who was fairly bothered to know what subject he could start that would prove more agreeable. "'Tis a sensible head," thought Charley, "although an ugly one, for 'tis plain enough the man does not like flattery." A third attempt, however, Charley was determined to make, and having failed in his observations as to the riding and coat of his fellow-traveller, thought he would just drop a trifling allusion to the wonderful headless horse, that was jogging on so sociably beside his old mare; and as Charley was considered about Carrick to be very knowing in horses, besides, being a full private in the Royal Mallow Light Horse Volunteers, which were every one of them mounted like real Hessians, he felt rather sanguine as to the result of his third attempt.

"To be sure, that's a brave horse your honour rides," recommenced the persevering Charley.

"You may say that, with your own ugly mouth," growled the head.

Charley, though not much flattered by the compliment, nevertheless chuckled at his success in obtaining an answer, and thus continued, "May be your honour wouldn't be after riding him across the country?"

"Will you try me, Charley?" said the head, with an inexpressible look of ghastly delight.

"Faith, and that's what I'd do," responded Charley, "only I'm afraid, the night being so dark, of laming the old mare, and I've every halfpenny of a hundred pounds on her heels."

This was true enough; Charley's courage was nothing dashed at the headless horseman's proposal; and there never was a steeple-chase, nor a fox-chase, riding or leaping in the country, that Charley Culnane was not at it, and foremost in it.

"Will you take my word," said the man who carried his head so snugly under his right arm, "for the safety of your mare?"

"Done," said Charley; and away they started, helter-skelter, over everything, ditch and wall, pop, pop, the old mare never went in such style, even in broad daylight, and Charley had just the start of his companion, when the hoarse voice called out, "Charley Culnane, Charley, man, stop for your life, stop!"

Charley pulled up hard. "Ay," said he, "you may beat me by the head, because it always goes so much before you; but if the bet was neck-and-neck, and that's the go between the old mare and Desdemona, I'd win it hollow!"

It appeared as if the stranger was well aware of what was passing in Charley's mind, for he suddenly broke out quite loquacious.

"Charley Culnane," says he, "you have a stout soul in you, and are every inch of you a good rider. I've tried you, and I ought to know; and that's the sort of man for my money. A hundred years it is since my horse and I broke our necks at the bottom of Kilcummer hill, and ever since I have been trying to get a man that dared to ride with me, and never found one before. Keep, as you have always done, at the tail of the hounds, never balk a ditch, nor turn away from a stone wall, and the headless horseman will never desert you nor the old mare."

Charley, in amazement, looked towards the stranger's right arm, for the purpose of seeing in his face whether or not he was in earnest, but behold! the head was snugly lodged in the huge pocket of the horseman's scarlet hunting-coat. The horse's head had ascended perpendicularly above them, and his extraordinary companion, rising quickly after his avant-courier, vanished from the astonished gaze of Charley Culnane.

Charley, as may be supposed, was lost in wonder, delight, and perplexity; the pelting rain, the wife's pudding, the new snaffle -

even the match against squire Jephson - all were forgotten; nothing could he think of, nothing could he talk of, but the headless horseman. He told it, directly that he got home, to Judy; he told it the following morning to all the neighbours; and he told it to the hunt on St. Stephen's Day, but what provoked him after all the pains he took in describing the head, the horse, and the man, was that one and all attributed the creation of the headless horseman to his friend Con Buckley's "X water parliament." This, however, should be told, that Charley's old mare beat Mr. Jephson's bay filly, Desdemona, by Diamond, and Charley pocketed his cool hundred; and if he didn't win by means of the headless horseman, I am sure I don't know any other reason for his doing so.

Tales From The Land Of Saints & Scholars

The Hill-Man and the Housewife

"The Hill-Man and the Housewife" is a gentle Irish folktale that explores the uneasy balance between the human world and the world of the fairies. Originally written by Juliana Horatia Ewing (1841–1885) and later adapted by Alfred Perceval Graves in The Irish Fairy Book (1909), the story tells of a kindly housewife who one day receives a visit from a mysterious little "hill-man", a being of the sidhe, the fairy folk who live beneath the green hills of Ireland.

Graves's adaptation preserves Ewing's warmth and domestic humour while deepening the Irish folkloric texture, the sense that the fairy world lies just beneath the surface of ordinary life.

It is well known that the good people cannot stand mean ways. Now, there once lived a housewife who had a sharp eye to her own good in this world, and gave alms of what she had no use, for the good of her soul.

One day a hill-man knocked at her door. "Can you lend us a saucepan, good mother?" said he. "There's a wedding in the hill, and all the pots are in use." "Is he to have one?" asked the servant girl who opened the door. "Ay, to be sure," said the house-wife.

But when the maid was taking a saucepan from the shelf, she pinched her arm and whispered sharply, "Not that, you stupid; get the old one out of the cupboard. It leaks, and the hill-men are so neat and such nimble workers that they are sure to mend it before they send it home. So one does a good turn to the good people and saves sixpence from the tinker."

The maid fetched the saucepan, which had been laid by till the tinker's next visit, and gave it to the dwarf, who thanked her and went away. The Hill-man and the Housewife

The saucepan was soon returned neatly mended and ready for use. At supper time the maid filled the pan with milk and set it on the fire for the children's supper, but in a few minutes the milk was so burnt and smoked that no one could touch it, and even the pigs would not drink the wash into which it was thrown.

Ah, you good-for-nothing slut!" cried the house-wife, as she this time filled the pan herself. "You would ruin the richest, with your careless ways; there's a whole quart of good milk spoilt at once." "And that's tuppence," cried a voice from the chimney, a queer whining voice like some old body who was always grumbling over something.

The house-wife had not left the saucepan for two minutes when the milk boiled over, and it was all burnt and smoked as before. "The pan must be dirty," cried the housewife in a rage, "and there are two full quarts of milk as good as thrown to the dogs." "And that's fourpence," said the voice in the chimney.

After a long scrubbing the saucepan was once more filled and set on the fire, but it was not the least use, the milk was burnt and smoked again, and the housewife burst into tears at the waste, crying out, "Never before did such a thing happen to me since I kept house! Three quarts of milk burnt for one meal!" "And that's sixpence," cried the voice from the chimney. "You didn't save the tinker after all," with which the hill-man himself came tumbling down the chimney, and went off laughing through the door. But from that time the saucepan was as good as any other.

Tales From The Land Of Saints & Scholars

The Horned Women

"The Horned Women", adapted by Joseph Jacobs in Celtic Fairy Tales (1892), is one of the darker and more unsettling pieces in his collection. The story tells of a wealthy housewife in Ireland who is visited late at night by a group of twelve witches, each wearing a single horn on her forehead.

The tale fuses Christian and pre-Christian imagery, echoing old Irish beliefs about witchcraft, nocturnal spirits, and protective charms. Its central figure, the "goodwife" menaced by demonic women, embodies the tension between domestic order and supernatural intrusion.

A rich woman sat up late one night carding and preparing wool, while all the family and servants were asleep. Suddenly a knock was given at the door, and a voice called, "Open! open!"

"Who is there?" said the woman of the house.

"I am the Witch of one Horn," was answered.

The mistress, supposing that one of her neighbours had called and required assistance, opened the door, and a woman entered, having in her hand a pair of wool-carders, and bearing a horn on her forehead, as if growing there. She sat down by the fire in silence, and began to card the wool with violent haste. Suddenly she paused, and said aloud, "Where are the women? they delay too long."

Then a second knock came to the door, and a voice called as before, "Open! open!"

The mistress felt herself obliged to rise and open to the call, and immediately a second witch entered, having two horns on her forehead, and in her hand a wheel for spinning wool.

"Give me place," she said, "I am the Witch of the two Horns," and she began to spin as quick as lightning.

And so the knocks went on, and the call was heard, and the witches entered, until at last twelve women sat round the fire - the first with one horn, the last with twelve horns.

And they carded the thread, and turned their spinning-wheels, and wound and wove, all singing together an ancient rhyme, but no word did they speak to the mistress of the house. Strange to hear, and frightful to look upon, were these twelve women, with their horns and their wheels; and the mistress felt near to death, and she tried to rise that she might call for help, but she could not move, nor could she utter a word or a cry, for the spell of the witches was upon her.

Then one of them called to her in Irish, and said, "Rise, woman, and make us a cake."

Then the mistress searched for a vessel to bring water from the well that she might mix the meal and make the cake, but she could find none.

And they said to her, "Take a sieve and bring water in it."

And she took the sieve and went to the well; but the water poured from it, and she could fetch none for the cake, and she sat down by the well and wept.

Then a voice came by her and said, "Take yellow clay and moss, and bind them together, and plaster the sieve so that it will hold."

This she did, and the sieve held the water for the cake; and the voice said again, "Return, and when you come to the north angle of the house, cry aloud three times and say, 'The mountain of the Fenian women and the sky over it is all on fire."

And she did so.

When the witches inside heard the call, a great and terrible cry broke from their lips, and they rushed forth with wild lamentations and shrieks, and fled away to Slievenamon, where was their chief abode. But the Spirit of the Well bade the mistress of the house to enter and prepare her home against the enchantments of the witches if they returned again.

And first, to break their spells, she sprinkled the water in which she had washed her child's feet, the feet-water, outside the door on the threshold; secondly, she took the cake which in her absence the witches had made of meal mixed with the blood drawn from the sleeping family, and she broke the cake in bits, and placed a bit in the mouth of each sleeper, and they were restored; and she took the cloth they had woven, and placed it half in and half out of the chest with the padlock; and lastly, she secured the door with a great crossbeam fastened in the jambs, so that the witches could not enter, and having done these things she waited.

Not long were the witches in coming back, and they raged and called for vengeance.

"Open! open!" they screamed, "open, feet-water!"

"I cannot," said the feet-water, "I am scattered on the ground, and my path is down to the Lough."

"Open, open, wood and trees and beam!" they cried to the door.

"I cannot," said the door, "for the beam is fixed in the jambs and I have no power to move."

"Open, open, cake that we have made and mingled with blood!" they cried again.

"I cannot," said the cake, "for I am broken and bruised, and my blood is on the lips of the sleeping children."

Then the witches rushed through the air with great cries, and fled back to Slievenamon, uttering strange curses on the Spirit of the Well, who had wished their ruin; but the woman and the house were left in peace, and a mantle dropped by one of the witches in her flight was kept hung up by the mistress in memory of that night; and this mantle was kept by the same family from generation to generation for five hundred years after.

Tales From The Land Of Saints & Scholars

The Jackdaw

"The Jackdaw," as included in Fairy and Folk Tales of the Irish Peasantry (1888), is one of the shorter and more moralistic pieces drawn from the Irish oral tradition. It tells of a jackdaw who grows discontented with his plain black feathers and envies the bright plumage of other birds.

The tale serves as a sharp parable about vanity, false pride, and the folly of self-disguise, a theme common in Irish moral folklore and in fables of wider European tradition.

Tom Moor was a linen draper in Sackville Street. His father when he died, left him an affluent fortune, and a shop of excellent trade.

As he was standing at his door one day a countryman came up to him with a nest of jackdaws, and accosting him, says, "Master, will you buy a nest of daws?" "No, I don't want any." "Master," replied the man, "I will sell them all cheap; you shall have the whole nest for nine-pence." "I don't want them," answered Tom Moor, "so go about your business."

As the man was walking away one of the daws popped out his head, and cried "Mawk, mawk." "Damn it," says Tom Moor, "that bird knows my name; halloo, countryman, what will you take for the bird?" "Why, you shall have him for threepence." Tom Moor bought him, had a cage made, and hung him up in the shop.

The journeymen took much notice of the bird, and would frequently tap at the bottom of the cage, and say, "Who are you? Who are you? Tom Moor of Sackville Street."

In a short time the jackdaw learned these words, and if he wanted victuals or water, would strike his bill against the cage, turn up the white of his eyes, cock his head, and cry, "Who are you? who are you? Tom Moor of Sackville Street."

Tom Moor was fond of gaming, and often lost large sums of money; finding his business neglected in his absence, he had a small hazard table set up in one corner of his dining-room, and invited a party of his friends to play at it.

The jackdaw had by this time become familiar; his cage was left open, and he hopped into every part of the house; sometimes he got into the dining-room, where the gentlemen were at play, and one of them being a constant winner, the others would say, "Damn it, how he nicks them." The bird learned these words also, and adding them to the former, would call, "Who are you? who are you? Tom Moor of Sackville Street. Damn it, how he nicks them."

Tom Moor, from repeated losses and neglect of business, failed in trade, and became a prisoner in the Fleet; he took his bird with him, and lived on the master's side, supported by friends, in a decent manner. They would sometimes ask what brought you here? when he used to lift up his hands and answer, "Bad company, by God." The bird learned this likewise, and at the end of the former words, would say, "What brought you here? Bad company, by God."

Some of Tom Moor's friends died, others went abroad, and by degrees he was totally deserted, and removed to the common side of the prison, where the jail distemper soon attacked him; and in the last stage of life, lying on a straw bed; the poor bird had been for two days without food or water, came to his feet, and striking his bill on the floor, calls out, "Who are you? Tom Moor of Sackville Street; damn it, how he nicks them, damn it, how he nicks them. What brought you here? bad company, by God, bad company, by God."

Tom Moor, who had attended to the bird, was struck with his words, and reflecting on himself, cried out, "Good God, to what a situation am I reduced! my father, when he died, left me a good fortune and an established trade. I have spent my fortune, ruined my business, and am now dying in a loathsome jail; and to complete all, keeping that poor thing confined without support. I will endeavour to do one piece of justice before I die, by setting him at liberty."

He made a struggle to crawl from his straw bed, opened the casement, and out flew the bird. A flight of jackdaws from the Temple were going over the jail, and Tom Moor's bird mixed among them. The gardener was then laying the plats of the Temple gardens, and as often as he placed them in the day the jackdaws pulled them up by night. They got a gun and attempted to shoot some of them; but, being cunning birds, they always placed one as a watch in the stump of a hollow tree; who, as soon as the gun was levelled cried "Mawk," and away they flew.

The gardeners were advised to get a net, and the first night it was spread they caught fifteen; Tom Moor's bird was amongst them. One of the men took the net into a garret of an uninhabited house, fastens the doors and windows, and turns the birds loose. "Now," said he, "you black rascals, I will be revenged of you." Taking hold of the first at hand, he twists her neck, and throwing him down, cries, "There goes one." Tom Moor's bird, who had hopped up to a beam at one corner of the room unobserved, as the man lays hold of the second, calls out, "Damn it, how he nicks them." The man alarmed, cries, "Sure I heard a voice, but the house is uninhabited, and the door is fast; it could only be imagination." On laying hold of the third, and twisting his neck, Tom's bird again says, "Damn it, how he nicks them." The man dropped the bird in his hand, and turning to where the voice came from, seeing the other with his mouth open, cries out, "Who are you?" to which the bird answered, "Tom Moor of Sackville Street, Tom Moor of Sackville Street." "The devil you are; and what brought you here." Tom Moor's bird, lifting up his pinions, answered, "Bad company, by God, bad company, by God." The fellow, frightened almost out of his wits, opened the door, ran downstairs, and out of the house, followed by all the birds, who by this means regained their liberty.

Tales From The Land Of Saints & Scholars

The King of the Black Desert

"The King of the Black Desert" is an Irish folktale originally collected by Douglas Hyde (1860–1949), a leading figure of the Gaelic Revival and later the first President of Ireland. It was later adapted by Alfred Perceval Graves in The Irish Fairy Book (1910), where it appears as one of the darker, more fantastical moral tales of Irish storytelling.

In Graves's retelling, adapted from Hyde's Irish-language source, the tale retains a lyrical yet sombre tone. The Black Desert becomes a landscape of exile and testing, its king a figure both demonic and sorrowful, embodying greed, enchantment, and isolation.

When O'Conor was king over Ireland he was living in Rathcroghan, of Connacht. He had one son, but he, when he grew up, was wild, and the King could not control him, because he would have his own will in everything.

One morning he went out, his hound at his foot and his hawk on his hand, and his fine black horse to bear him - and he went forward, singing a verse of a song to himself, until he came as far as a big bush that was growing on the brink of a glen. There was an old grey man sitting at the foot of the bush, and he said, "King's son, if you are able to play as well as you are able to sing songs, I would like to play a game with you." The King's son thought that it was a silly old man that was in it, and he alighted, threw bridle over branch, and sat down by the side of the old grey man.

The old man drew out a pack of cards and asked, "Can you play these?"

"I can," said the King's son.

"What shall we play for?" said the old grey man.

"Anything you wish," says the King's son.

"All right; if I win you must do for me anything I shall ask of you, and if you win I must do for you anything you ask of me," says the old grey man.

"I'm satisfied," says the King's son.

They played the game, and the King's son beat the old grey man. Then he said, "What would you like me to do for you, King's son?"

"I won't ask you to do anything for me," says the King's son. "I think that you are not able to do much."

"Don't mind that," said the old man. "You must ask me to do something. I never lost a bet yet that I wasn't able to pay it."

As I said, the King's son thought that it was a silly old man that was in it, and to satisfy him he said to him, "Take the head off my stepmother and put a goat's head on her for a week."

"I'll do that for you," said the old grey man.

The King's son went a-riding on his horse, his hound at his foot, his hawk on his hand, and he faced for another place, and never thought more about the old grey man until he came home.

He found a cry and great grief in the castle. The servants told him that an enchanter had come into the room where the Queen was, and had put a goat's head on her in place of her own head.

"By my hand, but that's a wonderful thing," says the King's son. "If I had been at home I'd have whipt the head off him with my sword."

There was great grief on the King, and he sent for a wise councillor, and asked him did he know how the thing happened to the Queen.

"Indeed, I cannot tell you that," said he, "it's a work of enchantment."

The King's son did not let on that he had any knowledge of the matter, but on the morrow morning he went out, his hound at his foot, his hawk on his hand, and his fine black horse to bear him, and he never drew rein until he came as far as the big bush on the brink of the glen. The old grey man was sitting there under the bush, and said, "King's son, will you have a game today?" The King's son got down and said, "I will." With that he threw bridle over branch and sat down by the side of the old man. He drew out the cards and asked the King's son did he get the thing he had won yesterday.

"That's all right," said the King's son.

"We'll play for the same bet to-day," says the old grey man.

"I'm satisfied," said the King's son.

They played - the King's son won. "What would you like me to do for you this time?" says the old grey man. The King's son thought and said to himself, "I'll give him a hard job this time." Then he said, "There's a field of seven acres at the back of my father's castle; let it be filled to-morrow morning with cows, and no two of them to be of one colour, or one height, or one age."

"That shall be done," says the old grey man.

The King's son went riding on his horse, his hound at his foot, his hawk on his hand, and faced for home. The King was sorrowful about the Queen; there were doctors out of every place in Ireland, but they could not do her any good.

On the morning of the next day the King's herd went out early, and he saw the field at the back of the castle filled with cows, and no two of them of the same colour, the same age, or the same height. He went in and told the King the wonderful news. "Go and drive them out," says the King. The herd got men, and went with them driving out the cows, but no sooner would he put them out on one side than they would come in on the other. The herd went to the King again, and told him that all the men that were in Ireland would not be able to put out these cows that were in the field. "They're enchanted cows," said the King.

When the King's son saw the cows, he said to himself, "I'll have another game with the grey old man to-day!"

That morning he went out, his hound at his foot, his hawk on his hand, and his fine black horse to bear him, and he never drew rein till he came as far as the big bush on the brink of the glen. The old grey man was there before him, and asked him would he have a game of cards.

"I will," says the King's son, "but you know well that I can beat you playing cards."

"We'll have another game, then," says the old grey man. "Did you ever play ball?"

"I did, indeed," said the King's son, "but I think that you are too old to play ball, and, besides that, we have no place here to play it."

"If you're contented to play, I'll find a place," says the old grey man.

"I'm contented," says the King's son.

"Follow me," says the old grey man.

The King's son followed him through the glen until he came to a fine green hill. There he drew out a little enchanted rod, spoke some words which the King's son did not understand, and after a moment the hill opened and the two went in, and they passed through a number of splendid halls until they came out into a garden. There was everything finer than another in that garden, and at the bottom of the garden there was a place for playing ball. They threw up a piece of silver to see who would have hand-in, and the old grey man got it.

They began then, and the old grey man never stopped until he won out the game. The King's son did not know what he would do. At last he asked the old man what he would desire him to do for him.

"I am King over the Black Desert, and you must find out myself and my dwelling-place within a year and a day, or I shall find you out and you shall lose your head."

Then he brought the King's son out the same way by which he went in. The green hill closed behind them, and the old grey man disappeared out of sight.

The King's son went home, riding on his horse, his hound at his foot, his hawk on his hand, and he sorrowful enough.

That evening the King observed that there was grief and great trouble on his young son, and when he went to sleep the King and every person that was in the castle heard heavy sighings and ravings from him. The King was in grief - a goat's head to be on the Queen - but he was seven times worse when they told him the (whole) story how it happened from beginning to end.

He sent for a wise councillor, and asked him did he know where the King of the Black Desert was living.

"I do not, indeed," said he, "but as sure as there's a tail on the cat, unless the young heir finds out that enchanter he will lose his head."

There was great grief that day in the castle of the King. There was a goat's head on the Queen, and the King's son was going searching for an enchanter, without knowing whether he would ever come back.

After a week the goat's head was taken off the Queen, and her own head was put upon her. When she heard of how the goat's head was put upon her, a great hate came upon her against the King's son, and she said, "that he may never come back, alive or dead."

Of a Monday morning he left his blessing with his father and his kindred; his travelling bag was bound upon his shoulder, and he went, his hound at his foot, his hawk on his hand, and his fine black horse to bear him.

He walked that day until the sun was gone beneath the shadow of the hills and till the darkness of the night was coming, without knowing where he could get lodgings. He noticed a large wood on his left-hand side, and he drew towards it as quickly as he could, hoping to spend the night under the shelter of the trees. He sat down at the foot of a large oak tree, and opened his travelling bag to take some food and drink, when he saw a great eagle coming towards him.

"Do not be afraid of me, King's son; I know you - you are the son of O'Conor, King of Ireland. I am a friend, and if you give me your horse to give to eat to four hungry birds that I have, I shall bear you farther than your horse would bear you, and, perhaps, I would put you on the track of him you are looking for."

"You can have the horse, and welcome," says the King's son, "although I'm sorrowful at parting from him."

"All right, I shall be here tomorrow at sunrise." With that she opened her great gob, caught hold of the horse, struck in his two sides against one another, took wing, and disappeared out of sight.

The King's son ate and drank his enough, put his travelling bag under his head, and it was not long till he was asleep, and he never awoke till the eagle came and said, "It is time for us to be going; there is a long journey before us. Take hold of your bag and leap up upon my back."

"But to my grief," says he, "I must part from my hound and my hawk."

"Do not be grieved," says she, "they will be here before you when you come back."

Then he leaped up on her back. She took wing, and off and away with her through the air. She brought him across hills and hollows, over a great sea, and over woods, till he thought that he was at the end of the world. When the sun was going under the shadow of the hills, she came to earth in the midst of a great desert, and said to him, "Follow the path on your right-hand side, and it will bring you to the house of a friend. I must return again to provide for my birds."

He followed the path, and it was not long till he came to the house, and he went in. There was an old grey man sitting in the corner. He rose and said, "A hundred thousand welcomes to you, King's son, from Rathcroghan of Connacht."

"I have no knowledge of you," said the King's son.

"I was acquainted with your grandfather," said the old grey man. "Sit down; no doubt there is hunger and thirst on you."

"I'm not free from them," said the King's son.

The old man then smote his two palms against one another, and two servants came and laid a board with beef, mutton, pork, and plenty of bread before the King's son, and the old man said to him,

Eat and drink your enough. Perhaps it may be a long time before you get the like again."

He ate and drank as much as he desired, and thanked him for it.

Then the old man said, "You are going seeking for the King of the Black Desert. Go to sleep now, and I will go through my books to see if I can find out the dwelling-place of that King." Then he smote his palms together, and a servant came, and he told him, "Take the King's son to his chamber." He took him to a fine chamber, and it was not long till he fell asleep.

On the morning of the next day the old man came and said, "Rise up, there is a long journey before you. You must do five hundred miles before midday."

"I could not do it," said the King's son.

"If you are a good rider I will give you a horse that will bring you over the journey."

"I will do as you say," said the King's son.

The old man gave him plenty to eat and to drink, and, when he was satisfied, he gave him a little white garron, and said, "Give the garron his head, and when he stops look up into the air, and you will see three swans as white as snow. Those are the three daughters of the King of the Black Desert. There will be a green napkin in the mouth of one of them, that is the youngest daughter, and there is not anyone alive except her who could bring you to the house of the King of the Black Desert. When the garron stops you will be near a lake. The three swans will come to land on the brink of that lake, and they will make three young women of themselves, and they will go into the lake swimming and dancing. Keep your eye on the green napkin, and when you get the young women in the lake, go and get the napkin, and do not part with it. Go into hiding under a tree, and when the young women will come out, two of them will make swans of themselves, and will go away in the air. Then the youngest daughter will say, "I will do anything for him who will give me my napkin." Come forward then and give her the napkin, and say there is nothing you want but to bring you to her father's house, and tell her you are a king's son from a powerful country."

The King's son did everything as the old man desired him, and when he gave the napkin to the daughter of the King of the Black Desert, he said, "I am the son of O'Conor, King of Connaught. Bring me to your father. Long am I seeking him."

"Wouldn't it be better for me to do something else for you?" said she.

"I do not want anything else," said he.

"If I show you the house will you not be satisfied?" said she.

"I will be satisfied," said he.

"Now," said she, "upon your life do not tell my father that it was I who brought you to his house, and I shall be a good friend to you; but let on," said she, "that you have great powers of enchantment."

"I will do as you say," says he.

Then she made a swan of herself, and said, "Leap up on my back and put your hands under my neck, and keep a hard hold."

He did so, and she shook her wings, and off and away with her over hills and over glens, over sea and over mountains, until she came to earth as the sun was going under. Then she said to him, "Do you see that great house yonder? That is my father's house. Farewell. Any time that you are in danger I shall be at your side." Then she went from him.

The King's son went to the house and went in, and who should he see sitting in a golden chair but the old grey man who had played the cards and the ball with him.

"King's son," said he, "I see that you have found me out before the day and the year. How long since you left home?"

"This morning, when I was rising out of my bed, I saw a rainbow. I gave a leap, spread my two legs on it, and slid as far as this."

"By my hand, it was a great feat you performed," said the old King.

"I could do a more wonderful thing than that if I chose," said the King's son.

"I have three things for you to do," says the old King, "and if you are able to do them, you shall have the choice of my three daughters for wife, and unless you are able to do them, you shall lose your head, as a good many other young men have lost it before you."

"Then," he said, "there be neither eating nor drinking in my house except once in the week, and we had it this morning."

"It's all one to me," said the King's son. "I could fast for a month if I were on a pinch."

"No doubt you can go without sleep also," says the old King.

I can, without doubt," said the King's son.

"You shall have a hard bed to-night, then," says the old King. "Come with me till I show it to you." He brought him out then and showed him a great tree with a fork in it, and said, "Get up there and sleep in the fork, and be ready with the rise of the sun."

He went up into the fork, but as soon as the old King was asleep the young daughter came and brought him into a fine room, and kept him there until the old King was about to rise. Then she put him out again into the fork of the tree.

With the rise of the sun the old King came to him, and said, "Come down now and come with me until I show you the thing that you have to do to-day."

He brought the King's son to the brink of a lake and showed him an old castle, and said to him, "Throw every stone in that castle out into the loch, and let you have it done before the sun goes down in the evening." He went away from him then.

The King's son began working, but the stones were stuck to one another so fast that he was not able to raise one of them, and if he were to be working until this day, there would not be one stone out of the castle. He sat down then, thinking what he ought to do, and it was not long until the daughter of the old King came to him and said, "What is the cause of your grief?" He told her the work which he had to do. "Let that put no grief on you; I will do it," said she. Then she gave him bread, meat, and wine, pulled out a little enchanted rod, struck a blow on the old castle, and in a moment every stone of it was at the bottom of the lake. "Now," said she, "do not tell my father that it was I who did the work for you."

When the sun was going down in the evening, the old King came and said, "I see that you have your day's work done."

"I have," said the King's son, "I can do any work at all."

The old King thought now that the King's son had great powers of enchantment, and he said to him, "Your day's work for to-morrow is to lift the stones out of the loch, and to set up the castle again as it was before."

He brought the King's son home, and said to him, "Go to sleep in the place where you were last night."

When the old King went to sleep the young daughter came and brought him into the fine chamber, and kept him there till the old King was about to rise in the morning. Then she put him out again in the fork of the tree.

At sunrise the old King came and said, "It's time for you to get to work."

"There's no hurry on me at all," says the King's son, "because I know I can readily do my day's work."

He then went to the brink of the lake, but he was not able to see a stone, the water was that black. He sat down on a rock, and it was not long until Finnuala - that was the name of the old King's daughter - came to him and said, "What have you to do to-day?" He told her, and she said, "Let there be no grief on you. I can do that work for you." Then she gave him bread, beef, mutton, and wine. After that she drew out the little enchanted rod, smote the water of the lake with it, and in a moment the old castle was set up as it had been the day before. Then she said to him, "On your life, don't tell my father that I did this work for you, or that you have any knowledge of me at all."

On the evening of that day the old King came and said, "I see that you have the day's work done."

"I have," said the King's son, "that was an easy-done job."

Then the old King thought that the King's son had more power of enchantment than he had himself, and he said, "You have only one other thing to do." He brought him home then, and put him to sleep in the fork of the tree, but Finnuala came and put him into the fine chamber, and in the morning she sent him out again into the tree. At sunrise the old King came to him, and said, "Come with me till I show you your day's work."

He brought the King's son to a great glen, and showed him a well, and said, "My grandmother lost a ring in that well, and do you get it for me before the sun goes under this morning."

Now, this well was one hundred feet deep and twenty feet round about, and it was filled with water, and there was an army out of hell watching the ring.

When the old King went away Finnuala came and asked, "What have you to do to-day?" He told her, and she said, "That is a difficult task, but I shall do my best to save your life." Then she gave him beef, bread, and wine. Then she made a diver of herself, and went down into the well. It was not long till he saw smoke and lightning coming up out of the well, and he heard a sound like thunder, and anyone who would be listening to that noise, he would think that the army of hell was fighting.

At the end of a while the smoke went away, the lightning and thunder ceased, and Finnuala came up with the ring. She handed the ring to the King's son, and said, "I won the battle, and your life is saved. But, look, the little finger of my right hand is broken. But perhaps it's a lucky thing that it was broken. When my father comes do not give him the ring, but threaten him stoutly. He will bring you, then, to choose your wife, and this is how you shall make your choice. I and my sisters will be in a room; there will be a hole in the door, and we shall all put our hands out in a cluster. You will put your hand through the hole, and the hand that you will keep hold of when my father will open the door, that is the hand of her you shall have for wife. You can know me by my broken little finger."

"I can; and the love of my heart you are, Finnuala," says the King's son.

On the evening of that day the old King came and asked, "Did you get my grandmother's ring?"

"I did, indeed," says the King's son. "There was an army out of hell guarding it, but I beat them; and I would beat seven times as many. Don't you know I'm a Connachtman?"

Give me the ring," says the old King.

"Indeed, I won't give it," says he. "I fought hard for it. But do you give me my wife; I want to be going."

The old King brought him in, and said, "My three daughters are in that room before you. The hand of each of them is stretched out, and she on whom you will keep your hold until I open the door, that one is your wife."

The King's son thrust his hand through the hole that was in the door, and caught hold of the hand with the broken little finger, and kept a tight hold of it until the old King opened the door of the room.

"This is my wife," said the King's son. "Give me now your daughter's fortune."

"She has no fortune to get, but the brown slender steed to bring you home, and that you may never come back, alive or dead!"

The King's son and Finnuala went riding on the slender brown steed, and it was not long till they came to the wood where the King's son left his hound and his hawk. They were there before him, together with his fine black horse. He sent the slender brown steed back then. He set Finnuala riding on his horse, and leaped up himself, his hound at his heel, his hawk on his hand, and he never stopped till he came to Rathcroghan.

There was great welcome before him there, and it was not long till himself and Finnuala were married. They spent a long, prosperous life. But it is scarcely that even the track of this old castle is to be found to-day in Rathcroghan of Connacht.

Tales From The Land Of Saints & Scholars

The Lad with the Goat-Skin

"The Lad with the Goat-Skin", as retold by Joseph Jacobs in Celtic Fairy Tales (1892), is an Irish folktale that follows a poor, ragged youth who ventures out into the world wearing nothing but a rough garment made from a goat's hide.

Jacobs's version preserves the earthy humour and oral rhythm of the Irish peasant storyteller, full of repetition, playfulness, and irony. The goat-skin itself symbolises both poverty and disguise, it marks the lad as an outcast, yet protects him as he moves between worlds of the ordinary and the magical.

Long ago, a poor widow woman lived down near the iron forge, by Enniscorth, and she was so poor she had no clothes to put on her son; so she used to fix him in the ash-hole, near the fire, and pile the warm ashes about him; and according as he grew up, she sunk the pit deeper. At last, by hook or by crook, she got a goat-skin, and fastened it round his waist, and he felt quite grand, and took a walk down the street. So says she to him next morning, "Tom, you thief, you never done any good yet, and you six foot high, and past nineteen; - take that rope and bring me a faggot from the wood."

"Never say it twice, mother," says Tom - "here goes."

When he had it gathered and tied, what should come up but a big giant, nine foot high, and made a lick of a club at him. Well become

Tom, he jumped a-one side, and picked up a ram-pike; and the first crack he gave the big fellow, he made him kiss the clod.

"If you have ever a prayer," says Tom, "now's the time to say it, before I make fragments of you."

"I have no prayers," says the giant, "but if you spare my life I'll give you that club; and as long as you keep from sin, you'll win every battle you ever fight with it."

Tom made no bones about letting him off; and as soon as he got the club in his hands, he sat down on the bresna, and gave it a tap with the kippeen, and says, "Faggot, I had great trouble gathering you, and run the risk of my life for you, the least you can do is to carry me home." And sure enough, the wind o' the word was all it wanted. It went off through the wood, groaning and crackling, till it came to the widow's door.

Well, when the sticks were all burned, Tom was sent off again to pick more; and this time he had to fight with a giant that had two heads on him. Tom had a little more trouble with him - that's all; and the prayers he said, was to give Tom a fife; that nobody could help dancing when he was playing it. Begonies, he made the big faggot dance home, with himself sitting on it. The next giant was a beautiful boy with three heads on him. He had neither prayers nor catechism no more nor the others; and so he gave Tom a bottle of green ointment, that wouldn't let you be burned, nor scalded, nor wounded. "And now," says he, "there's no more of us. You may come and gather sticks here till little Lunacy Day in Harvest, without giant or fairy-man to disturb you."

Well, now, Tom was prouder nor ten peacocks, and used to take a walk down street in the heel of the evening; but some o' the little boys had no more manners than if they were Dublin jackeens, and put out their tongues at Tom's club and Tom's goat-skin. He didn't like that at all, and it would be mean to give one of them a clout. At last, what should come through the town but a kind of a bellman, only it's a big bugle he had, and a huntsman's cap on his head, and a kind of a painted shirt. So this - he wasn't a bellman, and I don't know what to call him - bugle man, maybe, proclaimed that the King of Dublin's daughter was so melancholy that she didn't give a laugh for seven years, and that her father would grant her in marriage to whoever could make her laugh three times.

"That's the very thing for me to try," says Tom; and so, without burning any more daylight, he kissed his mother, curled his club at the little boys, and off he set along the Yalla highroad to the town of Dublin.

At last Tom came to one of the city gates, and the guards laughed and cursed at him instead of letting him in. Tom stood it all for a little time, but at last one of them - out of fun, as he said - drove his bayonet half an inch or so into his side. Tom done nothing but take the fellow by the scruff o' the neck and the waistband of his corduroys, and fling him into the canal. Some run to pull the fellow out, and others to let manners into the vulgarian with their swords and daggers; but a tap from his club sent them headlong into the moat or down on the stones, and they were soon begging him to stay his hands.

So at last one of them was glad enough to show Tom the way to the palace-yard; and there was the king, and the queen, and the princess, in a gallery, looking at all sorts of wrestling, and sword-playing, and long-dances, and mumming, all to please the princess; but not a smile came over her handsome face.

Well, they all stopped when they seen the young giant, with his boy's face, and long black hair, and his short curly beard - for his poor mother couldn't afford to buy razors - and his great strong arms, and bare legs, and no covering but the goat-skin that reached from his waist to his knees. But an envious wizened bit of a fellow, with a red head, that wished to be married to the princess, and didn't like how she opened her eyes at Tom, came forward, and asked his business very snappishly.

"My business," says Tom, says he, "is to make the beautiful princess, God bless her, laugh three times."

"Do you see all of them merry fellows and skilful swordsmen," says the other, "that could eat you up with a grain of salt, and not a mother's soul of them ever got a laugh from her these seven years?"

So the fellows gathered round Tom, and the bad man aggravated him till he told them he didn't care a pinch o' snuff for the whole bilin' of them; let them come on, six at a time, and try what they could do.

The king, who was too far off to hear what they were saying, asked what the stranger wanted.

"He wants," says the red-headed fellow, "to make hares of your best men."

"Oh!" says the king, "if that's the way, let one of them turn out and try his mettle."

So one stood forward, with sword and pot-lid, and made a cut at Tom. He struck the fellow's elbow with the club, and up over their heads flew the sword, and down went the owner of it on the gravel from a thump he got on the helmet. Another took his place, and another, and another, and then half a dozen at once, and Tom sent swords, helmets, shields, and bodies, rolling over and over, and themselves bawling out that they were kilt, and disabled, and damaged, and rubbing their poor elbows and hips, and limping away. Tom contrived not to kill anyone; and the princess was so amused, that she let a great sweet laugh out of her that was heard over all the yard.

"King of Dublin," says Tom, "I've quarter your daughter."

And the king didn't know whether he was glad or sorry, and all the blood in the princess's heart run into her cheeks.

So there was no more fighting that day, and Tom was invited to dine with the royal family. Next day, Redhead told Tom of a wolf, the size of a yearling heifer, that used to be serenading about the walls, and eating people and cattle; and said what a pleasure it would give the king to have it killed.

"With all my heart," says Tom, "send a jackeen to show me where he lives, and we'll see how he behaves to a stranger."

The princess was not well pleased, for Tom looked a different person with fine clothes and a nice green birredh over his long curly hair; and besides, he'd got one laugh out of her. However, the king gave his consent; and in an hour and a half the horrible wolf was walking into the palace-yard, and Tom a step or two behind, with his club on his shoulder, just as a shepherd would be walking after a pet lamb.

The king and queen and princess were safe up in their gallery, but the officers and people of the court that were patrolling about the great barn, when they saw the big beast coming in, gave themselves up, and began to make for doors and gates; and the wolf licked his chops, as if he was saying, "Wouldn't I enjoy a breakfast off a couple of you!"

The king shouted out, "O Tom with the Goat-skin, take away that terrible wolf, and you must have all my daughter."

But Tom didn't mind him a bit. He pulled out his flute and began to play like vengeance; and dickens a man or boy in the yard but began shovelling away heel and toe, and the wolf himself was obliged to get on his hind legs and dance "Tatther Jack Walsh," along with the rest. A good deal of the people got inside, and shut the doors, the way the hairy fellow wouldn't pin them; but Tom kept playing, and the outsiders kept dancing and shouting, and the wolf kept dancing and roaring with the pain his legs were giving him; and all the time he had his eyes on Redhead, who was shut out along with the rest. Wherever Redhead went, the wolf followed, and kept one eye on him and the other on Tom, to see if he would give him leave to eat him. But Tom shook his head, and never stopped the tune, and Redhead never stopped dancing and bawling, and the wolf dancing and roaring, one leg up and the other down, and he ready to drop out of his standing from fair tiresomeness.

When the princess seen that there was no fear of any one being kilt, she was so diverted by the stew that Redhead was in, that she gave another great laugh; and well become Tom, out he cried, "King of Dublin, I have two halves of your daughter."

"Oh, halves or alls," says the king, "put away that devil of a wolf, and we'll see about it."

So Tom put his flute in his pocket, and says he to the baste that was sitting on his currabingo ready to faint, "Walk off to your mountain, my fine fellow, and live like a respectable baste; and if ever I find you come within seven miles of any town, I'll - "

He said no more, but spit in his fist, and gave a flourish of his club. It was all the poor devil of a wolf wanted, and he put his tail between his legs, and took to his pumps without looking at man or mortal, and neither sun, moon, nor stars ever saw him in sight of Dublin again.

At dinner everyone laughed but the foxy fellow; and sure enough he was laying out how he'd settle poor Tom next day.

"Well, to be sure!" says he, "King of Dublin, you are in luck. There's the Danes murdering us to no end. Deuce run to Lusk with them! and if anyone can save us from them, it is this gentleman with the goat-skin. There is a flail hanging on the collar-beam, in hell, and neither Dane nor devil can stand before it."

"So," says Tom to the king, "will you let me have the other half of the princess if I bring you the flail?"

"No, no," says the princess, "I'd rather never be your wife than see you in that danger."

But Redhead whispered and nudged Tom about how shabby it would look to renege the adventure. So he asked which way he was to go, and Redhead directed him.

Well, he travelled and travelled, till he came in sight of the walls of hell; and bedad, before he knocked at the gates, he rubbed himself over with the greenish ointment. When he knocked, a hundred little imps popped their heads out through the bars, and axed him what he wanted.

"I want to speak to the big devil of all," says Tom, "open the gate."

It wasn't long till the gate was thrown open, and the Old Boy received Tom with bows and scrapes, and asked his business.

"My business isn't much," says Tom. "I only came for the loan of that flail that I see hanging on the collar-beam, for the king of Dublin to give a thrashing to the Danes."

"Well," says the other, "the Danes is much better customers to me;

but since you walked so far I won't refuse. Hand that flail," says he to a young imp; and he winked the far-off eye at the same time. So, while some were barring the gates, the young devil climbed up, and took down the flail that had the hand staff and booltheen both made out of red-hot iron. The little vagabond was grinning to think how it would burn the hands o' Tom, but the dickens a burn it made on him, no more nor if it was a good oak sapling.

"Thank you," says Tom. "Now would you open the gate for a body, and I'll give you no more trouble."

"Oh, tramp!" says Old Nick, "is that the way? It is easier getting inside them gates than getting out again. Take that tool from him, and give him a dose of the oil of stirrup."

So one fellow put out his claws to seize on the flail, but Tom gave him such a welt of it on the side of the head that he broke off one of his horns, and made him roar like a devil as he was. Well, they rushed at Tom, but he gave them, little and big, such a thrashing as they didn't forget for a while. At last says the old thief of all, rubbing his elbow, "Let the fool out; and woe to whoever lets him in again, great or small."

So out marched Tom, and away with him, without minding the shouting and cursing they kept up at him from the tops of the walls; and when he got home to the big bawn of the palace, there never was such running and racing as to see himself and the flail. When he had his story told, he laid down the flail on the stone steps, and bid no one for their lives to touch it. If the king, and queen, and princess, made much of him before, they made ten times more of him now; but Redhead, the mean scruff-hound, stole over, and thought to catch hold of the flail to make an end of him. His fingers hardly touched it, when he let a roar out of him as if heaven and earth were coming together, and kept flinging his arms about and dancing, that it was pitiful to look at him. Tom run at him as soon as he could rise, caught his hands in his own two, and rubbed them this way and that, and the burning pain left them before you could reckon one. Well the poor fellow, between the pain that was only just gone, and the comfort he was in, had the most comical face that you ever see, it was such a mixtherum-gatherum of laughing and crying. Everybody burst out a laughing - the princess could not stop no more than the rest; and then says Tom, "Now, ma'am, if there were fifty halves of you, I hope you'll give me them all."

Well, the princess looked at her father, and by my word, she came over to Tom, and put her two delicate hands into his two rough ones, and I wish it was myself was in his shoes that day!

Tom would not bring the flail into the palace. You may be sure no other body went near it; and when the early risers were passing next morning, they found two long clefts in the stone, where it was after burning itself an opening downwards, nobody could tell how far. But a messenger came in at noon, and said that the Danes were so frightened when they heard of the flail coming into Dublin, that they got into their ships, and sailed away.

Well, I suppose, before they were married, Tom got some man, like Pat Mara of Tomenine, to learn him the "principles of politeness," fluxions, gunnery, and fortification, decimal fractions, practice, and the rule of three direct, the way he'd be able to keep up a conversation with the royal family. Whether he ever lost his time learning them sciences, I'm not sure, but it's as sure as fate that his mother never more saw any want till the end of her days.

Tales From The Land Of Saints & Scholars

The Lazy Beauty and her Aunts

"The Lazy Beauty and Her Aunts" is a traditional Irish folk tale first collected by Patrick Kennedy, the 19th-century folklorist from County Wexford, and later adapted by W. B. Yeats for his Fairy and Folk Tales of the Irish Peasantry (1888, The Walter Scott Publishing Company). It is a variant of a widespread European story type that rewards virtue and industry while mocking vanity and idleness, akin to "The Three Spinners" found in German and English traditions.

The tale combines humour with a sly social commentary, turning a moral fable on its head. Idleness triumphs through cunning and feminine charm, while the virtues of toil are playfully undermined. In Yeats's hands, the story's rustic wit and light irony preserve the music of Irish peasant storytelling, where common sense often outsmarts convention and laughter is its own form of wisdom.

There was once a poor widow woman, who had a daughter that was as handsome as the day, and as lazy as a pig, saving your presence. The poor mother was the most industrious person in the townland, and was a particularly good hand at the spinning-wheel. It was the wish of her heart that her daughter should be as handy as herself; but she'd get up late, eat her breakfast before she'd finish her prayers, and then go about dawdling, and anything she handled seemed to be burning her fingers. She drawled her words as if it was a great trouble to her to speak, or as if her tongue was as lazy as her body.

Many a heart-scald her poor mother got with her, and still she was only improving like dead fowl in August.

Well, one morning that things were as bad as they could be, and the poor woman was giving tongue at the rate of a mill-clapper, who should be riding by but the king's son. "Oh dear, oh dear, good woman!" said he, "you must have a very bad child to make you scold so terribly. Sure it can't be this handsome girl that vexed you!" "Oh, please your Majesty, not at all," says the old dissembler. "I was only checking her for working herself too much. Would your majesty believe it? She spins three pounds of flax in a day, weaves it into linen the next, and makes it all into shirts the day after." "My gracious," says the prince, "she's the very lady that will just fill my mother's eye, and with her being the greatest spinner in the kingdom. Will you put on your daughter's bonnet and cloak, if you please, ma'am, and set her behind me? Why, my mother will be so delighted with her, that perhaps she'll make the girl her daughter-in-law in a week, that is, if the young woman herself is agreeable."

Well, between the confusion, and the joy, and the fear of being found out, the women didn't know what to do; and before they could make up their minds, young Anty (Anastasia) was set behind the prince, and away he and his attendants went, and a good heavy purse was left behind with the mother. She pullillued a long time after all was gone, in dread of something bad happening to the poor girl.

The prince couldn't judge of the girl's breeding or wit from the few answers he pulled out of her. The queen was struck in a heap when she saw a young country girl sitting behind her son, but when she saw her handsome face, and heard all she could do, she didn't think she could make too much of her. The prince took an opportunity of whispering her that if she didn't object to be his wife she must strive to please his mother. Well, the evening went by, and the prince and

Anty were getting fonder and fonder of one another, but the thought of the spinning used to send the cold to her heart every moment. When bedtime came, the old queen went along with her to a beautiful bedroom, and when she was bidding her good-night, she pointed to a heap of fine flax, and said, "You may begin as soon as you like tomorrow morning, and I'll expect to see these three pounds in nice thread the morning after." Little did the poor girl sleep that night. She kept crying and lamenting that she didn't mind her mother's advice better. When she was left alone next morning, she began with a heavy heart; and though she had a nice mahogany wheel and the finest flax you ever saw, the thread was breaking every moment. One while it was as fine as a cobweb, and the next as coarse as a little boy's whipcord. At last she pushed her chair back, let her hands fall in her lap, and burst out a-crying.

A small, old woman with surprising big feet appeared before her at the same moment, and said, "What ails you, you handsome colleen?" "An' haven't I all that flax to spin before tomorrow morning, and I'll never be able to have even five yards of fine thread of it put together." "An' would you think bad to ask poor Colliagh Cuslmōr (Old woman Big-foot) to your wedding with the young prince? If you promise me that, all your three pounds will be made into the finest of thread while you're taking your sleep to-night." "Indeed, you must be there and welcome, and I'll honour you all the days of your life." "Very well; stay in your room till tea-time, and tell the queen she may come in for her thread as early as she likes to-morrow morning." It was all as she said; and the thread was finer and evener than the gut you see with fly-fishers. "My brave girl you were!" says the queen. "I'll get my own mahogany loom brought into you, but you needn't do anything more to-day. Work and rest, work and rest, is my motto. To-morrow you'll weave all this thread, and who knows what may happen?"

The poor girl was more frightened this time than the last, and she was so afraid to lose the prince. She didn't even know how to put the warp in the gears, nor how to use the shuttle, and she was sitting in the greatest grief, when a little woman, who was mighty well-shouldered about the hips, all at once appeared to her, saying her name was Colliach Cromanmōr, and made the same bargain with her as Colliach Cushmōr. Great was the queen's pleasure when she found early in the morning a web as fine and white as the finest paper you ever saw. "The darling you were!" says she. "Take your ease with the ladies and gentlemen to-day, and if you have all this made into nice shirts to-morrow you may present one of them to my son, and be married to him out of hand."

Oh, wouldn't you pity poor Anty the next day, she was now so near the prince, and, maybe, would be soon so far from him. But she waited as patiently as she could with scissors, needle, and thread in hand, till a minute after noon. Then she was rejoiced to see the third old woman appear. She had a big red nose, and informed Anty that people called her Shron Mor Rua on that account. She was up to her as good as the others, for a dozen fine shirts were lying on the table when the queen paid her an early visit.

Now there was nothing talked of but the wedding, and I needn't tell you it was grand. The poor mother was there along with the rest, and at the dinner the old queen could talk of nothing but the lovely shirts, and how happy herself and the bride would be after the honeymoon, spinning, and weaving, and sewing shirts and shifts without end. The bridegroom didn't like the discourse, and the bride liked it less, and he was going to say something, when the footman came up to the head of the table and said to the bride, "Your ladyship's aunt, Colliach Cushmōr, bade me ask might she come in." The bride blushed and wished she was seven miles under the floor, but well became the prince. "Tell Mrs. Cushmōr," said he, "that any relation of my bride's will be always heartily welcome wherever she and I are." In came the woman with the big foot, and got a seat near the prince. The old queen didn't like it much, and after a few words she asked rather spitefully, "Dear ma'am, what's the reason your foot is so big?" "Musha, faith, your majesty, I was standing almost all my life at the spinning-wheel, and that's the reason." "I declare to you, my darling," said the prince, "I'll never allow you to spend one hour at the same spinning-wheel." The same footman said again, "Your ladyship's aunt, Colliach Cromanmōr, wishes to come in, if the genteels and yourself have no objection." Very sharoose (displeased) was Princess Anty, but the prince sent her welcome, and she took her seat, and drank healths apiece to the company. "May I ask, ma'am?" says the old queen, "why you're so wide half-way between the head and the feet?" "That, your majesty, is owing to sitting all my life at the loom." "By my sceptre," says the prince, "my wife shall never sit there an hour." The footman again came up. "Your ladyship's aunt, Colliach Shron Mor Rua, is asking leave to come into the banquet." More blushing on the bride's face, but the bridegroom spoke out cordially, "Tell Mrs. Shron Mor Rua she's doing us an honour." In came the old woman, and great respect she got near the top of the table, but the people down low put up their tumblers and glasses to their noses to hide the grins. "Ma'am," says the old queen, "will you tell us, if you please, why your nose is so big and red?" "Truth, your majesty, my head was bent down over the stitching all my life, and all the blood in my body ran into my nose." "My darling," said the prince to Anty, "if ever I see a needle in your hand, I'll run a hundred miles from you."

"And in truth, girls and boys, though it's a diverting story, I don't think the moral is good; and if any of you thuckeens go about imitating Anty in her laziness, you'll find it won't thrive with you as it did with her. She was beautiful beyond compare, which none of you are, and she had three powerful fairies to help her besides. There's no fairies now, and no prince or lord to ride by, and catch you idling or working; and maybe, after all, the prince and herself were not so very happy when the cares of the world or old age came on them."

Thus was the tale ended by poor old Shebale (Sybilla), Father Murphy's housekeeper, in Coolbawn, Barony of Bantry, about half a century since.

Tales From The Land Of Saints & Scholars

The Legend of Knockfierna

"The Legend of Knockfierna", adapted from Thomas Crofton Croker's Fairy Legends and Traditions of the South of Ireland (first published 1825–1828), tells of the haunted hill of Knockfierna in County Limerick, long believed to be the dwelling place of Donn Firinne, "Donn of Truth", one of the great fairy chieftains of Munster.

Croker's version blends the supernatural with the moral realism typical of early nineteenth-century Irish folklore collections. Knockfierna's story serves as both warning and wonder tale, a reminder that the old hills of Ireland are not mere scenery but living presences, to be respected and feared.

It is a very good thing not to be any way in dread of the fairies, for without doubt they have less power over a person; but to make too free with them, or to disbelieve in them altogether, is as foolish a thing as man, woman, or child can do.

It has been truly said, that "good manners are no burden," and that "civility costs nothing;" but there are some people fool-hardy enough to disregard doing a civil thing, which, whatever they may think, can never harm themselves or anyone else, and who at the same time will go out of their way for a bit of mischief, which never can serve them; but sooner or later they will come to know better, as you shall hear of Carroll O'Daly, a strapping young fellow up out of Connaught, whom they used to call, in his own country, "Devil Daly."

Carroll O'Daly used to go roving about from one place to another, and the fear of nothing stopped him; he would as soon pass an old churchyard or a regular fairy ground, at any hour of the night as go from one room into another, without ever making the sign of the cross, or saying, "Good luck attend you, gentlemen."

It so happened that he was once journeying, in the county of Limerick, towards "the Balbec of Ireland," the venerable town of Kilmallock; and just at the foot of Knockfierna he overtook a respectable-looking man jogging along upon a white pony. The night was coming on, and they rode side by side for some time, without much conversation passing between them, further than saluting each other very kindly; at last, Carroll O'Daly asked his companion how far he was going?

"Not far your way," said the farmer, for such his appearance bespoke him, "I'm only going to the top of this hill here."

"And what might take you there," said O'Daly, "at this time of the night?"

"Why then," replied the farmer, "if you want to know, 'tis the good people."

"The fairies you mean," said O'Daly.

"Whist! whist!" said his fellow-traveller, "or you may be sorry for it;" and he turned his pony off the road they were going, towards a little path which led up the side of the mountain, wishing Carroll O'Daly good night and a safe journey.

"That fellow," thought Carroll, "is about no good this blessed night, and I would have no fear of swearing wrong if I took my Bible oath that it is something else beside the fairies, or the good people, as he calls them, that is taking him up the mountain at this hour. The fairies!" he repeated, "is it for a well-shaped man like him to be going after little chaps like the fairies! To be sure some say there are such things, and more say not; but I know this, that never afraid would I be of a dozen of them, ay, of two dozen, for that matter, if they are no bigger than what I hear tell of."

Carroll O'Daly, whilst these thoughts were passing in his mind, had fixed his eyes steadfastly on the mountain, behind which the full moon was rising majestically. Upon an elevated point that appeared darkly against the moon's disk, he beheld the figure of a man leading a pony, and he had no doubt it was that of the farmer with whom he had just parted company.

A sudden resolve to follow flashed across the mind of O'Daly with the speed of lightning, for both his courage and curiosity had been worked up by his cogitations to a pitch of chivalry; and, muttering, "Here's after you, old boy!" he dismounted from his horse, bound him to an old thorn tree, and then commenced vigorously ascending the mountain.

Following as well as he could the direction taken by the figures of the man and pony, he pursued his way, occasionally guided by their partial appearance, and after toiling nearly three hours over a rugged and sometimes swampy path, came to a green spot on the top of the mountain, where he saw the white pony at full liberty grazing as quietly as may be. O'Daly looked around for the rider, but he was nowhere to be seen; he, however, soon discovered, close to where the pony stood, an opening in the mountain like the mouth of a pit, and he remembered having heard, when a child, many a tale about the "Poul-duve," or Black Hole of Knockfierna; how it was the entrance to the fairy castle which was within the mountain; and how a man whose name was Ahern, a land surveyor in that part of the country, had once attempted to fathom it with a line, and had been drawn down into it, and was never again heard of; with many other tales of the like nature.

"But" thought O'Daly, "these are old woman's stories, and since I've come up so far, I'll just knock at the castle door and see if the fairies are at home."

No sooner said than done; for, seizing a large stone, as big, ay, bigger than his two hands, he flung it with all his strength down into the Poul-duve of Knockfierna. He heard it bounding and tumbling about from one rock to another with a terrible noise, and he leaned his head over to try and hear when it would reach the bottom, and what should the very stone he had thrown in do but come up again with as much force as it had gone down, and gave him such a blow full in the face, that it sent him rolling down the side of Knockfierna, head over heels, tumbling from one crag to another, much faster than he came up. And in the morning Carroll O'Daly was found lying beside his horse; the bridge of his nose broken, which disfigured him for life; his head all cut and bruised, and both his eyes closed up, and as black as if Sir Daniel Donnelly had painted them for him.

Carroll O'Daly was never bold again in riding along near the haunts of the fairies after dusk; but small blame to him for that; and if ever he happened to be benighted in a lonesome place, he would make the best of his way to his journey's end, without asking questions, or turning to the right or to the left, to seek after the good people, or any who kept company with them.

The Legend of Knockshegowna

"The Legend of Knockshegowna", adapted from Thomas Crofton Croker's Fairy Legends and Traditions of the South of Ireland (1825–1828), is a lively Munster tale rooted in Ireland's deep fairy lore and its wry moral humour.

Croker's version, though framed as light folklore, preserves the older moral structure of the fairy cautionary tale, where mocking the unseen world invites retribution, and pride leads to enchantment or ruin. His tone balances rustic comedy with quiet unease, capturing how fairies in Irish tradition were both mischievous neighbours and moral enforcers.

In Tipperary is one of the most singularly shaped hills in the world. It has got a peak at the top like a conical nightcap thrown carelessly over your head as you awake in the morning. On the very point is built a sort of lodge, where in the summer the lady who built it and her friends used to go on parties of pleasure; but that was long after the days of the fairies, and it is, I believe, now deserted.

But before lodge was built, or acre sown, there was close to the head of this hill a large pasturage, where a herdsman spent his days and nights among the herd. The spot had been an old fairy ground, and the good people were angry that the scene of their light and airy gambols should be trampled by the rude hoofs of bulls and cows. The lowing of the cattle sounded sad in their ears, and the chief of the fairies of the hill determined in person to drive away the newcomers; and the way she thought of was this. When the harvest nights came on, and the moon shone bright and brilliant over the hill, and the cattle were lying down hushed and quiet, and the herdsman, wrapt in his mantle, was musing with his heart gladdened by the glorious company of the stars twinkling above him, she would come and dance before him, - now in one shape - now in another, - but all ugly and frightful to behold. One time she would be a great horse, with the wings of an eagle, and a tail like a dragon, hissing loud and spitting fire. Then in a moment she would change into a little man lame of a leg, with a bull's head, and a lambent flame playing round it. Then into a great ape, with duck's feet, and a turkey cock's tail. But I should be all day about it were I to tell you all the shapes she took. And then she would roar, or neigh, or hiss, or bellow, or howl, or hoot, as never yet was roaring, neighing, hissing, bellowing, howling, or hooting, heard in this world before or since. The poor herdsman would cover his face, and call on all the saints for help, but it was no use. With one puff of her breath she would blow away the fold of his great coat, let him hold it never so tightly over his eyes, and not a saint in heaven paid him the slightest attention. And to make matters worse, he never could stir; no, nor even shut his eyes, but there was obliged to stay, held by what power he knew not, gazing at these terrible sights until the hair of his head would lift his hat half a foot over his crown, and his teeth would be ready to fall out from chattering. But the cattle would scamper about mad, as if they were bitten by the fly; and this would last until the sun rose over the hill.

The poor cattle from want of rest were pining away, and food did them no good; besides, they met with accidents without end. Never a night passed that some of them did not fall into a pit, and get maimed, or, may be, killed. Some would tumble into a river and be drowned; in a word, there seemed never to be an end of the accidents. But what made the matter worse, there could not be a herdsman got to tend the cattle by night. One visit from the fairy drove the stoutest hearted almost mad. The owner of the ground did not know what to do. He offered double, triple, quadruple wages, but not a man could be found for the sake of money to go through the horror of facing the fairy. She rejoiced at the successful issue of her project, and continued her pranks. The herd gradually thinning, and no man daring to remain on the ground, the fairies came back in numbers, and gambolled as merrily as before, quaffing dew-drops from acorns, and spreading their feast on the heads of capacious mushrooms.

What was to be done? the puzzled farmer thought in vain. He found that his substance was daily diminishing, his people terrified, and his rent-day coming round. It is no wonder that he looked gloomy, and walked mournfully down the road. Now in that part of the world dwelt a man of the name of Larry Hoolahan, who played on the pipes better than any other player within fifteen parishes. A roving, dashing blade was Larry, and feared nothing. Give him plenty of liquor, and he would defy the devil. He would face a mad bull, or fight single-handed against a fair. In one of his gloomy walks the farmer met him, and on Larry's asking the cause of his down looks, he told him all his misfortunes. "If that is all ails you," said Larry, "make your mind easy. Were there as many fairies on Knockshegowna as there are potato blossoms in Eliogurty, I would face them. It would be a queer thing, indeed, if I, who never was afraid of a proper man, should turn my back upon a brat of a fairy not the bigness of one's thumb." "Larry," said the farmer, "do not talk so bold, for you know not who is hearing you; but if you make your words good, and watch my herds for a week on the top of the mountain, your hand shall be free of my dish till the sun has burnt itself down to the bigness of a farthing rush light."

The bargain was struck, and Larry went to the hilltop, when the moon began to peep over the brow. He had been regaled at the farmer's house, and was bold with the extract of barley-corn. So he took his seat on a big stone under a hollow of the hill, with his back to the wind, and pulled out his pipes. He had not played long when the voice of the fairies was heard upon the blast, like a slow stream of music. Presently they burst out into a loud laugh, and Larry could plainly hear one say, "What! another man upon the fairies' ring? Go to him, queen, and make him repent his rashness;" and they flew away. Larry felt them pass by his face as they flew, like a swarm of midges; and, looking up hastily, he saw between the moon and him a great black cat, standing on the very tip of its claws, with its back up, and mewing with the voice of a water-mill. Presently it swelled up towards the sky, and turning round on its left hind-leg, whirled till it fell to the ground, from which it started up in the shape of a salmon, with a cravat round its neck, and a pair of new top boots. "Go on, jewel," said Larry, "if you dance, I'll pipe;" and he struck up. So she turned into this, and that, and the other, but still Larry played on, as he well knew how. At last she lost patience, as ladies will do when you do not mind their scolding, and changed herself into a calf, milk-white as the cream of Cork, and with eyes as mild as those of the girl I love. She came up gentle and fawning, in hopes to throw him off his guard by quietness, and then to work him some wrong. But Larry was not so deceived; for when she came up, he, dropping his pipes, leaped upon her back.

Now from the top of Knockshegowna, as you look westward to the broad Atlantic, you will see the Shannon, queen of rivers, "spreading like a sea," and running on in gentle course to mingle with the ocean through the fair city of Limerick. It on this night shone under the moon, and looked beautiful from the distant hill. Fifty boats were gliding up and down on the sweet current, and the song of the fishermen rose gaily from the shore. Larry, as I said before, leaped upon the back of the fairy, and she, rejoiced at the opportunity, sprung from the hill-top, and bounded clear, at one jump, over the Shannon, flowing as it was just ten miles from the mountain's base. It was done in a second, and when she alighted on the distant bank, kicking up her heels, she flung Larry on the soft turf. No sooner was he thus planted, than he looked her straight in the face, and scratching his head, cried out, "By my word, well done! that was not a bad leap for a calf!"

She looked at him for a moment, and then assumed her own shape. "Laurence," said she, "you are a bold fellow; will you come back the way you went?" "And that's what I will," said he, "if you let me." So changing to a calf again, again Larry got on her back, and at another bound they were again upon the top of Knockshegowna. The fairy, once more resuming her figure, addressed him, "You have shown so much courage, Laurence," said she, "that while you keep herds on this hill you never shall be molested by me or mine. The day dawns, go down to the farmer, and tell him this; and if anything I can do may be of service to you, ask, and you shall have it." She vanished accordingly; and kept her word in never visiting the hill during Larry's life, but he never troubled her with requests. He piped and drank at the farmer's expense, and roosted in his chimney corner, occasionally casting an eye to the flock. He died at last, and is buried in a green valley of pleasant Tipperary, but whether the fairies returned to the hill of Knockshegowna after his death, is more than I can say.

Tales From The Land Of Saints & Scholars

The Legend of O'Donoghue

"The Legend of O'Donoghue" is a romantic and haunting tale drawn from the folklore of County Kerry, first recorded by Thomas Crofton Croker in his Fairy Legends and Traditions of the South of Ireland (1825–1828), and later adapted by W. B. Yeats in Fairy and Folk Tales of the Irish Peasantry (1888, The Walter Scott Publishing Company). The story centres on O'Donoghue Mór, the legendary chieftain of Killarney's Lakes, who was said to have ruled with justice and wisdom before vanishing one May morning into the waters of Lough Leane.

Yeats's adaptation preserves the tale's air of melancholy beauty, transforming Croker's antiquarian account into a lyrical vision of Ireland's living myth. The story embodies the Irish belief in the undying presence of ancestral spirits, protectors of land and people who inhabit the thresholds between worlds. It also reflects the Romantic fascination with Ireland's landscape as sacred and animate, where mist, mountain, and lake hold memory and promise.

In an age so distant that the precise period is unknown, a chieftain named O'Donoghue ruled over the country which surrounds the romantic Lough Lean, now called the lake of Killarney. Wisdom, beneficence, and justice distinguished his reign, and the prosperity and happiness of his subjects were their natural results. He is said to have been as renowned for his warlike exploits as for his pacific virtues; and as a proof that his domestic administration was not the less rigorous because it was mild, a rocky island is pointed out to strangers, called "O'Donoghue's Prison," in which this prince once confined his own son for some act of disorder and disobedience.

His end - for it cannot correctly be called his death - was singular and mysterious. At one of those splendid feasts for which his court was celebrated, surrounded by the most distinguished of his subjects, he was engaged in a prophetic relation of the events which were to happen in ages yet to come. His auditors listened, now wrapt in wonder, now fired with indignation, burning with shame, or melted into sorrow, as he faithfully detailed the heroism, the injuries, the crimes, and the miseries of their descendants. In the midst of his predictions he rose slowly from his seat, advanced with a solemn, measured, and majestic tread to the shore of the lake, and walked forward composedly upon its unyielding surface. When he had nearly reached the centre he paused for a moment, then, turning slowly round, looked toward his friends, and waving his arms to them with the cheerful air of one taking a short farewell, disappeared from their view.

The memory of the good O'Donoghue has been cherished by successive generations with affectionate reverence; and it is believed that at sunrise, on every May-day morning, the anniversary of his departure, he revisits his ancient domains. A favoured few only are in general permitted to see him, and this distinction is always an omen of good fortune to the beholders; when it is granted to many it is a sure token of an abundant harvest, a blessing, the want of which during this prince's reign was never felt by his people.

Some years have elapsed since the last appearance of O'Donoghue. The April of that year had been remarkably wild and stormy; but on May-morning the fury of the elements had altogether subsided. The air was hushed and still; and the sky, which was reflected in the serene lake, resembled a beautiful but deceitful countenance, whose smiles, after the most tempestuous emotions, tempt the stranger to believe that it belongs to a soul which no passion has ever ruffled.

The first beams of the rising sun were just gilding the lofty summit of Glenaa, when the waters near the eastern shore of the lake became suddenly and violently agitated, though all the rest of its surface lay smooth and still as a tomb of polished marble, the next morning a foaming wave darted forward, and, like a proud high-crested war-horse, exulting in his strength, rushed across the lake toward Toomies mountain. Behind this wave appeared a stately warrior fully armed, mounted upon a milk-white steed; his snowy plume waved gracefully from a helmet of polished steel, and at his back fluttered a light blue scarf. The horse, apparently exulting in his noble burden, sprung after the wave along the water, which bore him up like firm earth, while showers of spray that glittered brightly in the morning sun were dashed up at every bound.

The warrior was O'Donoghue; he was followed by numberless youths and maidens, who moved lightly and unconstrained over the watery plain, as the moonlight fairies glide through the fields of air; they were linked together by garlands of delicious spring flowers, and they timed their movements to strains of enchanting melody. When O'Donoghue had nearly reached the western side of the lake, he suddenly turned his steed, and directed his course along the wood-fringed shore of Glenaa, preceded by the huge wave that curled and foamed up as high as the horse's neck, whose fiery nostrils snorted above it. The long train of attendants followed with playful deviations the track of their leader, and moved on with unabated fleetness to their celestial music, till gradually, as they entered the narrow strait between Glenaa and Dinis, they became involved in the mists which still partially floated over the lakes, and faded from the view of the wondering beholders, but the sound of their music still fell upon the ear, and echo, catching up the harmonious strains, fondly repeated and prolonged them in soft and softer tones, till the last faint repetition died away, and the hearers awoke as from a dream of bliss.

Tales From The Land Of Saints & Scholars

The Little Weaver of Duleek Gate

"The Little Weaver of Duleek Gate" is a mischievous and whimsical Irish folktale, first told by Samuel Lover and later adapted by W. B. Yeats for his Irish Fairy Tales. The story centres on a poor but cheerful weaver who lives near Duleek Gate and spends his nights singing at his loom.

In Yeats's retelling, the tale takes on a gentle melancholy: the weaver's gift for song has made him beloved by the fairies, but it has also cost him his place in time. The story blends comedy and pathos, capturing the Irish sense that joy and sorrow, the real and the unreal, are never far apart.

You see, there was a weaver lived, once upon a time, in Duleek here, hard by the gate, and a very honest, industrious man he was, by all accounts. He had a wife, and of course they had children, and small blame to them, and plenty of them, so that the poor little weaver was obliged to work his fingers to the bone almost to get them the bit and the sup; but he didn't begrudge that, for he was an industrious creature, as I said before, and it was up early and down late with him, and the loom never standing still. Well, it was one morning that his wife called to him, and he sitting very busy throwing the shuttle; and says she, 'Come here,' says she, 'jewel, and eat your breakfast, now that it's ready.' But he never minded her, but went on working. So in a minute or two more, says she, calling out to him again, 'Arrah, leave off slaving yourself, my darling, and eat your bit o' breakfast while it is hot.'

'Leave me alone,' says he, and he drove the shuttle faster nor before.

Well, in a little time more, she goes over to him where he sat, and says she, coaxing him like, 'Thady, dear,' says she, 'the stirabout will be stone cold if you don't give over that weary work and come and eat it at once.'

'I'm busy with a pattern here that is breaking my heart,' says the weaver, 'and until I complete it and master it entirely, I won't quit.'

'Oh, think o' the lovely stirabout, that'll be spoilt entirely.'

'To the devil with the stirabout,' says he.

'God forgive you,' says she, 'for cursing your good breakfast.'

'Ay, and you too,' says he.

'Truth, you're as cross as two sticks this blessed morning, Thady,' says the poor wife, 'and it's a heavy handful I have of you when you are crooked in your temper; but stay there if you like, and let your stirabout grow cold, and not a one o' me'll ask you again;' and with that off she went, and the weaver, sure enough, was mighty crabbed, and the more the wife spoke to him the worse he got, which, you know, is only natural. Well, he left the loom at last, and went over to the stirabout, and what would you think but when he looked at it, it was as black as a crow; for, you see, it was in the height o' summer, and the flies lit upon it to that degree that the stirabout was fairly covered with them.

'Why, thin, bad luck to your impudence,' says the weaver, 'would no place serve you but that? and is it spoiling my breakfast you are, you dirty beasts?' And with that, being altogether crooked-tempered at the time, he lifted his hand, and he made one great slam at the dish o' stirabout, and killed no less than three score and tin flies at the one blow. It was three score and tin exactly, for he counted the carcasses one by one, and laid them out on a clean plate, for to view them.

Well, he felt a powerful spirit rising in him, when he seen the slaughter he done, at one blow; and with that he got as conceited as the very dickens, and not a stroke more work he'd do that day, but out he went, and was fractious and impudent to everyone he met, and was squaring up into their faces and saying, 'Look at that fist! that's the fist that killed three score and tin at one blow - Whoo!'

With that all the neighbours thought he was cracked, and faith, the poor wife herself thought the same when he came home in the evening, after spending every rap he had in drink, and swaggering about the place, and looking at his hand every minute.

'Indeed, an' your hand is very dirty, sure enough, Thady jewel,' says the poor wife; and true for her, for he rolled into a ditch coming home. 'You had better wash it, darling.'

'How dare you say dirty to the greatest hand in Ireland?' says he, going to beat her.

'Well, it's not dirty,' says she.

'It is throwing away my time I have been all my life,' says he, 'living with you at all, and stuck at a loom, nothing but a poor weaver, when it is Saint George or the Dragon I ought to be, which is two of the seven champions o' Christendom.'

'Well, suppose they christened him twice as much,' says the wife, 'sure, what's that to us?'

'Don't put in your prate,' says he, 'you ignorant strap,' says he. 'You're vulgar, woman - you're vulgar - mighty vulgar; but I'll have nothing more to say to any dirty sneaking trade again - devil a more weaving I'll do.'

'Oh, Thady dear, and what'll the children do then?'

'Let them go play marbles,' says he.

'That would be but poor feeding for them, Thady.'

'They shan't want for feeding,' says he, 'for it's a rich man I'll be soon, and a great man too.'

'Usha, but I'm glad to hear it, darling, - though I don't know how it's to be, but I think you had better go to bed, Thady.'

'Don't talk to me of any bed but the bed o' glory, woman,' says he, looking martial grand.

'Oh! God send we'll all be in glory yet,' says the wife, crossing herself, 'but go to sleep, Thady, for this present.'

'I'll sleep with the brave yet,' says he.

'Indeed, an' a brave sleep will do you a power o' good, my darling,' says she.

'And it's I that will be the knight!' says he.

'All night, if you please, Thady,' says she.

'None o' your coaxing,' says he. 'I'm determined on it, and I'll set off immediately, and be a knight errant.'

'A what?' says she.

'A knight errant, woman.'

'Lord, be good to me, what's that?' says she.

'A knight errant is a real gentleman,' says he, 'going round the world for sport, with a sword by his side, taking whatever he pleases for himself; and that's a knight errant,' says he.

Well, sure enough he went about among his neighbours the next day, and he got an old kettle from one, and a saucepan from another; and he took them to the tailor, and he sewed him up a suit o' tin clothes like any knight errant, and he borrowed a pot lid, and that he was very particular about, because it was his shield and he went to a friend o' his, a painter and glazier, and made him paint on his shield in big letters:

'I'M THE MAN OF ALL MEN,

THAT KILL'D THREE SCORE AND TEN

AT A BLOW.'

'When the people sees that,' says the weaver to himself, 'there's none will dare to come near me.'

And with that he told the wife to scour out the small iron pot for him, 'For,' says he, 'it will make an elegant helmet'; and when it was done, he put it on his head, and his wife said, 'Oh, murder, Thady jewel, is it putting a great heavy iron pot on your head you are, by way of a hat?'

'Certainly,' says he, 'for a knight errant should always have a weight on his brain.'

'But Thady dear,' says the wife, 'there's a hole in it, and it can't keep out the weather.'

'It will be the cooler,' says he, putting it on him, 'besides, if I don't like it, it is easy to stop it with a wisp o' straw, or the like o' that.'

'The three legs of it looks mighty queer, sticking up,' says she.

'Every helmet has a spike sticking out o' the top of it,' says the weaver, 'and if mine has three, it's only the grander it is.'

'Well,' says the wife, getting bitter at last, 'all I can say is, it isn't the first sheep's head was dressed in it.'

'Your servant, ma'am,' says he; and off he set.

Well, he was in want of a horse, and so he went to a field hard by, where the miller's horse was grazing, that used to carry the ground corn round the country.

'This is the identical horse for me,' says the weaver, 'he is used to carrying flour and male, and what am I but the flower o' chivalry in a coat o' mail; so that the horse won't be put out of his way in the least.'

But as he was riding him out of the field, who should see him but the miller.

'Is it stealing my horse you are, honest man?' says the miller.

'No,' says the weaver, 'I'm only going to exercise him,' says he, 'in the cool o' the evening; it will be good for his health.'

'Thank you kindly,' says the miller, 'but leave him where he is, and you'll oblige me.'

'I can't afford it,' says the weaver, running the horse at the ditch.

'Bad luck to your impudence,' says the miller, 'you've as much tin about you as a travelling tinker, but you've more brass. Come back here, you vagabond,' says he.

But he was too late; away galloped the weaver, and took the road to Dublin, for he thought the best thing he could do was to go to the King o' Dublin (for Dublin was a great place then, and had a king of its own), and he thought, maybe, the King o' Dublin would give him work. Well, he was four days going to Dublin, for the beast was not the best and the roads worse, not all as one as now; but there was no turnpikes then, glory be to God!

When he got to Dublin, he went straight to the palace, and when he got into the courtyard he let his horse go and graze about the place, for the grass was growing out between the stones; everything was flourishing then in Dublin, you see. Well, the king was looking out of his drawing-room window, for diversion, when the weaver came in; but the weaver pretended not to see him, and he went over to a stone seat, under the window - for, you see, there was stone seats all round about the place for the accommodation o' the people - for the king was a decent, obliging man; well, as I said, the weaver went over and lay down on one o' the seats, just under the king's window, and pretended to go asleep; but he took care to turn out the front of his shield that had the letters on it; well, my dear, with that, the king calls out to one of the lords of his court that was standing behind him, holding up the skirt of his coat, according to reason.

'Look here,' says he, 'what do you think of a vagabond like that coming under my very nose to go sleep? It is true I'm a good king,' says he, 'and I 'commodate the people by having seats for them to sit down and enjoy the recreation and contemplation of seeing me here, looking out a' my drawing-room window, for diversion; but that is no reason they are to make a hotel o' the place, and come and sleep here. Who is it at all?' says the king.

'Not a one o' me knows, please your majesty.'

'I think he must be a furriner,' says the king, 'because his dress is outlandish.'

'And doesn't know manners, more betoken,' says the lord.

'I'll go down and circumspect him myself,' says the king, 'folly me,' says he to the lord, waving his hand at the same time in the most dignacious manner.

Down he went accordingly, followed by the lord; and when he went over to where the weaver was lying, sure the first thing he seen was his shield with the big letters on it, and with that, says he to the lord, 'Bedad,' says he, 'this is the very man I want.'

'For what, please your majesty?' says the lord.

'To kill that vagabond dragon, to be sure,' says the king.

'Sure, do you think he could kill him,' says the lord, 'when all the stoutest knights in the land wasn't equal to it, but never came back, and was eaten up alive by the cruel deceiver.'

'Sure, don't you see there,' says the king, pointing at the shield, 'that he killed three score and ten at one blow? And the man that done that, I think, is a match for anything.'

So, with that, he went over to the weaver and shook him by the shoulder for to wake him, and the weaver rubbed his eyes as if just wakened, and the king says to him, 'God save you,' said he.

'God save you kindly,' says the weaver, pretending he was quite unaware who he was speaking to.

'Do you know who I am,' says the king, 'that you make so free, good man?'

'No, indeed,' says the weaver, 'you have the advantage o' me.'

'To be sure I have,' says the king, mighty high, 'sure, ain't I the King o' Dublin?' says he.

The weaver dropped down on his two knees in front of the king, and says he, 'I beg God's pardon and yours for the liberty I took; please your holiness, I hope you'll excuse it.'

'No offence,' says the king, 'get up, good man. And what brings you here?' says he.

'I'm in want o' work, please your reverence,' says the weaver.

'Well, suppose I give you work?' says the king.

'I'll be proud to serve you, my lord,' says the weaver.

'Very well,' says the king. 'You killed three score and ten at one blow, I understand',' says the king.

'Yes,' says the weaver, 'that was the last trifle o' work I done, and I'm afeard my hand 'll go out o' practice if I don't get some job to do at once.'

'You shall have a job immediately,' says the king. 'It is not threescore and ten or any fine thing like that; it is only a blaggard dragon that is disturbing the country and ruining my tenants with eating their poultry, and I'm lost for want of eggs,' says the king.

'Troth, then, please your worship,' says the weaver, 'you look as yellow as if you swallowed twelve yolks this minute.'

'Well, I want this dragon to be killed,' says the king. 'It will be no trouble in life to you; and I am only sorry that it isn't better worth your while, for he isn't worth fearing at all; only I must tell you, that he lives in the County Galway, in the middle of a bog, and he has an advantage in that.'

'Oh, I don't value it in the least,' says the weaver, 'for the last three score and ten I killed was in a soft place.'

'When will you undertake the job, then?' says the king.

'Let me at him at once,' says the weaver.

'That's what I like,' says the king, 'you're the very man for my money,' says he.

'Talking of money,' says the weaver, 'by the same token, I'll want a trifle o' change from you for my travelling charges.'

'As much as you please,' says the king; and with the word, he brought him into his closet, where there was an old stocking in an oak chest, bursting with golden guineas.

'Take as many as you please,' says the king; and sure enough, my dear, the little weaver stuffed his tin clothes as full as they could hold with them.

'Now, I'm ready for the road,' says the weaver.

'Very well,' says the king, 'but you must have a fresh horse,' says he.

'With all my heart,' says the weaver, who thought he might as well exchange the miller's old garron for a better.

And maybe it's wondering you are that the weaver would think of going to fight the dragon after what he heard about him, when he was pretending to be asleep, but he had no such notion; all he intended was, - to fob the gold, and ride back again to Duleek with his gains and a good horse. But, you see, cute as the weaver was, the king was cuter still; for these high quality, you see, is great deceivers; and so the horse the weaver was put on was learned on purpose; and sure, the minute he was mounted, away powered the horse, and the devil saw to it that he went but right down to Galway.

Well, for four days he was going evermore, until at last the weaver seen a crowd o' people running as if Old Nick was at their heels, and they shouting a thousand murders and crying, 'The dragon, the dragon!' and he couldn't stop the horse nor make him turn back, but away he pelted right in front of the terrible beast that was coming up to him, and there was the most nefarious smell o' sulphur, saving your presence, enough to knock you down; and, faith the weaver seen he had no time to lose, and so he threw himself off the horse and made to a tree that was growing nigh at hand, and away he clambered up into it as nimble as a cat; and not a minute had he to spare, for the dragon came up in a powerful rage, and he devoured the horse body and bones, in less than no time; and then he began to sniffle and scent about for the weaver, and at last he clapped his eye on him, where he was, up in the three, and says he, 'In truth, you might as well come down out o' that,' says he, 'for I'll have you as sure as eggs is meat.'

'Devil be damned if I'll go down,' says the weaver.

'Sorra care, I care,' says the dragon, 'for you're as good as ready money in my pocket this minute, for I'll lie under this three,' says he, 'and sooner or later you must fall to my share'; and sure enough he sat down, and began to pick his teeth with his tail, after the heavy breakfast he made that morning (for he ate a whole village, let alone the horse), and he got drowsy at last, and fell asleep; but before he went to sleep, he wound himself all around about the tree, all as one as a lady winding ribbon around her finger, so that the weaver could not escape.

Well, as soon as the weaver knew he was dead asleep, by the snoring of him - and every snore he let out of him was like a clap o' thunder - that minute the weaver began to creep down the tree, as cautious as a fox; and he was very nearly at the bottom, when, bad cess to it, a thieving branch he was depending on broke, and down he fell right a-top o' the dragon; but if he did, good luck was on his side, for where should he fall but with his two legs right across the dragon's neck, and, my jewel, he laid hold o' the beast's ears, and there he kept his grip, for the dragon wakened and endeavoured to bite him; but, you see, by reason the weaver was behind his ears, he could not come at him, and, with that, he endeavoured for to shake him off; but the devil be damned, he could not stir the weaver; and though he shook all the scales on his body, he could not turn the scale against the weaver.

'By the hokey, this is too bad entirely,' says the dragon, 'but if you won't let go,' says he, 'by the powers o' wildfire, I'll give you a ride that will astonish your seven small senses, my boy'; and, with that, away he flew like mad; and where do you think he did fly? Bedad, he flew straight for Dublin, devil a less. But the weaver being on his neck was a great distress to him, and he would rather have had him an inside passenger; but, anyway, he flew and he flew till he came slap up against the palace o' the king; for, being blind with the rage, he never seen it, and he knocked his brains out - that is, the small trifle he had - and down he fell speechless.

And you see, good luck would have it, that the King o' Dublin was looking out of his drawing-room window, for diversion, that day also, and when he seen the weaver riding on the fiery dragon (for he was blazing like a tar-barrel), he called out to his courtiers to come and see the show.

'By the powders o' war, here comes the knight errant,' says the king, 'riding the dragon that's all afire, and if he gets into the palace, you must be ready with the fire engines,' says he, 'for to put him out.'

But when they seen the dragon fall outside, they all run downstairs and scampered into the palace-yard for to circumspect the curiosity; and by the time they got down, the weaver had got off o' the dragon's neck, and running up to the king, says he, 'please your holiness,' says he, 'I did not think myself worthy of killing this facetious beast, so I brought him to yourself for to do him the honour of decrepitation by your own royal five fingers. But I tamed him first, before I allowed him the liberty for to dare to appear in your royal presence, and you'll oblige me if you'll just make your mark with your own hand upon the unruly beast's neck.'

And with that the king, sure enough, drew out his sword and took the head off the dirty brute as clean as a new pin. Well, there was great rejoicing in the court that the dragon was killed; and says the king to the little weaver, says he, 'You are a knight errant as it is, and so it would be of no use for to knight you over again; but I will make you a lord,' says he.

'O Lord!' says the weaver, thunderstruck like at his own good luck.

'I will,' says the king, 'and as you are the first man I ever heard tell of that rode a dragon, you shall be called Lord Mountdragon,' says he.

'And where's my estates, please your holiness?' says the weaver, who always had a sharp look-out after the main chance.

'Oh, I didn't forget that' says the king, 'it is my royal pleasure to provide well for you, and for that reason I make you a present of all the dragons in the world, and give you power over them from this day forwards,' says he.

'Is that all?' says the weaver.

'All!' says the king. 'Why, you ungrateful little vagabond, was the like ever given to any man before?'

'I believe not, indeed,' says the weaver, 'many thanks to your majesty.'

'But that is not all I'll do for you,' says the king, 'I'll give you my daughter too in marriage,' says he.

Now, you see, that was nothing more than what he promised the weaver in his first promise; for, by all accounts, the king's daughter was the greatest dragon ever was seen, and had the devil's own tongue, and a beard a yard long, which she pretended was put on her by way of a penance by Father Mulcahy, her confessor; but it was well known it was in the family for ages, and no wonder it was so long, by reason of that same.

Tales From The Land Of Saints & Scholars

The Mad Pudding of Ballyboulteen

"The Mad Pudding of Ballyboulteen" is a lively Irish folktale first told by William Carleton and later adapted by Alfred Perceval Graves in The Irish Fairy Book. It centres on a farmer's wife who, in a fit of bad temper and impatience, throws a half-cooked pudding out of her kitchen door.

Beneath its humour, the story reflects the Irish fondness for tales that blend the ordinary with the uncanny. The domestic world, kitchen, hearth, and village lane, is made strange and unpredictable, a reminder that mischief and magic lurk even in the most familiar places.

Moll Roe Rafferty, the daughter of old Jack Rafferty, was a fine young bouncing girl, large and lavish, with a pretty head of hair on her like scarlet, that being one of the reasons why she was called Roe or red; her arms and cheeks were much the colour of the hair, and her saddle nose was the prettiest thing of its kind that ever was on a face.

Well, anyhow, it was Moll Rafferty that was the dilsy. It happened that there was a nate vagabond in the neighbourhood, just as much overburdened with beauty as herself, and he was named Gusty Gillespie. Gusty was what they call a black-mouth Presbyterian, and wouldn't keep Christmas day, except what they call 'old style.' Gusty was rather good-looking, when seen in the dark, as well as

Moll herself; anyhow, they got attached to each other, and in the end everything was arranged for their marriage.

Now this was the first marriage that had happened for a long time in the neighbourhood between a Protestant and a Catholic, and faix, there was one of the bride's uncles, old Harry Connolly, a fairy man, who could cure all complaints with a secret he had, and as he didn't wish to see his niece married on such a fellow, he fought bitterly against the match. All Moll's friends, however, stood up for the marriage, barring him, and, of course, the Sunday was appointed that they were to be dovetailed together.

Well, the day arrived, and Moll, as became her, went to mass, and Gusty to meeting, after which they were to join one another in Jack Rafferty's, where the priest, Father Mc. Sorley, was to slip up after mass to take his dinner with them, and to keep Mister Mc. Shuttle, who was to marry them, company. Nobody remained at home but old Jack Rafferty and his wife, who stopped to dress the dinner, for, to tell the truth, it was to be a great let-out entirely. Maybe, if all was known, too, Father Mc. Sorley was to give them a cast of his office over and above the minister, in regard that Moll's friends were not altogether satisfied at the kind of marriage which Mc. Shuttle could give them. The sorrow may care about that - splice here, splice there - all I can say is that when Mrs. Rafferty was going to tie up a big bag pudding, in walks Harry Connolly, the fairy man, in a rage, and shouts out, 'Blood and blunderbusses, what are you here for?'

'Arrah, why, Harry? Why, avick?'

'Why, the sun's in the suds, and the moon in the high Horricks; there's a clip-stick coming on, and there you're both as unconcerned as if it was about to rain mether. Go out, and cross yourselves three times in the name o' the four Mandromarvins, for as prophecy says,

Fill the pot, Eddy, supernaculum - a blazing star's a rare spectaculum. Go out, both of you, and look at the sun, I say, and ye'll see the condition he's in - off!'

Begad, sure enough, Jack gave a bounce to the door, and his wife leaped like a two-year-old, till they were both got on a stile beside the house to see what was wrong in the sky.

'Arrah, what is it, Jack?' says she, 'can you see anything?'

'No,' says he, sorra the full of my eye of anything I can spy, barring the sun himself, that's not visible, in regard of the clouds. God guard us! I doubt there's something to happen.'

'If there wasn't Jack, what'd put Harry, that knows so much, in the state he's in?'

'I doubt it's this marriage,' says Jack. 'Between ourselves, it's not over and above religious of Moll to marry a black-mouth, but, it can't be helped now, though you see it's not a taste o' the sun is willing to show his face upon it.'

'As to that,' says his wife, winking with both her eyes, 'if Gusty's satisfied with Moll, it's enough. I know who'll carry the whip hand, anyhow; but in the meantime let us ask Harry within what ails the sun?'

Well, they accordingly went in, and put this question to him, 'Harry, what's wrong, ahagur? What is it now, for if anybody alive knows 'tis yourself?'

'Ah,' said Harry, screwing his mouth with a kind of a dry smile, 'the sun has a hard twist o' the colic; but never mind that, I tell you, you'll have a merrier wedding than you think, that's all'; and having said this, he put on his hat and left the house.

Now, Harry's answer relieved them very much, and so, after calling to him to be back for dinner, Jack sat down to take a shough o' the pipe, and the wife lost no time in tying up the pudding, and putting it in the pot to be boiled.

In this way things went on well enough for a while, Jack smoking away, and the wife cooking and dressing at the rate of a hunt. At last, Jack, while sitting, as I said, contentedly at the fire, thought he could perceive an odd dancing kind of motion in the pot that puzzled him a good deal.

'Katty,' says he, 'what the dickens is in this pot on the fire?'

'Nerra thing but the big pudding. Why do you ask?' says she.

'Why,' says he, 'if ever a pot took it into its head to dance a jig, and this did. Thunder and sparkles, look at it!'

Begad, and it was true enough; there was the pot bobbing up and down, and from side to side, jigging it away as merry as a grig; and it was quite aisy to see that it wasn't the pot itself, but what was inside of it, that brought about the hornpipe.

'Be the hole o' my coat,' shouted Jack, 'there's something alive in it, or it would never cut such capers!'

'Begorra, there is, Jack; something strange entirely has got into it. Wirra, man alive, what's to be done?'

Just as she spoke the pot seemed to cut the buckle in prime style, and after a spring that'd shame a dancing master, off flew the lid, and out bounced the pudding itself, hopping as nimble as a pea on a drum-head about the floor. Jack blessed himself, and Katty crossed herself. Jack shouted, and Katty screamed. 'In the name of goodness, keep your distance; no one here injured you!'

The pudding, however, made a set at him, and Jack leaped first on a chair, and then on the kitchen table, to avoid it. It then danced towards Katty, who was repeating her prayers at the top of her voice, while the cunning thief of a pudding was hopping and jigging it around her as if it was amused at her distress.

'If I could get the pitchfork,' says Jack, 'I'd deal with it - by goxty, I'd try its mettle.'

'No, no,' shouted Katty, thinking there was a fairy in it, 'let us speak it fair. Who knows what harm it might do? Easy, now,' says she to the pudding, 'easy, dear; don't harm honest people that never meant to offend you. It wasn't us - no, in truth, it was old Harry Connolly that bewitched you; pursue him, if you wish, but spare a woman like me!'

The pudding, bedad, seemed to take her at her word, and danced away from her towards Jack, who, like the wife, believing there was a fairy in it, and that speaking it fair was the best plan, thought he would give it a soft word as well as her.

'Please your honour,' said Jack, 'she only speaks the truth, and upon my voracity, we both feels much obliged to you for your quietness. Faith, it's quite clear that if you weren't a gentlemanly pudding, all out, you'd act otherwise. old Harry, the rogue, is your mark; he's Just gone down the road there, and if you go fast you'll overtake him. Be my song, your dancing-master did his duty, anyway. Thank your honour! God speed you, and may you never meet with a parson or alderman in your travels.'

Just as Jack spoke, the pudding appeared to take the hint, for it quietly hopped out, and as the house was directly on the roadside, turned down towards the bridge, the very way that old Harry went. It was very natural, of course, that Jack and Katty should go out to see how it intended to travel, and as the day was Sunday, it was but natural, too, that a greater number of people than usual were passing the road. This was a fact; and when Jack and his wife were seen following the pudding, the whole neighbourhood was soon up and after it.

'Jack Rafferty, what is it? Katty, ahagur, will you tell us what it means?'

'Why,' replied Katty, 'it's my big pudding that's bewitched, and it's out hot foot pursuing, here she stopped, not wishing to mention her brother's name - 'someone or other that surely put pishrogues on it.'

This was enough; Jack, now seeing that he had assistance, found his courage coming back to him; so says he to Katty, 'Go home,' says he, 'an' lose no time in making another pudding as good, and here's Paddy Scanlan's wife, Bridget, says she'll let you boil it on her fire, as you'll want our own to dress the rest of the dinner; and Paddy himself will lend me a pitchfork for pursuing to the morsel of that same pudding will escape, till I let the wind out of it, now that I've the neighbours to back and support me,' says Jack.

This was agreed to, and Katty went back to prepare a fresh pudding, while Jack and half the townland pursued the other with spades, graips, pitchforks, scythes, flails, and all possible description of instruments. On the pudding went, however, at the rate of about six Irish miles an hour, and such a chase was never seen. Catholics, Protestants, and Presbyterians were all after it, armed, as I said, and bad end to the thing, but its own activity could save it. Here it made a hop, there a prod was made at it; but off it went, and someone, as eager to get a slice at it on the other side, got the prod instead of the pudding. Big Frank Farrell, the miller, of Ballyboulteen, got a prod backwards that brought a hullabaloo out of him that you might hear at the other end of the parish. One got a slice of a scythe, another a whack of a flail, a third a rap of a spade, that made him look nine ways at once.

'Where is it going?' asked one. 'My life for you, it's on its way to Meeting. Three cheers for it, if it turns to Carntaul!' 'Prod the soul out of it if it's a Protestant'' shouted the others, 'if it turns to the left, slice it into pancakes. We'll have no Protestant' puddings here.'

Begad, by this time the people were on the point of beginning to have a regular fight about it, when, very fortunately, it took a short turn down a little by-lane that led towards the Methodist preaching-house, and in an instant all parties were in an uproar against it as a Methodist pudding. 'It's a Wesleyan,' shouted several voices; and by this and by that, into a Methodist chapel it won't put a foot today, or we'll lose a fall. Let the wind out of it. Come, boys, where's your pitchforks?'

The devil pursuing to the one of them, however, ever could touch the pudding, and Just when they thought they had it up against the gavel of the Methodist chapel, begad, it gave them the slip, and hops over to the left, clean into the river, and sails away before their eyes as light as an eggshell.

Now, it so happened that a little below this place the demesne wall of Colonel Bragshaw was built up to the very edge of the river on each side of its banks; and so, finding there was a stop put to their pursuit of it, they went home again, every man, woman, and child of them, puzzled to think what the pudding was at all, what it meant, or where it was going! Had Jack Rafferty and his wife been willing to let out the opinion they held about Henry Connolly bewitching it, there is no doubt of it but poor Harry might be badly treated by the crowd, when their blood was up. They had sense enough, however, to keep that to themselves, for Harry being an old bachelor, was a kind friend to the Raffertys. So, of course, there was all kinds of talk about it - some guessing this, and some guessing that - one party saying the pudding was of their side, and another denying it, and insisting it belonged to them, and so on.

In the meantime, Katty Rafferty, for 'fraid the dinner might come short, went home and made another pudding much about the same size as the one that had escaped, and bringing it over to their next neighbour, Paddy Scanlan's, it was put into a pot, and placed on the fire to boil, hoping that it might be done in time, especially as they were to have the minister, who loved a warm slice of a good pudding as well as ever a gentleman in Europe.

Anyhow, the day passed; Moll and Gusty were made man and wife, and no two could be more loving. Their friends that had been asked to the wedding were sauntering about in pleasant little groups till dinner-time, chatting and laughing; but above all things, striving to account for the vagaries of the pudding; for, to tell the truth, its adventures had now gone through the whole parish.

Well, at any rate, dinner-time was drawing near, and Paddy Scanlan was sitting comfortably with his wife at the fire, the pudding boiling before their eyes, when in walks Harry Connolly in a flutter, shouting, 'Blood and blunderbusses, what are you here for?'

'Arrah, why, Harry - why, avick?' said Mrs. Scanlan.

'Why,' said Harry, 'the sun's in the suds, and the moon in the high Horricks! Here's a clipstick coming on, and there you sit as unconcerned as if it was about to rain mether! Go out, both of you, and look at the sun, I say, and ye'll see the condition he's in - off!'

'Ay, but, Harry, what's that rolled up in the tail of your cothamore (big coat)?'

'Out with you,' says Harry, 'an' pray against the clipstick - the sky's falling!'

Begad, it was hard to say whether Paddy or the wife got out first, they were so much alarmed by Harry's wild, thin face and piercing eyes; so out they went to see what was wonderful in the sky, and kept looking and looking in every direction, but not a thing was to be seen, barring the sun shining down with great good-humour, and not a single cloud in the sky.

Paddy and the wife now came in laughing to scold Harry, who no doubt was a great wag in his way when he wished. 'Musha, bad scran to you, Harry...' and they had time to say no more, however, for, as they were going into the door, they met him coming out of it, with a reek of smoke out of his tail like a lime-kiln.

'Harry,' shouted Bridget, 'my soul to glory, but the tail of your cothamore's afire - you'll be burned. Don't you see the smoke that's out of it?'

Cross yourselves three times,' said Harry, without stopping or even looking behind him, 'for, as the prophecy says, Fill the pot, Eddy...'

They could hear no more, for Harry appeared to feel like a man that carried something a great deal hotter than he wished, as anyone might see by the liveliness of his motions, and the queer faces he was forced to make as he went along.

'What the dickens is he carrying in the skirts of his big coat?' asked Paddy.

'My soul to happiness, but maybe he has stolen the pudding,' said Bridget, 'for it's known that many a strange thing he does.'

They immediately examined the pot, but found that the pudding was there, as safe as tuppence, and this puzzled them the more to think what it was he could be carrying about with him in the manner he did. But little they knew what he had done while they were sky-gazing!

Well, anyhow, the day passed, and the dinner was ready, and no doubt but a fine gathering there was to partake of it. The Presbyterian minister met the Methodist preacher - a devilish stretcher of an appetite he had, in truth - on their way to Jack Rafferty's, and as he knew he could take the liberty, why, he insisted on his dining with him; for, after all, in them days, the clergy of all descriptions lived upon the best footing among one another, not all at one as now - but no matter. Well, they had nearly finished their dinner, when Jack Rafferty himself asked Katty for the pudding; but, just as he spoke, in it came, as big as a mess-pot.

'Gentlemen,' said he, 'I hope none of you will refuse tasting a bit of Katty's pudding; I don't mean the dancing one that took to its travels today, but a good solid fellow that she made since.'

'To be sure we won't,' replied the priest. 'So, Jack, put a trifle on them three plates at your right hand, and send them over here to the clergy, and maybe,' he said, laughing - for he was a droll, good-humoured man - 'maybe, Jack, we won't set you a proper example.'

'With a heart and a half, your reverence and gentlemen; in truth, it's not a bad example ever any of you set us at the likes, or ever will set us, I'll go bail. and sure, I only wish it was better fare I had for you; but we're humble people, gentlemen, and so you can't expect to meet here what you would in higher places.'

'Better a male of herbs,' said the Methodist preacher, 'where peace is...' He had time to get no further, however; for much to his amazement, the priest and the minister started up from the table, just as he was going to swallow the first mouthful of the pudding, and, before you could say Jack Robinson, the pudding started away at a lively jig down the floor.

At this moment a neighbour's son came running in, and told them that the parson was coming to see the new-married couple, and wish them all happiness; and the words were scarcely out of his mouth when he made his appearance. What to think, he knew not, when he saw the minister footing it away at the rate of a wedding. He had very little time, however, to think; for, before he could sit down, up starts the Methodist preacher, and, clapping his fists in his sides, chimes in in great style along with him.

'Jack Rafferty,' says he, and, by the way, Jack was his tenant, 'what the dickens does all this mean?' says he, 'I'm amazed!'

'The not a particle o' me can tell you,' says Jack, 'but will your reverence Just taste a morsel o' pudding, merely that the young couple may boast that you ate at their wedding; for, sure, if you wouldn't, who would?'

'Well,' says he, 'to gratify them, I will; so, just a morsel. But, Jack, this bates Bannagher,' says he again, putting the spoonful of pudding into his mouth, 'has there been drink here?'

'Oh, the devil a spud,' says Jack, 'for although there's plenty in the house, faith, it appears the gentlemen wouldn't wait for it. Unless they tuck it elsewhere, I can make nothing o' this.'

He had scarcely spoken when the parson, who was an active man, cut a caper a yard high, and before you could bless yourself, the three clergy were hard at work dancing, as if for a wager. Begad, it would be impossible for me to tell you the state the whole meeting was in when they see this. Some were hoarse with laughing; some turned up their eyes with wonder; many thought them mad; and others thought they had turned up their little fingers a trifle too often.

'Be goxty, it's a burning shame,' said one, 'to see three black-mouth clergy in such a state at this early hour!' 'Thunder and ounce, what's over them at all?' says others, 'why, one would think they were bewitched. Holy Moses, look at the caper the Methodist cuts! and as for the Rector, who would think he could handle his feet at such a rate! Be this, and be that, he cuts the buckle, and does the trebling step equal to Paddy Horaghan, the dancing-master himself! And see! Bad cess to the morsel of the person that's not too hard at Peace upon a trencher, and it upon a Sunday, too! Whirroo, gentlemen, the fun's in you, after all - whish! more power to you!'

The sorra's own fun they had, and no wonder; but judge of what they felt when all at once they saw old Jack Rafferty himself bouncing in among them, and footing it away like the best of them. Bedad, no play could come up to it, and nothing could be heard but laughing, shouts of encouragement, and clapping of hands like mad. Now, the minute Jack Rafferty left the chair, where he had been carving the pudding, old Harry Connolly come over and claps himself down in his place, in order to send it round, of course; and he was scarcely seated when who should make his appearance but Barney Hartigan, the piper. Barney, by the way, had been sent for early in the day, but being from home when the message for him went, he couldn't come any sooner.

'Begorra,' says Barney, 'you're early at the work gentlemen! But what does this mane? But devil may care, you shan't want the music, while there's a blast in the pipes, anyhow!' So saying he gave them Jig Polthogue, and after that, Kiss My Lady, in his best style.

In the meantime the fun went on thick and threefold, for it must be remembered that Harry, the old knave, was at the pudding; and maybe, he didn't serve it about in double-quick time, too! The first he helped was the bride, and before you could say chopstick she was at it hard and fast, before the Methodist preacher, who gave a jolly spring before her that threw them into convulsions. Harry liked this, and made up his mind soon to find partners for the rest; so he accordingly sent the pudding about like lightning; and, to make a long story short, barring the piper and himself, there wasn't a pair of heels in the house but was as busy at the dancing as if their lives depended on it.

'Barney,' says Harry, 'Just taste a morsel o' this pudding; devil be damned, it's such a bully of a pudding ever you ate. Here, your soul! try a snig of it - it's beautiful!'

'To be sure I will,' says Barney. 'I'm not the boy to refuse a good thing. But, Harry, be quick, for you know my hands is engaged, and it would be a thousand pities not to keep them in music, and they so well inclined. Thank you, Harry. Begad, that is a fine pudding. But, blood and turnips! what's this for?'

The word was scarcely out of his mouth when he bounced up, pipes and all, and dashed into the middle of the party. 'Hurroo! your souls, let us make a night of it! The Ballyboulteen boys forever! Go it, your reverence! Turn your partner, heel and toe, minister. Good! Well done, again! Whish! Hurroo! Here's for Ballyboulteen, and the sky over it!'

Bad luck to such a set ever was seen together in this world, or will again, I suppose. The worst, however, wasn't come yet, for Just as they were in the very heat and fury of the dance, what do you think comes hopping in among them but another pudding, as nimble and merry as the first! That was enough; they had all heard of it - the ministers among the rest - and most of them had seen the other pudding, and knew that there must be a fairy in it, sure enough. Well, as I said, in it comes to the thick o' them; but the very appearance of it was enough.

Off the three clergy danced, and off the whole weddingers danced after them, everyone making the best of their way home; but not a soul of them able to break out of the step if they were to be hanged for it. Truth, it wouldn't leave a laugh in you to see the parson dancing down the road on his way home, and the minister and Methodist preacher cutting the buckle as they went along in the opposite direction. To make short work of it, they all danced home at last with scarce a puff of wind in them; the bride and bridegroom danced away to bed; and now, boys, come and let us dance the Horo Lheig in the barn without.

But, you see, boys, before we go, and in order to make everything plain, I had as good tell you that Harry, in crossing the bridge of Ballyboulteen, a couple o' miles between Squire Bragshaw's demesne wall, saw the pudding floating down the river - the truth is, he was waiting for it; but, be this as it may, he took it out, for the water had made it as clean as a new pin, and tucking it up in the tail of his big coat, contrived to bewitch it in the same manner by getting a fairy to get into it, for, indeed, it was pretty well known that the same Harry was hand and glove with the good people. Others will tell you that it was half a pound of quicksilver he put into it, but that doesn't stand to reason. At any rate, boys, I have told you the adventures of the Mad Pudding of Ballyboulteen; but I don't wish to tell you many other things about it that happened - for 'fraid I'd tell a lie!

Tales From The Land Of Saints & Scholars

The Plaisham

"The Plaisham", adapted from Seumas MacManus's Donegal Fairy Stories, is a lively piece of Irish folklore that blends humour with the eerie mischief of the unseen world. The story tells of a crafty young man from Donegal who encounters the Plaisham, a fairy being known for luring mortals into trouble with tricks and illusions.

Beneath the comic charm and rustic dialogue lies a warning about pride, curiosity, and the thin line between the mortal world and the Otherworld. MacManus's retelling captures the Donegal cadence, full of wit and rhythm, showing how the old stories were told to entertain as much as to caution.

Nancy and Shamus were man and wife, and they lived all alone together for forty years; but at length a good-for-nothing streel of a fellow named Rory, who lived close by, thought what a fine thing it would be if Shamus would die, and he could marry Nancy, and get the house, farm, and all the stock. So he up and said to Nancy,

"What a pity it is for such a fine-looking woman as you to be bothered with that old, complaining, good-for-nothing crony of a man that's as full of pains and aches as an egg's full of meat. If you were free of him the morrow, the finest and handsomest young man in the parish would be proud to have you for a wife."

At first Nancy used to laugh at this; but at last, when he kept on at it, it began to prey on Nancy's mind, and she said to young Rory one day, "I don't believe a word, of what you say. Who would take me if Shamus was buried the morra?"

"Why," says Rory, "you'd have the pick of the parish. I'd take you myself."

"Is that true?" says Nancy.

"I pledge you my word," says Rory, "I would."

"Oh, well, even if you would yourself," says Nancy, "Shamus won't be buried tomorrow, or maybe, God help me, for ten years to come yet."

"You've all that in your own hands," says Rory.

"How's that?" says Nancy.

"Why, you can kill him off," says Rory.

"I wouldn't have the old creature's blood on my head," says Nancy.

"Neither you need," says Rory.

And then he sat down and began to tell Nancy how she could do away with Shamus and still not have his blood on her head.

Now there was a prince called Connal, who lived in a wee sod house close by Nancy and Shamus, but whose fathers before him, before their money was wasted, used to live in a grand castle. So, next day, over Nancy goes to this prince, and to him says, "Why, Prince Connal, isn't it a shame to see the likes of you living in the likes of that house?"

"I know it is," said he, "but I cannot do any better."

"Botheration," says Nancy, "you easily can."

"I wish you would tell me how," says Prince Connal.

"Why," says Nancy, "there's my Shamus has little or nothing to do, an' why don't you make him build you a castle?"

"Ah," says the prince, laughing, "sure, Shamus couldn't build me a castle."

Says Nancy, "You don't know Shamus, for there's not a thing in the wide world he couldn't do if he likes to; but he's that lazy, that if you don't break every bone in his body to make him do it, he won't do it."

"Is that so?" says Prince Connal.

"That's so," says Nancy. "So if you order Shamus to build you a castle an' have it up in three weeks, or that you'll take his life if he doesn't, you'll soon have a grand castle to live in," says she.

"Well, if that's so," says Prince Connal, "I'll not be long wanting a castle."

So on the very next morning, over he steps to Shamus's, calls Shamus out, and takes him with him to the place he had marked out for the site of his castle, and shows it to Shamus, and tells him he wants him to have a grand castle built and finished on that spot in three weeks' time.

"But," says Shamus, says he, "I never built a castle in my life. I know nothing about it, an' I couldn't have you a castle there in thirty- three years, let alone three weeks."

"O!" says the prince, says he, "I'm told there's no man in Ireland can build a castle better nor faster than you, if you only like to; and if you haven't that castle built on that ground in three weeks," says he, "I'll have your life. So now choose for yourself." And he walked away, and left Shamus standing there.

When Shamus heard this, he was a down-hearted man, for he knew that Prince Connal was a man of his word and would not stop at taking any man's life any more than he would from putting the breath out of a beetle. So down he sits and begins to cry; and while Shamus was crying there, up to him comes a Wee Red Man, and says to Shamus, "What are you crying about?"

"Ah, my poor man," says Shamus, says he, "don't be asking me, for there's no use in telling you, you could do nothing to help me."

"You don't know that" says the Wee Red Man, says he. "It's no harm to tell me anyhow."

So Shamus, to relieve his mind, ups and tells the Wee Red Man what Prince Connal had threatened to do to him if he had not a grand castle finished on that spot in three weeks.

Says the little man, says he, "Go to the Fairies' Glen at moonrise the night, and under the rocking stone at the head of the glen you'll find a white rod. Take that rod with you, and mark out the plan of the castle on this ground with it; then go back and leave the rod where you got it, and by the time you get back again your castle will be finished."

At moonrise that night Shamus, as you may be well assured, was at the rocking stone at the head of the Glen of the Fairies, and from under it he got a little white rod. He went to the hill where the Prince's castle was to be built, and with the point of the rod he marked out the plan of the castle, and then he went back and left the rod where he got it.

The next morning, when Prince Connal got up out of bed and went out of his little sod hut to take the air, his eyes were opened, I tell you, to see the magnificent castle that was standing finished and with the coping-stones on it on the hill above. He lost no time till he went over to thank Shamus for building him such a beautiful castle; and when Nancy heard that the castle was finished, it was she that was the angry woman.

She went out and looked at the castle, and she wondered and wondered, too, but she said nothing. She had a long chat with Rory that day again, and from Rory she went off to Prince Connal, and says she, "Now, didn't I tell you right well what Shamus could do?"

"I see you did," says Prince Connal, "and it is very thankful to you I am. I'm contented now for life," says he, "and I'll never forget yourself and Shamus."

"Contented!" says she, "why, that place isn't half finished yet."

"How's that?" says Prince Connal.

"Why," says she, "you need a beautiful river flowing past that castle, with lovely trees, and birds singing in the branches, and you should have the ocean roaring up beside it."

"But still," says Prince Connal, says he, "one can't have everything. This is a hundred miles from a river and a hundred miles from an ocean, and no trees ever grew on this hill, nor ever could grow on it, and no bird ever sang on it for the last three hundred years."

"Then all the more reason," says she, "why you should have all of them things."

"But I can't have them," says Prince Connal.

"Can't you?" says she. "Yes, you can. If you promise to have Shamus's life unless he has you all those things by your castle in three days, you'll soon have all you want," says Nancy.

"Well, well, that's wonderful," says Prince Connal, says he, "and I'll do it."

So he sets out, and goes to Shamus's house, and calls Shamus out to him to tell him that his castle was very bare-looking without something about it. Says he, "Shamus, I want you to put a beautiful river flowing past it, with plenty of trees and bushes along the banks, and also birds singing in them; and I want you to have the ocean roaring up by it also."

"But, Prince Connal," says Shamus, says he, "you know very well that I couldn't get you them things."

"Right well I know you can," says Prince Connal, "and I'll give you three days to have all those things done; and if you haven't them done at the end of three days, then I'll have your life." And away goes Prince Connal.

Poor Shamus, he sat down and began to cry at this, because he knew that he could not do one of these things. And as he was crying and crying he heard a voice in his ear, and looking up he saw the Wee Red Man.

"Shamus, Shamus," says he, "what's the matter with you?"

"O," says Shamus, says he, "there's no use in telling you what's the matter with me this time. Although you helped me before, there's not a man in all the world could do what I've got to do now."

"Well, anyhow," says the Wee Red Man, "if I can't do you any good, I'll do you no harm."

So Shamus, to relieve his mind, ups and tells the Wee Red Man what's the matter with him.

"Shamus," says the Wee Red Man, says he, "I'll tell you what you'll do. When the moon's rising to-night, be at the head of the Glen of the Fairies, and at the spring well there you'll find a cup and a leaf and a feather. Take the leaf and the feather with you, and a cup of water, and go back to the castle. Throw the water from you as far as you can throw it, and then blow the leaf off your right hand, and the feather off your left hand, and see what you'll see."

Shamus promised to do this. And when the moon rose that night, Shamus was at the spring well of the Glen of the Fairies, and he found there a cup, a leaf, and a feather. He lifted a cup of water and took it with him, and the leaf and the feather, and started for the castle. When he came there, he pitched the cup of water from him as far as he could pitch it, and at once the ocean, that was a hundred miles away, came roaring up beside the castle, and a beautiful river that had been flowing a hundred miles on the other side of the castle came flowing down past it into the ocean. Then he blew the leaf off his right hand, and all sorts of lovely trees and bushes sprang up along the riverbanks. Then he blew the feather off his left hand, and the trees and the bushes were filled with all sorts and varieties of lovely singing birds, that made the most beautiful music he ever had heard.

And maybe that was not a surprise to Prince Connal when he got up in the morning and went out. Off he tramped to Shamus's to thank Shamus and Nancy, and when Nancy heard this she was the angry woman.

That day she had another long confab with Rory, and from him she went off again to Prince Connal, and asked him how he liked his castle and all its surroundings.

He said he was a pleased and proud man, that he was thankful to her and her man, Shamus, and that he would never forget it to them the longest day of his life.

"O, but," says she, "you're not content. This night you'll have a great gathering of princes and lords and gentlemen feasting in your castle, and you'll surely want something to amuse them with. You must get a plaisham."

"What's a plaisham? "said Prince Connal.

"O," says Nancy, "it's the most wonderful and most amusing thing in the world; it will keep your guests in good humour for nine days and nine nights after they have seen it."

"Well," says Prince Connal, "that must be a fine thing entirely, and I'm sure I would be mighty anxious to have it. But," says he, "where would I get it or how would I get it?"

"Well," says Nancy, "that's easy. If you order Shamus to bring a plaisham to your castle by supper time this night, and promise to have his life if he hasn't it there, he'll soon get it for you."

"Well, if that's so," says Prince Connal, "I'll not be long wanting a plaisham."

So home went Nancy rejoicing this time, for she said to herself that poor old Shamus would not be long living now, because there was no such thing known in the whole wide world as a plaisham; and though Shamus might build castles, and bring oceans and rivers and trees and birds to them, all in one night, he could not get a thing that did not exist and was only invented by Rory.

Well, off to Shamus went Prince Connal without much loss of time, and called Shamus out of his little cabin. He told him he was heartily well pleased with all he had done for him. "But there's one thing more I want you to do, Shamus, and then I'll be content," says he. "This night I give a grand supper to the lords, ladies, and gentry of the country, and I want something to amuse them with; so at supper time you must bring me a plaisham."

"A plaisham! What's that?" says Shamus.

"I don't know," says Prince Connal.

"No more do I," says Shamus, "an' how do you expect me to fetch it to you then?"

"Well," says Prince Connal, says he, "this is all there is to be said about it -- if you haven't a plaisham at my castle door at supper time the night, you'll be a dead man."

"O, O," says Shamus, says he, and sat down on the ditch and began to cry, while Prince Connal went off home.

"Shamus, Shamus," says a voice in his ears, "what are you crying about now?"

Poor Shamus lifted his head and looked around, and there beside him stood the Wee Red Man.

"O!" says Shamus, says he, "don't mind asking me," he says, "for it's no use in telling you what's the matter with me now. You may build a castle for me," says he, "and you may bring oceans and rivers to it, and trees and birds; but you couldn't do anything to help me now."

"How do you know that?" said the Wee Red Man.

"O, I know it well," says Shamus, says he, you couldn't give me the thing that never was an' never will be!"

"Well," says the Wee Red Man, says he, "tell me what it is anyhow. If I can't do you any good, sure I can't do you any harm."

So, to relieve his mind, Shamus ups and tells him that Prince Connal had ordered him, within twenty-four hours, to have at his castle door a plaisham. "But," says Shamus, says he, "there never was such a thing as that."

"Sure enough," says the Wee Red Man, "there never was. But still, if Prince Connal wants it, we must try to get it for him. This night,

Shamus," says the Wee Red Man, says he, "go to the head of the Glen of the Fairies, to the sciog bush [Fairy thorn], where you'll find a bone ring hanging on a branch of the thorn. Take it with you back home. When you get home, young Rory will be chatting with your wife in the kitchen. Don't you go in there, but go into the byre [cowshed], and put the ring in the cow's nose; then lie quiet, and you'll soon have a plaisham to drive to Prince Connal's castle door."

Shamus thanked the Wee Red Man, and that night he went to the head of the Glen of the Fairies, and sure enough, he found the ring hanging from one of the branches of the sciog bush. He took it with him, and started for home. When he looked in through the kitchen window, there he saw Nancy and Rory sitting over the fire, chatting and confabbing about how they would get rid of him; but he said nothing, only went into the byre. He put the ring into the brannet cow's nose, and as soon as the ring went into it, the cow began to kick and rear and create a great tendherary of a noise entirely. Then Shamus got in under some hay in the corner.

It was no time at all until Nancy was out to find what was wrong with the brannet cow. She struck the cow with her fist to quiet her, but when she hit her, her fist stuck to the cow, and she could not get away.

Rory had come running out after Nancy to help her, and Nancy called, "Rory, Rory, pull me away from the cow."

Rory got hold of her to pull her away, but as he did so his hands stuck to Nancy, and he could not get away himself.

Up then jumped Shamus from under the hay in the corner. "Hup, Hup!" says Shamus, says he, "drive on the plaisham."

And out of the byre starts the cow with Nancy stuck to her, and Rory stuck to that, and heads toward the castle, with the cow rearing and rowting, and Nancy and Rory yelling and bawling. They made a terrible din entirely, and roused the whole countryside, who flocked out to see what the matter was.

Down past Rory's house the cow went, and Rory's mother, seeing him sticking to Nancy, ran out to pull him away; but when she laid her hand on Rory, she stuck to him; and "Hup, Hup!" says Shamus, says he, "drive on the plaisham.

So, on they went. And Rory's father ran after them to pull the mother away; but when he laid his hands on the mother, he stuck to her; and "Hup, Hup!" says Shamus, "drive on the plaisham."

On again they went, and next they passed where a man was cleaning out his byre. When the man saw the ridiculous string of them, he flung a graip [fork] and a graipful of manure at them, and it stuck to Rory's father; and "Hup, Hup!" says Shamus, says he, "drive on the plaisham." But the man ran after to save his graip, and when he got hold of the graip, he stuck to it; and "Hup, Hup!" says Shamus, says he, "drive on the plaisham."

On they went; and a tailor came flying out of his house with his lap-board in his hand. He struck the string of them with the lap-board, the lap-board stuck to the last man, and the tailor stuck to it; and "Hup, Hup!" says Shamus, says he, "drive on the plaisham."

Then they passed a cobbler's. He ran out with his heel-stick, and struck the tailor; but the heel-stick stuck to the tailor, and the cobbler stuck to the heel-stick; and "Hup, Hup!" says Shamus, says he, "drive on the plaisham."

Then on they went, and they next passed a blacksmith's forge. The blacksmith ran out, and struck the cobbler with his sledge. The sledge stuck to the cobbler, and the blacksmith stuck to the sledge; and "Hup, Hup!" says Shamus, says he, "drive on the plaisham."

When they came near the castle, they passed a great gentleman's house entirely, and the gentleman came running out, and got hold of the blacksmith to pull him away; but the gentleman stuck to the blacksmith, and could not get away himself; and "Hup, Hup!" says Shamus, says he, "drive on the plaisham."

The gentleman's wife, seeing him stuck, ran after her man to pull him away; but the wife stuck to the gentleman; and "Hup, Hup!" says Shamus, says he, "drive on the plaisham."

Then their children ran after them to pull the mother away, and they stuck to the mother; and "Hup, Hup!" says Shamus, says he, "drive on the plaisham."

Then the butler ran to get hold of the children, and he stuck to them; and the footman ran to get hold of the butler, and stuck to him; and the cook ran to get hold of the footman, and stuck to him; and the servants all ran to get hold of the cook, and they stuck to her; and "Hup, Hup!" says Shamus, says he, "drive on the plaisham." And on they went; and when they came up to the castle, the plaisham was a mile long, and the yelling and bawling and noise that they made could be heard anywhere within the four seas of Ireland. The racket was so terrible that Prince Connal and all his guests and all his servants and all in his house came running to the windows to see what the matter was, at all, at all; and when Prince Connal saw what was coming to his house, and heard the racket they were raising, he yelled to his Prime Minister to go and drive them off with a whip.

The Prime Minister ran meeting them, and took the whip to them; but the whip stuck to them, and he stuck to the whip; and "Hup, Hup!" says Shamus, says he, "drive on the plaisham."

Then Prince Connal ordered out all his other ministers and all of his servants to head it off and turn it away from his castle; but every one of the servants that got hold of it stuck to it; and "Hup, Hup!" says Shamus, says he, "drive on the plaisham."

And the plaisham moved on still for the castle. Then Prince Connal himself, with all his guests, ran out to turn it away; but when Prince Connal laid hands on the plaisham, he stuck to it; and when his guest laid hands on him, they stuck one by one to him; and "Hup, Hup!" says Shamus, says he, "drive on the plaisham."

And with all the racket and all the noise of the ranting, roaring, rearing, and rawting, in through the castle hall-door drove the plaisham, through and through and out at the other side. The castle itself fell down and disappeared, the bone ring rolled away from the cow's nose, and the plaisham all at once broke up, and when Prince Connal looked around, there was no castle at all, only the sod hut, and he went into it a sorry man.

And all the others slunk off home, right headily ashamed of themselves, for the whole world was laughing at them. Nancy, she went east; and Rory, he went west; and neither one of them was ever heard of more. As for Shamus, he went home to his own little cabin, and lived all alone, happy and contented, for the rest of his life, and may you and I do the same.

Tales From The Land Of Saints & Scholars

The Pursuit of the Gilla Dacker

"The Pursuit of the Gilla Dacker" is a sprawling, comic-heroic Irish tale that blends myth, satire, and adventure. The story is filled with the sharp humour and exaggeration typical of Fenian lore, its tone shifting easily between farce and grandeur.

At its heart, the tale is about pride and folly. In Graves's retelling, the rhythm of oral tradition remains clear: the repetitions, the high spirits, the sense that even heroes can be ridiculous. It stands as one of the liveliest and most human of the Fenian cycle tales.

Now, it chanced at one time during the chase, while they were hunting over the plain of Cliach, that Finn went to rest on the hill of Collkilla, which is now called Knockainy; and he had his hunting-tents pitched on a level spot near the summit, and some of his chief heroes tarried with him.

When the King and his companions had taken their places on the hill, the Feni unleashed their gracefully shaped, sweet-voiced hounds through the woods and sloping glens. And it was sweet music to Finn's ear, the cry of the long-snouted dogs, as they routed the deer from their covers and the badgers from their dens; the pleasant, emulating shouts of the youths; the whistling and signalling of the huntsmen; and the encouraging cheers of the mighty heroes, as they spread themselves through the glens and woods, and over the broad green plain of Cliach.

Then did Finn ask who of all his companions would go to the highest point of the hill directly over them to keep watch and ward and to report how the chase went on. For, he said, the Dedannans were ever on the watch to work the Feni mischief by their druidical spells, and more so during the chase than at other times.

Finn Ban Mac Bresal stood forward and offered to go; and, grasping his broad spears, he went to the top, and sat viewing the plain to the four points of the sky. And the King and his companions brought forth the chess-board and chess-men and sat them down to a game.

Finn Ban Mac Bresal had been watching only a little time when he saw on a plain to the east a Fomor of vast size coming towards the hill, leading a horse. As he came nearer Finn Ban observed that he was the ugliest-looking giant his eyes ever lighted on. He had a large, thick body, bloated and swollen out to a great size; clumsy, crooked legs; and broad, flat feet turned inwards. His hands and arms and shoulders were bony and thick and very strong-looking; his neck was long and thin; and while his head was poked forward, his face was turned up, as he stared straight at Finn Mac Bresal. He had thick lips, and long, crooked teeth; and his face was covered all over with bushy hair.

He was fully armed; but all his weapons were rusty and soiled and slovenly looking. A broad shield of a dirty, sooty colour, rough and battered, hung over his back; he had a long, heavy, straight sword at his left hip; and he held in his left hand two thick-handled, broad-headed spears, old and rusty, and seeming as if they had not been handled for years. In his right hand he held an iron club, which he dragged after him with its end on the ground; and, as it trailed along, it tore up a track as deep as the furrow a farmer ploughs with a team of oxen.

The horse he led was even larger in proportion than the giant himself, and quite as ugly. His great carcass was covered all over with tangled scraggy hair, of a sooty black; you could count his ribs and all the points of his big bones through his hide; his legs were crooked and knotty; his neck was twisted; and as for his jaws, they were so long and heavy that they made his head look twice too large for his body.

The giant held him by a thick halter, and seemed to be dragging him forward by main force, the animal was so lazy and so hard to move. Every now and then, when the beast tried to stand still, the giant would give him a blow on the ribs with his big iron club, which sounded as loud as the thundering of a great billow against the rough-headed rocks of the coast. When he gave him a pull forward by the halter, the wonder was that he did not drag the animal's head away from his body; and, on the other hand, the horse often gave the halter such a tremendous tug backwards that it was equally wonderful how the arm of the giant was not torn away from his shoulder.

When at last he had come up he bowed his head and bended his knee, and saluted the King with great respect.

Finn addressed him; and after having given him leave to speak he asked him who he was, and what was his name, and whether he belonged to one of the noble or ignoble races; also what was his profession or craft, and why he had no servant to attend to his horse.

The big man made answer and said, "King of the Feni, whether I come of a noble or of an ignoble race, that, indeed, I cannot tell, for I know not who my father and mother were. As to where I came from, I am a Fomor of Lochlann in the north; but I have no particular dwelling-place, for I am continually travelling about from one country to another, serving the great lords and nobles of the world, and receiving wages for my service.

"In the course of my wanderings I have often heard of you, Oh King, and of your greatness and splendour and royal bounty; and I have come now to ask you to take me into your service for one year; and at the end of that time I shall fix my own wages, according to my custom.

"You ask me also why I have no servant for this great horse of mine. The reason of that is this - at every meal I eat my master must give me as much food and drink as would be enough for a hundred men; and whosoever the lord or chief may be that takes me into his service, it is quite enough for him to have to provide for me, without having also to feed my servant.

Moreover, I am so very heavy and lazy that I should never be able to keep up with a company on a march if I had to walk; and this is my reason for keeping a horse at all.

"My name is the Gilla Dacker, and it is not without good reason that I am so called. For there never was a lazier or worse servant than I am, or one that grumbles more at doing a day's work for his master. And I am the hardest person in the world to deal with; for, no matter how good or noble I may think my master, or how kindly he may treat me, it is hard words and foul reproaches I am likely to give him for thanks in the end.

"This, Oh Finn, is the account I have to give of myself, and these are my answers to your questions."

"Well," answered Finn, "according to your own account you are not a very pleasant fellow to have anything to do with; and of a truth there is not much to praise in your appearance. But things may not be so bad as you say; and, anyhow, as I have never yet refused any man service and wages, I will not now refuse you."

Whereupon Finn and the Gilla Dacker made covenants, and the Gilla Dacker was taken into service for a year.

"And now," said the Gilla Dacker, "as to this same horse of mine, I find I must attend to him myself, as I see no one here worthy of putting a hand near him. So I will lead him to the nearest stud, as I am likely to do, and let him graze among your horses. I value him greatly, however, and it would grieve me very much if any harm were to befall him; so," continued he, turning to the King, "I put him under your protection, Oh King, and under the protection of all the Feni that are here present."

At this speech the Feni all burst out laughing to see the Gilla Dacker showing such concern for his miserable, worthless old skeleton of a horse.

Howbeit, the big man, giving not the least heed to their merriment, took the halter off the horse's head and turned him loose among the horses of the Feni.

But now, this same wretched-looking old animal, instead of beginning to graze, as everyone thought he would, ran in among the horses of the Feni, and began straightway to work all sorts of mischief. He cocked his long, hard, switchy tail straight out like a rod, and, throwing up his hind legs, he kicked about on this side and on that, maiming and disabling several of the horses. Sometimes he went tearing through the thickest of the herd, butting at them with his hard, bony forehead; and he opened out his lips with a vicious grin and tore all he could lay hold on with his sharp, crooked teeth, so that none were safe that came in his way either before or behind.

At last he left them, and was making straight across to a small field where Conan Mail's horses were grazing by themselves, intending to play the same tricks among them. But Conan, seeing this, shouted in great alarm to the Gilla Dacker to bring away his horse, and not let him work anymore mischief; and threatening, if he did not do so at once, to go himself and knock the brains out of the vicious old brute on the spot.

But the Gilla Dacker told Conan that he saw no way of preventing his horse from joining the others, except someone put the halter on him. "And" he said to Conan, "there is the halter; and if you are in any fear for your own animals, you may go yourself and bring him away from the field."

Conan was in a mighty rage when he heard this; and as he saw the big horse just about to cross the fence, he snatched up the halter, and, running forward with long strides, he threw it over the animal's head and thought to lead him back. But in a moment the horse stood stock still, and his body and legs became as stiff as if they were made of wood; and though Conan pulled and tugged with might and main, he was not able to stir him an inch from his place.

At last Fergus Finnvel, the poet, spoke to Conan and said, "I never would have believed, Conan Mail, that you could be brought to do horse-service for any knight or noble in the whole world; but now, indeed, I see that you have made yourself a horse-boy to an ugly foreign giant, so hateful-looking and low-born that not a man of the Feni would have anything to say to him. As you have, however, to mind this old horse in order to save your own, would it not be better for you to mount him and revenge yourself for all the trouble he is giving you, by riding him across the country, over the hill-tops, and down into the deep glens and valleys, and through stones and bogs and all sorts of rough places, till you have broken the heart in his big ugly body?"

Conan, stung by the cutting words of the poet and by the jeers of his companions, jumped upon the horse's back, and began to beat him mightily with his heels and with his two big heavy fists to make him go; but the horse seemed not to take the least notice, and never stirred.

"I know the reason he does not go," said Fergus Finnvel, "he has been accustomed to carry a horseman far heavier than you - that is to say, the Gilla Dacker; and he will not move till he has the same weight on his back."

At this Conan Mail called out to his companions, and asked which of them would mount with him and help to avenge the damage done to their horses.

"I will go," said Coil Croda the Battle Victor, son of Criffan; and up he went. But the horse never moved.

Dara Donn Mac Morna next offered to go, and mounted behind the others; and after him Angus Mac Art Mac Morna. And the end of it was that fourteen men of the Clann Baskin and Clann Morna got up along with Conan; and all began to thrash the horse together with might and main. But they were none the better for it, for he remained standing stiff and immovable as before. They found, moreover, that their seat was not at all an easy one - the animal's back was so sharp and bony.

When the Gilla Dacker saw the Feni beating his horse at such a rate he seemed very angry, and addressed the King in these words, "King of the Feni, I now see plainly that all the fine accounts I heard about you and the Feni are false, and I will not stay in your service - no, not another hour. You can see for yourself the ill-usage these men are giving my horse without cause; and I leave you to judge whether anyone could put up with it - anyone who had the least regard for his horse. The time is, indeed, short since I entered your service, but I now think it a great deal too long; so pay me my wages and let me go my ways."

But Finn said, "I do not wish you to go; stay on till the end of your year, and then I will pay you all I promised you."

"I swear," answered the Gilla Dacker, "that if this were the very last day of my year, I would not wait till morning for my wages after this insult. So, wages or no wages, I will now seek another master; but from this time forth I shall know what to think of Finn Mac Cumal and his Feni!"

With that the Gilla Dacker stood up as straight as a pillar, and, turning his face towards the south-west, he walked slowly away.

When the horse saw his master leaving the hill he stirred himself at once and walked quietly after him, bringing the fifteen men away on his back. And when the Feni saw this they raised a loud shout of laughter, mocking them.

The Gilla Dacker, after he had walked some little way, looked back, and, seeing that his horse was following, he stood for a moment to tuck up his skirts. Then, all at once changing his pace, he set out with long, active strides; and if you know what the speed of a swallow is flying across a mountain-side, or the dry fairy wind of a March day sweeping over the plains, then you can understand the swiftness of the Gilla Dacker as he ran down the hill-side towards the south-west.

Neither was the horse behindhand in the race; for though he carried a heavy load, he galloped like the wind after his master, plunging and bounding forward with as much freedom as if he had nothing at all on his back.

The men now tried to throw themselves off; but this, indeed, they were not able to do, for the good reason that they found themselves fastened firmly, hands and feet and all, to the horse's back.

And now Conan, looking round, raised his big voice and shouted to Finn and the Feni, asking them were they content to let their friends be carried off in that manner by such a horrible, foul-looking old spectre of a horse.

Finn and the others, hearing this, seized their arms and started off in pursuit. Now, the way the Gilla Dacker and his horse took was first through Fermore, which is at the present day called Hy Conall Gavra; next over the wide, heathy summit of Slieve Lougher; from that to Corca Divna; and they ran along by Slieve Mish till they reached Cloghan Kincat, near the deep green sea.

And so the great horse continued his course without stop or stay, bringing the sixteen Feni with him through the sea. Now, this is how they fared in the sea while the horse was rushing farther and farther to the west. They had always a dry, firm strand under them, for the waters retired before the horse; while behind them was a wild, raging sea, which followed close after and seemed ready every moment to topple over their heads.

But, though the billows were tumbling and roaring all round, neither horse nor riders were wetted by as much as a drop of brine or a dash of spray.

Then Finn spoke and asked the chiefs what they thought best to be done; and they told him they would follow whatsoever counsel he and Fergus Finnvel, the poet, gave them. Then Finn told Fergus to speak his mind; and Fergus said, "My counsel is that we go straightway to Ben Edar, where we shall find a ship ready to sail. For our forefathers, when they wrested the land from the gifted, bright-complexioned Dedannans, bound them by covenant to maintain this ship for ever, fitted with all things needful for a voyage, even to the smallest article, as one of the privileges of Ben Edar; so that if at any time one of the noble sons of Gael Glas wished to sail to distant lands from Erin, he should have a ship lying at hand in the harbour ready to begin his voyage."

They agreed to this counsel, and turned their steps without delay northwards towards Ben Edar. They had not gone far when they met two noble-looking youths, fully armed, and wearing over their armour beautiful mantles of scarlet silk, fastened by brooches of gold. The strangers saluted the King with much respect; and the King saluted them in return. Then, having given them leave to converse, he asked them who they were, where they had come, and who the prince or chief was that they served. And the elder answered, "My name is Feradach, and my brother's name is Foltlebar; and we are the two sons of the King of Innia. Each of us professes an art; and it has long been a point of dispute between us which art is the better, my brother's or mine. Hearing that there is not in the world a wiser or more far-seeing man than you are, Oh King, we have come to ask you to take us into your service among your household troops for a year, and at the end of that time to give judgment between us in this matter."

Finn asked them what the two arts were they professed.

"My art," answered Feradach, "is this. If at any time a company of warriors need a ship, give me only my joiner's axe and my crann-tavall, and I am able to provide a ship for them without delay. The only thing I ask them to do is this - to cover their heads close, and keep them covered, while I give the crann-tavall three blows of my axe. Then I tell them to uncover their heads; and lo, there lies the ship in harbour ready to sail!"

Then Foltlebar spoke and said, "This, Oh King, is the art I profess.

On land I can track the wild duck over nine ridges and nine glens, and follow her without being once thrown out till I drop upon her in her nest. And I can follow up a track on sea quite as well as on land if I have a good ship and crew."

Finn replied, "You are the very men I want; and I now take you both into my service. At this moment I need a good ship and a skilful pilot more than any two things in the whole world."

Whereupon Finn told them the whole story of the Gilla Dacker's doings from beginning to end. "And we are now," said he, "on our way to Ben Edar to seek a ship that we may follow this giant and his horse and rescue our companions."

Then Feradach said, "I will get you a ship - a ship that will sail as swiftly as a swallow can fly!"

And Foltlebar said, "I will guide your ship in the track of the Gilla Dacker till you lay hands on him, in whatsoever quarter of the world he may have hidden himself!"

And so they turned back to Cloghan Kincat. And when they had come to the beach Feradach told them to cover their heads, and they did so. Then he struck three blows of his axe on the crann-tavall; after which he made them look. And lo, they saw a ship fully fitted out with oars and sails and with all things needed for a long voyage riding before them in the harbour!

Then they went on board and launched their ship on the cold, bright sea; and Foltlebar was their pilot and steersman. And they set their sail and plied their slender oars, and the ship moved swiftly westward till they lost sight of the shores of Erin; and they saw nothing all round them but a wide girdle of sea. After some days' sailing a great storm came from the west, and the black waves rose up against them so that they had much ado to keep their vessel from sinking. But through all the roaring of the tempest, through the rain and blinding spray, Foltlebar never stirred from the helm or changed his course, but still kept close on the track of the Gilla Dacker.

At length the storm abated and the sea grew calm. And when the darkness had cleared away they saw to the west, a little way off, a vast rocky cliff towering over their heads to such a height that its head seemed hidden among the clouds. It rose up sheer from the very water, and looked at that distance as smooth as glass, so that at first sight there seemed no way to reach the top.

Foltlebar, after examining to the four points of the sky, found the track of the Gilla Dacker as far as the cliff, but no farther. And he accordingly told the heroes that he thought it was on the top of that rock the giant lived; and that, anyhow, the horse must have made his way up the face of the cliff with their companions.

When the heroes heard this they were greatly cast down and puzzled what to do; for they saw no way of reaching the top of the rock; and they feared they should have to give up the quest and return without their companions. And they sat down and looked up at the cliff with sorrow and vexation in their hearts.

Fergus Finnvel, the poet, then challenged the hero Dermat O'Dyna to climb the rock in pursuit of the Gilla Dacker, and he did so, and on reaching the summit found himself in a beautiful fairy plain. He fared across it and came to a great tree laden with fruit beside a well as clear as crystal. Hard by, on the brink of the well, stood a tall pillar stone, and on its top lay a golden-chased drinking horn. He filled the horn from the well and drank, but had scarcely taken it from his lips when he saw a fully armed wizard champion advancing to meet him with looks and gestures of angry menace. The wizard upbraided him for entering his territory without leave and for drinking out of his well from his drinking horn, and thereupon challenged him to fight. For four days long they fought, the wizard escaping from Dermat every even-fall by leaping into the well and disappearing down through it. But on the fourth evening Dermat closed with the wizard when about to spring into the water, and fell with him into the well.

On reaching the bottom the wizard wrested himself away and started running, and Dermat found himself in a strangely beautiful country with a royal palace hard by, in front of which armed knights were engaged in warlike exercises. Through them the wizard ran, but, when Dermat attempted to follow, his way was barred by their threatening weapons. Nothing daunted, he fell upon them in all his battle fury, and routed them so entirely that they fled and shut themselves up in the castle or took refuge in distant woods.

Overcome with his battle toil (and smarting all over with wounds) Dermat fell into a dead sleep, from which he was wakened by a friendly blow from the flat of a sword held by a young, golden-haired hero, who proved to be the brother of the Knight of Valour, King of that country of Tir-fa-tonn, whom in the guise of the Knight of the Fountain, Dermat had fought and chased away.

A part of the kingdom belonging to him had been seized by his wizard brother, and he now seeks and obtains Dermat's aid to win it back for him.

When Dermat at last meets Finn and the other Feni who had gone in pursuit of him into the Kingdom of Sorca, at the summit of the great rock, he is able to relate how he headed the men of the Knight of Valour against the Wizard King, and slew him and defeated his army.

"And now," continued he, bringing forth the Knight of Valour from among the strange host, "this is he who was formerly called the

Knight of Valour, but who is now the King of Tir-fa-tonn. Moreover, this King has told me, having himself found it out by his druidical art, that it was Avarta the Dedannan (the son of Illahan of the Many-coloured Raiment) who took the form of the Gilla Dacker, and who brought the sixteen Feni away to the Land of Promise, where he now holds them in bondage."

Then Foltlebar at once found the tracks of the Gilla Dacker and his horse. He traced them from the very edge of the rock across the plain to the sea at the other side; and they brought round their ship and began their voyage. But this time Foltlebar found it very hard to keep on the track; for the Gilla Dacker, knowing that there were not in the world men more skilled in following up a quest than the Feni, took great pains to hide all traces of the flight of himself and his horse; so that Foltlebar was often thrown out; but he always recovered the track after a little time.

And so they sailed from island to island and from bay to bay, over many seas and by many shores, ever following the track, till at length they arrived at the Land of Promise. And when they had made the land, and knew for a certainty that this was indeed the Land of Promise, they rejoiced greatly; for in this land Dermat O'Dyna had been nurtured by Mannanan Mac Lir of the Yellow Hair.

Then they held council as to what was best to be done; and Finn's advice was that they should burn and spoil the country in revenge of the outrage that had been done to his people. Dermat, however, would not hear of this. And he said, "Not so, Oh King. The people of this land are of all men the most skilled in druidic art; and it is not well that they should be at feud with us. Let us rather send to Avarta a trusty herald to demand that he should set our companions at liberty. If he does so, then we shall be at peace; if he refuse, then shall we proclaim war against him and his people, and waste this land with fire and sword till he be forced, even by his own people, to give us back our friends."

This advice was approved by all. And then Finn said, "But how shall heralds reach the dwelling of this enchanter; for the ways are not open and straight, as in other lands, but crooked and made for concealment, and the valleys and plains are dim and shadowy and hard to be traversed?"

But Foltlebar, nothing daunted by the dangers and the obscurity of the way, offered to go with a single trusty companion; and they took up the track and followed it without being once thrown out, till they reached the mansion of Avarta. There they found their friends amusing themselves on the green outside the palace walls; for, though kept captive in the island, yet were they in no wise restrained, but were treated by Avarta with much kindness. When they saw the heralds coming towards them their joy knew no bounds; they crowded round to embrace them, and asked them many questions regarding their home and their friends.

At last Avarta himself came forth and asked who these strangers were; and Foltlebar replied, "We are of the people of Finn Mac Cumal, who has sent us as heralds to you. He and his heroes have landed on this island guided hereby me; and he bade us tell you that he has come to wage war and to waste this land with fire and sword as a punishment for that you have brought away his people by foul spells, and even now keeps them in bondage."

When Avarta heard this he made no reply, but called a council of his chief men to consider whether they should send back to Finn an answer of war or of peace. And they, having much fear of the Feni, were minded to restore Finn's people and to give him his own award in satisfaction for the injury done to him; and to invite Finn himself and those who had come with him to a feast of joy and friendship in the house of Avarta.

Avarta himself went with Foltlebar to give this message. And after he and Finn had exchanged friendly greetings, he told them what the council had resolved; and Finn and Dermat and the others were glad at heart. And Finn and Avarta put hand in hand and made a league of friendship.

So they went with Avarta to his house, where they found their lost friends; and, being full of gladness, they saluted and embraced each other. Then a feast was prepared; and they were feasted for three days, and they ate and drank and made merry.

On the fourth day a meeting was called on the green to hear the award. Now, it was resolved to make amends on the one hand to Finn, as King of the Feni, and on the other to those who had been brought away by the Gilla Dacker. And when all were gathered together Finn was first asked to name his award; and this is what he said, "I shall not name an award, Oh Avarta; neither shall I accept an eric from you. But the wages I promised you when we made our covenant at Knockainy, that I will give you. For I am thankful for the welcome you have given us here; and I wish that there should be peace and friendship between us forever."

But Conan, on his part, was not so easily satisfied; and he said to Finn, "Little have you endured, Oh Finn, in this matter; and you mayst well waive your award. But had you, like us, suffered from the sharp bones and the rough carcass of the Gilla Dacker's monstrous horse in a long journey from Erin to the Land of Promise, across wide seas, through tangled woods, and over rough-headed rocks, you would then, methinks, name an award."

At this, Avarta and the others who had seen Conan and his

companions carried off on the back of the big horse could scarce keep from laughing; and Avarta said to Conan, "Name your award, and I will fulfil it every jot; for I have heard of you, Conan, and I dread to bring the gibes and taunts of your foul tongue on myself and my people."

"Well, then," said Conan, "my award is this - that you choose fifteen of the best and noblest men in the Land of Promise, among whom are to be your own best beloved friends; and that you cause them to mount on the back of the big horse, and that you yourself take hold of his tail. In this manner you shall fare to Erin, back again by the self-same track the horse took when he brought us here- through the same surging seas, through the same thick thorny woods, and over the same islands and rough rocks and dark glens. And this, Avarta, is my award," said Conan.

Now, Finn and his people were rejoiced exceedingly when they heard Conan's award - that he asked from Avarta nothing more than like for like. For they feared much that he might claim treasure of gold and silver, and thus bring reproach on the Feni.

Avarta promised that everything required by Conan should be done, binding himself in solemn pledges. Then the heroes took their leave; and having launched their ship on the broad, green sea, they sailed back by the same course to Erin. And they marched to their camping-place at Knockainy, where they rested in their tents.

Avarta then chose his men. And he placed them on the horse's back, and he himself caught hold of the tail; and it is not told how they fared till they made harbour and landing-place at Cloghan Kincat. They delayed not, but straightway journeyed over the self-same track as before till they reached Knockainy.

Finn and his people saw them afar off coming towards the hill with great speed; the Gilla Dacker, quite as large and as ugly as ever, running before the horse; for he had let go the tail at Cloghan Kincat. And the Feni could not help laughing heartily when they saw the plight of the fifteen chiefs on the great horse's back; and they said with one voice that Conan had made a good award that time.

When the horse reached the spot from which he had at first set out the men began to dismount. Then the Gilla Dacker, suddenly stepping forward, held up his arm and pointed earnestly over the heads of the Feni towards the field where the horses were standing; so that the heroes were startled, and turned round every man to look. But nothing was to be seen except the horses grazing quietly inside the fence.

Finn and the others now turned round again with intent to speak to the Gilla Dacker and bring him and his people into the tents; but much did they marvel to find them all gone. The Gilla Dacker and his great horse and fifteen nobles of the Land of Promise had disappeared in an instant; and neither Finn himself nor any of his chiefs ever saw them afterwards.

Tales From The Land Of Saints & Scholars

The Quest of the Sons of Turenn

"The Quest of the Sons of Turenn", as adapted by Thomas William Hazen Rolleston in The High Deeds of Finn and Other Bardic Romances of Ancient Ireland (1910), retells one of the most powerful and tragic of Ireland's mythic cycles. The story comes from the Mythological Cycle, centred on the Tuatha Dé Danann and their struggles with rival divine races.

Rolleston's retelling captures the grandeur and sorrow of the tale, emphasising the moral gravity beneath its adventure. The brothers achieve every task through courage, cunning, and brotherly loyalty, but their triumph comes at a cost. Through Rolleston's adaptation, it becomes not only a legend of divine heroism but a timeless warning about the ruin that follows vengeance.

Long ago, when the people of Dana yet held lordship in Erinn, they were sorely afflicted by hordes of sea-rovers named Fomorians who used to harry the country and carry off youths and maidens into captivity. They also imposed cruel and extortionate taxes upon the people, for every kneading trough, and every quern for grinding corn, and every flagstone for baking bread had to pay its tax. And an ounce of gold was paid as a poll-tax for every man, and if any man would not or could not pay, his nose was cut off. Under this tyranny the whole country groaned, but they had none who was able to band them together and to lead them in battle against their oppressors.

Now before this it happened that one of the lords of the Danaans named Kian had married with Ethlinn, daughter of Balor, a princess of the Fomorians. They had a son named Lugh Lamfada, or Lugh of the Long Arm, who grew up into a youth of surpassing beauty and strength. And if his body was noble and mighty, no less so was his mind, for lordship and authority grew to him by the gift of the Immortals, and whatever he proposed that would he perform, whatever it might cost in time or toil, in tears or in blood. Now this Lugh was not brought up in Erinn but in a far-off isle of the western sea, where the sea-god Mananan and the other Immortals nurtured and taught him, and made him fit alike for warfare or for sovereignty, when his day should come to work their will on earth. Here in due time came the report of the grievous and dishonouring oppression wrought by the Fomorians upon the people of Dana, and that report was heard by Lugh. Then Lugh said to his tutors "It were a worthy deed to rescue my father and the people of Erinn from this tyranny; let me go there and attempt it." And they said to him, "Go, and blessing and victory be with you." So Lugh armed himself and mounted his fairy steed, and called his friends and foster-brothers about him, and across the bright and heaving surface of the waters they rode like the wind, until they took land in Erinn.

Now the chiefs of the Danaan folk were assembled upon the Hill of Usnach, which is upon the western side of Tara in Meath, in order to meet there the stewards of the Fomorians and to pay them their tribute. As they awaited the arrival of the Fomorians they became aware of a company on horseback, coming from the west, before whom rode a young man who seemed to command them all, and whose countenance was as radiant as the sun upon a dry summer's day, so that the Danaans could scarcely gaze upon it. He rode upon a white horse and was armed with a sword, and on his head was a helmet set with precious stones. The Danaan folk welcomed him as he came among them, and asked him of his name and his business among them. As they were thus talking another band drew near, numbering nine times nine persons, who were the stewards of the Fomorians coming to demand their tribute. They were men of a fierce and swarthy countenance, and as they came haughtily and arrogantly forward, the Danaans all rose up to do them honour. Then Lugh said, "Why do you rise up before that grim and ill-looking band and not before us?"

Said the King of Erinn, "We needs must do so, for if they saw but a child of a month old sitting down when they came near they would hold it cause enough to attack and slay us."

"I am greatly minded to slay them," said Lugh; and he repeated it, "very greatly minded."

"That would be bad for us," said the King, "for our death and destruction would surely follow."

"Ye are too long under oppression," said Lugh, and gave the word for onset. So he and his comrades rushed upon the Fomorians, and in a moment the hillside rang with blows and with the shouting of warriors. In no long time all of the Fomorians were slain save nine men, and these were taken alive and brought before Lugh.

"Ye also should be slain," said Lugh, "but that I am minded to send you as ambassadors to your King. Tell him that he may seek homage and tribute where he will henceforth, but Ireland will pay him none for ever."

Then the Fomorians went northwards away, and the people of Dana made them ready for war, and made Lugh their captain and war-lord, for the sight of his face heartened them, and made them strong, and they marvelled that they had endured their slavery so long.

In the meantime word was brought to Balor of the Mighty Blows, King of the Fomorians, and to his queen Kethlinn of the Twisted Teeth, of the shame and destruction that had been done to their stewards, and they assembled a great host of the sea-rovers and manned their war-ships, and the Northern Sea was white with the foam of their oar blades as they swept down upon the shores of Erinn. And Balor commanded them, saying, "When you have utterly destroyed and subdued the people of Dana, then make fast your ships with cables to the land of Erinn, and tow it here to the north of us into the region of ice and snow, and it shall trouble us no longer." So the host of Balor took land by the Falls of Dara and began plundering and devastating the province of Connacht.

Then Lugh sent messengers abroad to bring his host together, and among them was his own father, Kian, son of Canta. And as Kian went northwards on his errand to rouse the Ulster men, and was now come to the plain of Murthemny nearby Dundealga, he saw three warriors armed and riding across the plain. Now these three were the sons of Turenn, by name Brian and Iuchar and Iucharba. And there was an ancient blood-feud between the house of Canta and the house of Turenn, so that they never met without bloodshed.

Then Kian thought to himself, "If my brothers Cu and Kethan were here there might be a pretty fight, but as they are three to one I would do better to fly." Now there was a herd of wild swine nearby; and Kian changed himself by druidic sorceries into a wild pig and fell to rooting up the earth along with the others.

When the sons of Turenn came up to the herd, Brian said, "Brothers, did you see the warrior who just now was journeying across the plain?"

"We saw him," said they.

"What is become of him?" said Brian.

"Truly, we cannot tell," said the brothers.

"It is good watch you keep in time of war!" said Brian, "but I know what has taken him out of our sight, for he struck himself with a magic wand, and changed himself into the form of one of yonder swine, and he is rooting the earth among them now. Wherefore," said Brian, "I deem that he is no friend to us."

"If so, we have no help for it," said they, "for the herd belongs to some man of the Danaans; and even if we set to and begin to kill the swine, the pig of druidism might be the very one to escape."

"Have you learned so little in your place of studies," said Brian, "that you cannot distinguish a druidic beast from a natural beast?" And with that he smote his two brothers with a magic wand, and changed them into two slender, fleet hounds, and they darted in among the herd. Then all the herd scattered and fled, but the hounds separated the druidic pig and chased it towards a wood where Brian awaited it. As it passed, Brian flung his spear, and it pierced the chest of the pig and brought it down. The pig screamed, "Evil have you done to cast at me."

Brian said, "That have the sound of human speech!"

"I am in truth a man," said the pig, "and I am Kian, son of Canta, and I pray you show me mercy."

"That will we," said Iuchar and Iucharba, "and sorry are we for what has happened."

"Nay," said Brian, "but I swear by the Wind and the Sun that if you had seven lives I would take them all."

"Grant me a favour then," said Kian.

"We shall grant it," said Brian.

"Let me," said Kian, "return into my own form that I may die in the shape of a man."

"I had rather kill a man than a pig," said Brian. Then Kian became a man again and stood before them, the blood trickling from his breast.

"I have outwitted you now," cried he, "for if you had killed a pig you would have paid a pig's eric, but now you shall pay the eric of a man. Never was greater eric in the land of Erinn than that which you shall pay; and I swear that the very weapons with which you slay me shall tell the tale to the avenger of blood."

"Then you shall be slain with no weapons at all," said Brian; and they picked up the stones on the Plain of Murthemny and rained them upon him till he was all one wound, and he died. So they buried him as deep as the height of a man, and went their way to join the host of Lugh.

When the host was assembled, Lugh led them into Connacht and smote the Fomorians and drove them to their ships, but of this the tale tells not here. But when the fight was done, Lugh asked of his comrades if they had seen his father in the fight and how it fared with him. They said they had not seen him. Then Lugh made search among the dead, and they found not Kian there. "Were Kian alive he would be here," said Lugh, "and I swear by the Wind and the Sun that I will not eat or drink till I know what has befallen him."

On their return the Danaan host passed by the Plain of Murthemny, and when they came near the place of the murder the stones cried aloud to Lugh. And Lugh listened, and they told him of the deed of the sons of Turenn. Then Lugh searched for the place of a new grave, and when he had found it he caused it to be dug, and the body of his father was raised up, and Lugh saw that it was but a litter of wounds.

And he cried out, "O wicked and horrible deed!" and he kissed his father and said, "I am sick from this sight, my eyes are blind from it, my ears are deaf from it, my heart stands still from it. Ye gods that I adore, why was I not here when this crime was done? a man of the children of Dana slain by his fellows." And he lamented long and bitterly. Then Kian was again laid in his grave, and a mound was heaped over it and a pillar-stone set thereon and his name written in Ogham, and a dirge was sung for him.

After that Lugh departed to Tara, to the Court of the High King, and he charged his people to say nothing of what had happened until he himself had made it known.

When he reached Tara with his victorious host the King placed Lugh at his own right hand before all the princes and lords of the Danaan folk. Lugh looked round about him, and saw the sons of Turenn sitting among the assembly; and they were among the best and strongest and the handsomest of those who were present at that time; nor had any borne themselves better in the fight with the sea-rovers. Then Lugh asked of the King that the chain of silence might be shaken; and the assembly heard it, and gave their attention to Lugh. And Lugh said, "O King, and you princes of the People of Dana, I ask what vengeance each of you would exact upon a man who had foully murdered your father?"

Then they were all astonished, and the King answered and said, "Surely it is not the father of Lugh Lamfada who has thus been slain?"

"You have said it," said Lugh, "and those who did the deed are listening to me now, and know it better than I."

The King said, "Not in one day would I slay the murderer of my father, but I would tear from him a limb day by day till he were dead."

And so spoke all the lords of the Danaans, and the Sons of Turenn among the rest.

"They have sentenced themselves, the murderers of my father," said Lugh. "Nevertheless I shall accept an eric from them, and if they will pay it, it shall be well; but if not, I shall not break the peace of the King's Assembly and of his sanctuary, but let them beware how they leave the Hall Tara until they have made me satisfaction."

"Had I slain your father," said the High King, "glad should I be to have an eric accepted for his blood."

Then the Sons of Turenn whispered among themselves. "It is to us that Lugh is speaking," said Iuchar and Iucharba, "let us confess and have the eric assessed upon us, for he has got knowledge of our deed."

"Nay," said Brian, "but he may be seeking for an open confession, and then perchance he would not accept an eric."

But the two brethren said to Brian, "Do you confess because you are the eldest, or if you do not, then we shall."

So Brian, son of Turenn, rose up and said to Lugh, "It is to us you have spoken, Lugh, since you know there is enmity of old time between our houses; and if you will have it that we have slain your father, then declare our eric and we shall pay it."

"I will take an eric from you," said Lugh, "and if it seem too great, I will remit a portion of it."

"Declare it, then," said the Sons of Turenn.

"This it is," said Lugh.

"Three apples.

"The skin of a pig.

"A spear.

"Two steeds and a chariot.

"Seven swine.

"A whelp of a dog.

"A cooking spit.

"Three shouts on a hill."

"We would not consider heavy hundreds or thousands of these things," said the Sons of Turenn, "but we misdoubt you have some secret purpose against us."

"I deem it no small eric," said Lugh, "and I call to witness the High King and lords of the Danaans that I shall ask no more; and do you on your side give me guarantees for the fulfilment of it."

So the High King and the lords of the Danaans entered into bonds with Lugh and with the Sons of Turenn that the eric should be paid and should wipe out the blood of Kian.

"Now," said Lugh, "it is better form to give you fuller knowledge of the eric. The three apples that I have demanded of you are the apples that grow in the garden of the Hesperides, in the east of the world, and none but these will do. Thus it is with them, they are the colour of bright gold, and as large as the head of a month-old child; the taste of them is like honey; if he who eats them has any running sore or evil disease it is healed by them; they may be eaten and eaten and never be less. I doubt, Oh young heroes, if you will get these apples, for those who guard them know well an ancient prophecy that one day three knights from the western world would come to attempt them.

"As for the skin of the pig, that is a treasure of Tuish, the King of Greece. If it be laid upon a wounded man it will make him whole and well, if only it overtake the breath of life in him. And do you know what is the spear that I demanded?"

"We do not," said they.

"It is the poisoned spear of Peisear, the King of Persia, and so fierce is the spirit of war in it that it must be kept in a pot of soporific herbs or it would fly out raging for death. And do you know what the two horses and the chariot are you must get?"

"We do not know," said they.

"The steeds and the chariot belong to Dobar, King of Sicily. They are magic steeds and can go indifferently over land and sea, nor can they be killed by any weapon unless they be torn in pieces and their bones cannot be found. And the seven pigs are the swine of Asal, King of the Golden Pillars, which may be slain and eaten every night and the next morning they are alive again.

"And the hound-whelp I asked of you is the whelp of the King of Iorroway, that can catch and slay any beast in the world; hard it is to get possession of that whelp.

"The cooking spit is one of the spits that the fairy women of the Island of Finchory have in their kitchen.

"And the hill on which you must give three shouts is the hill where dwells Mochaen in the north of Lochlann. Now Mochaen and his sons have it as a sacred ordinance that they permit not any man to raise a shout upon their hill. With him it was that my father was trained to arms, and if I forgave you his death, yet would Mochaen not forgive it.

"And now you know the eric which you have to pay for the slaying of Kian, son of Canta."

Astonishment and despair overcame the Sons of Turenn when they learned the meaning of the eric of Lugh, and they went home to tell the tidings to their father.

"This is an evil tale," said Turenn, "I doubt but death and doom shall come from your seeking of that eric, and it is but right they should. Yet it may be that you shall obtain the eric if Lugh or Mananan will help you to it. Go now to Lugh, and ask him for the loan of the fairy steed of Mananan, which was given him to ride over the sea into Erinn. He will refuse you, for he will say that the steed is but lent to him and he may not make a loan of a loan. Then ask him for the loan of Ocean Sweeper, which is the magic boat of Mananan, and that he must give, for it is a sacred ordinance with Lugh not to refuse a second petition."

So they went to Lugh, and it all fell out as Turenn had told them, and they went back to Turenn.

"Ye have done something towards the eric," said Turenn, "but not much. Yet Lugh would be well pleased that you brought him whatever might serve him when the Fomorians come to the battle again, and well pleased would he be that you might get your death in bringing it. Go now, my sons, and blessing and victory be with you."

Then the Sons of Turenn went down to the harbour on the Boyne river where the Boat of Mananan was, and Ethne their sister with them. And when they reached the place, Ethne broke into lamentations and weeping; but Brian said, "Weep not, dear sister, but let us go forth gaily to great deeds. Better a hundred deaths in the quest of honour than to live and die as cowards and sluggards." But Ethne said, "ye are banished from Erinn—never was there a sadder deed." Then they put forth from the river-mouth of the Boyne and soon the fair coasts of Erinn faded out of sight. "And now," said they among themselves, "what course shall we steer?"

"No need to steer the Boat of Mananan," said Brian; and he whispered to the Boat, "Bear us swiftly, Boat of Mananan, to the Garden of the Hesperides"; and the spirit of the Boat heard him and it leaped eagerly forward, lifting and dipping over the rollers and throwing up an arch of spray each side of its bows wherein sat a rainbow when the sun shone upon it; and so in no long time they drew nigh to the coast where was the far-famed garden of the Golden Apples.

"And now, how shall we set about the capture of the apples?" said Brian.

"Draw sword and fight for them," said Iuchar and Iucharba, "and if we are the stronger, we shall win them, and if not, we shall fall, as fall we surely must before the eric for Kian be paid."

"Nay," said Brian, "but whether we live or die, let not men say of us that we went blind and headlong to our tasks, but rather that we made the head help the hand, and that we deserved to win even though we lost. Now my counsel is that we approach the garden in the shape of three hawks, strong of wing, and that we hover about until the Wardens of the Tree have spent all their darts and javelins in casting at us, and then let us swoop down suddenly and bear off each of us an apple if we may."

So it was agreed; and Brian struck himself and each of the brothers with a druid wand, and they became three beautiful, fierce, and strong-winged hawks. When the Wardens perceived them, they shouted and threw showers of arrows and darts at them, but the hawks evaded all of these until the missiles were spent, and then seized each an apple in his talons. But Brian seized two, for he took one in his beak as well. Then they flew as swiftly as they might to the shore where they had left their boat. Now the King of that garden had three fair daughters, to whom the apples and the garden were very dear, and he transformed the maidens into three griffins, who pursued the hawks. And the griffins threw darts of fire, as it were lightning, at the hawks.

"Brian!" then cried Iuchar and his brother, "we are being burnt by these darts—we are lost unless we can escape them."

On this, Brian changed himself and his brethren into three swans, and they plunged into the sea, and the burning darts were quenched. Then the griffins gave over the chase, and the Sons of Turenn made for their boat, and they embarked with the four apples. Thus their first quest was ended.

After that they resolved to seek the pigskin from the King of Greece, and they debated how they should come before him. "Let us," said Brian, "assume the character and garb of poets and men of learning, for such are likely to come from Ireland and to travel foreign lands, and in that character shall the Greeks receive us best, for such men have honour among them." "It is well said," replied the brothers, "yet we have no poems in our heads, and how to compose one we know not."

Howbeit they dressed their hair in the fashion of the poets of Erinn, and went up to the palace of Tuish the King. The doorkeeper asked of them who they were, and what was their business.

"We are bards from Ireland," they said, "and we have come with a poem to the King."

"Let them be admitted," said the King, when the doorkeeper brought him that tale, "they have doubtless come thus far to seek a powerful patron."

So Brian and Iuchar and Iucharba came in and were made welcome, and were entertained, and then the minstrels of the King of Greece chanted the lays of that country before them. After that came the turn of the stranger bards, and Brian asked his brethren if they had anything to recite.

"We have not," said they, "we know but one art—to take what we want by the strong hand if we may, and if we may not, to die fighting."

"That is a difficult art too," said Brian, "let us see how we thrive with the poetry."

So he rose up and recited this lay:

"Mighty is your fame, Oh King,

Towering like a giant oak;

For my song I ask no thing

Save a pigskin for a cloak.

"When a neighbour with his friend

Quarrels, they are ear to ear;

Who on us their store shall spend

Shall be richer than they were.

"Armies of the storming wind—

Raging seas, the sword's fell stroke—

You have nothing to my mind

Save your pigskin for a cloak."

"That is a very good poem," said the King, "but one word of its meaning I do not understand."

"I will interpret it for you," said Brian, "Mighty is your fame, Oh King, towering like a giant oak. That is to say, as the oak surpasses all the other trees of the forest, so do you surpass all the kings of the world in goodness, in nobleness, and in liberality.

"A pigskin for a cloak. That is the skin of the pig of Tuish which I would fain receive as the reward for my lay."

"When a neighbour with his friend quarrels, they are ear to ear. That is to signify that you and I shall be about each other's ears over the skin, unless you are willing to give it to me. Such is the sense of my poem," said Brian, son of Turenn.

"I would praise your poem more," said the King, "if there were not so much about my pigskin in it. Little sense have you, Oh man of poetry, to make that request of me, for not to all the poets, scholars, and lords of the world would I give that skin of my own free will. But what I will do is this—I will give the full of that skin of red gold thrice over in reward for your poem."

"Thanks be to you," said Brian, "for that. I knew that I asked too much, but I knew also you would redeem the skin amply and generously. And now let the gold be duly measured out in it, for greedy am I, and I will not abate an ounce of it."

The servants of the King were then sent with Brian and his brothers to the King's treasure-chamber to measure out the gold. As they did so, Brian suddenly snatched the skin from the hands of him who held it, and swiftly wrapped it round his body. Then the three brothers drew sword and made for the door, and a great fight arose in the King's palace. But they hewed and thrust manfully on every side of them, and though sorely wounded they fought their way through and escaped to the shore, and drove their boat out to sea, when the skin of the magic pig quickly made them whole and sound again. And thus the second quest of the Sons of Turenn had its end.

"Let us now," said Brian, "go to seek the spear of the King of Persia."

"In what manner of guise shall we go before the King of Persia?" said his brothers.

"As we did before the King of Greece," said Brian.

"That guise served us well with the King of Greece," replied they, "nevertheless, O'Brian, this business of professing to be poets, when we are but swordsmen, is painful to us."

However, they dressed their hair in the manner of poets and went up boldly to the palace of King Peisear of Persia, saying, as before, that they were wandering bards from Ireland who had a poem to recite before the King; and as they passed through the courtyard they marked the spear drowsing in its pot of sleepy herbs. They were made welcome, and after listening to the lays of the King's minstrel, Brian rose and sang:

"This little Peisear cares for spears,
Since armies, when his face they see,
All overcome with panic fears
Without a wound they turn and flee.

"The Yew is monarch of the wood,

No other tree disputes its claim.

The shining shaft in venom stewed

Flies fiercely forth to kill and maim."

"Tis a very good poem," said the King, "but, Oh bard from Erinn, I do not understand your reference to my spear."

"It is merely this," replied Brian, "that I would like your spear as a reward for my poem."

Then the King stared at Brian, and his beard bristled with anger, and he said, "Never was a greater reward paid for any poem than not to adjudge you guilty of instant death for your request."

Then Brian flung at the king the fourth golden apple which he had taken from the Garden of the Hesperides, and it dashed out his brains. Immediately the brothers all drew sword and made for the courtyard. Here they seized the magic spear, and with it and with their swords they fought their way clear, not without many wounds, and escaped to their boat. And thus ended the third quest of the Sons of Turenn.

Now having come safely and victoriously through so many straits and perils, they began to be merry and hoped that all the eric might yet be paid. So they sailed away with high hearts to the Island of Sicily, to get the two horses and the chariot of the King, and the Boat of Mananan bore them swiftly and well.

Having arrived here, they debated among themselves as to how they should proceed; and they agreed to present themselves as Irish mercenary soldiers—for such were likely in those days to take service with foreign kings—until they should learn where the horses and the chariot were kept, and how they should come at them. Then they went forward, and found the King and his lords in the palace garden taking the air.

The Sons of Turenn then paid homage to him, and he asked them of their business.

"We are Irish mercenary soldiers," they said, "seeking our wages from the kings of the world." "Are you willing to take service with me?" said the King. "We are," said they, "and to that end are we come."

Then their contract of military service was made, and they remained at the King's court for a month and a fortnight, and did not in all that time come to see the steeds or the chariot. At last Brian said,

"Things are going ill with us, my brethren, in that we know no more at this day of the steeds or of the chariot than when we first arrived at this place."

"What shall we do, then?" said they.

"Let us do this," said Brian. "Let us gird on our arms and all our marching array, and tell the King that we shall quit his service unless he show us the chariot.

And so they did; and the King said, "Tomorrow shall be a gathering and parade of all my host, and the chariot shall be there, and you shall see it if you have a mind."

So the next day the steeds were yoked and the chariot was driven round a great plain before the King and his lords. Now these steeds could run as well on sea as on dry land, and they were swifter than the winds of March. As the chariot came round the second time, Brian and his brothers seized the horses' heads, and Brian took the charioteer by the foot and flung him out over the rail, and they all leaped into the chariot and drove away. Such was the swiftness of their driving that they were out of sight before the King and his men knew rightly what had befallen. And thus ended the fourth quest of the Sons of Turenn.

Next they betook themselves to the court of Asal, King of the Golden Pillars, to get the seven swine which might be eaten every night and they would be whole and well on the morrow morn.

But it had now been noised about every country that three young heroes from Erinn were plundering the kings of the world of their treasures in payment of a mighty eric; and when they arrived at the Land of the Golden Pillars they found the harbour guarded and a strait watch kept, that no one who might resemble the Sons of Turenn should enter.

But Asal the King came to the harbour-mouth and spoke with the heroes, for he was desirous to see those who had done the great deeds that he had heard of. He asked them if it were true that they had done such things, and why. Then Brian told him the story of the mighty eric which had been laid upon them, and what they had done and suffered in fulfilling it. "Why," said King Asal, "have you now come to my country?"

"For the seven swine," said Brian, "to take them with us as a part of that eric."

"How do you mean to get them?" asked the King.

"With your goodwill," replied Brian, "if so it may be, and to pay you therefore with all the wealth we now have, which is thanks and love, and to stand by your side hereafter in any strait or quarrel you may enter into. But if you will not grant us the swine, and we may not be quit of our eric without them, we shall even take them as we may, and as we have in olden days taken mighty treasures from mighty kings."

Then King Asal went into counsel with his lords, and he advised that the swine be given to the Sons of Turenn, partly for that he was moved with their desperate plight and the hardihood they had shown, and partly that they might get them whether or no. To this they all agreed, and the Sons of Turenn were invited to come ashore, where they were courteously and hospitably entertained in the King's palace. On the morrow the pigs were given to them, and great was their gladness, for never before had they won a treasure without toil and blood. And they vowed that, if they should live, the name of Asal should be made by them a great and shining name, for his compassion and generosity which he had shown them. This, then, was the fifth quest of the Sons of Turenn.

"And where do you voyage now?" said Asal to them.

"We go," said they, "to Iorroway for the hound's whelp which is there."

"Take me with you, then," said Asal, "for the King of Iorroway is husband to my daughter, and I may prevail upon him to grant you the hound without combat."

So the King's ship was manned and provisioned, and the Sons of Turenn laid up their treasures in the Boat of Mananan, and they all sailed joyfully forth to the pleasant kingdom of Iorroway. But here, too, they found all the coasts and harbours guarded, and entrance was forbidden them. Then Asal declared who he was, and him they allowed to land, and he journeyed to where his son-in-law, the King of Iorroway, was. To him Asal related the whole story of the sons of

Turenn, and why they were come to that kingdom.

"You were a fool," said the King of Iorroway, "to have come on such a mission. There are no three heroes in the world to whom the Immortals have granted such grace that they should get my hound either by favour or by fight."

"That is not a good word," said Asal, "for the treasures they now possess have made them yet stronger than they were, and these they won in the teeth of kings as strong as you." And much more he said to him to persuade him to yield up the hound, but in vain. So Asal took his way back to the haven where the Sons of Turenn lay, and told them his tidings.

Then the Sons of Turenn seized the magic spear, and the pigskin, and with a rush like that of three eagles descending from a high cliff upon a lamb-fold they burst upon the guards of the King of Iorroway. Fierce and fell was the combat that ensued, and many times the brothers were driven apart, and all but overborne by the throng of their foes. But at last Brian perceived where the King of Iorroway was directing the fight, and he cut his way to him, and having smitten him to the ground, he bound him and carried him out of the press to the haven-side where Asal was.

"There," he said, "is your son-in-law for you Asal, and I swear by my sword that I had more easily killed him thrice than once to bring him thus bound to you."

"That is very like," said Asal, "but now hold him to ransom."

So the people of Iorroway gave the hound to the Sons of Turenn as a ransom for their King, and the King was released, and friendship and alliance were made between them. And with joyful hearts the Sons of Turenn bade farewell to the King of Iorroway and to Asal, and departed on their way. Thus was the sixth of their quests fulfilled.

Now Lugh Lamfada desired to know how the Sons of Turenn had fared, and whether they had got any portion of the great eric that might be serviceable to him when the Fomorians should return for one more struggle. And by sorcery and divination it was revealed to him how they had thriven, and that nought remained to be won save the cooking-spit of the sea-nymphs, and to give the three shouts upon the hill. Lugh then by druidic art caused a spell of oblivion and forgetfulness to descend upon the Sons of Turenn, and put into their hearts withal a yearning and passion to return to their native land of Erinn. They forgot, therefore, that a portion of the eric was still to win, and they bade the Boat of Mananan bear them home with their treasures, for they deemed that they should now quit them of all their debt for the blood of Kian and live free in their father's home, having done such things and won such fame as no three brothers had ever done since the world began.

At the Brugh of Boyne, where they had started on their quest, their boat came ashore again, and as they landed they wept for joy, and falling on their knees they kissed the green sod of Erinn. Then they took up their treasures and journeyed to Ben Edar, where the High King of Ireland, and Lugh with him, were holding an Assembly of the People of Dana. But when Lugh heard that they were on their way he put on his cloak of invisibility and withdrew privily to Tara.

When the brethren arrived at Ben Edar, the High King of the lords of the Danaans gave them welcome and applause, for all were rejoiced that the stain of ancient feud and bloodshed should be wiped out, and that the Children of Dana should be at peace within their borders. Then they sought for Lugh to deliver over the eric, but he was not to be found. And Brian said, "He has gone to Tara to avoid us, having heard that we were coming with our treasures and weapons of war."

Word was then sent to Lugh at Tara that the Sons of Turenn were at Ben Edar, and the eric with them.

"Let them pay it over to the High King," said Lugh.

So it was done; and when Lugh had tidings that the High King had the eric, he returned to Ben Edar.

Then the eric was laid before him, and Brian said, "Is the debt paid, Oh Lugh, son of Kian?"

Lugh said, "Truly there is here the price of any man's death; but it is not lawful to give a quittance for an eric that is not complete. Where is the cooking-spit from the Island of Finchory? and have you given the three shouts upon the Hill of Mochaen?"

At this word Brian and Iuchar and Iucharba fell prone upon the ground, and were speechless awhile from grief and dismay. After a while they left the Assembly like broken men, with hanging heads and with heavy steps, and betook themselves to Dún Turenn, where they found their father, and they told him all that had befallen them since they had parted with him and set forth on the Quest. Thus they passed the night in gloom and evil forebodings, and on the morrow they went down once more to the place where the Boat of Mananan was moored. And Ethne their sister accompanied them, wailing and lamenting, but no words of cheer had they now to say to her, for now they began to comprehend that a mightier and a craftier mind had caught them in the net of fate. And whereas they had deemed themselves heroes and victors in the most glorious quest whereof the earth had record, they now knew that they were but as arrows in the hands of a laughing archer, who shoots one at a stag and one at the heart of a foe, and one, it may be, in sheer wantonness, and to try his bow, over a cliff edge into the sea.

There dwelt the red-haired ocean-nymphs

"There dwelt the red-haired ocean-nymphs"

However, they put forth in their magic boat, but in no wise could they direct it to the Isle of Finchory, and a quarter of a year they traversed the seaways and never could get tidings of that island. At last Brian fashioned for himself by magic art a water-dress, with a helmet of crystal, and into the depths of the sea he plunged. Here, the story tells, he searched here and there for a fortnight, till at last he found that island, which was an island indeed with the sea over it and around it and beneath it. There dwelt the red-haired ocean-nymphs in glittering palaces among the sea-flowers, and they wrought fair embroidery with gold and jewels, and sang, as they wrought, a fairy music like the chiming of silver bells. Three fifties of them sat or played in their great hall as Brian entered, and they gazed on him but spoke no word. Then Brian strode to the wide hearth, and without a word he seized from it a spit that was made of beaten gold, and turned again to go. But at that the laughter of the sea-maidens rippled through the hall and one of them said, "You are a bold man, Brian, and bolder than you know; for if your two brothers were here, the weakest of us could vanquish all the three. Nevertheless, take the spit for your daring; we had never granted it for your prayers."

So Brian thanked them and bade farewell, and he rose to the surface of the water. Ere long his brethren perceived him as he shouldered the waves on the bosom of the deep, and they sailed to where he was and took him on board. And thus ended the quest for the seventh portion of the eric of Kian.

After that their hopes revived a little, and they set sail for the land of Lochlann, in which was the Hill of Mochaen. When they had arrived at the hill Mochaen came out to meet them with his three sons, Corc and Conn and Hugh; nor did the Sons of Turenn ever behold a band of grimmer and mightier warriors than those four.

"What seek you here?" asked Mochaen of them They told him that it had been laid upon them to give three shouts upon the hill.

"It have been laid upon me," said Mochaen, "to prevent this thing."

Then Brian and Mochaen drew sword and fell furiously upon each other, and their fighting was like that of two hungry lions or two wild bulls, until at last Brian drove his sword into the throat of Mochaen, and he died.

With that the Sons of Mochaen and the Sons of Turenn rushed fiercely upon each other. Long and sore was the strife that they had, and the blood that fell made red the grassy place wherein they fought. Not one of them but received wounds that pierced him through and through, and that heroes of less hardihood had died of a score of times. But in the end the sons of Mochaen fell, and Brian, Iuchar, and Iucharba lay over them in a swoon like death.

After a while Brian's senses came back to him, and he said, "Do you live, dear brothers, or how is it with you?" "We are as good as dead," said they, "let us be."

"Arise," then said Brian, "for truly I feel death coming swiftly upon us, and we have yet to give the three shouts upon the hill."

"We cannot stir," said Iuchar and Iucharba. Then Brian rose to his knees and to his feet, and he lifted up his two brothers while the blood of all three streamed down to their feet, and they raised their voices as best they might, and gave three hoarse cries upon the Hill of Mochaen. And thus was the last of the epic fulfilled.

Then they bound up their wounds, and Brian placed himself between the two brothers, and slowly and painfully they made their way to the boat, and put out to sea for Ireland. And as they lay in the stupor of faintness in the boat, one murmured to himself, "I see the Cape of Ben Edar and the coast of Turenn, and Tara of the Kings." Then Iuchar and Iucharba entreated Brian to lift their heads upon his breast. "Let us but see the land of Erinn again," said they, "the hills around Tailtin, and the dewy plain of Bregia, and the quiet waters of the Boyne and our father's Dún thereby, and healing will come to us; or if death come we can endure it after that." Then Brian raised them up; and they saw that they were now nearby under Ben Edar; and at the Strand of the Bull they took land. They were then conveyed to the Dún of Turenn, and life was still in them when they were laid in their father's hall.

And Brian said to Turenn, "Go now, dear father, with all speed to Lugh at Tara. Give him the cooking-spit, and tell how you have found us after giving our three shouts upon the Hill of Mochaen. Then beseech him that he yield you the loan of the pigskin of the King of Greece, for if it be laid upon us while the life is yet in us, we shall recover. We have won the eric, and it may be that he will not pursue us to our death."

Turenn went to Lugh and gave him the spit of the sea-nymphs, and begged him for the lives of his sons.

Lugh was silent for a while, but his countenance did not change, and he said, "Thou, old man, see nought but the cloud of sorrow wherein you are encompassed. But I hear from above it the singing of the Immortal Ones, who tell one another the story of this land. Your sons must die; yet have I shown to them more mercy than they showed to Kian. I have forgiven them; nor shall they live to slay their own immortality, but the royal bards of Erinn and the old men in the chimney corners shall tell of their glory and their fate as long as the land shall endure."

Then Turenn bowed his white head and went sorrowfully back to Dún Turenn; and he told his sons of the words that Lugh had said. And with that the sons of Turenn kissed each other, and the breath of life departed from them, and they died. And Turenn died also, for his heart was broken in him; and Ethne his daughter buried them in one grave. Thus, then, ends the tale of the Quest of the Eric and the Fate of the Sons of Turenn.

Tales From The Land Of Saints & Scholars

The Red Pony

"The Red Pony" is a traditional Irish folktale first collected by W. Larminie in West Irish Folk Tales and Romances (1893), later retold in Alfred Perceval Graves's The Irish Fairy Book (1909). The story belongs to that familiar class of wonder tales in which courage, gratitude, and faithfulness lead to unexpected fortune.

Like many Irish tales gathered in the late nineteenth century, "The Red Pony" blends native mythic motifs with European folktale structures. It carries echoes of pre-Christian horse symbolism, the red horse as both guardian and messenger between worlds, while also reflecting the moral sensibilities prized by rural storytellers: loyalty repaid, humility rewarded, greed undone.

There was a poor man there. He had a great family of sons. He had no means to put them forward. He had them at school. One day, when they were coming from school, he thought that whichever of them was last at the door he would keep him out. It was the youngest of the family that was last at the door. The father shut the door. He would not let him in. The boy went weeping. He would not let him in till night came. The father he said would never let him in - that he had boys enough.

The lad went away. He was walking till night. He came to a house on the rugged side of a hill on a height, one feather giving it shelter and support. He went in. He got a place till morning. When he made his breakfast in the morning he was going. The man of the house made him a present of a red pony, a saddle, and bridle. He went riding on the pony. He went away with himself.

"Now," said the pony, "whatever thing you may see before you, don't touch it."

They went on with themselves. He saw a light before him on the high road. When he came as far as the light, there was an open box on the road, and a light coming out of it. He took up the box. There was a lock of hair in it.

"Are you going to take up the box?" said the pony.

"I am. I cannot go past it."

"It's better for you to leave it," said the pony.

He took up the box. He put it in his pocket. He was going with himself. A gentleman met him.

"Pretty is your little beast. Where are you going?"

"I am looking for service."

"I am in want of one like you among the stable-boys."

He hired the lad. The lad he said must get room for the little beast in the stable. The gentleman he said would get it. They went home then. He had eleven boys. When they were going out into the stable at ten o'clock each of them took a light with him but he. He took no candle at all with him.

Each of them went into his own stable. When he went into his stable, he opened the box. He left it in a hole in the wall. The light was great. It was twice as much as in the other stables. There was wonder on the boys - what was the reason of the light being so great, and he without a candle with him at all. They told the master they did not know what was the cause of the light with the last boy. They had given him no candle, and he had twice as much light as they had.

"Watch tomorrow night what kind of light he has," said the master.

They watched the night of the morrow. They saw the box in the hole that was in the wall, and the light coming out of the box. They told the master. When the boys came to the house, the King asked him what the reason was why he did not take a candle with him to the stable, as well as the other boys. The lad he said had a candle. The King he said had not. He asked him how he got the box from which the light came. He said he had no box. The King he said had, and that he must give it to him; that he would not keep him, unless he gave him the box. The boy gave it to him. The King opened it. He drew out the lock of hair, in which was the light.

"You must go," said the King, "and bring me the woman to whom the hair belongs."

The lad was troubled. He went out. He told the red pony.

"I told you not to take up the box. You will get more than that on account of the box. When you have made your breakfast to-morrow, put the saddle and bridle on me."

When he made his breakfast on the morning of the morrow, he put saddle and bridle on the pony. He went till they came to three miles of sea.

"Keep a good hold now. I am going to give a jump over the sea. When I arrive yonder, there is a fair on the strand. Everyone will be coming up to you to ask for a ride, because I am such a pretty little beast. Give no one a ride. You will see a beautiful woman drawing near you, her in whose hair was the wonderful light. She will come up to you. She will ask you to let her ride for a while. Say you will, and welcome. When she comes riding, I will be off."

When she came to the sea, she cleared the three miles at a jump. She came upon the land opposite, and everyone was asking for a ride upon the beast, she was that pretty. He was giving a ride to no one. He saw that woman in the midst of the people. She was drawing near. She asked him would he give her a little riding. He said he would give it, and a thousand welcomes. She went riding. She went quietly, till she got out of the crowd. When the pony came to the sea, she made the three-mile jump again, the beautiful woman along with her. She took her home to the King. There was great joy on the King to see her. He took her into the parlour. She said to him she would not marry anyone until he would get the bottle of healing water that was in the eastern world. The King said to the lad he must go and bring the bottle of healing water that was in the eastern world to the lady. The lad was troubled. He went to the pony. He told the pony he must go to the eastern world for the bottle of healing water that was in it, and bring it to the lady.

"My advice was good," said the pony, "on the day you took the box up. Put saddle and bridle on me."

He went riding on her. They were going till they came to the sea. She stood then.

"You must kill me," said the pony. "That, or I must kill you!"

"It is hard to me to kill you," said the boy. "If I kill you, there will be no way to myself."

He cut her down. He opened her up. She was not long opened when there came two black ravens and one small one. The two ravens went into the body. They drank their fill of the blood. When they came out, the little raven went in. He closed up the pony. He would not let the little bird come out till he got the bottle of healing water that was in the eastern world. The ravens were very troubled. They were begging him to let the little bird out. He said he would not let it out till they brought him the bottle. They went to seek the bottle. They came back, and there was no bottle with them. They were entreating him to let the bird out to them. He would not let out the bird till he got the bottle. They went away again for the bottle. They came again at evening. They were tossed and scorched, and they had the bottle. They came to the place where the pony was. They gave the bottle to the boy. He rubbed the healing water to every place where they were burned. Then he let out the little bird. There was great joy on them to see him. He rubbed some of the healing water to the place where he cut the pony. He spilt a drop into her ear. She arose as well as she ever was. He had a little bottle in his pocket. He put some of the healing water into it. They went home.

When the King perceived the pony coming, he rose out. He took hold of her with his two hands. He took her in. He smothered her with kisses, and drowned her with tears; he dried her with finest cloths of silk and satin.

This is what the lady was doing while they were away. She boiled pitch, and filled a barrel, and that boiling. Now she went beside it. She rubbed the healing water to herself. She came out; she went to the barrel. She gave a jump in and out of the barrel. Three times she went in and out. She said she would never marry anyone who could not do the same. The young King came. He went to the barrel. He fell half in, half out.

He was all boiled and burned. Another gentleman came. He gave a jump into the barrel. He was burned. He came not out till he died. After that there was no one going in or out. The barrel was there, and no one at all was going near it. The lad went up to it. He rubbed the healing water on himself. He came to the barrel. He jumped in and out three times. He was watching her. She came out. She said she would never marry anyone but him.

Came the priest of the pattens, and the clerk of the bells. The pair were married. The wedding lasted three days and three nights. When it was over, the lad went to look at the place where the pony was. He never remembered to go and see the pony during the wedding. He found nothing but a heap of bones. There were two champions and two girls playing cards. The lad went crying when he saw the bones of the pony. One of the girls asked what the matter with him was. He said it was all one to her - that she cared nothing for his troubles.

"I would like to get knowledge of the cause why you are crying."

"It was my pony who was here. I never remembered to see her during the wedding. I have nothing now but her bones. I don't know what I shall do after her. It was she who did all that I accomplished."

The girl went laughing.

"Would you know your pony if you saw her?"

"I would know," said he.

She laid aside the cards. She stood up.

"Isn't that your pony?" said she.

"It is," said he.

"I was the pony," said the girl, "and the two ravens who went in to drink my blood my two brothers. When the ravens came out, a little bird went in. You closed the pony. You would not let the little bird out till they brought the bottle of healing water that was in the eastern world. They brought the bottle to you. The little bird was my sister.

It was my brothers were the ravens. We were all under enchantments. It is my sister who is married to you. The enchantments are gone from us since she was married."

Tales From The Land Of Saints & Scholars

The Secret of Labra

"The Secret of Labra", as retold by Thomas William Hazen Rolleston in The High Deeds of Finn and Other Bardic Romances of Ancient Ireland (1910), draws from the rich mythic cycles of ancient Ireland, blending kingship, prophecy, and the endurance of lineage.

Rolleston's adaptation, drawing on medieval Irish sources such as Cath Maige Tuired and bardic legend, frames the tale as both tragic and transcendent. The secret's revelation frees Labra from shame, while restoring the natural order between the human and the divine. The story speaks to ancient Irish conceptions of truth (fírinne) as something that cannot be contained by force or fear.

In very ancient days there was a King in Ireland named Labra, who was called Labra the Sailor for a certain voyage that he made. Now Labra was never seen save by one man, once a year, without a hood that covered his head and ears. But once a year it was his habit to let his hair be cropped, and the person to do this was chosen by lot, for the King was accustomed to put to death instantly the man who had cropped him. And so it happened that on a certain year the lot fell on a young man who was the only son of a poor widow, who dwelt nearby the palace of the King. When she heard that her son had been chosen she fell on her knees before the King and begged him, with tears, that her son, who was her only support and all she had in the world, might not suffer death as was customary. The King was moved by her grief and her entreaties, and at last he consented that the young man should not be slain provided that he vowed to keep secret to the day of his death what he should see. The youth agreed to this and he vowed by the Sun and the Wind that he would never, so long as he lived, reveal to man what he should learn when he cropped the King's hair.

So he did what was appointed for him and went home. But when he did so he had no peace for the wonder of the secret that he had learned preyed upon his mind so that he could not rest for thinking of it and longing to reveal it, and at last he fell into a wasting sickness from it, and was near to die. Then there was brought to see him a wise druid, who was skilled in all maladies of the mind and body, and after he had talked with the youth he said to his mother, "Your son is dying of the burden of a secret which he may not reveal to any man, but until he reveals it he will have no ease. Let him, therefore, walk along the highway till he comes to a place where four roads meet. Let him then turn to the right, and the first tree that he shall meet on the roadside let him tell the secret to it, and so it may be he shall be relieved, and his vow will not be broken."

The mother told her son of the druid's advice, and next day he went upon his way till he came to four crossroads, and he took the road upon the right, and the first tree he found was a great willow-tree. So the young man laid his cheek against the bark, and he whispered the secret to the tree, and as he turned back homeward he felt lightened of his burden, and he leaped and sang, and before many days were past he was as well and light-hearted as ever he had been in his life.

Some while after that it happened that the King's harper, namely Craftiny, broke the straining-post of his harp and went out to seek for a piece of wood wherewith to mend it. And the first timber he found that would fit the purpose was the willow-tree by the crossroads. He cut it down, therefore, and took as much as would give him a new straining-post, and he bore it home with him and mended his harp with it. That night he played after meat before the King and his lords as he was used to doing, but whatever he played and sang the folk that listened to him seemed to hear only one thing, "Two horse's ears have Labra the Sailor."

Then the King plucked off his hood, and after that he made no secret of his ears and none suffered on account of them thenceforward.

Tales From The Land Of Saints & Scholars

The Snow, the Crow, and the Blood

"The Snow, the Crow, and the Blood" is one of Seumas MacManus's darker Donegal tales, first appearing in his Donegal Fairy Stories (1900), a collection that mingles Irish folklore with the rhythms of the oral storyteller's voice. The story follows a bleak and elemental path, steeped in the Donegal landscape, harsh winters, lonely glens, and the uneasy balance between the mortal world and the uncanny. Its title alone captures the contrast at the heart of the tale: purity, cunning, and violence. In MacManus's hands, natural imagery becomes moral weather. The snow is innocence or perhaps inevitability; the crow, a familiar messenger of fate; and the blood, the price of interference in what should be left alone.

The Snow, the Crow, and the Blood remains a fine example of that art: haunting, concise, and full of weathered truth.

One day in the dead of winter, when the snow lay like a linen tablecloth over the world, Jack, the King of Ireland's son, went out to shoot. He saw a crow, and he shot it, and it fell down on the snow. Jack went up to it, and he thought he never saw anything blacker than that crow, or redder than its blood, nor anything whiter than the snow round about.

He said to himself, "I'll never rest till I get a wife whose hair is as black as that crow, whose cheeks are as red as that blood, and whose skin is as white as that snow."

So he went home, and told his father and mother this. He said he was going to set off before him and look for such a girl.

The King and Queen told Jack that it would be impossible ever to get a girl that would answer that description, and tried to persuade Jack from setting out, but Jack wouldn't be persuaded.

He started off with his father's and his mother's blessing, and a hundred guineas that his father had given him in his pocket. He travelled away and away very far, and about the middle of the day on the second day out, passing a graveyard, he saw a crowd there wrangling over a corpse. He went in and inquired what was the matter, and he found there were bailiffs wanting to seize the corpse for a debt of a hundred guineas. Jack was sorry for the poor corpse, so he put his hand in his pocket, took out the hundred guineas, and paid them down; and then the friends of the corpse thanked him heartily and buried the body.

That very same evening Jack was overtaken by a little red man who asked him where he was going.

Says Jack, "I'm going in search of a wife."

"Well," says the little red man, "such a handsome young fellow as you won't have to go far."

"Far enough," says Jack, "because the girl I want must have hair as black as the blackest crow, cheeks as red as the reddest blood, and skin as white as the whitest snow."

"Then," said the little red man, "there's only one such woman in the world, and she is the Princess of the East. There's many a brave young man went there before you to court her, but none of them ever came back alive again.

"For life or for death," says Jack, "I'll never rest until I reach the Princess of the East and court her."

"Well," said the little red man, "you'll want a boy with you. Let me be your boy."

"But I have no money to pay you," says Jack. "That will be alright," says the little red man. "I'll go with you."

That night late they reached a great castle. "This castle," says the little red man, "is the castle of the Giant of the Cloak of Darkness."

"Oh," says Jack, "I've heard of that terrible giant. We'll pass on, and look for somewhere else to stop."

"No other place we'll stop than here," says the little red man, knocking at the gates.

Jack was too brave to run away, so he stood by the little red man till a great and terrible giant came to the gates and opened them, and asked them what they wanted.

"We want supper and a bed for the night," says the red fellow.

"That's good," says the giant. "I want supper and bed too. I'll make my supper off you both, and my bed on your bones." And then he let a terrible laugh out of him that made the hair stand up on poor Jack's head.

But in a flash, the wee red fellow whips out his sword and struck out at the giant, and the giant then pulled out his, and struck out at the wee red man. Both of them fell to it hard and fast, and they fought a terrible fight for a long time; but in the end the wee red man ran the giant through the heart and killed him.

Then he took Jack in, and they spread for themselves a grand supper with the best of everything eatable and drinkable, and had a good sleep, and in the morning they started off, the wee red fellow taking with him the Cloak of Darkness belonging to the giant he had killed.

They travelled on and on that day, and at night they reached another castle.

"What castle is this?" says Jack.

"This," says the wee red man, "is the castle of the Giant of the Purse of Plenty."

"Then," says Jack, "I've heard of that terrible giant. We'll push on and look for somewhere else to stop tonight."

"Nowhere else than here we'll stop," says the wee red man. "No danger ever frightened me in all my life before, and it's too late to begin to learn fright now."

And before Jack could say anything he had knocked at the gates, and a giant with two heads came out roaring, and asked them what they wanted and what brought them there.

"We don't want much," says the little red man, "only what every traveller expects -- a sweet supper and a soft bed."

"I want both myself, too," says the giant, "and I'll make a sweet supper off you both, and a soft bed of your bones."

Then he laughed an awful laugh that shook the castle and made the hair stand up on poor Jack's head.

But that minute the wee red man whipped out his sword and made at him, and the giant whipped out his and made at the wee red man; and both of them fell to and had a fight long and hard, but at length the wee red man ran his sword through the giant's heart and killed him.

Then they went in, and spread for themselves a grand supper and a fine bed, in which they slept soundly till morning. And in the morning they went off, the little red man taking with him the Purse of Plenty.

All that day they travelled on before them, and when night fell they came to another great castle.

"What castle is this?" says Jack.

"This," says the little red man, "is the castle of the Giant of the Sword of Light."

"Oh," says Jack, "I've heard of that terrible giant and his awful sword, and," he says, "I want to get out of his neighbourhood as fast as possible."

"Fear never made me turn my back on man or mortal yet," says the little red man, "and I don't think I'll begin this late in life. As we're here, we'll lodge here this night."

So on the gates he rattled, and out came a frightful giant, with three great heads on him, and he roared so that the hills shook; and he asked them what they were doing here and what they wanted.

"We are two poor travellers on a journey," says the little red man, "and as night fell on us we thought we would ask you to give us bed and board for the night."

"Ha! Ha!" says the giant, laughing a terrible laugh. "I'll board myself on you two this night, and I'll bed me on your bones."

And at that he drew from his scabbard the terrible Sword of Light, whose flash travelled thrice round the world every time it was drawn, and whose lightest stroke killed any being, natural or enchanted.

But that instant the little red man drew around him the Cloak of Darkness, so that he should disappear from the giant's eyes, and drawing his own sword he began whacking and hacking, hewing and cutting the giant, while the giant couldn't see him to strike him in return, and in two minutes the wee red man had run his sword through the giant's heart and killed him.

He and Jack went into the castle, and they made a hearty supper and slept soundly in the softest beds they could get, and in the morning they went off again, the wee red man taking with him the Sword of Light.

Having the Purse of Plenty, they could not know want from this forward. So they went on their journey right merrily. They travelled far and long until at length they came into the East, and pushed on for the castle of the Princess. And when they came to where the Princess lived, they took their horses (for they were now riding two beautiful steeds) to a blacksmith's forge and had them shod with gold. And when they had had them shod, they rode up to the castle. By the wee red fellow's order, they didn't wait to knock at any gates, but put their golden spurs to their horses and leaped them over the castle walls.

When the servants and soldiers saw the pair come bounding over the castle walls upon horses shod with gold, they ran out in wonder. From the Purse of Plenty the red fellow, as Jack's servant, pulled out handfuls and handfuls of silver and of gold and scattered them among the crowd.

Then the servants quickly brought word to the Princess of the East of the beautiful and rich gentleman who had come, with his servant, to court her. They told her how they had both leaped the castle walls on horses shod with gold, and that they threw away their gold in handfuls.

She sent word for Jack to be brought to her, and when Jack came into her presence, he was enchanted with the look of her; for her hair was so black, her cheeks and lips were so red, and her skin was so white, he had never seen in all his life any one so beautiful.

"I understand you have come to court me," says she.

"That I have," says Jack.

"Well," says she, "to everyone that comes to court me, I give three tasks. If anyone performs the three tasks I give him he will win me; but if he fails in any one of the three, he will lose his head. Are you willing to try on such conditions?" says she.

"I'll try," says Jack, "upon any conditions."

She took him out then into the Garden of Heads, and showed him three hundred and sixty-five rose bushes, and for every flower there was a man's head on every one of three hundred and sixty-four of the bushes.

"There's one bush without a flower yet, Jack," says she, "but in less than three days I hope to see your head flowering on it."

Then she took him into the castle again, and treated him to a fine supper. And when they had finished supper and drunk their wine and chatted, she got up to bid him good-night.

She took out of her hair a gold comb, and showed it to him. "Now," she says, "I will wear that golden comb all night, and I'll spend this night from midnight to cockcrow neither on the earth nor under the earth. Yet you must have that comb for me in the morning, and it must be taken from my head between midnight and cockcrow." Then she stuck the comb into her hair again and went off.

Poor Jack acknowledged to himself that he had a task before him which he couldn't do. He wandered down the stairs and out of the castle, and went meandering into the garden in low spirits.

The wee red man soon came to him and asked him what the matter was.

"Oh, matter enough," says Jack, and commenced telling him all.

"Keep up your heart," says the wee red man, "and I'll see what I can do for you,"

So the little red man went and got his Cloak of Darkness, and then watched till midnight outside the Princess's door.

Just one second before the stroke of midnight, the Princess came out of her room with the golden comb in her hair, and went off to Hell. The little red man threw his Cloak of Darkness around him, and followed her.

She didn't stop till she came to Hell, where she went in, and the little red man went in after her.

The Devil was very glad to see her, and he kissed her, and the two sat down side by side and began to chat. And as they couldn't see the wee red man for his Cloak of Darkness, he came up behind and snatched the gold comb out of her hair, and went off with it; and when he came to earth, he gave the comb to Jack.

In the morning when the Princess of the East appeared at breakfast, Jack handed her gold comb to her across the table. She was furious, and the eyes of her flashed fire. That night she showed him a diamond ring on her finger, and she said she would not be on earth or under the earth between midnight and cockcrow, yet he must get that ring between those two times, and have it for her in the morning.

And when she went away, Jack went down to the garden, and was wandering about there when the wee red man came up to him and asked him what the matter was, and he told the wee red man.

"Well," says the wee red man, "I'll try what I can do." And so he took his Cloak of Darkness and watched for her that night again, and just before midnight, she came out and went off. He followed her, and she didn't stop till she was in Hell, where the Devil was very glad to see her and kissed her, and they sat down side by side to chat.

The little red fellow, with his Cloak of Darkness, came up beside her and waited, and the first opportunity he got, he snatched the ring off her finger, and went off and gave it to Jack.

So when she came down to breakfast the next morning Jack handed her over the table her diamond ring; and this morning she was doubly as furious as on the morning before. "Well," she said, "you've done two of the tasks, but the third you never will do."

So that night she told him, "I will spend all the time between midnight and cockcrow neither on the earth nor under the earth; and I want you to have for me in the morning the lips I shall have kissed while I have been away. Your head I'll surely have now, for the sword was never yet made by mortal man that can cut those lips." Then she went away.

Poor Jack, he wandered out into the garden very downhearted at this, and sure and certain that he would lose his head in the morning.

The little red man came up to him and asked him what the matter was. Jack told him and the red fellow said, "Keep up your heart, and I'll see what can be done." And he reminded Jack that he had the Sword of Light, which was never made by mortal man.

He threw his Cloak of Darkness about him, took the Sword of Light, and watched by the Princess's door. Just before midnight she came out and went off, and he followed her to Hell, where the Devil welcomed her with a kiss, and as he did so the little red man raised the Sword of Light and cut off his lips and left as fast as he could.

So in the morning Jack handed them across the table to the Princess, who was shaking with rage, and then he demanded her hand in marriage. And she had to consent.

As soon as they were married, the little red man said to Jack, "I have a wedding present for you." So he gave him ten blackthorns and told him to break one of these blackthorns on his wife every morning for ten mornings, and if he followed out his instructions faithfully, he would have a good wife on the tenth day.

Seeing the little red man had been such a good friend to him, Jack consented to do this. He broke a blackthorn on her every morning for ten mornings, and for every blackthorn he broke on her she was dispossessed of a devil. And on the tenth day she had lost all her rage and all her fury and all the devils, and she was the best and most perfect girl, as well as the most beautiful one, in all the world.

The little red man on the tenth day asked Jack if he remembered when he set out on his travels paying a hundred guineas to get a corpse buried. Jack he said did.

"Then," said the little red man, "it was I whom you buried, and I have tried to repay you a little. Now, good-bye, and may you and your wife prosper ever after."

The little red man disappeared, and Jack and his beautiful wife lived long and happily.

Tales From The Land Of Saints & Scholars

The Spirit Horse

"The Spirit Horse", adapted from Thomas Crofton Croker's Fairy Legends and Traditions of the South of Ireland (first published between 1825 and 1828), is one of those eerie Irish folktales that straddles the boundary between the living world and the supernatural. It tells of a spectral horse that appears by night to lure or carry away those who encounter it, often travellers returning late from fairs or taverns.

Croker's version, like much of his work, preserves the rhythms of oral storytelling, mixing humour and terror with the cadence of local speech. Beneath the folklore lies a moral layer: a caution against arrogance, drink, and wandering too far from the safety of hearth and faith. Yet The Spirit Horse is more than a warning, it is a study in the uncanny, showing how the natural and supernatural bleed together in Irish tradition.

The history of Morty Sullivan ought to be a warning to all young men to stay at home, and to live decently and soberly if they can, and not to go roving about the world. Morty, when he had just turned fourteen, ran away from his father and mother, who were a mighty respectable old couple, and many and many a tear they shed on his account. It is said they both died heart-broken for his loss. All they ever learned about him was that he went on board of a ship bound to America.

Thirty years after the old couple had been laid peacefully in their graves, there came a stranger to Beerhaven inquiring after them - it was their son Morty; and, to speak the truth of him, his heart did seem full of sorrow when he heard that his parents were dead and gone; - but what else could he expect to hear? Repentance generally comes when it is too late.

Morty Sullivan, however, as an atonement for his sins, was recommended to perform a pilgrimage to the blessed chapel of Saint Gobnate, which is in a wild place called Ballyvourney.

This he readily undertook, and willing to lose no time, commenced his journey the same afternoon. He had not proceeded many miles before the evening came on. There was no moon, and the star-light was obscured by a thick fog, which ascended from the valleys. His way was through a mountainous country, with many cross-paths and byways, so that it was difficult for a stranger like Morty to travel without a guide. He was anxious to reach his destination, and exerted himself to do so; but the fog grew thicker and thicker, and at last he became doubtful if the track he was in led to the blessed chapel of Saint Gobnate. But seeing a light which he imagined not to be far off, he went towards it, and when he thought himself close to it, the light suddenly seemed at a great distance, twinkling dimly through the fog. Though Morty felt some surprise at this, he was not disheartened, for he thought that it was a light sent by the holy Saint Gobnate to guide his feet through the mountains to her chapel.

And thus did he travel for many a mile, continually, as he believed, approaching the light, which would suddenly start off to a great distance. At length he came so close as to perceive that the light came from a fire, seated beside which he plainly saw an old woman; - then, indeed, his faith was a little shaken, and much did he wonder that both the fire and the old woman should travel before him, so many weary miles, and over such uneven roads.

"In the holy names of the pious Gobnate, and of her preceptor Saint Abban," said Morty, "how can that burning fire move on so fast before me, and who can that old woman be sitting beside the moving fire?"

These words had no sooner passed Morty's lips than he found himself, without taking another step, close to this wonderful fire, beside which the old woman was sitting munching her supper. With every wag of the old woman's jaw her eyes would roll fiercely upon Morty, as if she was angry at being disturbed; and he saw with more astonishment than ever that her eyes were neither black, nor blue, nor grey, nor hazel, like the human eye, but of a wild red colour, like the eye of a ferret. If before he wondered at the fire, much greater was his wonder at the old woman's appearance; and stout-hearted as he was, he could not but look upon her with fear - judging, and judging rightly, that it was for no good purpose her supping in so unfrequented a place, and at so late an hour, for it was near midnight. She said not one word, but munched and munched away, while Morty looked at her in silence. - "What's your name?" at last demanded the old hag, a sulphurous puff coming out of her mouth, her nostrils distending, and her eyes growing redder than ever, when she had finished her question.

Plucking up all his courage, "Morty Sullivan," replied he "at your service;" meaning the latter words only in civility.

"Ubbubbo!" said the old woman, "we'll soon see that;" and the red fire of her eyes turned into a pale green colour. Bold and fearless as Morty was, yet much did he tremble at hearing this dreadful exclamation, he would have fallen down on his knees and prayed to Saint Gobnate, or any other saint, for he was not particular; but he was so petrified with horror, that he could not move in the slightest way, much less go down on his knees.

"Take hold of my hand, Morty," said the old woman, "I'll give you a horse to ride that will soon carry you to your journey's end." So saying, she led the way, the fire going before them; - it is beyond mortal knowledge to say how, but on it went, shooting out bright tongues of flame, and flickering fiercely.

Presently they came to a natural cavern in the side of the mountain, and the old hag called aloud in a most discordant voice for her horse! In a moment a jet-black steed started from its gloomy stable, the rocky floor whereof rung with a sepulchral echo to the clanging hoofs.

"Mount, Morty, mount!" cried she, seizing him with supernatural strength, and forcing him upon the back of the horse. Morty finding human power of no avail, muttered, "O that I had spurs!" and tried to grasp the horse's mane; but he caught at a shadow; it nevertheless bore him up and bounded forward with him, now springing down a fearful precipice, now clearing the rugged bed of a torrent, and rushing like the dark midnight storm through the mountains.

The following morning Morty Sullivan was discovered by some pilgrims (who came that way after taking their rounds at Gougane Barra) lying on the flat of his back, under a steep cliff, down which he had been flung by the Phooka. Morty was severely bruised by the fall, and he is said to have sworn on the spot, by the hand of O'Sullivan (and that is no small oath), never again to take a full quart bottle of whisky with him on a pilgrimage.

Tales From The Land Of Saints & Scholars

The Story of Deirdre

"The Story of Deirdre", adapted by Joseph Jacobs from older Gaelic sources and included in his Celtic Fairy Tales (1892), retells one of Ireland's most tragic legends, drawn from the Ulster Cycle. Deirdre is born under a dark prophecy that she will bring ruin and sorrow to the men who love her.

In Jacobs's version, the language is pared back but still lyrical, retaining the sorrow and fatal beauty of the original bardic tale. His adaptation brought Deirdre's story, the "sorrowful tale of the sons of Usnach", to an English-speaking audience, preserving its themes of love, betrayal, and destiny while softening some of the older saga's harsher political and mythic edges.

There was a man in Ireland once who was called Malcolm Harper. The man was a right good man, and he had a goodly share of this world's goods. He had a wife, but no family. What did Malcolm hear but that a soothsayer had come home to the place, and as the man was a right good man, he wished that the soothsayer might come near them. Whether it was that he was invited or that he came of himself, the soothsayer came to the house of Malcolm.

"Are you doing any soothsaying?" says Malcolm.

"Yes, I am doing a little. Are you in need of soothsaying?"

"Well, I do not mind taking soothsaying from you, if you had soothsaying for me, and you would be willing to do it.

"Well, I will do soothsaying for you. What kind of soothsaying do you want?"

"Well, the soothsaying I wanted was that you would tell me my lot or what will happen to me, if you can give me knowledge of it."

"Well, I am going out, and when I return, I will tell you."

And the soothsayer went forth out of the house and he was not long outside when he returned.

"Well," said the soothsayer, "I saw in my second sight that it is on account of a daughter of yours that the greatest amount of blood shall be shed that has ever been shed in Erin since time and race began. And the three most famous heroes that ever were found will lose their heads on her account."

After a time a daughter was born to Malcolm, he did not allow a living being to come to his house, only himself and the nurse. He asked this woman, "Will you yourself bring up the child to keep her in hiding far away where eye will not see a sight of her nor ear hear a word about her?"

The woman she said would, so Malcolm got three men, and he took them away to a large mountain, distant and far from reach, without the knowledge or notice of anyone. He caused there a hillock, round and green, to be dug out of the middle, and the hole thus made to be covered carefully over so that a little company could dwell there together. This was done.

Deirdre and her foster-mother dwelt in the bothy mid the hills without the knowledge or the suspicion of any living person about them and without anything occurring, until Deirdre was sixteen years of age. Deirdre grew like the white sapling, straight and trim as the rash on the moss. She was the creature of fairest form, of loveliest aspect, and of gentlest nature that existed between earth and heaven in all Ireland - whatever colour of hue she had before, there was nobody that looked into her face but she would blush fiery red over it.

The woman that had charge of her, gave Deirdre every information and skill of which she herself had knowledge and skill. There was not a blade of grass growing from root, nor a bird singing in the wood, nor a star shining from heaven but Deirdre had a name for it. But one thing, she did not wish her to have either part or parley with any single living man of the rest of the world. But on a gloomy winter night, with black, scowling clouds, a hunter of game was wearily travelling the hills, and what happened but that he missed the trail of the hunt, and lost his course and companions. A drowsiness came upon the man as he wearily wandered over the hills, and he lay down by the side of the beautiful green knoll in which Deirdre lived, and he slept. The man was faint from hunger and wandering, and benumbed with cold, and a deep sleep fell upon him. When he lay down beside the green hill where Deirdre was, a troubled dream came to the man, and he thought that he enjoyed the warmth of a fairy broch, the fairies being inside playing music. The hunter shouted out in his dream, if there was any one in the broch, to let him in for the Holy One's sake. Deirdre heard the voice and said to her foster-mother, "O foster-mother, what cry is that?" "It is nothing at all, Deirdre - merely the birds of the air astray and seeking each other. But let them go past to the bosky glade. There is no shelter or house for them here." "Oh, foster-mother, the bird asked to get inside for the sake of the God of the Elements, and you yourself tell me that anything that is asked in His name we ought to do. If you will not allow the bird that is being benumbed with cold, and done to death with hunger, to be let in, I do not think much of your language or your faith. But since I give credence to your language and to your faith, which you taught me, I will myself let in the bird." And Deirdre arose and drew the bolt from the leaf of the door, and she let in the hunter. She placed a seat in the place for sitting, food in the place for eating, and drink in the place for drinking for the man who came to the house. "Oh, for this life and raiment, you man that came in, keep restraint on your tongue!" said the old woman. "It is not a great thing for you to keep your mouth shut and your tongue quiet when you get a home and shelter of a hearth on a gloomy winter's night."

"Well," said the hunter, "I may do that - keep my mouth shut and my tongue quiet, since I came to the house and received hospitality from you; but by the hand of your father and grandfather, and by your own two hands, if some other of the people of the world saw this beauteous creature you have here hid away, they would not long leave her with you, I swear."

"What men are these you refer to?" said Deirdre.

"Well, I will tell you, young woman," said the hunter.

"They are Naois, son of Uisnech, and Allen and Arden his two brothers."

"What like are these men when seen, if we were to see them?" said Deirdre.

"Why, the aspect and form of the men when seen are these," said the hunter, "they have the colour of the raven on their hair, their skin like swan on the wave in whiteness, and their cheeks as the blood of the brindled red calf, and their speed and their leap are those of the salmon of the torrent and the deer of the grey mountain side. And Naois is head and shoulders over the rest of the people of Erin."

"However they are," said the nurse, "be you off from here and take another road. And King of Light and Sun! in good sooth and certainty, little are my thanks for yourself or for her that let you in!"

The hunter went away, and went straight to the palace of King Connachar. He sent word in to the king that he wished to speak to him if he pleased. The king answered the message and came out to speak to the man. "What is the reason of your journey?" said the king to the hunter.

"I have only to tell you, Oh king," said the hunter, "that I saw the fairest creature that ever was born in Erin, and I came to tell you of it."

"Who is this beauty and where is she to be seen, when she was not seen before till you saw her, if you did see her?"

"Well, I did see her," said the hunter. "But, if I did, no man else can see her unless he get directions from me as to where she is dwelling."

"And will you direct me to where she dwells? and the reward of your directing me will be as good as the reward of your message," said the king.

"Well, I will direct you, Oh king, although it is likely that this will not be what they want," said the hunter.

Connachar, King of Ulster, sent for his nearest kinsmen, and he told them of his intent. Though early rose the song of the birds mid the rocky caves and the music of the birds in the grove, earlier than that did Connachar, King of Ulster, arise, with his little troop of dear friends, in the delightful twilight of the fresh and gentle May; the dew was heavy on each bush and flower and stem, as they went to bring Deirdre forth from the green knoll where she stayed. Many a youth was there who had a lithe leaping and lissom step when they started whose step was faint, failing, and faltering when they reached the bothy on account of the length of the way and roughness of the road.

"Yonder, now, down in the bottom of the glen is the bothy where the woman dwells, but I will not go nearer than this to the old woman," said the hunter.

Connachar with his band of kinsfolk went down to the green knoll where Deirdre dwelt and he knocked at the door of the bothy. The nurse replied, "No less than a king's command and a king's army could put me out of my bothy to-night. And I should be obliged to you, were you to tell who it is that wants me to open my bothy door."

"It is I, Connachar, King of Ulster." When the poor woman heard who was at the door, she rose with haste and let in the king and all that could get in of his retinue.

When the king saw the woman that was before him that he had been in quest of, he thought he never saw in the course of the day nor in the dream of night a creature so fair as Deirdre and he gave his full heart's weight of love to her. Deirdre was raised on the topmost of the heroes' shoulders and she and her foster-mother were brought to the Court of King Connachar of Ulster.

With the love that Connachar had for her, he wanted to marry Deirdre right off there and then, whether or not she wanted to marry him. But she said to him, "I would be obliged to you if you will give me the respite of a year and a day." He said, "I will grant you that, hard though it is, if you will give me your unfailing promise that you will marry me at the year's end." And she gave the promise. Connachar got for her a woman-teacher and merry modest maidens fair that would lie down and rise with her, that would play and speak with her. Deirdre was clever in maidenly duties and wifely understanding, and Connachar thought he never saw with bodily eye a creature that pleased him more.

Deirdre and her women companions were one day out on the hillock behind the house enjoying the scene, and drinking in the sun's heat. What did they see coming but three men a-journeying. Deirdre was looking at the men that were coming, and wondering at them. When the men neared them, Deirdre remembered the language of the huntsman, and she said to herself that these were the three sons of Uisnech, and that this was Naois, he having what was above the bend of the two shoulders above the men of Erin all. The three brothers went past without taking any notice of them, without even glancing at the young girls on the hillock. What happened but that love for Naois struck the heart of Deirdre, so that she could not but follow after him. She girded up her raiment and went after the men that went past the base of the knoll, leaving her women attendants there. Allen and Arden had heard of the woman that Connachar, King of Ulster, had with him, and they thought that, if Naois, their brother, saw her, he would have her himself, more especially as she was not married to the King. They perceived the woman coming, and called on one another to hasten their step as they had a long distance to travel, and the dusk of night was coming on. They did so.

She cried, "Naois, son of Uisnech, will you leave me?" "What piercing, shrill cry is that - the most melodious my ear ever heard, and the shrillest that ever struck my heart of all the cries I ever heard?"

"It is anything else but the wail of the wave-swans of Connachar," said his brothers.

"No! yonder is a woman's cry of distress," said Naois, and he swore he would not go further until he saw from whom the cry came, and

Naois turned back.

Naois and Deirdre met, and Deirdre kissed Naois three times, and a kiss each to his brothers. With the confusion that she was in, Deirdre went into a crimson blaze of fire, and her colour came and went as rapidly as the movement of the aspen by the stream side. Naois thought he never saw a fairer creature, and Naois gave Deirdre the love that he never gave to thing, to vision, or to creature but to herself.

Then Naois placed Deirdre on the topmost height of his shoulder, and told his brothers to keep up their pace, and they kept up their pace. Naois thought that it would not be well for him to remain in Erin on account of the way in which Connachar, King of Ulster, his uncle's son, had gone against him because of the woman, though he had not married her; and he turned back to Alba, that is, Scotland. He reached the side of Loch-Ness and made his habitation there. He could kill the salmon of the torrent from out his own door, and the deer of the grey gorge from out his window. Naois and Deirdre and Allen and Arden dwelt in a tower, and they were happy so long a time as they were there.

By this time the end of the period came at which Deirdre had to marry Connachar, King of Ulster. Connachar made up his mind to take Deirdre away by the sword whether she was married to Naois or not. So he prepared a great and gleeful feast. He sent word far and wide through Erin all to his kinspeople to come to the feast. Connachar thought to himself that Naois would not come though he should bid him; and the scheme that arose in his mind was to send for his father's brother, Ferchar Mac Ro, and to send him on an embassy to Naois.

He did so; and Connachar said to Ferchar, "Tell Naois, son of

Uisnech, that I am setting forth a great and gleeful feast to my friends and kinspeople throughout the wide extent of Erin all, and that I shall not have rest by day nor sleep by night if he and Allen and Arden be not partakers of the feast."

Ferchar Mac Ro and his three sons went on their journey, and reached the tower where Naois was dwelling by the side of Loch Etive. The sons of Uisnech gave a cordial kindly welcome to Ferchar Mac Ro and his three sons, and asked of him the news of Erin. "The best news that I have for you," said the hardy hero, "is that Connachar, King of Ulster, is setting forth a great sumptuous feast to his friends and kinspeople throughout the wide extent of Erin all, and he has vowed by the earth beneath him, by the high heaven above him, and by the sun that wends to the west, that he will have no rest by day nor sleep by night if the sons of Uisnech, the sons of his own father's brother, will not come back to the land of their home and the soil of their nativity, and to the feast likewise, and he has sent us on embassy to invite you."

"We will go with you," said Naois.

"We will," said his brothers.

But Deirdre did not wish to go with Ferchar Mac Ro, and she tried every prayer to turn Naois from going with him - she said, "I saw a vision, Naois, and do you interpret it to me," and then Deirdre sang:

O Naois, son of Uisnech, hear
What was shown in a dream to me.

There came three white doves out of the South

Tales From The Land Of Saints & Scholars

Flying over the sea,

And drops of honey were in their mouth

From the hive of the honey-bee.

O Naois, son of Uisnech, hear,

What was shown in a dream to me.

I saw three grey hawks out of the south

Come flying over the sea,

And the red red drops they bare in their mouth

They were dearer than life to me.

Said Naois, "It is nought but the fear of woman's heart, and a dream of the night, Deirdre. The day that Connachar sent the invitation to his feast will be unlucky for us if we don't go, Oh Deirdre."

"You will go there," said Ferchar Mac Ro, "and if Connachar show kindness to you, show you kindness to him; and if he will display wrath towards you display your wrath towards him, and I and my three sons will be with you."

"We will," said Daring Drop. "We will," said Hardy Holly. "We will," said Fiallan the Fair.

"I have three sons, and they are three heroes, and in any harm or danger that may befall you, they will be with you, and I myself will be along with them." And Ferchar Mac Ro gave his vow and his word in presence of his arms that, in any harm or danger that came in the way of the sons of Uisnech, he and his three sons would not leave head on live body in Erin, despite sword or helmet, spear or shield, blade or mail, be they ever so good.

Deirdre was unwilling to leave Alba, but she went with Naois. Deirdre wept tears in showers and she sang:

Dear is the land, the land over there,

Alba full of woods and lakes;

Bitter to my heart is leaving you,

But I go away with Naois.

Ferchar Mac Ro did not stop till he got the sons of Uisnech away with him, despite the suspicion of Deirdre.

The coracle was put to sea,

The sail was hoisted to it;

And the second morrow they arrived

On the white shores of Erin.

As soon as the sons of Uisnech landed in Erin, Ferchar Mac Ro sent word to Connachar, king of Ulster, that the men whom he wanted were come, and let him now show kindness to them. "Well," said Connachar, "I did not expect that the sons of Uisnech would come, though I sent for them, and I am not quite ready to receive them. But there is a house down yonder where I keep strangers, and let them go down to it today, and my house will be ready before tomorrow."

But he that was up in the palace felt it long that he was not getting word as to how matters were going on for those down in the house of the strangers. "Go you, Gelban Grednach, son of Lochlin's King, go you down and bring me information as to whether her former hue and complexion are on Deirdre. If they be, I will take her out with edge of blade and point of sword, and if not, let Naois, son of Uisnech, have her for himself," said Connachar.

Gelban, the cheering and charming son of Lochlin's King, went down to the place of the strangers, where the sons of Uisnech and Deirdre were staying. He looked in through the bicker-hole on the door-leaf. Now she that he gazed upon used to go into a crimson blaze of blushes when anyone looked at her. Naois looked at Deirdre and knew that someone was looking at her from the back of the door-leaf. He seized one of the dice on the table before him and fired it through the bicker-hole, and knocked the eye out of Gelban Grednach the Cheerful and Charming, right through the back of his head. Gelban returned back to the palace of King Connachar.

"You were cheerful, charming, going away, but you are cheerless, charmless, returning. What has happened to you, Gelban? But have you seen her, and are Deirdre's hue and complexion as before?" said Connachar.

"Well, I have seen Deirdre, and I saw her also truly, and while I was looking at her through the bicker-hole on the door, Naois, son of Uisnech, knocked out my eye with one of the dice in his hand. But of a truth and verity, although he put out even my eye, it were my desire still to remain looking at her with the other eye, were it not for the hurry you told me to be in," said Gelban.

"That is true," said Connachar, "let three hundred bravo heroes go down to the abode of the strangers, and let them bring hereto me Deirdre, and kill the rest."

Connachar ordered three hundred active heroes to go down to the abode of the strangers and to take Deirdre up with them and kill the rest. "The pursuit is coming," said Deirdre.

"Yes, but I will myself go out and stop the pursuit," said Naois.

"It is not you, but we that will go," said Daring Drop, and Hardy Holly, and Fiallan the Fair, "it is to us that our father entrusted your defence from harm and danger when he himself left for home." And the gallant youths, full noble, full manly, full handsome, with beauteous brown locks, went forth girt with battle arms fit for fierce fight and clothed with combat dress for fierce contest fit, which was burnished, bright, brilliant, bladed, blazing, on which were many pictures of beasts and birds and creeping things, lions and lithe-limbed tigers, brown eagle and harrying hawk and adder fierce; and the young heroes laid low three-thirds of the company.

Connachar came out in haste and cried with wrath, "Who is there on the floor of fight, slaughtering my men?"

"We, the three sons of Ferchar Mac Ro."

"Well," said the king, "I will give a free bridge to your grandfather, a free bridge to your father, and a free bridge each to you three brothers, if you come over to my side tonight."

"Well, Connachar, we will not accept that offer from you nor thank you for it. Greater by far do we prefer to go home to our father and tell the deeds of heroism we have done, than accept anything on these terms from you. Naois, son of Uisnech, and Allen and Arden are as nearly related to yourself as they are to us, though you are so keen to shed their blood, and you would shed our blood also,

Connachar." And the noble, manly, handsome youths with beauteous, brown locks returned inside. "We are now," said they, "going home to tell our father that you are now safe from the hands of the king." And the youths all fresh and tall and lithe and beautiful, went home to their father to tell that the sons of Uisnech were safe. This happened at the parting of the day and night in the morning twilight time, and Naois said they must go away, leave that house, and return to Alba.

Naois and Deirdre, Allan and Arden started to return to Alba. Word came to the king that the company he was in pursuit of were gone. The king then sent for Duanan Gacha Druid, the best magician he had, and he spoke to him as follows, "Much wealth have I expended on you, Duanan Gacha Druid, to give schooling and learning and magic mystery to you, if these people get away from me today without care, without consideration or regard for me, without chance of overtaking them, and without power to stop them."

"Well, I will stop them," said the magician, "until the company you send in pursuit return." And the magician placed a wood before them through which no man could go, but the sons of Uisnech marched through the wood without halt or hesitation, and Deirdre held on to Naois's hand.

"What is the good of that? that will not do yet," said Connachar. "They are off without bending of their feet or stopping of their step, without heed or respect to me, and I am without power to keep up to them or opportunity to turn them back this night."

"I will try another plan on them," said the druid; and he placed before them a grey sea instead of a green plain. The three heroes stripped and tied their clothes behind their heads, and Naois placed Deirdre on the top of his shoulder.

They stretched their sides to the stream,
And sea and land were to them the same,
The rough grey ocean was the same
As meadow-land green and plain.

"Though that be good, Oh Duanan, it will not make the heroes return," said Connachar, "they are gone without regard for me, and without honour to me, and without power on my part to pursue them or to force them to return this night."

"We shall try another method on them, since yon one did not stop them," said the druid. And the druid froze the grey ridged sea into hard rocky knobs, the sharpness of sword being on the one edge and the poison power of adders on the other. Then Arden cried that he was getting tired, and nearly giving over. "Come you, Arden, and sit on my right shoulder," said Naois. Arden came and sat on Naois's shoulder. Arden was long in this posture when he died; but though he was dead Naois would not let him go. Allen then cried out that he was getting faint and nigh-well giving up. When Naois heard his prayer, he gave forth the piercing sigh of death, and asked Allen to lay hold of him and he would bring him to land.

Allen was not long when the weakness of death came on him and his hold failed. Naois looked around, and when he saw his two well-beloved brothers dead, he cared not whether he lived or died, and he gave forth the bitter sigh of death, and his heart burst.

"They are gone," said Duanan Gacha Druid to the king, "and I have done what you desired me. The sons of Uisnech are dead and they will trouble you no more; and you have your wife hale and whole to yourself."

"Blessings for that upon you and may the good results accrue to me, Duanan. I count it no loss what I spent in the schooling and teaching of you. Now dry up the flood, and let me see if I can behold Deirdre," said Connachar. And Duanan Gacha Druid dried up the flood from the plain and the three sons of Uisnech were lying together dead, without breath of life, side by side on the green meadow plain and Deirdre bending above showering down her tears.

Then Deirdre said this lament, "Fair one, loved one, flower of beauty; beloved upright and strong; beloved noble and modest warrior. Fair one, blue-eyed, beloved of your wife; lovely to me at the trysting-place came your clear voice through the woods of Ireland. I cannot eat or smile henceforth. Break not today, my heart. Soon enough shall I lie within my grave. Strong are the waves of sorrow, but stronger is sorrow's self, Connachar."

The people then gathered round the heroes' bodies and asked Connachar what was to be done with the bodies. The order that he gave was that they should dig a pit and put the three brothers in it side by side. Deirdre kept sitting on the brink of the grave, constantly asking the gravediggers to dig the pit wide and free. When the bodies of the brothers were put in the grave, Deirdre said:

Come over here, Naois, my love,

Let Arden close to Allen lie;

If the dead had any sense to feel,

Ye would have made a place for Deirdre.

The men did as she told them. She jumped into the grave and lay down by Naois, and she was dead by his side.

The king ordered the body to be raised from out the grave and to be buried on the other side of the loch. It was done as the king bade, and the pit closed. Thereupon a fir shoot grew out of the grave of Deirdre and a fir shoot from the grave of Naois, and the two shoots united in a knot above the loch. The king ordered the shoots to be cut down, and this was done twice, until, at the third time, the wife whom the king had married caused him to stop this work of evil and his vengeance on the remains of the dead.

Tales From The Land Of Saints & Scholars

The Story of the Children of Lir

"The Story of the Children of Lir", as retold by Thomas William Hazen Rolleston in The High Deeds of Finn and Other Bardic Romances of Ancient Ireland (1910), is one of Ireland's most haunting myths of loss, endurance, and transformation. It tells of King Lir, whose four children, Fionnuala, Aodh, Fiachra, and Conn, are cursed by their jealous stepmother, Aoife, to live as swans for nine hundred years.

Rolleston's version, adapted from older bardic and oral traditions, softens some of the rawness of earlier tellings but retains the story's deep emotional core. His prose emphasises both the natural beauty of Ireland's mythic landscape and the spiritual symbolism of transformation and redemption. In his hands, the Children of Lir become not just tragic figures but emblems of Ireland itself, enduring exile, change, and the passing of ages with quiet, unbroken dignity.

Long ago there dwelt in Ireland the race called by the name of De Danaan, or People of the Goddess Dana. They were a folk who delighted in beauty and gaiety, and in fighting and feasting, and loved to go gloriously apparelled, and to have their weapons and household vessels adorned with jewels and gold. They were also skilled in magic arts, and their harpers could make music so enchanting that a man who heard it would fight, or love, or sleep, or forget all earthly things, as they who touched the strings might will him to do. In later times the Danaans had to dispute the sovereignty of Ireland with another race, the Children of Miled, whom men call the Milesians, and after much fighting they were vanquished. Then, by their sorceries and enchantments, when they could not prevail against the invaders, they made themselves invisible, and they have dwelt ever since in the Fairy Mounds and raths of Ireland, where their shining palaces are hidden from mortal eyes. They are now called the Shee, or Fairy Folk of Erinn, and the faint strains of unearthly music that may be heard at times by those who wander at night near to their haunts come from the harpers and pipers who play for the People of Dana at their revels in the bright world underground.

At the time when the tale begins, the People of Dana were still the lords of Ireland, for the Milesians had not yet come. They were divided it is said, into many families and clans; and it seemed good to them that their chiefs should assemble together, and choose one to be king and ruler over the whole people. So they met in a great assembly for this purpose, and found that five of the greatest lords all desired the sovereignty of Erin. These five were Bóv the Red, and Ilbrech of Assaroe, and Lir from the Hill of the White Field, which is on Slieve Fuad in Armagh; and Midir the Proud, who dwelt at Slieve Callary in Longford; and Angus of Brugh na Boyna, which is now Newgrange on the river Boyne, where his mighty mound is still to be seen. All the Danaan lords saving these five went into council together, and their decision was to give the sovereignty to Bóv the Red, partly because he was the eldest, partly because his father was the Dagda, mightiest of the Danaans, and partly because he was himself the most deserving of the five.

All were content with this, save only Lir, who thought himself the fittest for royal rule; so he went away from the assembly in anger, taking leave of no one. When this became known, the Danaan lords would have pursued Lir, to burn his palace and inflict punishment and wounding on himself for refusing obedience and fealty to him whom the assembly had chosen to reign over them. But Bóv the Red forbade them, for he would not have war among the Danaans; and he said, "I am nonetheless King of the People of Dana because this man will not do homage to me."

Thus it went on for a long time. But at last a great misfortune befell Lir, for his wife fell ill, and after three nights she died. Sorely did Lir grieve for this, and he fell into a great dejection of spirit, for his wife was very dear to him and was much thought of by all folk, so that her death was counted one of the great events of that time.

Now Bóv the Red came before long to hear of it, and he said, "If Lir would choose to have my help and friendship now, I can serve him well, for his wife is no longer living, and I have three maidens, daughters of a friend, in fosterage with me, namely, Eva and Aoife and Elva, and there are none fairer and of better name in Erin; one of these he might take to wife." And the lords of the Danaans heard what he said, and answered that it was true and well bethought. So messengers were sent to Lir, to say that if he were willing to yield the sovereignty to Bóv the Red, he might make alliance with him and wed one of his foster-children. To Lir, having been thus gently entreated, it seemed good to end the feud, and he agreed to the marriage. So the following day he set out with a train of fifty chariots from the Hill of the White Field and journeyed straight for the palace of Bóv the Red, which was by Lough Derg on the River Shannon.

Arriving there, he found about him nothing but joy and glad faces, for the renewal of amity and concord; and his people were welcomed, and well entreated, and handsomely entertained for the night.

And there sat the three maidens on the same couch with the Danaan Queen, and Bóv the Red bade Lir choose which one he would have to wife.

"The maidens are all fair and noble," said Lir, "but the eldest is first in consideration and honour, and it is she that I will take, if she be willing."

"The eldest is Eva," said Bóv the Red, "and she will wed you if it be pleasing to you." "It is pleasing," said Lir, and the pair were wedded the same night. Lir abode for fourteen days in the palace of Bóv the Red, and then departed with his bride, to make a great wedding-feast among his own people.

In due time after this Eva, wife of Lir, bore him two fair children at a birth, a daughter and a son. The daughter's name was called Fionnuala of the Fair Shoulder, and the son's name was Hugh. And again she bore him two sons, Fiachra and Conn; and at their birth she died. At this Lir was sorely grieved and afflicted, and but for the great love he bore to his four children he would gladly have died too.

When the folk at the palace of Bóv the Red heard that, they also were sorely grieved at the death of their foster-child, and they lamented her with keening and with weeping. Bóv the Red said, "We grieve for this maiden on account of the good man we gave her to, and for his friendship and fellowship; howbeit our friendship shall not be sundered, for we shall give him to wife her sister, namely Aoife."

Word of this was brought to Lir, and he went once more to Lough Derg to the palace of Bóv the Red and there he took to wife Aoife, the fair and wise, and brought her to his own home. And Aoife held the children of Lir and of her sister in honour and affection; for indeed no one could behold these four children without giving them the love of his soul.

For love of them, too, came Bóv the Red often to the house of Lir, and he would take them to his own house at times and let them spend a while there, and then to their own home again. All of the People of Dana who came visiting and feasting to Lir had joy and delight in the children, for their beauty and gentleness; and the love of their father for them was exceeding great, so that he would rise very early every morning to lie down among them and play with them.

Only, alas! a fire of jealousy began to burn at last in the breast of Aoife, and hatred and bitter ill-will grew in her mind towards the children of Lir. And she feigned an illness, and lay under it for the most of a year, meditating a black and evil deed. At last she said that a journey from home might recover her, and she bade her chariot be yoked and set out, taking with her the four children. Fionnuala was sorely unwilling to go with her on that journey, for she had a misgiving, and a premonition of treachery and of kin-slaying against her in the mind of Aoife. Yet she was not able to avoid the mischief that was destined for her.

So Aoife journeyed away from the Hill of the White Field, and when she had come some way she spoke to her people and said, "Kill me, I pray ye, the four children of Lir, who have taken the love of their father from me, and you may ask of me what reward you will." "Not so," said they, "by us they shall never be killed; it is an evil deed that you have thought of, and evil it is but to have spoken of it."

When they would not consent to her will, she drew a sword and would have slain the children herself, but her womanhood overcame her and she could not. So they journeyed on westward till they came to the shores of Loch Derryvaragh, and there they made a halt and the horses were out spanned. Aoife bade the children bathe and swim in the lake, and they did so. Then Aoife by Druid spells and witchcraft put upon each of the children the form of a pure white swan, and she cried to them:

"Out on the lake with you, children of Lir!
Cry with the waterfowl over the mere!
Breed and seed of you ne'er shall I see;
Woeful the tale to your friends shall be."

Then the four swans turned their faces towards the woman, and Fionnuala spoke to her and said, "Evil is your deed, Aoife, to destroy us thus without a cause, and think not that you shalt escape punishment for it. Assign us even some period to the ruin and destruction that you have brought upon us."

"I shall do that," said Aoife, "and it is this. In your present forms shall you abide, and none shall release you till the woman of the South be mated with the man of the North. Three hundred years shall you be upon the waters of Derryvaragh, and three hundred upon the Straits of Moyle between Erinn and Alba, and three hundred in the seas by Erris and Inishglory, and then shall the enchantment have an end."

Upon this, Aoife was smitten with repentance, and she said, "Since I may not henceforth undo what has been done, I give you this, that you shall keep your human speech, and you shall sing a sad music such as no music in the world can equal, and you shall have your reason and your human will, that the bird-shape may not wholly destroy you." Then she became as one possessed, and cried wildly like a prophetess in her trance:

"Ye with the white faces! Ye with the stammering Gaelic on your tongues!
Soft was your nurture in the King's house -
Now shall you know the buffeting wind
Nine hundred years upon the tide.

"The heart of Lir shall bleed!
None of his victories shall stead him now!
Woe to me that I shall hear his groan,
Woe that I have deserved his wrath!"

Then they caught and yoked her horses, and Aoife went on her way till she reached the palace of Bóv the Red. Here she and her folk were welcomed and entertained, and Bóv the Red inquired of her why she had not brought with her the children of Lir.

"I brought them not," she replied, "because Lir loves you not, and he fears that if he sends his children to you, you would capture them and hold them for hostages."

"That is strange," said Bóv the Red, "for I love those children as if they were my own." And his mind misgave him that some treachery had been wrought; and he sent messengers privily northwards to the Hill of the White Field. "For what have you come?" asked Lir. "Even to bring your children to Bóv the Red," said they. "Did they not reach you with Aoife?" said Lir. "Nay," said the messengers, "but Aoife said you would not permit them to go with her."

Then fear and trouble came upon Lir, for he surmised that Aoife had wrought evil upon the children. So his horses were yoked and he set out upon his road south-westward, until he reached the shores of Loch Derryvaragh. But as he passed by that water, Fionnuala saw the train of horsemen and chariots, and she cried to her brothers to come near to the shore, "for," said she, "these can only be the company of our father who have come to follow and seek for us."

Lir, by the margin of the lake, saw the four swans and heard them talking with human voices, and he halted and spoke to them. Then said Fionnuala, "Know, Oh Lir, that we are your four children, and that she who has wrought this ruin upon us is your wife and our mother's sister, through the bitterness of her jealousy." Lir was glad to know that they were at least living, and he said, "Is it possible to put your own forms upon you again?" "It is not possible," said Fionnuala, "for all the men on earth could not release us until the woman of the South be mated with the man of the North." Then Lir and his people cried aloud in grief and lamentation, and Lir entreated the swans to come on land and abide with him since they had their human reason and speech. But Fionnuala said, "That may not be, for we may not company with men any longer, but abide on the waters of Erinn nine hundred years. But we have still our Gaelic speech, and moreover we have the gift of uttering sad music, so that no man who hears it thinks aught worth in the world save to listen to that music for ever. Do you abide by the shore for this night and we shall sing to you.

So Lir and his people listened all night to the singing of the swans, nor could they move nor speak till morning, for all the high sorrows of the world were in that music, and it plunged them in dreams that could not be uttered.

Next day Lir took leave of his children and went on to the palace of

Bóv the Red. Bóv reproached him that he had not brought with him his children. "Woe is me," said Lir, "it was not I that would not bring them; but Aoife there, your own foster-child and their mother's sister, put upon them the forms of four snow-white swans, and there they are on the Loch of Derryvaragh for all men to see; but they have kept still their reason and their human voice and their Gaelic."

Bóv the Red started when he heard this, and he knew that what Lir had said was true. Fiercely he turned to Aoife, and said, "This treachery will be worse, Aoife, for you than for them, for they shall be released in the end of time, but your punishment shall be forever." Then he smote her with a druid wand and she became a Demon of the Air, and flew shrieking from the hall, and in that form she abides to this day.

As for Bóv the Red, he came with his nobles and attendants to the shores of Loch Derryvaragh, and there they made an encampment, and the swans conversed with them and sang to them. And as the thing became known, other tribes and clans of the People of Dana would also come from every part of Erinn and stay awhile to listen to the swans and depart again to their homes; and most of all came their own friends and fellow-pupils from the Hill of the White Field. No such music as theirs, say the historians of ancient times, ever was heard in Erinn, for foes who heard it were at peace, and men stricken with pain or sickness felt their ills no more; and the memory of it remained with them when they went away, so that a great peace and sweetness and gentleness was in the land of Erinn for those three hundred years that the swans abode in the waters of Derryvaragh.

But one day Fionnuala said to her brethren, "Do you know, my dear ones, that the end of our time here is come, all but this night only?" Then great sorrow and distress overcame them, for in the converse with their father and kinsfolk and friends they had half forgotten that they were no longer men, and they loved their home on Loch Derryvaragh, and feared the angry waves of the cold northern sea. But early next day they came to the lough-side to speak with Bóv the Red and with their father, and to bid them farewell, and Fionnuala sang to them her last lament. Then the four swans rose in the air and flew northward till they were seen no more, and great was the grief among those they left behind; and Bóv the Red let it be proclaimed throughout the length and breadth of Erin that no man should henceforth presume to kill a swan, lest it might chance to be one of the children of Lir.

Far different was the dwelling-place which the swans now came to, from that which they had known on Loch Derryvaragh. On either side of them, to north and south, stretched a wide coast far as the eye could see, beset with black rocks and great precipices, and by it ran fiercely the salt, bitter tides of an ever-angry sea, cold, grey, and misty; and their hearts sank to behold it and to think that there they must abide for three hundred years.

Ere long, one night, there came a thick murky tempest upon them, and Fionnuala said, "In this black and violent night, my brothers, we may be driven apart from each other; let us therefore appoint a meeting-place where we may come together again when the tempest passed over us." And they settled to meet at the Seal Rock, for this rock they had now all learned to know.

By midnight the hurricane descended upon the Straits of Moyle, and the waves roared upon the coast with a deafening noise, and thunder bellowed from the sky, and lightning was all the light they had. The swans were driven apart by the violence of the storm, and when at last the wind fell and the seas grew calm once more, Fionnuala found herself alone upon the ocean-tide not far from the Seal Rock. And thus she made her lament:

"Woe is me to be yet alive!
My wings are frozen to my sides.
Well-nigh has the tempest shattered my heart,
And my comely Hugh parted from me!

"O my beloved ones, my Three,
Who slept under the shelter of my feathers,
Shall you and I ever meet again
Until the dead rise to life?

"Where is Flachra, where is Hugh?
Where is my fair Conn?
Shall I henceforth bear my part alone?
Woe is me for this disastrous night!"

Fionnuala remained upon the Seal Rock until the morrow morn, watching the tossing waters in all directions around her, until at last she saw Conn coming towards her, and his head drooping and feathers drenched and disarrayed. Joyfully did the sister welcome him; and before long, behold, Fiachra also approaching them, cold and wet and faint, and the speech was frozen in him that not a word he spake could be understood. So Fionnuala put her wings about him, and said, "If but Hugh came now, how happy should we be!"

In no long time after that they saw Hugh also approaching them across the sea, and his head was dry and his feathers fair and unruffled, for he had found shelter from the gale. Fionnuala put him under her breast, and Conn under her right wing and Fiachra under her left, and covered them wholly with her feathers. "O children," she said to them, "evil though you think this night to have been, many such a one shall we know from this time forward."

So there the swans continued, suffering cold and misery upon the tides of Moyle; and one while they would be upon the coast of Alba and another upon the coast of Erinn, but the waters they might not leave. At length there came upon them a night of bitter cold and snow such as they had never felt before, and Fionnuala sang this lament:

"Evil is this life.

The cold of this night,

The thickness of the snow,

The sharpness of the wind -

"How long have they lain together,

Under my soft wings,

The waves beating upon us,

Conn and Hugh and Fiachra?

"Aoife has doomed us,

Us, the four of us,

To-night to this misery -

Evil is this life."

Thus for a long time they suffered, till at length there came upon the Straits of Moyle a night of January so piercing cold that the like of it had never been felt. And the swans were gathered together upon the Seal Rock. The waters froze into ice around them, and each of them became frozen in his place, so that their feet and feathers clung to the rock; and when the day came and they strove to leave the place, the skin of their feet and the feathers of their breasts clove to the rock, they came naked and wounded away.

"Woe is me, Oh children of Lir," said Fionnuala, "we are now indeed in evil case, for we cannot endure the salt water, yet we may not be away from it; and if the saltwater gets into our sores we shall perish of it." And thus she sang:

"Tonight we are full of keening;

No plumage to cover our bodies;

And cold to our tender feet

Are the rough rocks all awash.

"Cruel to us was Aoife,

Who played her magic upon us?

And drove us out to the ocean,

Four wonderful, snow-white swans.

"Our bath is the frothing brine
In the bay by red rocks guarded,
For mead at our father's table
We drink of the salt blue sea.

"Three sons and a single daughter -
In clefts of the cold rocks dwelling,
The hard rocks, cruel to mortals.
- We are full of keening to-night."

So they went forth again upon the Straits of Moyle, and the brine was grievously sharp and bitter to them, but they could not escape it nor shelter themselves from it. Thus they were, till at last their feathers grew again and their sores were healed.

On one day it happened that they came to the mouth of the river Bann in the north of Erinn, and there they perceived a fair host of horsemen riding on white steeds and coming steadily onward from the south-west "Do you know who yon riders are, children of Lir?" asked Fionnuala. "We know not," said they, "but it is like they are some party of the People of Dana." Then they moved to the margin of the land, and the company they had seen came down to meet them; and behold, it was Hugh and Fergus, the two sons of Bóv the Red, and their nobles and attendants with them, who had long been seeking for the swans along the coast of the Straits of Moyle.

Most lovingly and joyfully did they greet each other and the swans inquired concerning their father Lir, and Bóv the Red, and the rest of their kinsfolk.

"They are well," said the Danaans, "and at this time they are all assembled together in the palace of your father at the Hill of the White Field, where they are holding the Festival of the Age of Youth. They are happy and gay and have no weariness or trouble, save that you are not among them, and that they have not known where you were since you left them at Lough Derryvaragh."

"That is not the tale of our lives," said Fionnuala.

After that the company of the Danaans departed and brought word of the swans to Bóv the Red and to Lir, who were rejoiced to hear that they were living, "for," said they, "the children shall obtain relief in the end of time." And the swans went back to the tides of Moyle and abode there till their time to be in that place had expired.

When that day had come, Fionnuala declared it to them, and they rose up wheeling in the air, and flew westward across Ireland till they came to the Bay of Erris, and there they abode as was ordained. Here it happened that among those of mortal MEN whose dwellings bordered on the bay was a young man of gentle blood, by name Evric, who having heard the singing of the swans came down to speak with them, and became their friend. After that he would often come to hear their music, for it was very sweet to him; and he loved them greatly, and they him. All their story they told him, and he it was who set it down in order, even as it is here narrated.

Much hardship did they suffer from cold and tempest in the waters of the Western Sea, yet not so much as they had to bear by the coasts of the ever-stormy Moyle, and they knew that the day of redemption was now drawing near. In the end of the time Fionnuala said,

"Brothers, let us fly to the Hill of the White Field, and see how Lir our father and his household are faring." So they arose and set forward on their airy journey until they reached the Hill of the White Field, and thus it was that they found the place, namely, desolate and thorny before them, with nought but green mounds where once were the palaces and homes of their kin, and forests of nettles growing over them, and never a house nor a hearth. And the four drew closely together and lamented aloud at that sight, for they knew that old times and things had passed away in Erinn, and they were lonely in a land of strangers, where no man lived who could recognise them when they came to their human shapes again. They knew not that Lir and their kin of the People of Dana yet dwelt invisible in the bright world within the Fairy Mounds, for their eyes were holden that they should not see, since other things were destined for them than to join the Danaan folk and be of the company of the immortal Shee.

So they went back again to the Western Sea until the holy Patrick came into Ireland and preached the Faith of the One God and of the Christ. But a man of Patrick's men, namely the Saint Mochaovóg, came to the Island of Inishglory in Erris Bay, and there built himself a little church of stone, and spent his life in preaching to the folk and in prayer. The first night he came to the island the swans heard the sound of his bell ringing at matins on the following morn, and they leaped in terror, and the three brethren left Fionnuala and fled away. Fionnuala cried to them, "What ails you, beloved brothers?" "We know not," said they, "but we have heard a thin and dreadful voice, and we cannot tell what it is." "That is the voice of the bell of Mochaovóg," said Fionnuala, "and it is that bell which shall deliver us and drive away our pains, according to the will of God."

Then the brethren came back and hearkened to the chanting of the cleric until matins were performed. "Let us chant our music now," said Fionnuala. So they began, and chanted a solemn, slow, sweet, fairy song in adoration of the High King of Heaven and of Earth.

Mochaovóg heard that, and wondered, and when he saw the swans he spoke to them and inquired them. They told him they were the children of Lir. "Praised be God for that," said Mochaovóg. "Surely it is for your sakes that I have come to this island above every other island that is in Erinn. Come to land now, and trust in me that your salvation and release are at hand."

So they came to land, and dwelt with Mochaovóg in his own house, and there they kept the canonical hours with him and heard mass. And Mochaovóg caused a good craftsman to make chains of silver for the swans, and put one chain between Fionnuala and Hugh and another between Conn and Fiachra; and they were a joy and solace of mind to the Saint, and their own woe and pain seemed to them dim and far off as a dream.

Now at this time it happened that the King of Connacht was Lairgnen, son of Colman, and he was betrothed to Deoca, daughter of the King of Munster. And so it was that when Deoca came northward to be wedded to Lairgnen she heard the tale of the swans and of their singing, and she prayed the king that he would obtain them for her, for she longed to possess them. But Lairgnen would not ask them of Mochaovóg. Then Deoca set out homeward again, and vowed that she would never return to Lairgnen till she had the swans; and she came as far as the church of Dalua, which is now called Kildaloe, in Clare. Then Lairgnen sent messengers for the birds to Mochaovóg, but he would not give them up.

At this Lairgnen was very wroth, and he went himself to Mochaovóg, and he found the cleric and the four birds at the altar.

But Lairgnen seized upon the birds by their silver chains, two in each hand dragged them away to the place where Deoca was; and Mochaovóg followed them. But when they came to Deoca and she had laid her hands upon the birds, behold, their covering of feathers fell off and in their places were three shrunken and feeble old men and one lean and withered old woman, fleshless and bloodless from extreme old age. And Lairgnen was struck with amazement and fear, and went out from that place.

Then Fionnuala said to Mochaovóg, "Come now and baptize us quickly, for our end is near. And if you are grieved at parting from us, know that also to us it is a grief. Do you make our grave when we are dead, and place Conn at my right side and Fiachra at my left, and Hugh before my face, for thus they were likely to be when I sheltered them on many a winter night by the tides of Moyle."

So Mochaovóg baptized the three brethren and their sister; and shortly afterwards they found peace and death, and they were buried even as Fionnuala had said. And over their tomb a stone was raised, and their names and lineage graved on it in branching Ogham; and lamentation and prayers were made for them, and their souls won to heaven.

But Mochaovóg was sorrowful, and grieved after them so long as he lived on earth.

Tales From The Land Of Saints & Scholars

The Storyteller at Fault

"The Storyteller at Fault", adapted from Joseph Jacobs' Celtic Fairy Tales (1892), is a brief yet deftly moral tale drawn from the Irish oral tradition. It tells of a celebrated storyteller whose gift for invention begins to betray him.

Jacobs' adaptation captures both the humour and the dry, moral clarity of the Irish tradition. The story belongs to that familiar Celtic class of cautionary anecdotes where cunning teeters on folly. It pokes gentle fun at storytellers themselves, those who weave endlessly, half-prisoners of their own art, and reflects a culture that prizes quickness of mind but also the wisdom to stop talking before the audience leaves.

At the time when the Tuatha De Dannan held the sovereignty of Ireland, there reigned in Leinster a king, who was remarkably fond of hearing stories. Like the other princes and chieftains of the island, he had a favourite storyteller, who held a large estate from his Majesty, on condition of telling him a new story every night of his life, before he went to sleep. Many indeed were the stories he knew, so that he had already reached a good old age without failing even for a single night in his task; and such was the skill he displayed that whatever cares of state or other annoyances might prey upon the monarch's mind, his storyteller was sure to send him to sleep.

One morning the storyteller arose early, and as his custom was, strolled out into his garden turning over in his mind incidents which he might weave into a story for the king at night. But this morning he found himself quite at fault; after pacing his whole demesne, he returned to his house without being able to think of anything new or strange. He found no difficulty in "there was once a king who had three sons" or "one day the king of all Ireland," but further than that he could not get. At length he went into breakfast, and found his wife much perplexed at his delay.

"Why don't you come to breakfast, my dear?" said she.

"I have no mind to eat anything," replied the storyteller, "long as I have been in the service of the king of Leinster, I never sat down to breakfast without having a new story ready for the evening, but this morning my mind is quite shut up, and I don't know what to do. I might as well lie down and die at once. I'll be disgraced forever this evening, when the king calls for his storyteller."

Just at this moment the lady looked out of the window.

"Do you see that black thing at the end of the field?" said she.

"I do," replied her husband.

They drew nigh, and saw a miserable looking old man lying on the ground with a wooden leg placed beside him.

"Who are you, my good man?" asked the storyteller.

"Oh, then, 'tis little matter who I am. I'm a poor, old, lame, decrepit, miserable creature, sitting down here to rest awhile."

"An' what are you doing with that box and dice I see in your hand?"

"I am waiting here to see if anyone will play a game with me," replied the beggar man.

"Play with you! Why what has a poor old man like you to play for?"

"I have one hundred pieces of gold in this leathern purse," replied the old man.

"You may as well play with him," said the storyteller's wife, "and perhaps you'll have something to tell the king in the evening."

A smooth stone was placed between them, and upon it they cast their throws.

It was but a little while and the storyteller lost every penny of his money.

"Much good may it do you, friend," said he. "What better hap could I look for, fool that I am!"

"Will you play again?" asked the old man.

"Don't be talking, man. You have all my money."

"Haven't you chariot and horses and hounds?"

"Well, what of them!"

"I'll stake all the money I have against yours."

"Nonsense, man! Do you think for all the money in Ireland, I'd run the risk of seeing my lady tramp home on foot?"

"Maybe you'd win," said the bocough.

"Maybe I wouldn't," said the storyteller.

"Play with him, husband," said his wife. "I don't mind walking, if you do, love."

"I never refused you before," said the storyteller, "and I won't do so now."

Down he sat again, and in one throw lost houses, hounds, and chariot.

"Will you play again?" asked the beggar.

"Are you making game of me, man; what else have I to stake?"

"I'll stake all my winnings against your wife," said the old man.

The storyteller turned away in silence, but his wife stopped him.

"Accept his offer," said she. "This is the third time, and who knows what luck you may have? You'll surely win now."

They played again, and the storyteller lost. No sooner had he done so, than to his sorrow and surprise, his wife went and sat down near the ugly old beggar.

"Is that the way you're leaving me?" said the storyteller.

"Sure I was won," said she. "You would not cheat the poor man, would you?"

"Have you any more to stake?" asked the old man.

"You know very well I have not," replied the storyteller.

"I'll stake the whole now, wife and all, against your own self," said the old man.

Again they played, and again the storyteller lost.

"Well! here I am, and what do you want with me?"

"I'll soon let you know," said the old man, and he took from his pocket a long cord and a wand.

"Now," he said to the storyteller, "what kind of animal would you rather be, a deer, a fox, or a hare? You have your choice now, but you may not have it later."

To make a long story short, the storyteller made his choice of a hare; the old man threw the cord round him, struck him with the wand,

and lo! a long-eared, frisking hare was skipping and jumping on the green.

But it wasn't for long; who but his wife called the hounds, and set them on him. The hare fled, the dogs followed. Round the field ran a high wall, so that run as he might, he couldn't get out, and mightily diverted were beggar and lady to see him twist and double.

In vain did he take refuge with his wife, she kicked him back again to the hounds, until at length the beggar stopped the hounds, and with a stroke of the wand, panting and breathless, the storyteller stood before them again.

"And how did you like the sport?" said the beggar.

"It might be sport to others," replied the storyteller looking at his wife, "for my part I could well put up with the loss of it."

"Would it be asking too much," he went on to the beggar, "to know who you are at all, or where you come from, or why you take a pleasure in plaguing a poor old man like me?"

"Oh!" replied the stranger, "I'm an odd kind of good-for-little fellow, one day poor, another day rich, but if you wish to know more about me or my habits, come with me and perhaps I may show you more than you would make out if you went alone."

"I'm not my own master to go or stay," said the storyteller, with a sigh.

The stranger put one hand into his wallet and drew out of it before their eyes a well-looking middle-aged man, to whom he spoke as follows, "By all you heard and saw since I put you into my wallet, take charge of this lady and of the carriage and horses, and have them ready for me whenever I want them."

Scarcely had he said these words when all vanished, and the

storyteller found himself at the Foxes' Ford, near the castle of Red Hugh O'Donnell. He could see all but none could see him.

O'Donnell was in his hall, and heaviness of flesh and weariness of spirit were upon him.

"Go out," he said to his doorkeeper, "and see who or what may be coming."

The doorkeeper went, and what he saw was a lank, grey Beggarman; half his sword bared behind his haunch, his two shoes full of cold road-a-wayish water sousing about him, the tips of his two ears out through his old hat, his two shoulders out through his scant tattered cloak, and in his hand a green wand of holly.

"Save you, O'Donnell," said the lank grey Beggarman.

"And you likewise," said O'Donnell. "From where come you, and what is your craft?"

"I come from the outmost stream of earth,

From the glens where the white swans glide,

A night in Islay, a night in Man,

A night on the cold hillside."

"It's the great traveller you are," said O'Donnell.

"Maybe you've learnt something on the road."

"I am a juggler," said the lank grey Beggarman, "and for five pieces of silver you shall see a trick of mine."

"You shall have them," said O'Donnell; and the lank grey

Beggarman took three small straws and placed them in his hand.

"The middle one," said he, "I'll blow away; the other two I'll leave."

"You cannot do it," said one and all.

But the lank grey Beggarman put a finger on either outside straw and, whiff, away he blew the middle one.

"Tis a good trick," said O'Donnell; and he paid him his five pieces of silver.

"For half the money," said one of the chief's lads, "I'll do the same trick."

"Take him at his word, O'Donnell."

The lad put the three straws on his hand, and a finger on either outside straw and he blew; and what happened but that the fist was blown away with the straw.

"You are sore, and you will be sorer," said O'Donnell.

"Six more pieces, O'Donnell, and I'll do another trick for you," said the lank grey Beggarman.

"Six shalt you have."

"Can you see my two ears! One I'll move but not t'other."

"Tis easy to see them, they're big enough, but you can never move one ear and not the two together."

The lank grey Beggarman put his hand to his ear, and he gave it a pull.

O'Donnell laughed and paid him the six pieces.

"Call that a trick," said the fistless lad, "anyone can do that," and so saying, he put up his hand, pulled his ear, and what happened was that he pulled away ear and head.

"Sore you are; and sorer you will be," said O'Donnell.

"Well, O'Donnell," said the lank grey Beggarman, "strange are the tricks I've shown you, but I'll show you a stranger one yet for the same money."

"You have my word for it," said O'Donnell.

With that the lank grey Beggarman took a bag from under his armpit, and from out the bag a ball of silk, and he unwound the ball and he flung it slantwise up into the clear blue heavens, and it became a ladder; then he took a hare and placed it upon the thread, and up it ran; again he took out a red-eared hound, and it swiftly ran up after the hare.

"Now," said the lank grey Beggarman, "has any one a mind to run after the dog and on the course?"

"I will," said a lad of O'Donnell's.

"Up with you then," said the juggler, "but I warn you if you let my hare be killed I'll cut off your head when you come down."

The lad ran up the thread and all three soon disappeared. After looking up for a long time, the lank grey Beggarman said, "I'm afraid the hound is eating the hare, and that our friend has fallen asleep."

Saying this he began to wind the thread, and down came the lad fast asleep; and down came the red-eared hound and in his mouth the last morsel of the hare.

He struck the lad a stroke with the edge of his sword, and so cast his head off. As for the hound, if he used it no worse, he used it no better.

"It's little I'm pleased, and sore I'm angered," said O'Donnell, "that a hound and a lad should be killed at my court."

"Five pieces of silver twice over for each of them," said the juggler, "and their heads shall be on them as before."

"You shalt get that," said O'Donnell.

Five pieces, and again five were paid him, and lo! the lad had his head and the hound his. And though they lived to the uttermost end of time, the hound would never touch a hare again, and the lad took good care to keep his eyes open.

Scarcely had the lank grey Beggarman done this when he vanished from out their sight, and no one present could say if he had flown through the air or if the earth had swallowed him up.

He moved as wave tumbling o'er wave

As whirlwind following whirlwind,

As a furious wintry blast,

So swiftly, sprucely, cheerily,

Right proudly,

And no stop made

Until he came

To the court of Leinster's King,

He gave a cheery light leap

O'er top of turret,

Of court and city

Of Leinster's King.

Heavy was the flesh and weary the spirit of Leinster's king. 'Twas the hour he was likely to hear a story, but send he might right and left, not a jot of tidings about the storyteller could he get.

"Go to the door," he said to his doorkeeper, "and see if a soul is in sight who may tell me something about my storyteller."

The doorkeeper went, and what he saw was a lank grey Beggarman, half his sword bared behind his haunch, his two old shoes full of cold road-a-wayish water sousing about him, the tips of his two ears out through his old hat, his two shoulders out through his scant tattered cloak, and in his hand a three-stringed harp.

"What can you do?" said the doorkeeper.

"I can play," said the lank grey Beggarman.

"Never fear," added he to the storyteller, "thou shalt see all, and not a man shall see you."

When the king heard a harper was outside, he bade him in.

"It is I that have the best harpers in the five-fifths of Ireland," said he, and he signed them to play. They did so, and if they played, the lank grey Beggarman listened.

"Heard you ever the like?" said the king.

"Did you ever, Oh king, hear a cat purring over a bowl of broth, or the buzzing of beetles in the twilight, or a shrill tongued old woman scolding your head off?"

"That I have often," said the king.

"More melodious to me," said the lank grey Beggarman, "were the worst of these sounds than the sweetest harping of your harpers."

When the harpers heard this, they drew their swords and rushed at him, but instead of striking him, their blows fell on each other, and soon not a man but was cracking his neighbour's skull and getting his own cracked in turn.

When the king saw this, he thought it hard the harpers weren't content with murdering their music, but must needs murder each other.

"Hang the fellow who began it all," said he, "and if I can't have a story, let me have peace."

Up came the guards, seized the lank grey Beggarman, marched him to the gallows and hanged him high and dry. Back they marched to the hall, and who should they see but the lank grey Beggarman seated on a bench with his mouth to a flagon of ale.

"Never welcome you in," cried the captain of the guard, "didn't we hang you this minute, and what brings you here?"

"Is it me myself, you mean?"

"Who else?" said the captain.

"May your hand turn into a pig's foot with you when you think of tying the rope; why should you speak of hanging me?"

Back they scurried to the gallows, and there hung the king's favourite brother.

Back they hurried to the king who had fallen fast asleep.

"Please your Majesty," said the captain, "we hanged that strolling vagabond, but here he is back again as well as ever."

"Hang him again," said the king, and off he went to sleep once more.

They did as they were told, but what happened was that they found the king's chief harper hanging where the lank grey Beggarman should have been.

The captain of the guard was sorely puzzled.

"Are you wishful to hang me a third time?" said the lank grey Beggarman.

"Go where you will," said the captain, "and as fast as you please if you'll only go far enough. It's

trouble enough you've given us already."

"Now you're reasonable," said the Beggarman, "and since you've given up trying to hang a stranger because he finds fault with your music, I don't mind telling you that if you go back to the gallows you'll find your friends sitting on the sward none the worse for what has happened."

As he said these words he vanished; and the storyteller found himself on the spot where they first met, and where his wife still was with the carriage and horses.

"Now," said the lank grey Beggarman, "I'll torment you no longer. There's your carriage and your horses, and your money and your wife; do what you please with them."

"For my carriage and my houses and my hounds," said the storyteller,

"I thank you; but my wife and my money you may keep."

"No," said the other. "I want neither, and as for your wife, don't think ill of her for what she did, she couldn't help it."

"Not help it! Not help kicking me into the mouth of my own hounds! Not help casting me off for the sake of a beggarly old"

"I'm not as beggarly or as old as you think. I am Angus of the Bruff;

many a good turn you've done me with the King of Leinster. This morning my magic told me the difficulty you were in, and I made up my mind to get you out of it. As for your wife there, the power that changed your body changed her mind. Forget and forgive as man and wife should do, and now you have a story for the King of Leinster when he calls for one;" and with that he disappeared.

It's true enough he now had a story fit for a king. From first to last he told all that had befallen him; so long and loud laughed the king that he couldn't go to sleep at all. And he told the storyteller never to trouble for fresh stories, but every night as long as he lived he listened again and he laughed afresh at the tale of the lank grey Beggarman.

The Three Crowns

"The Three Crowns" is a traditional Irish folktale first recorded by Patrick Kennedy and later adapted by Alfred Perceval Graves in The Irish Fairy Book (1910). The story follows the classic quest pattern of Celtic folklore, weaving together motifs of enchantment, courage, and moral testing. It tells of three brothers who set out to win their fortunes, each facing supernatural trials and temptations.

At its heart, the tale is a moral allegory dressed in mythic clothing. It speaks to the Irish fascination with luck and destiny, but also to the deeper belief that integrity and humility are the truest forms of magic. The three crowns themselves echo the triadic symbols that recur throughout Celtic lore, body, mind, and spirit; land, sea, and sky; past, present, and future. Like many of Kennedy's collected tales, The Three Crowns captures the lingering twilight between the Christian and the older mythic worlds, where fairies, saints, and mortals still shared a moral universe.

There was once a king, some place or other, and he had three daughters. The two eldest were very proud and uncharitable, but the youngest was as good as they were bad. Well, three princes came to court them, and two of them were the moral of the two eldest ladies, and one was just as lovable as the youngest. They were all walking down to a lake one day that lay at the bottom of the lawn, just like the one at Castleboro', and they met a poor beggar. The King wouldn't give him anything, and the eldest princes wouldn't give him anything, nor their sweethearts; but the youngest daughter and her true love did give him something, and kind words along with it, and that was better nor all.

When they got to the edge of the lake, what did they find but the most beautiful boat you ever saw in your life; and says the eldest, "I'll take a sail in this fine boat;" and says the second eldest, "I'll take a sail in this fine boat;" and says the youngest, "I won't take a sail in that fine boat, for I'm afraid it's an enchanted one." But the others persuaded her to go in, and her father was just going in after her, when up sprung on the deck a little man only seven inches high, and he ordered him to stand back. Well, all the men put their hands to their swords; and if the same swords were only thraneens they weren't able to draw them, for all strength was left their arms. Seven Inches loosened the silver chain that fastened the boat and pushed away; and after grinning at the four men, says he to them, "Bid your daughters and your brides farewell for a while. That wouldn't have happened you three, only for your want of charity. You," says he to the youngest, "needn't fear; you'll recover your princess all in good time, and you and she will be as happy as the day is long. Bad people, if they were rolling stark naked in gold, would not be rich. Banacht lath!" Away they sailed, and the ladies stretched out their hands, but weren't able to say a word.

Well, they were crossing the lake while a cat would be licking her ear, and the poor men couldn't stir hand nor foot to follow them. They saw Seven Inches handing the three princesses out of the boat, and letting them down by a nice basket and windlass into a draw-well that was convenient, but king nor princes never saw an opening before in the same place. When the last lady was out of sight the men found the strength in their arms and legs again. Round the lake they ran, and never drew rein till they came to the well and windlass, and there was the silk rope rolled on the axle, and the nice white basket hanging to it. "Let me down," says the youngest prince, "I'll die or recover them again." "No," says the second daughter's sweetheart, "I'm entitled to my turn before you." "And" says the other, "I must get first turn, in right of my bride." So they gave way to him, and in he got into the basket, and down they let him. First they lost sight of him, and then, after winding off a hundred perches of the silk rope, it slackened, and they stopped turning. They waited two hours, and then they went to dinner, because there was no chuck made at the rope.

Guards were set till morning, and then down went the second prince, and, sure enough, the youngest of all got himself let down on the third day. He went down perches and perches, while it was as dark about him as if he was in a big pot with the cover on. At last he saw a glimmer far down, and in a short time he felt the ground. Out he came from the big lime-kiln, and lo and behold you, there was a wood and green fields, and a castle in a lawn, and a bright sky over all. "It's in Tir-na-n Oge I am," says he. "Let's see what sort of people are in the castle." On he walked across fields and lawn, and no one was there to keep him out or let him into the castle; but the big hall door was wide open. He went from one fine room to another that was finer, and at last he reached the handsomest of all, with a table in the middle; and such a dinner as was laid upon it! The prince was hungry enough, but he was too mannerly to go eat without being invited. So he sat by the fire, and he did not wait long till he heard steps, and in came Seven Inches and the youngest sister by the hand. Well, prince and princess flew into one another's arms, and says the little man, says he, "Why aren't you eating?" "I think, sir," says he, "it was only good manners to wait to be asked." "The other princes didn't think so," says he. "Each of them fell to without leave nor license, and only gave me the rough side o' his tongue when I told them they were making more free than welcome. Well, I don't think they feel much hunger now. There they are, good marvel instead of flesh and blood," says he, pointing to two statues, one in one corner and the other in the other corner of the room. The prince was frightened, but he was afraid to say anything, and Seven Inches made him sit down to dinner between himself and his bride, and he'd be as happy as the day is long, only for the sight of the stone men in the corner. Well, that day went by, and when the next came, says Seven Inches to him, "Now, you'll have to set out that way," pointing to the sun, "and you'll find the second princess in a giant's castle this evening, when you'll be tired and hungry, and the eldest princess tomorrow evening; and you may as well bring them here with you. You need not ask leave of their masters; they're only housekeepers with the big fellows. I suppose, if they ever get home, they'll look on poor people as if they were flesh and blood like themselves."

Away went the prince, and bedad it's tired and hungry he was when he reached the first castle at sunset. Oh, wasn't the second princess glad to see him! And if she didn't give him a good supper it's a wonder. But she heard the giant at the gate, and she hid the prince in a closet. Well, when he came in, he snuffed, and he snuffed, an' says he, "Be (by) the life, I smell fresh mate." "Oh," says the princess, "it's only the calf I got killed to-day." "Ay, ay," says he, "is supper ready?" "It is," says she; and before he rose from the table he hid three-quarters of the calf and a keg of wine. "I think," says he when all was done, "I smell fresh mate still." "It's sleepy you are," says she, "go to bed." "When will you marry me?" says the giant, "you're putting me off too long." "St. Tibb's Eve," says she. "I wish I knew how far off that is," says he; and he fell asleep with his head in the dish.

Next day he went out after breakfast, and she sent the prince to the castle where the eldest sister was. The same thing happened there; but when the giant was snoring, the princess wakened up the prince, and they saddled two steeds in the stables, and magh go bragh (the field for ever) with them. But the horses' heels struck the stones outside the gate, and up got the giant, and after them he made. He roared, and he shouted, and the more he shouted the faster ran the horses; and just as the day was breaking he was only twenty perches behind. But the prince didn't leave the Castle of Seven Inches without being provided with something good. He reined in his steed, and flung a short, sharp knife over his shoulder, and up sprung a thick wood between the giant and themselves. They caught the wind that blew before them, and the wind that blew behind them did not catch them. At last they were near the castle where the other sister lived; and there she was, waiting for them under a high hedge, and a fine steed under her.

But the giant was now in sight, roaring like a hundred lions, and the other giant was out in a moment, and the chase kept on. For every two springs the horses gave the giants gave three, and at last they were only seventy perches off. Then the prince stopped again and flung the second skian behind him. Down went all the flat field, till there was a quarry between them a quarter of a mile deep, and the bottom filled with black water; and before the giants could get round it the prince and princesses were inside the domain of the great magician, where the high thorny hedge opened of itself to everyone that he chose to let in.

Well, to be sure, there was joy enough between the three sisters till the two eldest saw their lovers turned into stone. But while they were shedding tears for them Seven Inches came in and touched them with his rod. So they were flesh and blood and life once more, and there was great hugging and kissing, and all sat down to a nice breakfast, and Seven Inches sat at the head of the table.

When breakfast was over he took them into another room, where there was nothing but heaps of gold and silver and diamonds, and silks and satins; and on a table there was lying three sets of crowns. A gold crown was in a silver crown, and that was lying in a copper crown. He took up one set of crowns and gave it to the eldest princess; and another set, and gave it to the second princess; and another set, and gave it to the youngest princess of all; and says he, "Now you may all go to the bottom of the pit, and you have nothing to do but stir the basket, and the people that are watching above will draw you up, princesses first, princes after. But remember, ladies, you are to keep your crowns safe, and be married in them all the same day. If you be married separately, or if you be married without your crowns, a curse will follow - mind what I say."

So they took leave of him with great respect, and walked arm-in-arm to the bottom of the draw-well. There was a sky and a sun over them and a great high wall, and the bottom of the draw-well was inside the arch. The youngest pair went last, and says the princess to the prince, "I'm sure the two princes don't mean any good to you. Keep these crowns under your cloak, and if you are obliged to stay last, don't get into the basket, but put a big stone, or any heavy thing, inside, and see what will happen."

So when they were inside the dark cave they put in the eldest princess first, and she stirred the basket and up she went, but first she gave a little scream. Then the basket was let down again, and up went the second princess, and then up went the youngest; but first she put her arms round her prince's neck and kissed him, and cried a little. At last it came to the turn of the youngest prince, and well became him - instead of going into the basket he put in a big stone.

He drew on one side and listened, and after the basket was drawn up about twenty perch down came itself and the stone like thunder, and the stone was made brishe of on the flags.

Well, my poor prince had nothing for it but to walk back to the castle; and through it and round it he walked, and the finest of eating and drinking he got, and a bed of bog-down to sleep on, and fine walks he took through gardens and lawns, but not a sight could he get, high or low, of Seven Inches. Well, I don't think any of us would be tired of this way of living forever! Maybe we would. Anyhow, the prince got tired of it before a week, he was so lonesome for his true love; and at the end of a month he didn't know what to do with himself.

One morning he went into the treasure room and took notice of a beautiful snuff-box on the table that he didn't remember seeing there before. He took it in his hands and opened it, and out Seven Inches walked on the table. "I think, prince," says he, "you're getting a little tired of my castle?" "Ah!" says the other, "if I had my princess here, and could see you now and then, I'd never see a dismal day." "Well, you're long enough here now, and you're wanting there above. Keep your bride's crowns safe, and whenever you want my help, open this snuff-box. Now take a walk down the garden, and come back when you're tired."

Well, the prince was going down a gravel walk with a quickset hedge on each side and his eyes on the ground, and he thinking on one thing and another. At last he lifted his eyes, and there he was outside of a smith's bawn gate that he had often passed before, about a mile away from the palace of his betrothed princess. The clothes he had on him were as ragged as you please, but he had his crowns safe under his old cloak.

So the smith came out, and says he, "It's a shame for a strong big fellow like you to be on the sthra, and so much work to be done. Are you any good with hammer and tongs? Come in and bear a hand, and I'll give you diet and lodging and a few thirteens when you earn them." "Never say't twice," says the prince, "I want nothing but to be employed." So he took the sledge and pounded away at the red-hot bar that the smith was turning on the anvil to make into a set of horseshoes.

Well, they weren't long powdering away, when a stronshuch (idler) of a tailor came in; and when the smith asked him what news he had, he got the handle of the bellows and began to blow to let out all he had heard for the last two days. There were so many questions and answers at first that, if I told them all, it would be bed-time before I'd be done. So here is the substance of the discourse; and before he got far into it the forge was half filled with women knitting stockings and men smoking.

You all heard how the two princesses were unwilling to be married till the youngest would be ready with her crowns and her sweetheart. But after the windlass loosened accidentally when they were pulling up her bridegroom that was to be, there was no more sign of a well or a rope or a windlass than there is on the palm of your hand. So the buckeens that were courting the eldest ladies wouldn't give peace nor ease to their lovers nor the King till they got consent to the marriage, and it was to take place this morning. Myself went down out of curiosity; and to be sure I was delighted with the grand dresses of the two brides and the three crowns on their heads - gold, silver, and copper - one inside the other. The youngest was standing by, mournful enough, in white, and all was ready. The two bridegrooms came walking in as proud and grand as you please, and up they were walking to the altar rails when, my dear, the boards opened two yards wide under their feet, and down they went among the dead men and the coffins in the vaults. Oh, such screeching as the ladies gave! and such running and racing and peeping down as there was; but the clerk soon opened the door of the vault, and up came the two heroes, and their fine clothes covered an inch thick with cobwebs and mould.

So the King said they should put off the marriage, "For," says he, "I see there is no use in thinking of it till my youngest gets her three crowns and is married along with the others. I'll give my youngest daughter for a wife to whoever brings three crowns to me like the others; and if he doesn't care to be married, some other one will, and I'll make his fortune." "I wish," says the smith, "I could do it; but I was looking at the crowns after the princesses got home, and I don't think there's a black or a white smith on the face of the earth could imitate them." "Faint heart never won fair lady," says the prince. "Go to the palace, and ask for a quarter of a pound of gold, a quarter of a pound of silver, and a quarter of a pound of copper. Get one crown for a pattern, and my head for a pledge, and I'll give you out the very things that are wanted in the morning." "Ubbabow," says the smith, "are you in earnest?" "Faith, I am so," says he. "Go! Worse than lose you can't."

To make a long story short, the smith got the quarter of a pound of gold, and the quarter of a pound of silver, and the quarter of a pound of copper, and gave them and the pattern crown to the prince. He shut the forge door at nightfall, and the neighbours all gathered in the bawn, and they heard him hammering, hammering, hammering, from that to daybreak, and every now and then he'd pitch out through the window bits of gold, silver, or copper; and the idlers scrambled for them, and cursed one another, and prayed for the good luck of the workman.

Well, just as the sun was thinking to rise he opened the door and brought the three crowns he got from his true love, and such shouting and huzzaing as there was! The smith asked him to go along with him to the palace, but he refused; so off set the smith, and the whole townland with him; and wasn't the King rejoiced when he saw the crowns! "Well," says he to the smith, "you're a married man, and what's to be done?" "Faith, your majesty, I didn't make them crowns at all; it was a big shuler (vagrant) of a fellow that took employment with me yesterday." "Well, daughter, will you marry the fellow that made these crowns?" "Let me see them first, father." So when she examined them she knew them right well, and guessed it was her true love that had sent them. "I will marry the man that these crowns came from," says she.

Well," said the King to the eldest of the two princes, "go up to the smith's forge, take my best coach, and bring home the bridegroom." He was very unwilling to do this, he was so proud, but he did not wish to refuse. When he came to the forge he saw the prince standing at the door, and beckoned him over to the coach. "Are you the fellow," says he, "that made them crowns?" "Yes," says the other. "Then," says he, "maybe you'd give yourself a brushing, and get into that coach; the King wants to see you. I pity the princess." The young prince got into the carriage, and while they were on the way he opened the snuff-box, and out walked Seven Inches, and stood on his thigh. "Well," says he, "what trouble is on you now?" "Master," says the other, "please to let me back in my forge, and let this carriage be filled with paving-stones." No sooner said than done. The prince was sitting in his forge, and the horses wondered what was after happening to the carriage.

When they came to the palace yard the King himself opened the carriage door to pay respect to the new son-in-law. As soon as he turned the handle a shower of stones fell on his powdered wig and his silk coat, and down he fell under them. There was great fright, and some tittering, and the King, after he wiped blood from his forehead, looked very cross at the eldest prince.

"My liege," says he, "I'm very sorry for this accident, but I'm not to blame. I saw the young smith get into the carriage, and we never stopped a minute since." "It's uncivil you were to him. Go," says he to the other prince, "and bring the young prince here, and be polite." "Never fear," says he.

But there's some people that couldn't be good-natured if they were to be made heirs of Damer's estate. Not a bit civiler was the new messenger than the old, and when the King opened the carriage door a second time it's a shower of mud that came down on him; and if he didn't fume and splutter and shake himself it's no matter. "There's no use," says he, "going on this way. The fox never got a better messenger than himself."

So he changed his clothes and washed himself, and out he set to the smith's forge. Maybe he wasn't polite to the young prince, and asked him to sit along with himself. The prince begged to be allowed to sit in the other carriage, and when they were half-way he opened his snuff-box.

"Master," says he, "I'd wished to be dressed now according to my rank."

"You shall be that" says Seven Inches. "And now I'll bid you farewell. Continue as good and kind as you always were; love your wife, and that's all the advice I'll give you." So Seven Inches vanished; and when the carriage door was opened in the yard, out walks the prince, as fine as hands and pins could make him, and the first thing he did was to run over to his bride and embrace her very heartily.

Everyone had great joy but the two other princes. There was not much delay about the marriages that were all celebrated on the same day, and the youngest prince and princess were the happiest married couple you ever heard of in a story.

Tales From The Land Of Saints & Scholars

The Three Wishes

"The Three Wishes", originally collected by the Irish writer William Carleton and later adapted by W. B. Yeats for his 1888 anthology Fairy and Folk Tales of the Irish Peasantry (The Walter Scott Publishing Company), is a humorous moral tale drawn from the rich oral storytelling traditions of rural Ireland. The story follows a poor but well-meaning couple who are granted three wishes by a supernatural visitor, usually a fairy or other spirit, as a reward for some small act of kindness.

Like many Irish folk stories gathered in the nineteenth century, The Three Wishes carries the familiar themes of contentment, humility, and the danger of human impatience when faced with the enchantments of the Otherworld. Carleton's version, rooted in his keen ear for peasant dialogue and Yeats's later literary retelling, balances laughter with quiet sympathy for ordinary lives caught between faith and superstition.

In ancient times there lived a man called Billy Dawson, and he was known to be a great rogue. They say he was descended from the family of the Dawsons, which was the reason, I suppose, of his carrying their name upon him.

Billy, in his youthful days, was the best hand at doing nothing in all Europe; devil a mortal could come next or near him at idleness; and, in consequence of his great practice that way, you may be sure that if any man could make a fortune by it he would have done it.

Billy was the only son of his father, barring two daughters; but they have nothing to do with the story I'm telling you. Indeed it was kind father and grandfather for Billy to be handy at the knavery as well as at the idleness; for it was well known that not one of their blood ever did an honest act, except with a roguish intention. In short, they were all together a decent connection, and a credit to the name. As for Billy, all the villainy of the family, both plain and ornamental, came down to him by way of legacy; for it so happened that the father, in spite of all his cleverness, had nothing but his roguery to leave him.

Billy, to do him justice, improved the fortune he got, and every day advanced him farther into dishonesty and poverty, until, at the long run, he was acknowledged on all hands to be the completest swindler and the poorest vagabond in the whole parish.

Billy's father, in his young days, had often been forced to acknowledge the inconvenience of not having a trade, in consequence of some nice point in law, called the "Vagrant Act," that sometimes troubled him. On this account he made up his mind to give Bill an occupation, and he accordingly bound him to a blacksmith; but whether Bill was to live or die by forgery was a puzzle to his father, - though the neighbours said that both was most likely. At all events, he was put apprentice to a smith for seven years, and a hard card his master had to play in managing him. He took the proper method, however, for Bill was so lazy and roguish that it would vex a saint to keep him in order.

"Bill," says his master to him one day that he had been sunning himself about the ditches, instead of minding his business, "Bill, my boy, I'm vexed to the heart to see you in such a bad state of health.

You're very ill with that complaint called an All-overness; however," says he, "I think I can cure you. Nothing will bring you about but three or four sound doses every day of a medicine called 'the oil o' the hazel.' Take the first dose now," says he; and he immediately banged him with a hazel cudgel until Bill's bones ached for a week afterwards.

"If you were my son," said his master, "I tell you that, as long as I could get a piece of advice growing convenient in the hedges, I'd have you a different youth from what you are. If working was a sin, Bill, was no more an innocent boy that ever broke bread than you would be. Good people are scarce, you think; but however that may be, I throw it out as a hint, that you must take your medicine till you're cured, whenever you happen to get unwell in the same way."

From this moment he kept Bill's nose to the grinding-stone; and whenever his complaint returned, he never failed to give him a hearty dose for his improvement.

In the course of time, however, Bill was his own man and his own master; but it would puzzle a saint to know whether the master or the man was the more precious youth in the eyes of the world.

He immediately married a wife, and devil a doubt of it, but if he kept her in whiskey and sugar, she kept him in hot water. Bill drank and she drank; Bill fought and she fought; Bill was idle and she was idle; Bill whacked her and she whacked Bill. If Bill gave her one black eye, she gave him another; just to keep herself in countenance. Never was there a blessed pair so well met; and a beautiful sight it was to see them both at breakfast-time, blinking at each other across the potato-basket, Bill with his right eye black, and she with her left.

In short, they were the talk of the whole town, and to see Bill of a morning staggering home drunk, his shirt sleeves rolled up on his smutted arms, his breast open, and an old tattered leather apron, with one corner tucked up under his belt, singing one minute, and fighting with his wife the next; - she, reeling beside him, with a discoloured eye, as aforesaid, a dirty ragged cap on one side of her head, a pair of Bill's old slippers on her feet, a squalling child on her arm - now cuffing and dragging Bill, and again kissing and hugging him! Yes, it was a pleasant picture to see this loving pair in such a state!

This might do for a while, but it could not last. They were idle, drunken, and ill-conducted; and it was not to be supposed that they would get a farthing candle on their words. They were, of course, driven to great straits; and faith, they soon found that their fighting, and drinking, and idleness made them the laughing-sport of the neighbours; but neither brought food to their children, put a coat upon their backs, nor satisfied their landlord when he came to look for his own. Still, the never a one of Bill but was a funny fellow with strangers, though, as we said, the greatest rogue unhanged.

One day he was standing against his own anvil, completely in a brown study - being brought to his wit's end how to make out a breakfast for the family. The wife was scolding and cursing in the house, and the naked creatures of children squalling about her knees for food. Bill was fairly at an ambush, and knew not where or how to turn himself, when a poor withered old beggar came into the forge, tottering on his staff. A long white beard fell from his chin, and he looked as thin and hungry that you might blow him, one would think, over the house. Bill at this moment had been brought to his senses by distress, and his heart had a touch of pity towards the old man; for, on looking at him a second time, he clearly saw starvation and sorrow in his face.

"God save you, honest man!" said Bill.

The old man gave a sigh, and raising himself with great pain, on his staff, he looked at Bill in a very beseeching way.

"Musha, God save you kindly!" says he, "maybe you could give a poor, hungry, helpless old man a mouthful of something to ait? You see yourself I'm not able to work; if I was, I'd scorn to be beholding to anyone."

"Faith, honest man," said Bill, "if you knew who you're speaking to, you'd as soon ask a monkey for a churn-staff as me for either mate or money. There's not a blackguard in the three kingdoms so fairly on the shaughran as I am for both the one and the other. The wife within is sending the curses thick and heavy on me, and the children's playing the cat's melody to keep her in comfort. Take my word for it, poor man, if I had either mate or money I'd help you, for I know particularly well what it is to want them at the present speaking; an empty sack won't stand, neighbour."

So far Bill told him truth. The good thought was in his heart, because he found himself on a footing with the beggar; and nothing brings down pride, or softens the heart, like feeling what it is to want.

"Why, you are in a worse state than I am," said the old man, "you have a family to provide for, and I have only myself to support."

"You may kiss the book on that, my old worthy," replied Bill, "but come, what I can do for you I will; plant yourself up here beside the fire, and I'll give it a blast or two of my bellows that will warm the old blood in your body. It's a cold, miserable, snowy day, and a good heat will be of service."

"Thank you kindly," said the old man, "I am cold, and a warming at your fire will do me good, sure enough. Oh, it is a bitter, bitter day; God bless it!" He then sat down, and Bill blew a rousing blast that soon made the stranger edge back from the heat. In a short time he felt quite comfortable, and when the numbness was taken out of his joints, he buttoned himself up and prepared to depart.

"Now," says he to Bill, "you hadn't the food to give me, but what you could you did. Ask any three wishes you choose, and be they what they may, take my word for it, they shall be granted."

Now, the truth is, that Bill, though he believed himself a great man in point of 'cuteness, wanted, after all, a full quarter of being square; for there is always a great difference between a wise man and a knave. Bill was so much of a rogue that he could not, for the blood of him, ask an honest wish, but stood scratching his head in a puzzle.

"Three wishes!" said he. "Why, let me see - did you say three?"

"Ay," replied the stranger, "three wishes - that was what I said."

"Well," said Bill, "here goes, - aha! - let me alone, my old worthy! - faith I'll overreach the parish, if what you say is true. I'll cheat them in dozens, rich and poor, old and young. Let me alone, man, - I have it here;" and he tapped his forehead with great glee. "Faith, you're the sort to meet of a frosty morning, when a man wants his breakfast; and I'm sorry that I have neither money nor credit to get a bottle of whiskey, that we might take our morning together."

"Well, but let us hear the wishes," said the old man, "my time is short, and I cannot stay much longer."

"Do you see this sledge-hammer?" said Bill, "I wish, in the first place, that whoever takes it up in their hands may never be able to lay it down till I give them lave; and that whoever begins to sledge with it may never stop sledging till it's my pleasure to release him."

"Secondly - I have an arm-chair, and I wish that whoever sits down in it may never rise out of it till they have my consent."

"And thirdly - that whatever money I put into my purse, nobody may have power to take it out of it but myself!"

"You devil's rip!" says the old man in a passion, shaking his staff across Bill's nose, "why did you not ask something that would serve you both here and hereafter? Sure it's as common as the market-cross, that there's not a vagabond in his Majesty's dominions stands more in need of both."

"Oh! by the elevens," said Bill, "I forgot that altogether! Maybe you'd be civil enough to let me change one of them? The sorra prettier wish ever was made than I'll make, if you'll give me another chance."

"Get out, you reprobate," said the old fellow, still in a passion. "Your day of grace is past. Little you knew who was speaking to you all this time. I'm St. Moroky, you blackguard, and I gave you an opportunity of doing something for yourself and your family; but you neglected it, and now your fate is cast, you dirty, bog-trotting profligate. Sure, it's well known what you are! Aren't you a by-word in everybody's mouth, you and your scold of a wife? By this and by that, if ever you happen to come across me again, I'll send you to where you won't freeze, you villain!"

He then gave Bill a rap of his cudgel over the head, and laid him at his length beside the bellows, kicked a broken coal-scuttle out of his way, and left the forge in a fury.

When Billy recovered himself from the effects of the blow, and began to think on what had happened, he could have quartered himself with vexation for not asking great wealth as one of the wishes at least; but now the die was cast on him, and he could only make the most of the three he pitched upon.

He now bethought him how he might turn them to the best account, and here his cunning came to his aid. He began by sending for his wealthiest neighbours on pretence of business; and when he got them under his roof, he offered them the arm-chair to sit down in. He now had them safe, nor could all the art of man relieve them except worthy Bill was willing. Bill's plan was to make the best bargain he could before he released his prisoners; and let him alone for knowing how to make their purses bleed. There wasn't a wealthy man in the country he did not fleece. The parson of the parish bled heavily; so did the lawyer; and a rich attorney, who had retired from practice, swore that the Court of Chancery itself was paradise compared to Bill's chair.

This was all very good for a time. The fame of his chair, however, soon spread; so did that of his sledge. In a short time neither man, woman, nor child would darken his door; all avoided him and his fixtures as they would a spring-gun or man-trap. Bill, so long as he fleeced his neighbours, never wrought a hand's turn; so that when his money was out, he found himself as badly off as ever. In addition to all this, his character was fifty times worse than before; for it was the general belief that he had dealings with the old boy. Nothing now could exceed his misery, distress, and ill-temper. The wife and he and their children all fought among one another. Everybody hated them, cursed them, and avoided them. The people thought they were acquainted with more than Christian people ought to know. This, of course, came to Bill's ears, and it vexed him very much.

One day he was walking about the fields, thinking of how he could raise the wind once more; the day was dark, and he found himself, before he stopped, in the bottom of a lonely glen covered by great bushes that grew on each side. "Well," thought he, when every other means of raising money failed him, "it's reported that I'm in league with the old boy, and as it's a folly to have the name of the connection without the profit, I'm ready to make a bargain with him any day; -

so," said he, raising his voice, "Nick, you sinner, if you be convenient and willing, why stand out here; show your best leg - here's your man."

The words were hardly out of his mouth when a dark, sober-looking old gentleman, not unlike a lawyer, walked up to him. Bill looked at the foot and saw the hoof. - "Morrow, Nick," says Bill.

"Morrow, Bill," says Nick. "Well, Bill, what's the news?"

"Devil a much myself hears of late," says Bill, "is there anything fresh below?"

"I can't exactly say, Bill; I spend little of my time down now; the Tories are in office, and my hands are consequently too full of business here to pay much attention to anything else."

"A fine place this, sir," says Bill, "to take a constitutional walk in; when I want an appetite I often come this way myself - hem! High feeding is very bad without exercise."

"High feeding! Come, come, Bill, you know you didn't taste a morsel these four-and-twenty hours."

"You know that's a bounce, Nick. I eat a breakfast this morning that would put a stone of flesh on you, if you only smelt at it."

"No matter; this is not to the purpose. What's that you were muttering to yourself a while ago? If you want to come to the brunt, here I'm for you."

"Nick," said Bill, "you're complete; you want nothing barring a pair of Brian O'Lynn's breeches."

Bill, in fact, was bent on making his companion open the bargain, because he had often heard that, in that case, with proper care on his own part, he might defeat him in the long run. The other, however, was his match.

"What was the nature of Brian's garment," inquired Nick. "Why, you know the song," said Bill -

"Brian O'Lynn had no breeches to wear,

So he got a sheep's skin for to make him a pair;

With the fleshy side out and the woolly side in,

They'll be pleasant and cool, says Brian O'Lynn.'

"A cool pair would serve you, Nick."

"You're mighty waggish to-day, Mister Dawson."

"And good right I have," said Bill, "I'm a man snug and well to do in the world; have lots of money, plenty of good eating and drinking, and what more need a man wish for?"

"True," said the other, "in the meantime it's rather odd that so respectable a man should not have six inches of unbroken cloth in his apparel. You are as naked a tatterdemalion as I ever laid my eyes on; in full dress for a party of scare-crows, William."

"That's my own fancy, Nick; I don't work at my trade like a gentleman. This is my forge dress, you know."

"Well, but what did you summon me here for?" said the other, "you may as well speak out, I tell you; for, my good friend, unless you do, I shan't. Smell that."

"I smell more than that," said Bill, "and by the way, I'll thank you to give me the windy side of you - curse all sulphur, I say. There, that's what I call an improvement in my condition. But as you are so stiff," says Bill, "why, the short and long of it is - that - hem - you see I'm - tut - sure you know I have a thriving trade of my own, and that if I like I needn't be at a loss; but in the meantime I'm rather in a kind of a so - so - don't you take?"

And Bill winked knowingly, hoping to trick him into the first proposal.

"You must speak above-board, my friend," says the other. "I'm a man of few words, blunt and honest. If you have anything to say, be plain. Don't think I can be losing my time with such a pitiful rascal as you are."

"Well," says Bill, "I want money, then, and am ready to come into terms. What have you to say to that, Nick?"

"Let me see - let me look at you," says his companion, turning him about. "Now, Bill, in the first place, are you not as finished a scarecrow as ever stood upon two legs?"

"I play second fiddle to you there again," says Bill.

"There you stand, with the blackguards' coat of arms quartered under your eye, and - - "

"Don't make little of blackguards," said Bill, "nor speak disparagingly of your own crest."

"Why, what would you bring, you brazen rascal, if you were fairly put up at auction?"

"Faith, I'd bring more bidders than you would," said Bill, "if you were to go off at auction tomorrow. I tell you they should bid downwards to come to your value, Nicholas. We have no coin small enough to purchase you."

"Well, no matter," said Nick. "If you are willing to be mine at the expiration of seven years, I will give you more money than ever the rascally breed of you was worth."

"Done!" said Bill, "but no disparagement to my family, in the meantime; so down with the hard cash, and don't be a fool."

The money was accordingly paid down! but as nobody was present, except the giver and receiver, the amount of what Bill got was never known.

"Won't you give me a luck-penny?" said the old gentleman.

"Tut," said Billy, "so prosperous an old fellow as you cannot want it; however, bad luck to you, with all my heart! and it's rubbing grease to a fat pig to say so. Be off now, or I'll commit suicide on you. Your absence is a cordial to most people, you infernal old profligate. You have injured my morals even for the short time you have been with me; for I don't find myself so virtuous as I was."

"Is that your gratitude, Billy?"

"Is it gratitude you speak of, man? I wonder you don't blush when you name it. However, when you come again, if you bring a third eye in your head you will see what I mane, Nicholas, ahagur."

The old gentleman, as Bill spoke, hopped across the ditch, on his way to Downing-street, where of late 'tis thought he possesses much influence.

Bill now began by degrees to show off; but still wrought a little at his trade to blindfold the neighbours. In a very short time, however, he became a great man. So long indeed as he was a poor rascal, no decent person would speak to him; even the proud serving-men at the "Big House" would turn up their noses at him. And he well deserved to be made little of by others, because he was mean enough to make little of himself. But when it was seen and known that he had oceans of money, it was wonderful to think, although he was now a greater blackguard than ever, how those who despised him before began to come round him and court his company. Bill, however, had neither sense nor spirit to make those sunshiny friends know their distance; not he - instead of that he was proud to be seen in decent company, and so long as the money lasted, it was, "hail fellow, well met," between himself and every fair-faced sponger who had a horse under him, a decent coat to his back, and a good appetite to eat his dinners. With riches and all, Bill was the same man still; but, somehow or other, there is a great difference between a rich profligate and a poor one, and Bill found it so to his cost in both cases.

Before half the seven years was passed, Bill had his carriage, and his equipages; was hand and glove with my Lord This, and my Lord That; kept hounds and hunters; was the first sportsman at the Curragh; patronised every boxing ruffian he could pick up; and betted night and day on cards, dice, and horses. Bill, in short, should be a blood, and except he did all this, he could not presume to mingle with the fashionable bloods of his time.

It's an old proverb, however, that "what is got over the devil's back is sure to go off under it;" and in Bill's case this proved true. In short, the old boy himself could not supply him with money so fast as he made it fly; it was "come easy, go easy," with Bill, and so sign was on it, before he came within two years of his time he found his purse empty.

And now came the value of his summer friends to be known. When it was discovered that the cash was no longer flush with him - that stud, and carriage, and hounds were going to the hammer - whish! off they went, friends, relations, pot-companions, dinner-eaters, black-legs, and all, like a flock of crows that had smelt gunpowder. Down Bill soon went, week after week, and day after day, until at last he was obliged to put on the leather apron, and take to the hammer again; and not only that, for as no experience could make him wise, he once more began his tap-room brawls, his quarrels with Judy, and took to his "high feeding" at the dry potatoes and salt. Now, too, came the cutting tongues of all who knew him, like razors upon him. Those that he scorned because they were poor and himself rich, now paid him back his own with interest; and those that he measured himself with, because they were rich, and who only countenanced him in consequence of his wealth, gave him the hardest word in their cheeks. The devil mend him! He deserved it all, and more if he had got it.

Bill, however, who was a hardened sinner, never fretted himself down an ounce of flesh by what was said to him, or of him. Not he; he cursed, and fought, and swore, and schemed away as usual, taking in every one he could; and surely none could match him at villainy of all sorts, and sizes.

At last the seven years became expired, and Bill was one morning sitting in his forge, sober and hungry, the wife cursing him, and the children squalling, as before; he was thinking how he might defraud some honest neighbour out of a breakfast to stop their mouths and his own too, when who walks into him but old Nick, to demand his bargain.

"Morrow, Bill!" says he with a sneer.

"The devil welcome you!" says Bill, "but you have a fresh memory."

"A bargain's a bargain between two honest men, any day," says Satan, "when I speak of honest men, I mean yourself and me, Bill;" and he put his tongue in his cheek to make game of the unfortunate rogue he had come for.

"Nick, my worthy fellow," said Bill, "have bowels; you wouldn't do a shabby thing; you wouldn't disgrace your own character by putting more weight upon a falling man. You know what it is to get a come down yourself, my worthy; so just keep your toe in your pump, and walk off with yourself somewhere else. A cool walk will serve you better than my company, Nicholas."

"Bill, it's no use in shirking," said his friend, "your swindling tricks may enable you to cheat others, but you won't cheat me, I guess. You want nothing to make you perfect in your way but to travel; and travel you shall under my guidance, Billy. No, no - I'm not to be swindled, my good fellow. I have rather a - a - better opinion of myself, Mr. D., than to think that you could outwit one Nicholas Clutie, Esq. - ahem!"

"You may sneer, you sinner," replied Bill, "but I tell you that I have outwitted men who could buy and sell you to your face. Despair, you villain, when I tell you that no attorney could stand before me."

Satan's countenance got blank when he heard this; he wriggled and fidgeted about, and appeared to be not quite comfortable.

"In that case, then," says he, "the sooner I deceive you the better; so turn out for the Low Countries."

"Is it come to that in earnest?" said Bill, "and are you going to act the rascal at the long run?"

"Pon honour, Bill."

"Have patience, then, you sinner, till I finish this horseshoe - it's the last of a set I'm finishing for one of your friend the attorney's horses. And here, Nick, I hate idleness, you know it's the mother of mischief; take this sledgehammer, and give a dozen strokes or so, till I get it out of hands, and then here's with you, since it must be so."

He then gave the bellows a puff that blew half a peck of dust in Clubfoot's face, whipped out the red-hot iron, and set Satan sledging away for bare life.

"Faith," says Bill to him, when the shoe was finished, "it's a thousand pities ever the sledge should be out of your hand; the great Parra Gow was a child to you at sledging, you're such an able tyke. Now just exercise yourself till I bid the wife and children goodbye, and then I'm off."

Out went Bill, of course, without the slightest notion of coming back; no more than Nick had that he could not give up the sledging, and indeed neither could he, but was forced to work away as if he was sledging for a wager. This was just what Bill wanted. He was now compelled to sledge on until it was Bill's pleasure to release him; and so we leave him very industriously employed, while we look after the worthy who outwitted him.

In the meantime, Bill broke cover, and took to the country at large; wrought a little journey-work wherever he could get it, and in this way went from one place to another, till, in the course of a month, he walked back very coolly into his own forge, to see how things went on in his absence. There he found Satan in a rage, the perspiration pouring from him in torrents, hammering with might and main upon the naked anvil. Bill calmly leaned his back against the wall, placed his hat on the side of his head, put his hands into his breeches pockets, and began to whistle Shaun Gow's hornpipe. At length he says, in a very quiet and good-humoured way -

"Morrow, Nick!"

"Oh!" says Nick, still hammering away - "Oh! you double-distilled villain, may the most refined, ornamental, double-rectified, super-extra, and original collection of curses that ever was gathered into a single nosegay of ill-fortune, shine in the buttonhole of your conscience while your name is Bill Dawson! I denounce you as a double-milled villain, a finished, hot-pressed knave, in comparison of whom all the other knaves I ever knew, attorneys included, are honest men. I brand you as the pearl of cheats, a tip-top take-in. I denounce you, I say again, for the villainous treatment I have received at your hands in this most untoward and unfortunate transaction between us; for unfortunate, in every sense, is he that has anything to do with such a prime and finished impostor."

"You're very warm, Nicky," says Bill, "what puts you into a passion, you old sinner? Sure if it's your own will and pleasure to take exercise at my anvil, I'm not to be abused for it. Upon my credit, Nicky, you ought to blush for using such blackguard language, so unbecoming your grave character. You cannot say that it was I set you a hammering at the empty anvil, you profligate. However, as you are so industrious, I simply say it would be a thousand pities to take you from it. Nick, I love industry in my heart, and I always encourage it; so work away, it's not often you spend your time so creditably. I'm afraid if you weren't at that you'd be worse employed."

"Bill, have bowels," said the operative, "you wouldn't go to lay more weight on a falling man, you know; you wouldn't disgrace your character by such a piece of iniquity as keeping an inoffensive gentleman, advanced in years, at such an unbecoming and rascally job as this. Generosity's your top virtue, Bill; not but that you have many other excellent ones, as well as that, among which, as you say yourself, I reckon industry; but still it is in generosity you shine. Come, Bill, honour bright, and release me."

"Name the terms, you profligate."

"You're above terms, William; a generous fellow like you never thinks of terms."

"Goodbye, old gentleman!" said Bill, very coolly, "I'll drop in to see you once a month."

"No, no, Bill, you infern-a-a- you excellent, worthy, delightful fellow, not so fast; not so fast. Come, name your terms, you sland - - my dear Bill, name your terms."

"Seven years more."

"I agree; but..."

"And the same supply of cash as before, down on the nail here."

"Very good; very good. You're rather simple, Bill; rather soft, I must confess. Well, no matter. I shall yet turn the tab - a - hem! You are an exceedingly simple fellow, Bill; still there will come a day, my dear Bill - there will come - - "

"Do you grumble, you vagrant? Another word, and I double the terms."

"Mum, William - mum; tace is Latin for a candle."

"Seven years more of grace, and the same measure of the needful that I got before. Ay or no?"

"Of grace, Bill! Ay! ay! ay! There's the cash. I accept the terms. Oh blood! the rascal - of grace!! Bill!"

"Well, now drop the hammer, and vanish," says Billy, "but what would you think to take this sledge, while you stay, and give me a - - eh! why in such a hurry?" he added, seeing that Satan withdrew in double-quick time.

"Hollo! Nicholas!" he shouted, "come back; you forgot something!" and when the old gentleman looked behind him, Billy shook the hammer at him, on which he vanished altogether.

Billy now got into his old courses; and what shows the kind of people the world is made of, he also took up with his old company. When they saw that he had the money once more, and was sowing it about him in all directions, they immediately began to find excuses for his former extravagance.

"Say what you will," said one, "Bill Dawson's a spirited fellow, and bleeds like a prince."

"He's a hospitable man in his own house, or out of it, as ever lived," said another.

"His only fault is," observed a third, "that he is, if anything, too generous, and doesn't know the value of money; his fault's on the right side, however."

"He has the spunk in him," said a fourth, "keeps a capital table, prime wines, and a standing welcome for his friends."

"Why," said a fifth, "if he doesn't enjoy his money while he lives, he won't when he's dead; so more

power to him, and a wider throat to his purse."

Indeed, the very persons who were cramming themselves at his expense despised him at heart. They knew very well, however, how to take him on the weak side. Praise his generosity, and he would do anything; call him a man of spirit, and you might fleece him to his face. Sometimes he would toss a purse of guineas to this knave, another to that flatterer, a third to a bully, and a fourth to some broken down rake - and all to convince them that he was a sterling friend - a man of mettle and liberality. But never was he known to help a virtuous and struggling family - to assist the widow or the fatherless, or to do any other act that was truly useful. It is to be supposed the reason of this was, that as he spent it, as most of the world do, in the service of the devil, by whose aid he got it, he was prevented from turning it to a good account. Between you and me, dear reader, there are more persons acting after Bill's fashion in the same world than you dream about.

When his money was out again, his friends played him the same rascally game once more. No sooner did his poverty become plain, than the knaves began to be troubled with small fits of modesty, such as an unwillingness to come to his place when there was no longer anything to be got there. A kind of virgin bashfulness prevented them from speaking to him when they saw him getting out on the wrong side of his clothes. Many of them would turn away from him in the prettiest and most delicate manner when they thought he wanted to borrow money from them - all for fear of putting him to the blush by asking it. Others again, when they saw him coming towards their houses about dinner hour, would become so confused, from mere gratitude, as to think themselves in another place; and their servants, seized, as it were, with the same feeling, would tell Bill that their masters were "not at home."

At length, after travelling the same villainous round as before, Bill was compelled to betake himself, as the last remedy, to the forge; in other words, he found that there is, after all, nothing in this world that a man can rely on so firmly and surely as his own industry. Bill, however, wanted the organ of common sense; for his experience - and it was sharp enough to leave an impression - ran off him like water off a duck.

He took to his employment sorely against his grain; but he had now no choice. He must either work or starve, and starvation is like a great doctor - nobody tries it till every other remedy fails them. Bill had been twice rich; twice a gentleman among blackguards, but always a blackguard among gentlemen; for no wealth or acquaintance with decent society could rub the rust of his native vulgarity off him. He was now a common blinking sot in his forge; a drunken bully in the tap-room, cursing and brow-beating everyone as well as his wife; boasting of how much money he had spent in his day; swaggering about the high doings he carried on; telling stories about himself and Lord This at the Curragh; the dinners he gave - how much they cost him, and attempting to extort credit upon the strength of his former wealth. He was too ignorant, however, to know that he was publishing his own disgrace, and that it was a mean-spirited thing to be proud of what ought to make him blush through a deal board nine inches thick.

He was one morning industriously engaged in a quarrel with his wife, who, with a three-legged stool in her hand, appeared to mistake his head for his own anvil; he, in the meantime, paid his addresses to her with his leather apron, when who steps in to jog his memory about the little agreement that was between them, but old Nick. The wife, it seems, in spite of all her exertions to the contrary, was getting the worst of it; and Sir Nicholas, willing to appear a gentleman of great gallantry, thought he could not do less than take up the lady's quarrel, particularly as Bill had laid her in a sleeping posture. Now Satan thought this too bad; and as he felt himself under many obligations to the sex, he determined to defend one of them on the present occasion; so as Judy rose, he turned upon the husband, and floored him by a clever facer.

"You unmanly villain," said he, "is this the way you treat your wife? 'Pon honour, Bill, I'll chastise you on the spot. I could not stand by, a spectator of such ungentlemanly conduct, without giving up all claim to gallant - - " Whack! the word was divided in his mouth by the blow of a churn-staff from Judy, who no sooner saw Bill struck, than she nailed Satan, who "fell" once more.

"What, you villain! that's for striking my husband like a murderer behind his back," said Judy, and she suited the action to the word, "that's for interfering between man and wife. Would you murder the poor man before my face? eh? If he bates me, you shabby dog you, who has a better right? I'm sure it's nothing out of your pocket. Must you have your finger in every pie?"

This was anything but idle talk; for at every word she gave him a remembrance, hot and heavy. Nicholas backed, danced, and hopped; she advanced, still drubbing him with great perseverance, till at length he fell into the redoubtable arm-chair, which stood exactly behind him. Bill, who had been putting in two blows for Judy's one, seeing that his enemy was safe, now got between the devil and his wife, a situation that few will be disposed to envy him.

"Tenderness, Judy," said the husband, "I hate cruelty. Go put the tongs in the fire, and make them red hot. Nicholas, you have a nose," said he.

Satan began to rise, but was rather surprised to find that he could not budge.

"Nicholas," says Bill, "how is your pulse? you don't look well; that is to say, you look worse than usual."

The other attempted to rise, but found it a mistake.

"I'll thank you to come along," said Bill. "I have a fancy to travel under your guidance, and we'll take the Low Countries in our way, won't we? Get to your legs, you sinner; you know a bargain's a bargain between two honest men, Nicholas; meaning yourself and me. Judy, are the tongs hot?"

Satan's face was worth looking at, as he turned his eyes from the husband to the wife, and then fastened them on the tongs, now nearly at a furnace heat in the fire, conscious at the same time that he could not move out of the chair.

"Billy," said he, "you won't forget that I rewarded your generosity the last time I saw you, in the way of business." "Faith, Nicholas, it fails me to remember any generosity I ever showed you. Don't be womanish. I simply want to see what kind of stuff your nose is made of, and whether it will stretch like a rogue's conscience. If it does, we will flatter it up the chimney with red-hot tongs, and when this old hat is fixed on the top of it, let us alone for a weather-cock." "Have a fellow-feeling, Mr. Dawson; you know we ought not to dispute. Drop the matter, and I give you the next seven years." "We know all that," says Billy, opening the red-hot tongs very coolly. "Mr. Dawson," said Satan, "if you cannot remember my friendship to yourself, don't forget how often I stood your father's friend, your grandfather's friend, and the friend of all your relations up to the tenth generation. I intended, also, to stand by your children after you, so long as the name of Dawson, and a respectable one it is, might last." "Don't be blushing, Nick," says Bill, "you are too modest; that was ever your failing; hold up your head, there's money bid for you. I'll give you such a nose, my good friend, that you will have to keep an outrider before you, to carry the end of it on his shoulder." "Mr. Dawson, I pledge my honour to raise your children in the world as high as they can go; no matter whether they desire it or not." "That's very kind of you," says the other, "and I'll do as much for your nose."

He gripped it as he spoke, and the old boy immediately sung out; Bill pulled, and the nose went with him like a piece of warm wax. He then transferred the tongs to Judy, got a ladder, resumed the tongs, ascended the chimney, and tugged stoutly at the nose until he got it five feet above the roof. He then fixed the hat upon the top of it, and came down.

"There's a weather-cock," said Billy, "I defy Ireland to show such a beauty. Faith, Nick, it would make the prettiest steeple for a church, in all Europe, and the old hat fits it to a shaving."

In this state, with his nose twisted up the chimney, Satan sat for some time, experiencing the novelty of what might be termed a peculiar sensation. At last the worthy husband and wife began to relent.

"I think," said Bill, "that we have made the most of the nose, as well as the joke; I believe, Judy, it's long enough." "What is?" says Judy.

"Why, the joke," said the husband.

"Faith, and I think so is the nose," said Judy.

"What do you say yourself, Satan?" said Bill.

"Nothing at all, William," said the other, "but that - ha! ha! - it's a good joke - an excellent joke, and a goodly nose, too, as it stands. You were always a gentlemanly man, Bill, and did things with a grace; still, if I might give an opinion on such a trifle - - "

"It's no trifle at all," says Bill, "if you spake of the nose." "Very well, it is not," says the other, "still, I am decidedly of opinion, that if you could shorten both the joke and the nose without further violence, you would lay me under very heavy obligations, which I shall be ready to acknowledge and repay as I ought." "Come," said Bill, "shell out once more, and be off for seven years. As much as you came down with the last time, and vanish."

The words were scarcely spoken, when the money was at his feet, and Satan invisible. Nothing could surpass the mirth of Bill and his wife at the result of this adventure. They laughed till they fell down on the floor.

It is useless to go over the same ground again. Bill was still incorrigible. The money went as the devil's money always goes. Bill caroused and squandered, but could never turn a penny of it to a good purpose. In this way, year after year went, till the seventh was closed, and Bill's hour come. He was now, and had been for some time past, as miserable a knave as ever. Not a shilling had he, nor a shilling's worth, with the exception of his forge, his cabin, and a few articles of crazy furniture. In this state he was standing in his forge as before, straining his ingenuity how to make out a breakfast, when Satan came to look after him. The old gentleman was sorely puzzled how to get at him. He kept skulking and sneaking about the forge for some time, till he saw that Bill hadn't a cross to bless himself with. He immediately changed himself into a guinea, and lay in an open place where he knew Bill would see him. "If," said he, "I once get into his possession, I can manage him." The honest smith took the bait, for it was well gilded; he clutched the guinea, put it into his purse, and closed it up. "Ho! ho!" shouted the devil out of the purse, "you're caught, Bill; I've secured you at last, you knave you. Why don't you despair, you villain, when you think of what's before you?" "Why, you unlucky old dog," said Bill, "is it there you are? Will you always drive your head into every loophole that's set for you? Faith, Nick achora, I never had you bagged till now."

Satan then began to tug and struggle with a view of getting out of the purse, but in vain.

"Mr. Dawson," said he, "we understand each other. I'll give the seven years additional, and the cash on the nail." "Be easy, Nicholas. You know the weight of the hammer, that's enough. It's not a whipping with feathers you're going to get, anyhow. Just be easy." "Mr. Dawson, I grant I'm not your match. Release me, and I double the cash. I was merely trying your temper when I took the shape of a guinea."

"Faith and I'll try yours before I leave it, I've a notion." He immediately commenced with the sledge, and Satan sang out with a considerable want of firmness. "Am I heavy enough!" said Bill.

"Lighter, lighter, William, if you love me. I haven't been well latterly, Mr. Dawson - I have been delicate - my health, in short, is in a very precarious state, Mr. Dawson." "I can believe that" said Bill, "and it will be more so before I have done with you. Am I doing it right?" "Bill," said Nick, "is this gentlemanly treatment in your own respectable shop? Do you think, if you dropped into my little place, that I'd act this rascally part towards you? Have you no compunction?" "I know," replied Bill, sledging away with vehemence, "that you're notorious for giving your friends a warm welcome. Devil an old youth more so; but you must be dealing in bad coin, must you? However, good or bad, you're in for a sweat now, you sinner. Am I doing it pretty?"

"Lovely, William - but, if possible, a little more delicate."

"Oh, how delicate you are! Maybe a cup o' tea would serve you, or a little small gruel to compose your stomach."

"Mr. Dawson," said the gentleman in the purse, "hold your hand and let us understand one another. I have a proposal to make." "Hear the sinner anyhow," said the wife. "Name your own sum," said Satan, "only set me free." "No, the sorra may take the toe you'll budge till you let Bill off," said the wife, "hold him hard, Bill, barring he sets you clear of your engagement." "There it is, my posy," said Bill, "that's the condition. If you don't give me up, here's at you once more - and you must double the cash you gave the last time, too. So, if you're of that opinion, say ay - leave the cash and be off."

The money again appeared in a glittering heap before Bill, upon which he exclaimed - "The ay has it, you dog. Take to your pumps now, and fair weather after you, you vagrant; but Nicholas - Nick -

here, here - - " The other looked back, and saw Bill, with a broad grin upon him, shaking the purse at him - "Nicholas come back," said he. "I'm short a guinea." Nick shook his fist, and disappeared.

It would be useless to stop now, merely to inform our readers that Bill was beyond improvement. In short, he once more took to his old habits, and lived on exactly in the same manner as before. He had two sons - one as great a blackguard as himself, and who was also named after him; the other was a well-conducted, virtuous young man, called James, who left his father, and having relied upon his own industry and honest perseverance in life, arrived afterwards to great wealth, and built the town called Castle Dawson; which is so called from its founder until this day.

Bill, at length, in spite of all his wealth, was obliged, as he himself said, "to travel", in other words, he fell asleep one day, and forgot to awaken; or, in still plainer terms, he died.

Now, it is usual, when a man dies, to close the history of his life and adventures at once; but with our hero this cannot be the case. The moment Bill departed, he very naturally bent his steps towards the residence of St. Moroky, as being, in his opinion, likely to lead him towards the snuggest berth he could readily make out. On arriving, he gave a very humble kind of a knock, and St. Moroky appeared.

"God save your Reverence!" said Bill, very submissively.

"Be off; there's no admittance here for so poor a youth as you are," said St Moroky.

He was now so cold and fatigued that he cared little where he went, provided only, as he said himself, "he could rest his bones, and get an air of the fire." Accordingly, after arriving at a large black gate, he knocked, as before, and was told he would get instant admittance the moment he gave his name.

"Billy Dawson," he replied.

"Off, instantly," said the porter to his companions, "and let his Majesty know that the rascal he dreads so much is here at the gate."

Such a racket and tumult were never heard as the very mention of Billy Dawson created.

In the meantime, his old acquaintance came running towards the gate with such haste and consternation, that his tail was several times nearly tripping up his heels.

"Don't admit that rascal," he shouted, "bar the gate - make every chain, and lock and bolt, fast - I won't be safe - and I won't stay here, nor none of us need stay here, if he gets in - my bones are sore yet after him. No, no - begone you villain - you'll get no entrance here - I know you too well."

Bill could not help giving a broad, malicious grin at Satan, and, putting his nose through the bars, he exclaimed - "Ha! you old dog, I have you afraid of me at last, have I?"

He had scarcely uttered the words, when his foe, who stood inside, instantly tweaked him by the nose, and Bill felt as if he had been gripped by the same red-hot tongs with which he himself had formerly tweaked the nose of Nicholas.

Bill then departed, but soon found that in consequence of the inflammable materials which strong drink had thrown into his nose, that organ immediately took fire, and, indeed, to tell the truth, kept burning night and day, winter and summer, without ever once going out, from that hour to this.

Such was the sad fate of Billy Dawson, who has been walking without stop or stay, from place to place, ever since; and in consequence of the flame on his nose, and his beard being tangled like a wisp of hay, he has been christened by the country folk Will-o'-the-Wisp, while, as it were, to show the mischief of his disposition, the circulating knave, knowing that he must seek the coldest bogs and quagmires in order to cool his nose, seizes upon that opportunity of misleading the unthinking and tipsy night travellers from their way, just that he may have the satisfaction of still taking in as many as possible.

Tales From The Land Of Saints & Scholars

The Vengeance of Mesgedra

"The Vengeance of Mesgedra:" is a tragic tale drawn from the Fenian Cycle of Irish mythology, retold by Thomas William Hazen Rolleston in The High Deeds of Finn and Other Bardic Romances of Ancient Ireland (1910). The story follows Mesgedra, a king of Leinster, and his companion, Conall Cernach, a hero of the Red Branch of Ulster.

In Rolleston's retelling, the tale is both heroic and moral: a meditation on how pride and the relentless code of honour can destroy even the noblest warriors. It also reflects the bardic fascination with fate and retribution, how ancient wrongs ripple through generations. Rolleston's adaptation, drawn from earlier Irish sources including The Book of Leinster and The Book of the Dun Cow, softens some of the medieval ferocity, turning the episode into a story of dignity undone by duty.

Atharna the bard, surnamed The Extortionate, was the chief poet and satirist of Ulster in the reign of Conor mac Nessa. Greed and arrogance were in his heart and poison on his tongue, and the kings and lords of whom he asked rewards for his poems dared not refuse him aught, partly because of the poisonous satires and lampoons which he would otherwise make upon them for their niggardliness, and partly for that in Ireland at that day it was deemed shameful to refuse to a bard whatsoever he might ask. Once it was said that he asked of a sub-king, namely Eochy mac Luchta, who was famed for hospitality and generosity, the single thing that Eochy would have been grieved to give, namely his eye, and Eochy had but one eye. But the King plucked it out by the roots and gave it to him; and Atharna went away disappointed, for he had looked that Eochy would ransom his eye at a great price.

Now Conor mac Nessa, King of Ulster, and all the Ulster lords, having grown very powerful and haughty, became ill neighbours to all the other kingdoms in Ireland. On fertile Leinster above all they fixed their eyes, and sought for an opportunity to attack and plunder the province. Conor resolved at last to move Atharna to go to the King of Leinster, in the hope that he himself might be rid of Atharna, by the King of Leinster killing him for his insolence and his exactions, and that he might avenge the death of his bard by the invasion of Leinster.

Atharna therefore set out for Leinster accompanied by his train of poets and harpers and gillies and arrived at the great Dún of Mesgedra the King, at Naas in Kildare. Here he dwelt for twelve months wasting the substance of the Leinstermen and in the end when he was minded to return to Ulster he went before the King Mesgedra and the lords of Leinster and demanded his poet's fee.

"What is your demand, Atharna?" asked Mesgedra.

"So many cattle and so many sheep," answered Atharna, "and store of gold and raiment, and of the fairest dames and maidens of Leinster forty-five, to grind at my querns in Dún Atharna."

"It shall be granted you," said the King. Then Atharna feared some mischief, for the King and the nobles of Leinster had not seemed like men on whom shameful conditions are laid, nor had they offered to ransom their women. Atharna therefore judged that the Leinstermen might fall upon him to recover their booty when he was once beyond the border, for within their own borders they might not affront a guest. He sent, therefore, a swift messenger to Conor mac Nessa, bidding him come with a strong escort as quickly as he might, to meet Atharna's band on the marches of Leinster, and convey him safely home.

Atharna then departed from Naas with a great herd of sheep and cattle and other spoils, and with thrice fifteen of the noble women of Leinster. He went leisurely, meaning to strike the high road to Emania from Dublin; but when he came there the Liffey was swollen with rain, and the ford at Dublin might not be crossed. He caused, therefore, many great hurdles to be made, and these were set in the river, and over them a causeway of boughs was laid, so that his cattle and spoils came safely across. Hence is the town of that place called to this day in Gaelic the City of the Hurdle Ford.

On the next day Conor and the Ulstermen met him, but a great force of the men of Leinster was also marching from Naas to the border, to recover their womenfolk, even as Atharna had expected. The Leinstermen then broke the battle on the company from Ulster, and defeated them, driving them with the cows of Atharna on to the sea cape of Ben Edar (Howth), but they recovered the women. On Ben Edar did King Conor with the remnant of his troop then fortify themselves, making a great fosse across the neck of land by which Ben Edar is joined to the mainland, and here they were besieged, with hard fighting by day and night, expecting that help should come to them from Ulster, where they had sent messengers to tell of their distress.

Now Conall of the Victories was left behind to rule in Emania when Conor set forth to Leinster, and he now, on hearing how the King was beset, assembled a great host and marched down to Ben Edar.

Here he attacked the host of Leinster, and a great battle was fought, many being slain on both sides, and the King of Leinster, Mesgedra, lost his left hand in the fight. In the end the men of Leinster were routed, and fled, and Mesgedra drove in his chariot past the City of the Hurdle Ford and Naas to the fords of Liffey at Clane. Here there was a sacred oak tree where druid rites and worship were performed, and that oak tree was sanctuary, so that within its shadow, guarded by mighty spells, no man might be slain by his enemy.

Now Conall Cearnach had followed hard on the track of Mesgedra, and when he found him beneath the oak, he drove his chariot round and round the circuit of the sanctuary, bidding Mesgedra come forth and do battle with him, or be counted a dastard among the kings of Erinn. But Mesgedra said, "Is it the fashion of the champions of Ulster to challenge one-armed men to battle?"

Then Conall let his charioteer bind one of his arms to his side, and again he taunted Mesgedra and bade him come forth.

Mesgedra then drew sword, and between him and Conall there was a fierce fight until the Liffey was reddened with their blood. At last, by a chance blow of the sword of Mesgedra, the bonds of Conall's left arm were severed.

"On your head be it," said Conall, "if you release me again."

Then he caused his arm to be bound up once more, and again they met, sword to sword, and again in the fury of the fight Mesgedra cut the thongs that bound Conall's arm. "The gods themselves have doomed you," shouted Conall then, and he rushed upon Mesgedra and in no long time he wounded him to death.

"Take my head," said Mesgedra then, "and add my glory to your glory, but be well assured this wrong shall yet be avenged by me upon Ulster," and he died.

Then Conall cut off the head of Mesgedra and put it in his chariot, and also took the chariot of Mesgedra and fared northwards. Ere long he met a chariot and fifty women accompanying it. In it was Buan the Queen, wife of Mesgedra, returning from a visit to Meath.

"Who are you, woman?" said Conall.

"I am Buan, wife of Mesgedra the King."

"You are to come with me," then said Conall.

"Who have commanded this?" said Buan.

"Mesgedra the King," said Conall.

"By what token dost you lay these commands upon me?"

"Behold his chariot and his horses," said Conall.

"He gives rich gifts to many a man," answered the Queen.

Then Conall showed her the head of her husband.

"This is my token," said he.

"It is enough," said Buan. "But give me leave to bewail him before I go into captivity."

Then Buan rose up in her chariot and raised for Mesgedra a keen of sorrow so loud and piercing that her heart broke with it, and she fell backwards on the road and died.

Conall Cearnach then buried her there, and laid the head of her husband by her side; and the fair hazel tree that grew from her grave by the fords of Clane was called Coll Buana, or the Hazel Tree of Buan.

But before Conall buried the head of Mesgedra he caused the brain to be taken out and mixed with lime to make a bullet for a sling, for so it was customary to do when a great warrior had been killed; and the brain-balls thus made were accounted to be the deadliest of missiles.

So when Leinster had been harried and plundered and its king and queen thus slain, the Ulstermen drew northward again, and the brain-ball was laid up in the Dún of King Conor at Emania.

Years afterwards it happened that the Wolf of Connacht, namely Ket, son of Maga, came disguised within the borders of Ulster in search of prey, and he entered the palace precincts of Conor in Emania. There he saw two jesters of the King, who had gotten the brain-ball from the shelf where it lay, and were rolling it about the courtyard. Ket knew it for what it was, and put it out of sight of the jesters and took it away with him while they made search for it. Thenceforth Ket carried it ever about with him in his girdle, hoping that he might yet use it to destroy some great warrior among the Ulstermen.

One day thereafter Ket made a foray on the men of Ross, and carried away a spoil of cattle. The host of Ulster and King Conor with them overtook him as he went homeward. The men of Connacht had also mustered to the help of Ket, and both sides made them ready for battle.

Now a river, namely Brosna, ran between them, and on a hill at one side of this were assembled a number of the noble women of Connacht, who desired greatly to look on the far-famed Ultonian warriors, and above all on Conor the King, whose presence was said to be royal and stately beyond any man that was then living in Erinn. Among the bushes, close to the women, Ket hid himself, and lay still but watchful.

Now Conor, seeing none but womenfolk close to him at this point, and being willing to show them his splendour, drew near to the bank on his side of the stream. Then Ket leaped up, whirling his sling, and the bullet hummed across the river and smote King Conor on the temple. And his men carried him off for dead, and the men of Connacht broke the battle on the Ulstermen, slaying many, and driving the rest of them back to their own place. This battle was thenceforth called the Battle of the Ford of the Sling-cast, or Athnurchar; and so the place is called to this day.

When Conor was brought home to Emania his chief physician, Fingen, found the ball half buried in his temple. "If the ball be taken out," said Fingen, "he will die; if it remain he will live, but he will bear the blemish of it."

"Let him bear the blemish," said the Ulster lords, "that is a small matter compared with the death of Conor."

Then Fingen stitched the wound over with a thread of gold, for Conor had curling golden hair, and bade him keep himself from all violent movements and from all vehement passions, and not to ride on horseback, and he would do well.

After that Conor lived for seven years, and he went not to war during that time, and all cause of passion was kept far from him. Then one day at broad noon the sky darkened, and the gloom of night seemed to spread over the world, and all the people feared, and looked for some calamity. Conor called to him his chief druid, namely Bacarach, and inquired of him as to the cause of the gloom.

The druid then went with Conor into a sacred grove of oaks and performed the rites of divination, and in a trance he spoke to Conor, saying, "I see a hill near a great city, and three high crosses on it. To one of them is nailed the form of a young man who is like unto one of the Immortals. Round him stand soldiers with tall spears, and a great crowd waiting to see him die."

"Is he, then, a malefactor?"

"Nay," said the druid, "but holiness, innocence, and truth have come to earth in him, and for this cause have the druids of his land doomed him to die, for his teaching was not as theirs. And the heavens are darkened for wrath and sorrow at the sight."

Then Conor leaped up in a fury, crying, "They shall not slay him, they shall not slay him! Would I could be there with the host of Ulster, and thus would I scatter his foes"; and with that he snatched his sword and began striking at the trees that stood thickly about him in the druid grove. Then with the heat of his passion the sling-ball burst from his head, and he fell to the ground and died. Thus was fulfilled the vengeance of Mesgedra upon Conor mac Nessa, King of Ulster.

Tales From The Land Of Saints & Scholars

The Witches' Excursion

"The Witches' Excursion" is a lively Irish folktale first collected by Patrick Kennedy and later adapted by W. B. Yeats in his 1888 anthology Fairy and Folk Tales of the Irish Peasantry (The Walter Scott Publishing Company). The story blends dark humour with rustic superstition, portraying a group of witches who gather in secret to perform their nightly rites.

In Yeats's adaptation, the tone becomes more literary and folkloric, balancing the eerie spectacle of supernatural flight with a keen interest in the social world the tale emerged from. The story mirrors the everyday anxieties of nineteenth-century Ireland, poverty, gossip, and moral judgement, through the lens of fantasy.

Shemus Rua (Red James) awakened from his sleep one night by noises in his kitchen. Stealing to the door, he saw half-a-dozen old women sitting round the fire, jesting and laughing, his old housekeeper, Madge, quite frisky and gay, helping her sister crones to cheering glasses of punch. He began to admire the impudence and imprudence of Madge, displayed in the invitation and the riot, but recollected on the instant her officiousness in urging him to take a comfortable posset, which she had brought to his bedside just before he fell asleep. Had he drunk it, he would have been just now deaf to the witches' glee. He heard and saw them drink his health in such a mocking style as nearly to tempt him to charge them, besom in hand, but he restrained himself.

The jug being emptied, one of them cried out, "Is it time to be gone?" and at the same moment, putting on a red cap, she added:

"By yarrow and rue,

And my red cap too,

Hie over to England."

Making use of a twig which she held in her hand as a steed, she gracefully soared up the chimney, and was rapidly followed by the rest. But when it came to the housekeeper, Shamus interposed. "By your leave, ma'am," said he, snatching twig and cap. "Ah, you deceitful old crocodile! If I find you here on my return, there'll be wigs on the green:

'By yarrow and rue,

And my red cap too,

Hie over to England."

The words were not out of his mouth when he was soaring above the ridge pole, and swiftly ploughing the air. He was careful to speak no word (being somewhat conversant with witch-lore), as the result would be a tumble, and the immediate return of the expedition.

In a very short time they had crossed the Wicklow hills, the Irish Sea, and the Welsh mountains, and were charging, at whirlwind speed, the hall door of a castle. Shamus, only for the company in which he found himself, would have cried out for pardon, expecting to be mummy against the hard oak door in a moment; but, all bewildered, he found himself passing through the keyhole, along a passage, down a flight of steps, and through a cellar-door key-hole before he could form any clear idea of his situation.

Waking to the full consciousness of his position, he found himself sitting on a stillion, plenty of lights glimmering round, and he and his companions, with full tumblers of frothing wine in hand, hobnobbing and drinking healths as jovially and recklessly as if the liquor was honestly come by, and they were sitting in Shamus's own kitchen. The red birredh had assimilated Shamus's nature for the time being to that of his unholy companions. The heady liquors soon got into their brains, and a period of unconsciousness succeeded the ecstasy, the headache, the turning round of the barrels, and the "scattered sight" of poor Shamus. He woke up under the impression of being roughly seized, and shaken, and dragged upstairs, and subjected to a disagreeable examination by the lord of the castle, in his state parlour. There was much derision among the whole company, gentle and simple, on hearing Shamus's explanation, and, as the thing occurred in the dark ages, the unlucky Leinster man was sentenced to be hung as soon as the gallows could be prepared for the occasion.

The poor Hibernian was in the cart proceeding on his last journey, with a label on his back, and another on his breast, announcing him as the remorseless villain who for the last month had been draining the casks in my lord's vault every night. He was surprised to hear himself addressed by his name, and in his native tongue, by an old woman in the crowd. "Ach, Shamus, alanna! is it going to die you are in a strange place without your cappeen d'yarrag?" These words infused hope and courage into the poor victim's heart. He turned to the lord and humbly asked leave to die in his red cap, which he supposed had dropped from his head in the vault. A servant was sent for the headpiece, and Shamus felt lively hope warming his heart while placing it on his head. On the platform he was graciously allowed to address the spectators, which he proceeded to do in the usual formula composed for the benefit of flying stationers - "Good people all, a warning take by me;" but when he had finished the line, "My parents reared me tenderly," he unexpectedly added - "By yarrow and rue," etc., and the disappointed spectators saw him shoot up obliquely through the air in the style of a sky-rocket that had missed its aim. It is said that the lord took the circumstance much to heart, and never afterwards hung a man for twenty-four hours after his offence.

Tales From The Land Of Saints & Scholars

The Wonderful Tune

"The Wonderful Tune" is one of the best-known tales from Thomas Crofton Croker's Fairy Legends and Traditions of the South of Ireland (first published 1825–1828), a collection that helped define early nineteenth-century Irish folklore for an English-speaking audience. The story centres on Maurice Connor, a blind piper from Kinsale whose music is said to charm not only people but the very elements of nature.

Croker's tale, like much of his work, reflects both the allure and the peril of crossing the boundary between the human and the supernatural. It captures the deep connection between Irish identity and music, the idea that song is not merely art but a living bridge between worlds.

Maurice Connor was the king, and that's no small word, of all the pipers in Munster. He could play jig and planxty without end, and Ollistrum's March, and the Eagle's Whistle, and the Hen's Concert, and odd tunes of every sort and kind. But he knew one, far more surprising than the rest, which had in it the power to set everything dead or alive dancing.

In what way he learned it is beyond my knowledge, for he was mighty cautious about telling how he came by so wonderful a tune. At the very first note of that tune, the brogues began shaking upon the feet of all who heard it - old or young it mattered not - just as if their brogues had the ague; then the feet began going - going - going from under them, and at last up and away with them, dancing like mad! - whisking here, there, and everywhere, like a straw in a storm - there was no halting while the music lasted!

Not a fair, nor a wedding, nor a patron in the seven parishes round, was counted worth the speaking of without "blind Maurice and his pipes." His mother, poor woman, used to lead him about from one place to another, just like a dog.

Down through Iveragh - a place that ought to be proud of itself, for 'tis Daniel O'Connell's country - Maurice Connor and his mother were taking their rounds. Beyond all other places Iveragh is the place for stormy coast and steep mountains, as proper a spot it is as any in Ireland to get yourself drowned, or your neck broken on the land, should you prefer that. But, notwithstanding, in Ballinskellig bay there is a neat bit of ground, well fitted for diversion, and down from it towards the water, is a clean smooth piece of strand - the dead image of a calm summer's sea on a moonlight night, with just the curl of the small waves upon it.

Here it was that Maurice's music had brought from all parts a great gathering of the young men and the young women - Oh the darlings! - for 'twas not every day the strand of Trafraska was stirred up by the voice of a bagpipe. The dance began; and as pretty a rinkafadda it was as ever danced. "Brave music," said everybody, "and well done," when Maurice stopped.

"More power to your elbow, Maurice, and a fair wind in the bellows," cried Paddy Dorman, a hump-backed dancing-master, who was there to keep order. "Tis a pity," said he, "if we'd let the piper run dry after such music, 'twould be a disgrace to Iveragh, that didn't come on it since the week of the three Sundays." So, as well became him, for he was always a decent man, says he, "Did you drink, piper?"

"I will, sir," says Maurice, answering the question on the safe side, for you never yet knew piper or schoolmaster who refused his drink.

"What will you drink, Maurice?" says Paddy.

"I'm no ways particular," says Maurice, "I drink anything, and give God thanks, barring raw water; but if 'tis all the same to you, mister Dorman, may be you wouldn't lend me the loan of a glass of whiskey."

"I've no glass, Maurice," said Paddy, "I've only the bottle."

"Let that be no hindrance," answered Maurice, "my mouth just holds a glass to the drop; often I've tried it, sure."

So Paddy Dorman trusted him with the bottle - more fool was he; and, to his cost, he found that though Maurice's mouth might not hold more than the glass at one time, yet owing to the hole in his throat, it took many a filling.

"That was no bad whisky neither," says Maurice, handing back the empty bottle.

"By the holy frost, then!" says Paddy, "tis but cold comfort there's in that bottle now; and 'tis your word we must take for the strength of the whisky, for you've left us no sample to judge by...", and to be sure Maurice had not.

Now I need not tell any gentleman or lady with common understanding, that if he or she was to drink an honest bottle of whiskey at one pull, it is not at all the same thing as drinking a bottle of water; and in the whole course of my life, I never knew more than five men who could do so without being overtaken by the liquor. Of these Maurice Connor was not one, though he had a stiff head enough of his own - he was fairly tipsy. Don't think I blame him for it, 'tis often a good man's case; but true is the word that says, "when liquor's in, sense is out;" and puff, at a breath, before you could say "Lord save us!" out he blasted his wonderful tune.

'Twas really then beyond all belief or telling the dancing Maurice himself could not keep quiet; staggering now on one leg, now on the other, and rolling about like a ship in a cross sea, trying to humour the tune. There was his mother too, moving her old bones as light as the youngest girl of them all; but her dancing, no, nor the dancing of all the rest, is not worthy the speaking about to the work that was going on down on the strand. Every inch of it covered with all manner of fish jumping and plunging about to the music, and every moment more and more would tumble in out of the water, charmed by the wonderful tune. Crabs of monstrous size spun round and round on one claw with the nimbleness of a dancing-master, and twirled and tossed their other claws about like limbs that did not belong to them. It was a sight surprising to behold. But perhaps you may have heard of Father Florence Conry, a Franciscan Friar, and a great Irish poet; bolg an dana, as they used to call him - a wallet of poems. If you have not he was as pleasant a man as one would wish to drink with of a hot summer's day; and he has rhymed out all about the dancing fishes so neatly, that it would be a thousand pities not to give you his verses; so here's my hand at an upset of them into English:

"The big seals in motion,

Like waves of the ocean,

Or gouty feet prancing,

Came heading the gay fish,

Tales From The Land Of Saints & Scholars

Crabs, lobsters, and crayfish,
Determined on dancing.

"The sweet sounds they follow'd,
The gasping cod swallow'd;
'Twas wonderful, really!
And turbot and flounder,
'Mid fish that were rounder,
Just caper'd as gaily.

"John-dory's came tripping;
Dull hake, by their skipping
To frisk it seem'd given;
Bright mackerel went springing,
Like small rainbows winging
Their flight up to heaven.

"The whiting and haddock
Left salt-water paddock,
This dance to be put in:
Where skate with flat faces
Edged out some odd plaices;
But soles kept their footing.

"Sprats and herrings in powers
Of silvery showers
All number outnumbered;
And great ling so lengthy
Were there in such plenty,
The shore was encumbered.

"The scallop and oyster
Their two shells did roister,
Like castanets fitting;
While limpets moved clearly,
And rocks very nearly
With laughter were splitting."

Never was such a hullabaloo in this world, before or since, 'twas as if heaven and earth were coming together; and all out of Maurice Connor's wonderful tune!

In the height of all these doings, what should there be dancing among the outlandish set of fishes but a beautiful young woman - as beautiful as the dawn of day! She had a cocked hat upon her head; from under it her long green hair - just the colour of the sea - fell down behind, without hindrance to her dancing. Her teeth were like rows of pearl; her lips for all the world looked like red coral; and she had an elegant gown, as white as the foam of the wave, with little rows of purple and red seaweeds settled out upon it; for you never yet saw a lady, under the water or over the water, who had not a good notion of dressing herself out.

Up she danced at last to Maurice, who was flinging his feet from under him as fast as hops - for nothing in this world could keep still while that tune of his was going on - and says she to him, chanting it out with a voice as sweet as honey -

"I'm a lady of honour

Who live in the sea;

Come down, Maurice Connor,

And be married to me.

"Silver plates and gold dishes

You shall have, and shall be

The king of the fishes,

When you're married to me."

Drink was strong in Maurice's head, and out he chanted in return for her great civility. It is not every lady, may be, that would be after making such an offer to a blind piper; therefore 'twas only right in him to give her as good as she gave herself - so says Maurice:

"I'm obliged to you, madam:

Off a gold dish or plate,

If a king, and I had them,
I could dine in great state.

"With your own father's daughter
I'd be sure to agree;
But to drink the salt water
Wouldn't do so with me!"

The lady looked at him quite amazed, and swinging her head from side to side like a great scholar, "Well," says she, "Maurice, if you're not a poet, where is poetry to be found?"

In this way they kept on at it, framing high compliments; one answering the other, and their feet going with the music as fast as their tongues. All the fish kept dancing too. Maurice heard the clatter, and was afraid to stop playing lest it might be displeasing to the fish, and not knowing what so many of them may take it into their heads to do to him if they got vexed.

Well, the lady with the green hair kept on coaxing of Maurice with soft speeches, till at last she persuaded him to promise to marry her, and be king over the fishes, great and small. Maurice was well fitted to be their king, if they wanted one that could make them dance; and he surely would drink, barring the salt water, with any fish of them all.

When Maurice's mother saw him, with that unnatural thing in the form of a green-haired lady as his guide, and he and she dancing down together so lovingly to the water's edge through the thick of the fishes, she called out after him to stop and come back. "Oh then," says she, "as if I was not widow enough before, there he is going away from me to be married to that scaly woman. And who knows but 'tis grandmother I may be to a hake or a cod - Lord help and pity me, but 'tis a mighty unnatural thing! - and may be 'tis boiling and eating my own grandchild I'll be, with a bit of salt butter, and I not knowing it! - Oh Maurice, Maurice, if there's any love or nature left in you, come back to your own old mother, who reared you like a decent Christian!"

Then the poor woman began to cry and ullagoane so finely that it would do any one good to hear her.

Maurice was not long getting to the rim of the water; there he kept playing and dancing on as if nothing was the matter, and a great thundering wave coming in towards him ready to swallow him up alive; but as he could not see it, he did not fear it. His mother it was who saw it plainly through the big tears that were rolling down her cheeks; and though she saw it, and her heart was aching as much as ever mother's heart ached for a son, she kept dancing, dancing, all the time for the bare life of her. Certain it was she could not help it, for Maurice never stopped playing that wonderful tune of his.

He only turned the bothered ear to the sound of his mother's voice, fearing it might put him out in his steps, and all the answer he made back was -

"Whisht with you, mother - sure I'm going to be king over the fishes down in the sea, and for a token of luck, and a sign that I am alive and well, I'll send you in, every twelvemonth on this day, a piece of burned wood to Trafraska." Maurice had not the power to say a word more, for the strange lady with the green hair, seeing the wave just upon them, covered him up with herself in a thing like a cloak with a big hood to it, and the wave curling over twice as high as their heads, burst upon the strand, with a rush and a roar that might be heard as far as Cape Clear.

That day twelvemonth the piece of burned wood came ashore in Trafraska. It was a queer thing for Maurice to think of sending all the way from the bottom of the sea. A gown or a pair of shoes would have been something like a present for his poor mother; but he had said it, and he kept his word. The bit of burned wood regularly came ashore on the appointed day for as good, ay, and better than a hundred years. The day is now forgotten, and may be that is the reason why people say how Maurice Connor has stopped sending the luck-token to his mother. Poor woman, she did not live to get as much as one of them; for what through the loss of Maurice, and the fear of eating her own grandchildren, she died in three weeks after the dance - some say it was the fatigue that killed her, but whichever it was, Mrs. Connor was decently buried with her own people.

Seafaring men have often heard off the coast of Kerry, on a still night, the sound of music coming up from the water; and some, who have had good ears, could plainly distinguish Maurice Connor's voice singing these words to his pipes:

"Beautiful shore, with your spreading strand,

Your crystal water, and diamond sand;

Never would I have parted from thee

But for the sake of my fair lady."

Tales From The Land Of Saints & Scholars

The Wooing of Becfola

"The Wooing of Becfola", adapted from James Stephens's Irish Fairy Tales (1910), is a tale that blends courtly romance, myth, and moral fable in Stephens's lyrical, ironic style. Set in the heroic age of Ireland, it follows Becfola, a woman of rare beauty who becomes queen through marriage to the High King Dermot.

Throughout the story, Stephens's prose fuses mythic cadence with modern psychological insight. The fairies and transformations are not mere fantasy but mirrors for human frailty. Becfola's fate, her disappearance into legend, suggests that beauty and longing are twin forces that can't be reconciled within mortal bounds. As with much of Stephens's work, The Wooing of Becfola reimagines older Irish material with humour, empathy, and a subtle critique of the idealised Celtic past.

Chapter I

We do not know where Becfola came from. Nor do we know for certain where she went to. We do not even know her real name, for the name Becfola, "Dowerless" or "Small-dowered," was given to her as a nickname. This only is certain, that she disappeared from the world we know of, and that she went to a realm where even conjecture may not follow her.

It happened in the days when Dermod, son of the famous Ae of Slane, was monarch of all Ireland. He was unmarried, but he had many foster-sons, princes from the Four Provinces, who were sent by their fathers as tokens of loyalty and affection to the Ard-Ri, and his duties as a foster-father were righteously acquitted. Among the young princes of his household there was one, Crimthann, son of Ae, King of Leinster, whom the High King preferred to the others over whom he held fatherly sway. Nor was this wonderful, for the lad loved him also, and was as eager and intelligent and modest as becomes a prince.

The High King and Crimthann would often set out from Tara to hunt and hawk, sometimes unaccompanied even by a servant; and on these excursions the king imparted to his foster-son his own wide knowledge of forest craft, and advised him generally as to the bearing and duties of a prince, the conduct of a court, and the care of a people.

Dermod mac Ae delighted in these solitary adventures, and when he could steal a day from policy and affairs he would send word privily to Crimthann. The boy, having donned his hunting gear, would join the king at a place arranged between them, and then they ranged abroad as chance might direct.

On one of these adventures, as they searched a flooded river to find the ford, they saw a solitary woman in a chariot driving from the west.

"I wonder what that means?" the king exclaimed thoughtfully.

"Why should you wonder at a woman in a chariot?" his companion inquired, for Crimthann loved and would have knowledge.

"Good, my Treasure," Dermod answered, "our minds are astonished when we see a woman able to drive a cow to pasture, for it has always seemed to us that they do not drive well."

Crimthann absorbed instruction like a sponge and digested it as rapidly.

"I think that is justly said," he agreed.

"But" Dermod continued, "when we see a woman driving a chariot of two horses, then we are amazed indeed."

When the machinery of anything is explained to us we grow interested, and Crimthann became, by instruction, as astonished as the king was.

"In good truth," said he, "the woman is driving two horses."

"Had you not observed it before?" his master asked with kindly malice.

"I had observed but not noticed," the young man admitted.

"Further," said the king, "surmise is aroused in us when we discover a woman far from a house; for you will have both observed and noticed that women are home-dwellers, and that a house without a woman or a woman without a house are imperfect objects, and although they be but half observed, they are noticed on the double."

"There is no doubting it," the prince answered from a knitted and thought-tormented brow.

"We shall ask this woman for information about herself," said the king decidedly.

"Let us do so," his ward agreed

"The king's majesty uses the words 'we' and 'us' when referring to the king's majesty," said Dermod, "but princes who do not yet rule territories must use another form of speech when referring to themselves."

"I am very thoughtless," said Crimthann humbly.

The king kissed him on both cheeks.

"Indeed, my dear heart and my son, we are not scolding you, but you must try not to look so terribly thoughtful when you think. It is part of the art of a ruler."

"I shall never master that hard art," lamented his fosterling.

"We must all master it," Dermod replied. "We may think with our minds and with our tongues, but we should never think with our noses and with our eyebrows."

The woman in the chariot had drawn nigh to the ford by which they were standing, and, without pause, she swung her steeds into the shallows and came across the river in a tumult of foam and spray.

"Does she not drive well?" cried Crimthann admiringly.

"When you are older," the king counselled him, "you will admire that which is truly admirable, for although the driving is good the lady is better."

He continued with enthusiasm, "She is in truth a wonder of the world and an endless delight to the eye."

She was all that and more, and, as she took the horses through the river and lifted them up the bank, her flying hair and parted lips and all the young strength and grace of her body went into the king's eye and could not easily come out again.

Nevertheless, it was upon his ward that the lady's gaze rested, and if the king could scarcely look away from her, she could, but only with an equal effort, look away from Crimthann.

"Halt there!" cried the king.

"Who should I halt for?" the lady demanded, halting all the same, as is the manner of women, who rebel against command and yet receive it.

"Halt for Dermod!"

"There are Dermods and Dermods in this world," she quoted.

"There is yet but one Ard-Ri'," the monarch answered.

She then descended from the chariot and made her reverence.

"I wish to know your name?" said he.

But at this demand the lady frowned and answered decidedly, "I do not wish to tell it."

"I wish to know also where you come from and to what place you are going?"

"I do not wish to tell any of these things."

"Not to the king!"

"I do not wish to tell them to anyone."

Crimthann was scandalised.

"Lady," he pleaded, "you will surely not withhold information from the Ard-Ri'?"

But the lady stared as royally on the High King as the High King did on her, and whatever it was he saw in those lovely eyes, the king did not insist.

He drew Crimthann apart, for he withheld no instruction from that lad.

"My heart," he said, "we must always try to act wisely, and we should only insist on receiving answers to questions in which we are personally concerned."

Crimthann imbibed all the justice of that remark.

"Thus I do not really require to know this lady's name, nor do I care from what direction she comes."

"You do not?" Crimthann asked.

"No, but what I do wish to know is, will she marry me?"

"By my hand that is a notable question," his companion stammered.

"It is a question that must be answered," the king cried triumphantly. "But" he continued, "to learn what woman she is, or where she comes from, might bring us torment as well as information. Who knows in what adventures the past has engaged her!"

And he stared for a profound moment on disturbing, sinister horizons, and Crimthann meditated there with him.

"The past is hers," he concluded, "but the future is ours, and we shall only demand that which is pertinent to the future."

He returned to the lady.

"We wish you to be our wife," he said. And he gazed on her benevolently and firmly and carefully when he said that, so that her regard could not stray otherwise. Yet, even as he looked, a tear did well into those lovely eyes, and behind her brow a thought moved of the beautiful boy who was looking at her from the king's side.

But when the High King of Ireland asks us to marry him we do not refuse, for it is not a thing that we shall be asked to do every day in the week, and there is no woman in the world but would love to rule it in Tara.

No second tear crept on the lady's lashes, and, with her hand in the king's hand, they paced together towards the palace, while behind them, in melancholy mood, Crimthann mac Ae led the horses and the chariot.

Chapter II

They were married in a haste which equalled the king's desire; and as he did not again ask her name, and as she did not volunteer to give it, and as she brought no dowry to her husband and received none from him, she was called Becfola, the Dowerless.

Time passed, and the king's happiness was as great as his expectation of it had promised. But on the part of Becfola no similar tidings can be given.

There are those whose happiness lies in ambition and station, and to such a one the fact of being queen to the High King of Ireland is a satisfaction at which desire is sated. But the mind of Becfola was not of this temperate quality, and lacking Crimthann, it seemed to her that she possessed nothing.

For to her mind he was the sunlight in the sun, the brightness in the moonbeam; he was the savour in fruit and the taste in honey; and when she looked from Crimthann to the king she could not but consider that the right man was in the wrong place. She thought that crowned only with his curls Crimthann mac Ae was more nobly diademed than are the masters of the world, and she told him so.

His terror on hearing this unexpected news was so great that he meditated immediate flight from Tara; but when a thing has been uttered once it is easier said the second time and on the third repetition it is patiently listened to.

After no great delay Crimthann mac Ae agreed and arranged that he and Becfola should fly from Tara, and it was part of their understanding that they should live happily ever after.

One morning, when not even a bird was astir, the king felt that his dear companion was rising. He looked with one eye at the light that stole greyly through the window, and recognised that it could not in justice be called light.

"There is not even a bird up," he murmured.

And then to Becfola.

"What is the early rising for, dear heart?"

"An engagement I have," she replied.

"This is not a time for engagements," said the calm monarch.

"Let it be so," she replied, and she dressed rapidly.

"And what is the engagement?" he pursued.

"Raiment that I left at a certain place and must have. Eight silken smocks embroidered with gold, eight precious brooches of beaten gold, three diadems of pure gold."

"At this hour," said the patient king, "the bed is better than the road."

"Let it be so," said she.

"And moreover," he continued, "a Sunday journey brings bad luck."

"Let the luck come that will come," she answered.

"To keep a cat from cream or a woman from her gear is not work for a king," said the monarch severely.

The Ard-Ri' could look on all things with composure, and regard all beings with a tranquil eye; but it should be known that there was one deed entirely hateful to him, and he would punish its commission with the very last rigour - this was, a transgression of the Sunday. During six days of the week all that could happen might happen, so far as Dermod was concerned, but on the seventh day nothing should happen at all if the High King could restrain it. Had it been possible he would have tethered the birds to their own green branches on that day, and forbidden the clouds to pack the upper world with stir and colour. These the king permitted, with a tight lip, perhaps, but all else that came under his hand felt his control.

It was his custom when he arose on the morn of Sunday to climb to the most elevated point of Tara, and gaze there on every side, so that he might see if any fairies or people of the Shi' were disporting themselves in his lordship; for he absolutely prohibited the usage of the earth to these beings on the Sunday, and woe's worth was it for the sweet being he discovered breaking his law.

We do not know what ill he could do to the fairies, but during Dermod's reign the world said its prayers on Sunday and the Shi' folk stayed in their hills.

It may be imagined, therefore, with what wrath he saw his wife's preparations for her journey, but, although a king can do everything, what can a husband do...? He rearranged himself for slumber.

"I am no party to this untimely journey," he said angrily.

"Let it be so," said Becfola.

She left the palace with one maid, and as she crossed the doorway something happened to her, but by what means it happened would be hard to tell; for in the one pace she passed out of the palace and out of the world, and the second step she trod was in Faery, but she did not know this.

Her intention was to go to Cluain da chaillech to meet Crimthann, but when she left the palace she did not remember Crimthann anymore.

To her eye and to the eye of her maid the world was as it always had been, and the landmarks they knew were about them. But the object for which they were travelling was different, although unknown, and the people they passed on the roads were unknown, and were yet people that they knew.

They set out southwards from Tara into the Duffry of Leinster, and after some time they came into wild country and went astray. At last Becfola halted, saying, "I do not know where we are."

The maid replied that she also did not know.

"Yet," said Becfola, "if we continue to walk straight on we shall arrive somewhere."

They went on, and the maid watered the road with her tears.

Night drew on them; a grey chill, a grey silence, and they were enveloped in that chill and silence; and they began to go in expectation and terror, for they both knew and did not know that which they were bound for.

As they toiled desolately up the rustling and whispering side of a low hill the maid chanced to look back, and when she looked back she screamed and pointed, and clung to Becfola's arm. Becfola followed the pointing finger, and saw below a large black mass that moved jerkily forward.

"Wolves!" cried the maid. "Run to the trees yonder," her mistress ordered. "We will climb them and sit among the branches."

They ran then, the maid moaning and lamenting all the while.

"I cannot climb a tree," she sobbed, "I shall be eaten by the wolves."

And that was true.

But her mistress climbed a tree, and drew by a hand's breadth from the rap and snap and slaver of those steel jaws. Then, sitting on a branch, she looked with angry woe at the straining and snarling horde below, seeing many a white fang in those grinning jowls, and the smouldering, red blink of those leaping and prowling eyes.

Chapter III

But after some time the moon arose and the wolves went away, for their leader, a sagacious and crafty chief, declared that as long as they remained where they were, the lady would remain where she was; and so, with a hearty curse on trees, the troop departed. Becfola had pains in her legs from the way she had wrapped them about the branch, but there was no part of her that did not ache, for a lady does not sit with any ease upon a tree.

For some time she did not care to come down from the branch. "Those wolves may return," she said, "for their chief is crafty and sagacious, and it is certain, from the look I caught in his eye as he departed, that he would rather taste of me than eat any woman he has met."

She looked carefully in every direction to see if one might discover them in hiding; she looked closely and lingeringly at the shadows under distant trees to see if those shadows moved; and she listened on every wind to try if she could distinguish a yap or a yawn or a sneeze. But she saw or heard nothing; and little by little tranquillity crept into her mind, and she began to consider that a danger which is past is a danger that may be neglected.

Yet before she descended she looked again on the world of jet and silver that dozed about her, and she spied a red glimmer among distant trees.

"There is no danger where there is light," she said, and she thereupon came from the tree and ran in the direction that she had noted.

In a spot between three great oaks she came upon a man who was roasting a wild boar over a fire. She saluted this youth and sat beside him. But after the first glance and greeting he did not look at her again, nor did he speak.

When the boar was cooked he ate of it and she had her share. Then he arose from the fire and walked away among the trees. Becfola followed, feeling ruefully that something new to her experience had arrived, "for," she thought, "it is usual that young men should not speak to me now that I am the mate of a king, but it is very unusual that young men should not look at me."

But if the young man did not look at her she looked well at him, and what she saw pleased her so much that she had no time for further cogitation. For if Crimthann had been beautiful, this youth was ten times more beautiful. The curls on Crimthann's head had been indeed as a benediction to the queen's eye, so that she had eaten the better and slept the sounder for seeing him. But the sight of this youth left her without the desire to eat, and, as for sleep, she dreaded it, for if she closed an eye she would be robbed of the one delight in time, which was to look at this young man, and not to cease looking at him while her eye could peer or her head could remain upright.

They came to an inlet of the sea all sweet and calm under the round, silver-flooding moon, and the young man, with Becfola treading on his heel, stepped into a boat and rowed to a high-jutting, pleasant island. There they went inland towards a vast palace, in which there was no person but themselves alone, and there the young man went to sleep, while Becfola sat staring at him until the unavoidable peace pressed down her eyelids and she too slumbered.

She was awakened in the morning by a great shout.

"Come out, Flann, come out, my heart!"

The young man leaped from his couch, girded on his harness, and strode out. Three young men met him, each in battle harness, and these four advanced to meet four other men who awaited them at a little distance on the lawn. Then these two sets of four fought together with every warlike courtesy but with every warlike severity, and at the end of that combat there was but one man standing, and the other seven lay tossed in death.

Becfola spoke to the youth.

"Your combat has indeed been gallant" she said.

"Alas," he replied, "if it has been a gallant deed it has not been a good one, for my three brothers are dead and my four nephews are dead."

"Ah me!" cried Becfola, "why did you fight that fight?"

"For the lordship of this island, the Isle of Fedach, son of Dali."

But, although Becfola was moved and horrified by this battle, it was in another direction that her interest lay; therefore she soon asked the question which lay next her heart, "Why would you not speak to me or look at me?"

"Until I have won the kingship of this land from all claimants, I am no match for the mate of the High King of Ireland," he replied.

And that reply was like balm to the heart of Becfola.

"What shall I do?" she inquired radiantly. "Return to your home," he counselled. "I will escort you there with your maid, for she is not really dead, and when I have won my lordship I will go seek you in Tara."

"You will surely come," she insisted.

"By my hand," said he, "I will come."

These three returned then, and at the end of a day and night they saw far off the mighty roofs of Tara massed in the morning haze. The young man left them, and with many a backward look and with dragging, reluctant feet, Becfola crossed the threshold of the palace, wondering what she should say to Dermod and how she could account for an absence of three days' duration.

Chapter IV

IT was so early that not even a bird was yet awake, and the dull grey light that came from the atmosphere enlarged and made indistinct all that one looked at, and swathed all things in a cold and livid gloom.

As she trod cautiously through dim corridors Becfola was glad that, saving the guards, no creature was astir, and that for some time yet she need account to no person for her movements. She was glad also of a respite which would enable her to settle into her home and draw about her the composure which women feel when they are surrounded by the walls of their houses, and can see about them the possessions which, by the fact of ownership, have become almost a part of their personality. Sundered from her belongings, no woman is tranquil, her heart is not truly at ease, however her mind may function, so that under the broad sky or in the house of another she is not the competent, precise individual which she becomes when she sees again her household in order and her domestic requirements at her hand.

Becfola pushed the door of the king's sleeping chamber and entered noiselessly. Then she sat quietly in a seat gazing on the recumbent monarch, and prepared to consider how she should advance to him when he awakened, and with what information she might stay his inquiries or reproaches.

"I will reproach him," she thought. "I will call him a bad husband and astonish him, and he will forget everything but his own alarm and indignation."

But at that moment the king lifted his head from the pillow and looked kindly at her. Her heart gave a great throb, and she prepared to speak at once and in great volume before he could formulate any question. But the king spoke first, and what he said so astonished her that the explanation and reproach with which her tongue was thrilling fled from it at a stroke, and she could only sit staring and bewildered and tongue-tied.

"Well, my dear heart," said the king, "have you decided not to keep that engagement?"

"I...I...!" Becfola stammered.

"It is truly not an hour for engagements," Dermod insisted, "for not a bird of the birds has left his tree; and" he continued maliciously, "the light is such that you could not see an engagement even if you met one."

"I," Becfola gasped. "I...!"

"A Sunday journey," he went on, "is a notorious bad journey. No good can come from it. You can get your smocks and diadems to-morrow. But at this hour a wise person leaves engagements to the bats and the staring owls and the round-eyed creatures that prowl and sniff in the dark. Come back to the warm bed, sweet woman, and set on your journey in the morning."

Such a load of apprehension was lifted from Becfola's heart that she instantly did as she had been commanded, and such a bewilderment had yet possession of her faculties that she could not think or utter a word on any subject.

Yet the thought did come into her head as she stretched in the warm gloom that Crimthann the son of Ae must be now attending her at

Cluain da chaillech, and she thought of that young man as of something wonderful and very ridiculous, and the fact that he was waiting for her troubled her no more than if a sheep had been waiting for her or a roadside bush.

She fell asleep.

Chapter V

In the morning as they sat at breakfast four clerics were announced, and when they entered the king looked on them with stern disapproval.

"What is the meaning of this journey on Sunday?" he demanded.

A lank-jawed, thin-browed brother, with uneasy, intertwining fingers, and a deep-set, venomous eye, was the spokesman of those four.

"Indeed," he said, and the fingers of his right hand strangled and did to death the fingers of his left hand, "indeed, we have transgressed by order."

"Explain that."

"We have been sent to you hurriedly by our master, Molasius of Devenish."

"A pious, a saintly man," the king interrupted, "and one who does not countenance transgressions of the Sunday."

"We were ordered to tell you as follows," said the grim cleric, and he buried the fingers of his right hand in his left fist, so that one could not hope to see them resurrected again. "It was the duty of one of the Brothers of Devenish," he continued, "to turn out the cattle this morning before the dawn of day, and that Brother, while in his duty, saw eight comely young men who fought together."

"On the morning of Sunday," Dermod exploded.

The cleric nodded with savage emphasis.

"On the morning of this self-same and instant sacred day."

"Tell on," said the king wrathfully.

But terror gripped with sudden fingers at Becfola's heart.

"Do not tell horrid stories on the Sunday," she pleaded. "No good can come to any one from such a tale."

"Nay, this must be told, sweet lady," said the king. But the cleric stared at her glumly, forbiddingly, and resumed his story at a gesture.

"Of these eight men, seven were killed."

"They are in hell," the king said gloomily.

"In hell they are," the cleric replied with enthusiasm.

"And the one that was not killed?"

"He is alive," that cleric responded.

"He would be," the monarch assented. "Tell your tale."

"Molasius had those seven miscreants buried, and he took from their unhallowed necks and from their lewd arms and from their unblessed weapons the load of two men in gold and silver treasure."

"Two men's load!" said Dermod thoughtfully.

"That much," said the lean cleric. "No more, no less. And he has sent us to find out what part of that hellish treasure belongs to the Brothers of Devenish and how much is the property of the king."

Becfola again broke in, speaking graciously, regally, hastily, "Let those Brothers have the entire of the treasure, for it is Sunday treasure, and as such it will bring no luck to anyone."

The cleric again looked at her coldly, with a harsh-lidded, small-set, grey-eyed glare, and waited for the king's reply.

Dermod pondered, shaking his head as to an argument on his left side, and then nodding it again as to an argument on his right.

"It shall be done as this sweet queen advises. Let a reliquary be formed with cunning workmanship of that gold and silver, dated with my date and signed with my name, to be in memory of my grandmother who gave birth to a lamb, to a salmon, and then to my father, the Ard-Ri'. And, as to the treasure that remains over, a pastoral staff may be beaten from it in honour of Molasius, the pious man."

"The story is not ended," said that glum, spike-chinned cleric.

The king moved with jovial impatience.

"If you continue it," he said, "it will surely come to an end sometime. A stone on a stone makes a house, dear heart, and a word on a word tells a tale."

The cleric wrapped himself into himself, and became lean and menacing. He whispered, "Besides the young man, named Flann, who was not slain, there was another person present at the scene and the combat and the transgression of Sunday."

"Who was that person?" said the alarmed monarch.

The cleric spiked forward his chin, and then butted forward his brow.

"It was the wife of the king," he shouted. "It was the woman called Becfola. It was that woman," he roared, and he extended a lean, inflexible, unending first finger at the queen.

"Dog!" the king stammered, starting up.

"If that be in truth a woman," the cleric screamed.

"What do you mean?" the king demanded in wrath and terror.

"Either she is a woman of this world to be punished, or she is a woman of the Shi' to be banished, but this holy morning she was in the Shi', and her arms were about the neck of Flann."

The king sank back in his chair stupefied, gazing from one to the other, and then turned an unseeing, fear-dimmed eye towards Becfola.

"Is this true, my pulse?" he murmured.

"It is true," Becfola replied, and she became suddenly to the king's eye a whiteness and a stare. He pointed to the door.

"Go to your engagement," he stammered. "Go to that Flann."

"He is waiting for me," said Becfola with proud shame, "and the thought that he should wait wrings my heart."

She went out from the palace then. She went away from Tara, and in all Ireland and in the world of living men she was not seen again, and she was never heard of again.

Tales From The Land Of Saints & Scholars

Historical Notes

This section contains some brief biographical notes about the original collectors and their books featured in this collection. These notes have been adapted from those primarily on Wikipedia along with other supporting sources and notes.

Joseph Jacobs

Joseph Jacobs was an Australian-born folklorist, literary critic, historian, and social scientist whose work helped shape the modern understanding of English and European folk traditions. Born in Sydney in 1854 to a Jewish family of Prussian descent, Jacobs was educated first in Australia and later in England, where he attended St. John's College, Cambridge. From early on, he showed a keen interest in history, languages, and the stories that bind cultures together.

Though he trained as a scholar of literature and history, Jacobs is best remembered as one of the foremost collectors and editors of English folklore. His work revived and popularised many of the world's best-loved fairy tales, including *Jack and the Beanstalk*, *Goldilocks and the Three Bears*, *The Three Little Pigs*, *Jack the Giant Killer*, and *The History of Tom Thumb*. These tales first appeared in *English Fairy Tales* (1890) and *More English Fairy Tales* (1893), collections that combined careful research with vivid retelling. His editions became definitive for generations of English-speaking readers, shaping how these stories are still told today.

Jacobs's passion for comparative folklore led him beyond England's borders. He compiled and edited collections of Jewish, Celtic, Indian, and European fairy tales, introducing readers to the breadth of the world's oral traditions. His work was distinguished by a desire to preserve the tone, humour, and moral imagination of the original storytellers, rather than smoothing them into Victorian gentility. In this, Jacobs differed from contemporaries like the Brothers Grimm or Andrew Lang, striving instead for authenticity and cultural respect.

Beyond his collections of tales, Jacobs was an active editor and scholar. He produced critical editions of *The Fables of Bidpai* and *The Fables of Aesop*, wrote extensively on the migration and transformation of folklore motifs, and edited several versions of *The Thousand and One Nights*. He was deeply involved with The Folklore Society in England and served as editor of its journal, *Folklore*. His expertise and editorial rigor helped to formalize folklore studies as a serious academic discipline.

Jacobs also made important contributions to Jewish scholarship and cultural history. In 1896, he travelled to the United States to lecture on The Philosophy of Jewish History at Gratz College in Philadelphia and before audiences of the Council of Jewish Women in New York, Philadelphia, and Chicago. Four years later, he moved permanently to America to take up the role of revising editor for the monumental *Jewish Encyclopaedia* (1901–1906), overseeing contributions from more than six hundred writers and scholars. He also worked closely with the Jewish Publication Society and the American Jewish Historical Society, helping to advance Jewish intellectual life in the English-speaking world.

Joseph Jacobs married Georgina Horne, with whom he had two sons and a daughter. He continued writing and editing until his death at his home in Yonkers, New York, on 30 January 1916, aged sixty-two.

During his lifetime, Jacobs was recognized as one of the leading folklorists of his generation, a scholar who bridged cultures and preserved voices from the deep past. His collections remain some of the most beloved in the English language, cherished both for their storytelling charm and their deep respect for the traditions they represent.

Selected Bibliography

- English Fairy Tales (1890)
- Celtic Fairy Tales (1892)
- More English Fairy Tales (1893)
- Indian Fairy Tales (1892)
- The Fables of Aesop (1894)
- Europa's Fairy Book (1916)
- Jewish Fairy Tales and Legends (1919, posthumous)
- The Fables of Bidpai (1895)
- The Thousand and One Nights (editor, various editions)
- The Story of Geographical Discovery: How the World Became Known (1899)
- The Jews of Angevin England: Documents and Records from Latin and Hebrew Sources (1893)
- Studies in Biblical Archaeology (1894)
- An Inquiry into the Sources of the History of the Jews in Spain (1894)

William Butler Yeats

William Butler Yeats (1865–1939) stands among the most influential literary figures of the twentieth century, an Irish poet and dramatist whose imagination reshaped modern verse, yet whose deep engagement with folklore and the occult made him equally a chronicler of Ireland's older, half-vanished spiritual world. His reputation as a Nobel laureate and national poet sometimes obscures another dimension of his work: Yeats as folklorist, collector, and interpreter of the Irish supernatural tradition. Through that lens, Yeats appears not only as an artist but as an intermediary, bridging the oral and the written, the rural and the literary, the past and the modern nation in search of its soul.

William Butler Yeats was born on 13 June 1865 in Sandymount, County Dublin, the eldest child of the painter John Butler Yeats and Susan Pollexfen, whose Sligo lineage would become central to his imaginative geography. The family divided its time between Dublin, London, and the west of Ireland. Sligo, in particular, where Yeats spent many childhood holidays, would become his "country of the heart", a landscape alive with stories of fairies, holy wells, and uncanny visitations.

Educated in Dublin and London, Yeats showed an early interest in myth, mysticism, and art rather than formal study. In 1885, he began publishing poems in the *Dublin University Review*, and two years later co-founded the Dublin Hermetic Society, reflecting a lifelong fascination with the unseen world. His early immersion in Irish folklore was also encouraged by contact with the nationalist revival then stirring in Dublin, the movement that sought to recover Ireland's language, legends, and cultural independence from British influence.

Yeats's first major publication, *Fairy and Folk Tales of the Irish Peasantry* (1888), established him as both folklorist and literary figure. The volume, published by Walter Scott in London, was an anthology of tales drawn from earlier collections by Thomas Crofton Croker, Patrick Kennedy, Lady Wilde (his future mother-in-law), and others, interwoven with stories Yeats himself gathered through conversation in Sligo and Galway.

In his preface, Yeats declared that the Irish "still believe in fairies with a vividness of belief unknown in other lands," positioning folklore not as quaint superstition but as a living expression of the national imagination. He edited, condensed, and reframed the material with a poet's ear, shaping a prose style that retained the rhythms of oral speech while aspiring to literary grace. His second collection, *Irish Fairy Tales* (1892), and its expanded successor, *The Celtic Twilight* (1893), deepened that project.

The Celtic Twilight was subtitled Faerie and Folklore, but it was also a spiritual autobiography. Yeats recorded encounters with "old men and women who still see the fairies" and infused them with his own symbolism. The work stands midway between ethnography and visionary prose, a hybrid that would influence later folklorists and writers alike. He wrote of folklore as revelation: "I have desired, like every artist, to create a little world out of the beautiful, pleasant, and significant things of this marred and clumsy world."

In the 1890s, Yeats became a leading figure in the Irish Literary Revival, alongside Lady Gregory, J.M. Synge, and Douglas Hyde. His folklore work during this period turned toward dramatization. With Lady Gregory, he founded the Irish Literary Theatre (later the Abbey Theatre), envisioning a stage rooted in Ireland's mythic consciousness rather than imitating English realism. Plays such as *The Countess Cathleen* (1892), *The Land of Heart's Desire* (1894), and *Cathleen ni Houlihan* (1902) reimagined folk motifs, the fatal beauty of the fairy world, the sacrificial female spirit of Ireland, and the perilous border between mortal and supernatural realms.

Yeats also drew upon the mythic cycles of early Irish literature, particularly the Ulster and Fenian cycles. He found in Cuchulain and Finn not remote heroes but archetypes for a modern Ireland seeking renewal through mythic self-understanding. His editorial work with Lady Gregory on *Gods and Fighting Men* (1904) and *Cuchulain of Muirthemne* (1902) brought these legends to wider audiences, often filtered through Lady Gregory's prose but shaped by Yeats's vision.

Yeats's folklore interests cannot be separated from his involvement with mysticism. He joined the Hermetic Order of the Golden Dawn in 1890, delving into ritual magic, symbolism, and the idea that myth was a coded form of spiritual truth. For Yeats, folklore was not merely sociological material but a fragment of the same esoteric wisdom that underpinned all religions and philosophies. His poetry of this period, *The Wind Among the Reeds* (1899), *In the Seven Woods* (1903), translates folk and occult imagery into visionary lyricism.

His study of folk belief also informed his theories of artistic creation. In essays such as *Magic* (1901), Yeats argued that "the borders of our minds are ever shifting," and that imagination could summon real presences. Folklore, to him, was evidence of that porous boundary—the collective dream of a people materialising as myth.

After Ireland's independence, Yeats's focus turned increasingly to politics and metaphysics, but folklore remained a deep current beneath his later work. His poetry of maturity, *The Tower* (1928), *The Winding Stair* (1933), revisits fairy lore, ancestral memory, and the supernatural landscape of Sligo, now transfigured by age and scepticism. "The fairies have gone from the countryside," he wrote, "but the poets still follow their shadows."

As a senator in the Irish Free State (1922–1928), Yeats argued that myth and tradition were essential to national identity. His folkloric scholarship, though less active, found renewed life in essays such as *The Philosophy of Shelley's Poetry* and *A Vision* (1925, revised 1937), where he transformed the structures of myth into a private cosmology.

Yeats died in January 1939 at Roquebrune-Cap-Martin, France, and was reburied in Drumcliff, County Sligo, in 1948, beneath Ben Bulben, the mountain he had mythologised in verse. His epitaph, taken from his poem *Under Ben Bulben*, reads:

Cast a cold eye,

On life, on death.

Horseman, pass by!

Yeats's folklore work stands at the intersection of art, anthropology, and nationalism. Unlike later field folklorists such as Seán Ó Súilleabháin or Marie-Louise Sjoestedt, he did not pursue strict documentation. Instead, he sought to translate oral belief into literary myth. His approach combined the precision of a collector with the intuition of a visionary: he recorded stories, shaped them into art, and treated them as evidence of an imaginative continuity between Ireland's rural life and its ancient myths.

Modern scholars often debate whether Yeats's romantic vision distorted the folk tradition. Yet his collections preserved material that might otherwise have been lost, and his influence helped inspire later systematic folkloric research in Ireland. More importantly, he redefined folklore as a living art, one that could serve both poetry and nation.

Select Bibliography

Primary Works by Yeats (Folklore and Related Writing):

- Fairy and Folk Tales of the Irish Peasantry (London: Walter Scott, 1888)
- Irish Fairy Tales (London: T. Fisher Unwin, 1892)
- The Celtic Twilight: Faerie and Folklore (London: A. H. Bullen, 1893; rev. ed. 1902)
- The Secret Rose (London: Lawrence & Bullen, 1897)
- Ideas of Good and Evil (London: A. H. Bullen, 1903) — includes essay "Magic"
- The Wanderings of Oisin and Other Poems (London: Kegan Paul, 1889)
- A Vision (London: T. Werner Laurie, 1925; rev. 1937)

Collaborative and Related Works:

- Lady Gregory, Cuchulain of Muirthemne (1902), edited and introduced by Yeats
- Lady Gregory, Gods and Fighting Men (1904), introduced by Yeats
- Yeats & Lady Gregory, The Unicorn from the Stars and Other Plays (1908)

Alfred Perceval Graves

Alfred Perceval Graves (1846–1931) was born in Dublin on 22 July 1846, the second son of Charles Graves, later Church of Ireland bishop of Limerick, and Selina Cheyne. His upbringing moved between an academic household in Ireland and schooling in England. University followed at Trinity College Dublin, where he began publishing in student and literary magazines. In 1869 he entered the British civil service as a Home Office clerk, transferring in 1874 to the inspectorate of schools, a practical career he would keep while building, in parallel, a life in letters.

Graves' first book, *Songs of Killarney* (1873), set the tone for much that followed. He possessed a poet's ear trained on Irish melody and narrative, and a wish to place traditional idiom in contemporary circulation. Its success opened the door to regular magazine work and drew him into the widening circle of the Irish literary revival in London. In 1891 he helped found the Irish Literary Society (ILS), serving eight years as honorary secretary and later as president. Through the ILS, alongside figures such as W. B. Yeats, Douglas Hyde, and others, he worked to normalise Irish subject-matter on London platforms and to connect literature with song.

Graves' strongest contribution as a folklorist lay in song collection and mediation rather than in philological fieldwork. He collaborated with classically trained composers to restore and republish traditional airs with newly fashioned or adapted words, and to bring those songs into drawing rooms, concert halls and schools. His partnership with Charles Villiers Stanford produced *Songs of Old Ireland* (Boosey, 1882), a fifty-song landmark that worked from Petrie-manuscript sources and offered performable, pianistic settings. Stanford's editorial authority on the airs and Graves' texts brought credibility with musicians and accessibility with general audiences.

He continued this work in *Irish Songs and Ballads* (Novello, 1893) and *Songs of Erin, Op. 76* (Boosey, 1901), again with Stanford, and in *Irish Folk-Songs* (Boosey, 1897), whose airs were arranged by the younger composer Charles Wood. These volumes, designed for domestic music-making, were part anthology, part revival. They stabilised melodies, supplied singable English-language texts, and, crucially, named sources. In doing so they helped to move Irish traditional repertoire from fragile oral exchange into durable print and performance culture.

The publishing programme mapped onto Graves' organisational work. He played a visible role in the early Folk-Song movement in Britain and Ireland, and was associated with the creation of the Irish Folk Song Society (1904), whose journal published airs and ballads with attention to "the old traditional scales". Graves' name appears among the energies that brought that society into being, and its first phase, steered with Charlotte Milligan Fox, exemplifies the hybrid method he favoured, with musicians and writers working together to document and disseminate tradition.

As a writer of words to traditional tunes, he could be deft and popular. *Father O'Flynn*, set to the jig *Top of Cork Road* and long since welded to the tune's identity, became an anthem of clerical cheerfulness and a calling card for its author. The song's "original" is often linked to the Kerry parish priest Michael Walsh, a collector himself, and in microcosm, this hints at Graves' world, in which tradition bearers, editors and performers overlap.

Graves' editorial interests were not confined to song. With *The Irish Fairy Book* (T. F. Unwin, 1909), he turned to prose tradition, assembling and introducing a representative set of tales and legends for a general readership, and commissioning illustrations by George Denham. It is an "edited" book in the nineteenth-century sense, curatorial, introductory, and aimed at cultural education as much as entertainment.

Graves was a bridge figure. He did not claim ethnographic neutrality, making singable paraphrases, writing new lyrics to old airs, and arguing, explicitly in prefaces and implicitly by practice, that popularisation was itself a form of preservation. His volumes carry attributions, sketch histories of tunes, and mark the chain of transmission, Petrie manuscripts here, collectors such as P. W. Joyce there, while reaching beyond specialist circles to choirs, parlours and music-schools. The approach drew collaborators (Stanford, Wood), institutional footing (ILS; Folk-Song Society networks), and readers who might otherwise never have met the old songs.

He kept his public work largely non-partisan. Obituaries noticed that he "kept clear of politics" while stirring fresh interest in the folk-songs of Ireland, Wales and the Highlands within the revival's often sharp cultural debates, a that stance helped him function as a convenor. Late in life he settled at Harlech in north Wales, learned Welsh well enough to be welcomed as a bard at the National Eisteddfod (Bangor, 1902), and maintained his cross-Celtic sympathies to the end.

Graves married twice, first to Jane Cooper (d. 1886), with whom he had five children, and then to Amalie von Ranke, with whom he had five more, among them the poet Robert Graves. In old age he set his memory in order in *To Return to All That* (1930), a quietly pointed title in dialogue with his son's memoir. The book records a long career spent shuttling between administration and art, and offers first-hand testimony of the literary and musical circles in which his song-collecting matured. He died at Harlech on 27 December 1931.

Selected bibliography

- Songs of Killarney. London: Bradbury, Agnew, 1873.
- Irish Songs and Ballads. Manchester: A. Ireland & Co., 1880; expanded ed. London: Novello, Ewer, 1893 (music arranged by C. V. Stanford).
- Songs of Old Ireland: A Collection of Fifty Irish Melodies. Words by A. P. Graves; music arranged by C. V. Stanford. London: Boosey, 1882.
- The Irish Song Book: With Original Irish Airs. Edited by A. P. Graves. London: T. Fisher Unwin, 1894 (and later eds.).
- Irish Folk-Songs. Words by A. P. Graves; airs arranged by Charles Wood. London: Boosey, 1897.
- Songs of Erin, Op. 76: A Collection of Fifty Irish Folk Songs. Words by A. P. Graves; music arranged by C. V. Stanford. London: Boosey, 1901.
- The Irish Fairy Book. Edited by A. P. Graves; illus. George Denham. London: T. F. Unwin, 1909.
- Irish Literary and Musical Studies. London: Elkin Mathews, 1913; New York: Scribner's, 1914.
- To Return to All That: An Autobiography. London: Jonathan Cape; Dublin: Talbot Press, 1930.

Tales From The Land Of Saints & Scholars

Seumas McManus

Seumas MacManus (1868–1960) was born James McManus on 31 December 1868 in Mountcharles (Irish: Ros Mhic Thriúin), a village in the parish of Inver near Lough Erne, County Donegal, Ireland. His father, Patrick MacManus, was a merchant and small farmer, and his mother Mary Molloy provided the local roots and oral traditions of the region. From his early years Seumas was steeped in the folklore of the north-western Irish Gaeltacht: stories told by the fireside, by the craggy shore counties, among fishermen and farmers, children and elders alike.

Educated locally, MacManus worked first as a teacher in Donegal, but it was the power of story-telling that steadily drew him away from the classroom and into full-time authorship. He married Ethna Carbery (born Anna Johnston, a poet and nationalist figure from County Antrim) in 1901 and the couple lived at Revlin House near Donegal town for a period, deeply engaged in the Irish cultural revival.

MacManus's contribution to Irish folklore lies less in archival field-work than in the art of retelling folk-tales in a literary form accessible to international audiences while still preserving a sense of the vernacular voice. Collating and adapting stories from the oral tradition of Donegal and surrounding districts, he published dozens of volumes spanning fairy-tales, folk-tales, ballads, local humour and Irish history.

Among his early works, *Through the Turf Smoke: The Love, Lore, and Laughter of Old Ireland* (1899) and *Donegal Fairy Stories* (1900) showcased his narrative style: clean, conversational, rooted in memory and place. He frequently toured the United States, lecturing on Irish folklore and connecting Irish diaspora audiences with the storytelling traditions of "the old country". His recorded visits at the University of Notre Dame illustrate that he was welcomed as both entertainer and cultural narrator, urging listeners to understand the tales as living, many-voiced forms, not simply as relics.

While MacManus did not conduct systematic folklore surveys in the modern academic sense, he performed an important bridging role between the oral tradition and printed literature. He emphasised the role of the seanchaí (traditional story-teller) and insisted that stories were meant to be told aloud rather than merely read.

He wrote: "These tales were made … for the passing of long nights, for the shortening of weary journeys … Be not content with reading them …"

He credited his informants, local storytellers in Donegal, with joyful regard and sought to retain the regional colour and dialect-inflection of their speech. This gives his published tales a sense of authenticity and vitality. You feel the peat-smoke, the hearth-light, the salt-wind of the coasts. At the same time, MacManus did adapt for his audience. He smoothed some of the dialect, reorganised episodes, added dramatic structure, and inserted narrative links to engage the reader rather than a purely oral audience.

MacManus's work also sits in the context of the Irish Literary Revival. He numbered among those who valued folklore as a repository of national memory (though he did not adopt the more myth-saturated style of Yeats or Gregory). Rather, his emphasis remained on community, humour, work, struggle, the everyday heroic and the subtle world of folk belief.

In addition to his folklore collections, MacManus turned his hand to popular history. His *The Story of the Irish Race: A Popular History of Ireland* (first published 1921) remains perhaps his most ambitious single volume, being a sweeping narrative from earliest legends to modern times, aimed at a lay audience. The intersection of folklore, history and cultural narrative was central to his worldview: that the stories of the common people (their jokes, beliefs, traditions) were a vital strand of the national story.

MacManus continued publishing well into the mid-20th century. He died in New York City on 23 October 1960. He left a legacy not only of dozens of printed volumes but of an international audience for Irish story-telling, and a model of how folk-tales might be preserved in readable form without losing their spark. Scholars of folklore may note that his methodology lacks the rigorous field-notes and indexing of later collectors, but his strength lies in style, transmission and bridging the vernacular and literate worlds. As one contemporary remarked, "the world lost something it may never recover when it lost the art of story-telling."

Selected Bibliography

- MacManus, Seumas. Through the Turf Smoke: The Love, Lore, and Laughter of Old Ireland. New York: Doubleday & McClure, 1899.
- MacManus, Seumas. In Chimney Corners: Merry Tales of Irish Folk-Lore. Dublin: M. H. Gill & Son, 1899.
- MacManus, Seumas. Donegal Fairy Stories. New York: McClure, Phillips & Co., 1900.
- MacManus, Seumas. The Story of the Irish Race: A Popular History of Ireland. New York: Macmillan, 1921; revised 4th ed. 1944.

- MacManus, Seumas. The Well o' the World's End. Dublin: [publisher], 1939.
- MacManus, Seumas. Hibernian Nights: Twenty-Two Tales of Irish Mystery and Magic. New York: [publisher], 1963.
- MacManus, Seumas. The Bold Heroes of Hungry Hill, and Other Irish Folk Tales. Dublin: [publisher], 1951.

Thomas William Hazen Rolleston

Thomas William Hazen Rolleston (1857–1920) was born on 1 May 1857 at Glasshouse, Shinrone, County Offaly, the son of a county court judge. He was educated at St Columba's College and at Trinity College Dublin, an upbringing that placed him at the focal point between Anglo-Irish institutions and a deepening curiosity about Irish tradition. His early adult years included a spell in the German states, which sharpened his interest in European letters and in translation. Returning to Dublin, he helped to found the *Dublin University Review* in 1885, a short-lived but influential platform for the emerging Irish Literary Revival. It printed some of W. B. Yeats's earliest poems and gathered kindred spirits around questions of language, heritage and culture.

In the late 1880s Rolleston became a visible organiser within the Revival's networks. He edited *Poems and Ballads of Young Ireland* (1888), an anthology that brought together Yeats, Douglas Hyde and others and that later commentators treated as an early marker of the movement's collective voice. He also took a hand in the practical work of cultural economy as the first managing director of the Irish Industries' Society, which aimed to sustain traditional crafts. By the 1890s he had moved to London, joined the Rhymers' Club, and became a founder-member of the Irish Literary Society, moving easily between salons and study, journalism and advocacy.

Rolleston's most enduring contribution lies in his work as a folklorist and mythographer. Two books in particular set his name before general readers and students alike. *The High Deeds of Finn, and Other Bardic Romances of Ancient Ireland* (1910), richly illustrated by Stephen Reid, retold Fenian and other heroic materials in clear, rhythmic prose, attentive to the narrative pulse rather than the academic footnote. It is an artefact of the Revival's double ambition: to make ancient tradition readable to a modern audience and to present it as a literature in its own right.

The following year he published *Myths and Legends of the Celtic Race* (1911), the book by which he is most widely remembered. It ranges across Irish and Welsh cycles, the religion of the Celts, invasion myths, heroic biography and wonder-tale, interweaving synopsis, commentary and cultural history. Written for the intelligent general reader, it treats "Celtic" as a literary-historical category rather than an ethnic chemistry, and it provides a framework that shaped anglophone understanding of Celtic material for much of the twentieth century. Although later scholarship has refined or corrected parts of his synthesis, the reach and balance of the volume keep it in circulation as a classic of interpretation and retelling.

Rolleston's editorial work complemented his folkloric books. With Stopford A. Brooke he co-edited *A Treasury of Irish Poetry in the English Tongue* (1900), an anthology that placed Irish verse within an accessible canon for British and American readers and offered biographical and critical notes that bridged scholarship and taste. The anthology appeared in several impressions on both sides of the Atlantic, and it helped anchor the Revival's poets within a long view of Irish writing in English.

Beyond folklore and poetry, Rolleston was a nimble man of letters. He wrote a brisk *Life of Gotthold Ephraim Lessing* (1889), translated and commented on German literature, and attempted larger syntheses such as *Parallel Paths: A Study in Biology, Ethics and Art* (1908), a curious, ambitious book that sought common structures across natural science, moral thought and aesthetics. These works show the same instinct visible in his mythography: to find pattern, analogy and continuity rather than to isolate disciplines.

As a cultural organiser, Rolleston often stood in the productive tension between Yeats's mythic theatre, Hyde's language movement and the practicalities of publication. He could be a conciliator and, at times, a critic. Yeats later called him an "intimate enemy", a phrase that speaks less of personal hostility than of the closeness of their intellectual sparring within a small, intense milieu. Rolleston's administrative work for the Irish Industries' Society and his links to the Gaelic League underline a persistent theme: the folklore of a people has to be housed in viable institutions if it is to outlast fashion.

During the First World War he served in London as a librarian within the Ministry of Information's censorship department, his knowledge of Irish and of minor languages being pressed into bureaucratic service. He had settled in Hampstead by 1908 and died there on 5 December 1920. In biographical outline he looks like a typical late-Victorian man of letters, for in his chosen labours he helped to conserve, interpret and popularise the heroic and wonder-tale traditions of Ireland for a modern literary public.

Rolleston approached Irish tradition as a storyteller with a historian's conscience. In *High Deeds of Finn* he worked from manuscript sources and nineteenth-century editions but thinned the apparatus in favour of pace and clarity. The book's introduction and headnotes mark sources and cycles without swamping the reader, a balance that helped the volume travel beyond Ireland. In *Myths and Legends of the Celtic Race* he widened the lens to a pan-Celtic view. There he attempted a topology of story: mythic origins, divine dramatis personae, heroic sagas, and the after-life of tales in literature. He aimed for comparative breadth rather than philological depth, and in doing so he created a map that later readers could refine. The books' endurance is due not only to subject matter but to tone: an educated, companionable voice that neither patronises the oral source nor pretends to a neutrality he did not claim.

Rolleston was also a connector. The anthologies he edited and the review he founded stitched folklore to poetry, and poetry to public life. In that sense he sits alongside Standish O'Grady, Lady Gregory and others as a mediator between archive and audience. If Yeats gave the Revival its theatre and dream, Rolleston helped to give it a bookshelf that ordinary readers could carry home.

Selected bibliography

Folklore, myth, anthology

- The High Deeds of Finn, and Other Bardic Romances of Ancient Ireland (London: George G. Harrap, 1910). Illus. Stephen Reid.
- Myths and Legends of the Celtic Race (London: George G. Harrap, 1911).
- Stopford A. Brooke and T. W. Rolleston, eds., A Treasury of Irish Poetry in the English Tongue (London: Smith, Elder, 1900; New York: Macmillan, later printings).
- Poems and Ballads of Young Ireland (Dublin: M. H. Gill, 1888) [editor and contributor].

Other major works

- Life of Gotthold Ephraim Lessing (London: Walter Scott, 1889).
- Parallel Paths: A Study in Biology, Ethics and Art (London: Duckworth, 1908).

James Stephens

James Stephens (1880–1950) occupies a singular place in early twentieth-century Irish letters. He was a writer whose work bridged the mythic and the modern, the dreamlike humour of folklore and the intellectual ferment of literary Dublin. He was, at once, poet, novelist, folklorist, and nationalist, a man whose slight physical stature belied the scope of his imagination. Though his life was touched by poverty, displacement, and contradiction, Stephens's literary voice became one of the most distinctive of the Irish Revival, uniting the lyric tradition of Celtic mythology with a sharp, modern consciousness.

Stephens's origins were humble and, like much else in his life, partly veiled in myth. He himself claimed to have been born on 2 February 1882, the same day and year as James Joyce, perhaps out of whimsy or a sense of poetic kinship. Official records, however, indicate that he was born at the Rotunda Hospital, Dublin, on 9 February 1880, the son of Francis Stephens, a van-man and messenger for a stationer, and Charlotte Collins.

His father died when James was only two years old. His mother remarried when he was six, and the young boy, wandering the streets of Dublin and caught begging, was sent to the Meath Protestant Industrial School for Boys in Blackrock. There he spent the rest of his childhood, an experience that left him with both resilience and a lifelong sympathy for the marginalised.

Stephens was later adopted by a family with whom he grew up alongside two brothers, Tom and Dick. He attended school with them and became known for his small stature, barely 4 feet 10 inches in height, but also for his surprising athleticism and fierce determination. Known affectionately as "Tiny Tim," he excelled in running competitions and was fascinated by the tales of military courage told within his adoptive household. His dream of becoming a soldier was thwarted by his height, but the romanticism of heroism and struggle would later echo through his literary retellings of Irish myth.

By the turn of the century, Stephens had begun working as a solicitor's clerk while immersing himself in the growing ferment of Irish cultural nationalism. He took up the Irish language, learned to speak and write it fluently, and embraced socialism and republicanism. His friendship with Thomas MacDonagh, poet, revolutionary, and one of the leaders executed after the Easter Rising of 1916, was especially influential. Through MacDonagh, Stephens entered the literary circles of Dublin and began contributing to The Irish Review, the progressive periodical associated with Patrick Pearse's bilingual school, St Enda's.

It was during this period that Stephens came under the mentorship of the poet, mystic, and editor George William Russell, known as "Æ". Under Æ's encouragement, Stephens published his first collection of poetry, *Insurrections* (1909). The title was prophetic as it captured not only the rising mood of Irish nationalism but also Stephens's belief in the revolutionary potential of imagination itself.

In 1915, Stephens was appointed registrar of the National Gallery of Ireland, a position he held until 1925. It provided him financial stability during a decade of intense literary productivity.

Stephens's true creative identity took shape in his reimagining of Irish myth and folklore. His prose retellings possess a musicality and wit that set them apart from both the earnest romanticism of earlier Celtic Revivalists and the arch scholarship of later folklorists. His Ireland is not a museum of the ancient past, but a living, breathing landscape where gods, heroes, and peasants share the same rhythms of speech and irony.

Irish Fairy Tales (1920) and *Deirdre* (1923) exemplify this gift. Drawing from the mythological cycles preserved in early Irish literature, the *Tuatha Dé Danann*, the *Red Branch* heroes, and the Ulster sagas, Stephens refashioned these materials into fluid, lyrical narratives, rich in humour and compassion. He often emphasised the humanity of his mythical figures. Deirdre becomes less a tragic symbol and more a living woman, while the gods of the Tuatha Dé are dreamers and schemers with recognisably mortal temperaments.

Stephens's folkloric writing was not simple transcription. It was transformation. His voice combined the cadences of oral storytelling with the psychological insight of modernism. Through a light but deliberate irony, he allowed ancient myth to mirror the political and spiritual uncertainties of modern Ireland. As such, he stands as a bridge between the oral tradition of the seanchaí and the literary modernism of Yeats and Joyce.

Stephens's novels further developed this unique synthesis of folklore, satire, and philosophy. *The Crock of Gold* (1912), his best-known work, blends mythic characters, fairies, gods, and philosophers, with the earthy humour of rural Ireland. The story's playful treatment of metaphysics and sensuality makes it one of the most enduringly original books of the Irish Revival. It has remained in print for over a century and is often cited as a companion piece to Yeats's own mythic vision.

In *The Demi-Gods* (1914) and *Etched in Moonlight* (1928), Stephens continued to blend mythic imagination with social commentary. These novels depict wandering figures who move through a landscape both mystical and absurd, revealing the tensions between spiritual idealism and worldly confusion. His prose style, lyrical, ironic, at times rhapsodic, owes much to oral tradition, yet his structural experimentation marks him as a literary modernist.

Stephens's later life was marked by travel and literary friendships. Dividing his time between Dublin, London, and Paris, he became part of the expatriate Irish literary network of the interwar years. During the 1930s he formed a friendship with James Joyce, who admired *The Crock of Gold* and believed they shared the same birthday. Joyce, fearing he might not live to finish *Finnegans Wake*, even proposed that Stephens complete the book, signing it "JJ & S", a punning nod to "Jameson & Sons." The plan was never realised, as Joyce eventually finished the work himself, but the exchange reveals the mutual regard between two very different masters of Irish modernism.

During his final decade, Stephens found new audiences through regular broadcasts on the BBC, where his gift for oral storytelling came alive once again. His distinctive voice, half-poet, half-seanchaí, made him a natural broadcaster, and his readings introduced many listeners in Britain and Ireland to the rhythms of Irish folklore and myth.

Stephens died in 1950, leaving behind a body of work that remains singular in its mixture of lyric beauty, laughter, and mythic depth.

Selected Bibliography

Poetry

- Insurrections (1909)
- The Adventures of Seumas Beg: The Rocky Road to Dublin (1915)

- Reincarnations (1918)
- Collected Poems (1926)
- Kings and the Moon (1938)

Novels and Prose Works

- The Charwoman's Daughter (1912)
- The Crock of Gold (1912)
- Here Are Ladies (1913)
- The Demi-Gods (1914)
- The Adventures of Seumas Beg (1915)
- The Insurrection in Dublin (1916) – a vivid eyewitness account of the Easter Rising
- Irish Fairy Tales (1920)
- Deirdre (1923)
- Etched in Moonlight (1928)
- In the Land of Youth (1924) – retellings from Irish mythology
- Collected Poems (1926)

Broadcasts and Later Work

- BBC radio readings, 1930s–1940s (various series and adaptations)

Tales From The Land Of Saints & Scholars

About the Editor

Clive Gilson was born in 1962 into a household steeped in sport and rhythm. His father was a senior amateur and lower-league professional footballer, while his mother, equally formidable, was an award-winning ballroom dancer. Their spirited household didn't just hum with ambition, it danced to it.

After earning a degree in History from Leeds University, Clive took an unexpected turn into the then-nascent world of information technology in the late 1980s. Yet, the call of story and stage never left him. Alongside a thriving tech career, he freelanced as a journalist and book reviewer, earning one small by-line in the national press, and also spent over a decade performing in village halls and professional theatres across the south of England.

A true inheritor of his family's sporting zeal, Clive later pivoted into live sports broadcasting. In the 1990s, he became a trusted rugby 'stato' for the BBC, ITV, EuroSport, and TVNZ, bringing insight and analysis to major tournaments including the Heineken Cup, Six Nations, World Sevens, and Rugby World Cups.

As a writer, Clive has made his mark across genres. His debut novel, *Songs of Bliss*, was published in 2017, followed by *A Solitude of Stars* in 2019. Since then, he has released three acclaimed short story collections, *The Mechanic's Curse*, *The Insomniac Booth*, and, in 2025, *Melodies in Black Ink*.

He is also an award-winning poet and the author of a biography detailing the life of a former professional footballer, namely his father. Since 2018, Clive has served as Managing Editor of the Firesides Tales Project, a global storytelling initiative that has published over 30 collections of folktales, fairy tales, myths, and legends from around the world.

Today, Clive continues to write fiction rich in folklore, memory, and quiet transformation, combining his deep love of narrative with a lifelong fascination with the human spirit.

For more about his work, visit clivegilson.com, where stories are always waiting to be found.

Tales From The Land Of Saints & Scholars

ORIGINAL FICTION BY CLIVE GILSON

- *Songs of Bliss*
- *Out of the Walled Garden*
- *The Mechanic's Curse*
- *The Insomniac Booth*
- *A Solitude of Stars (Cry Havoc, part 1)*
- *A Symphony Of Sorrows (Cry Havoc, part 2)*
- *Melodies In Black Ink*
- *Acts Of Faith*

AS EDITOR – *FIRESIDE TALES – Western Europe*

- *Tales From the Land of Dragons* – Welsh Folk & Fairy Tales
- *Tales From the Land of The Brave* – Scottish Folk & Fairy Tales
- *Tales From the Land of Saints And Scholars* – Irish Folk & Fairy Tales
- *Tales From the Land of Hope And Glory* – English Folk & Fairy Tales
- *Tales from Gallia* – French Folk & Fairy Tales

AS EDITOR – *FIRESIDE TALES – Northern Europe*

- *Tales From Lands of Snow and Ice* – Scandinavian Folk & Fairy Tales
- *Tales From the Viking Isles* – Icelandic Folk & Fairy Tales
- *Tales From the Forest Lands* – Finnish Folk & Fairy Tales
- *Tales From the Old Norse* – Scandinavian Folk & Fairy Tales
- *Tales from Germania* – German Folk & Fairy Tales

AS EDITOR – *FIRESIDE TALES – Southern Europe*

- *Tales From the Land of Rabbits* – Spanish & Portuguese Folk & Fairy Tales
- *Tales Told by Bulls and Wolves* – Italian Folk & Fairy Tales
- *Tales of Fire and Bronze* – Greek Folk & Fairy Tales

AS EDITOR – *FIRESIDE TALES – Eastern Europe*

- *Tales From The Samodivi* – Balkan Folk & Fairy Tales
- *Tales From the Land of the Strigoi* – Romanian Folk & Fairy Tales

Tales From The Land Of Saints & Scholars

- *Tales Told by the Wind Mother* – Hungarian Folk & Fairy Tales

AS EDITOR – *FIRESIDE TALES* – North America

- *Okaraxta* - Tales from The Great Plains
- *Tibik-Kîzis* – Tales from The Great Lakes & Canada
- *Jóhonaa'éí* – Tales from America's Southwest
- *Qugaaĝix̂* - First Nation Tales from Alaska & The Arctic
- *Karahkwa* - First Nation Tales from America's Eastern States
- *Pot-Likker* - Folklore, Fairy Tales, and Settler Stories from America

AS EDITOR – *FIRESIDE TALES* – Africa

- *Arokin Tales* – Folklore & Fairy Tales from West Africa
- *Hadithi Tales* – Folklore & Fairy Tales from East Africa
- *Inkathaso Tales* – Folklore & Fairy Tales from Southern Africa
- *Tarubadur Tales* – Folklore & Fairy Tales from North Africa
- *Elephant And Frog* – Folklore from Central Africa

AS EDITOR – *FIRESIDE TALES* – Middle East

- *Tales From The Meddahs* – Turkish Folk & Fairy Tales
- *Tales From The Hakawati* – Arabic Folk & Fairy Tales
- *Tales Told By Balebos & Gusan* – Jewish & Armenian Folk & Fairy Tales

AS EDITOR – *FIRESIDE TALES* – Asia & The Far East

- *Tales Told By The Kathaakaar* – Folk & Fairy Tales from India
- *Tales Of The Gùshì Yuan* – Chinese Folk & Fairy Tales

AS EDITOR – *FIRESIDE TALES* – Animal Tales

- *Dog Tails* – Folk & Fairy Tales featuring our canine chums
- *Cat Tails* – Folk & Fairy Tales featuring our feline friends
- *Horse Tails* – Folk & Fairy Tales featuring our equine friends
- *Pig Tails* – Folk & Fairy Tales featuring our porcine friends

Tales From The Land Of Saints & Scholars

AS EDITOR – *FIRESIDE TALES* – *South & Central America*

- *Tales From The Caribbean* – Folk & Fairy Tales from Caribbean islands
- *Tales From Central America* – Central American Folk & Fairy Tales
- *Tales Told From South America* – South American Folk & Fairy Tales

Tales From The Land Of Saints & Scholars

Reviews

I have edited Clive Gilson's books for over a decade now – he's prolific and can turn his hand to many genres. poetry, short fiction, contemporary novels, folklore, and science fiction – and the common theme is that none of them ever fails to take my breath away. There's something in each story that is either memorably poignant, hauntingly unnerving, or sidesplittingly funny - *Lorna Howarth, The Write Factor*

Ragged A**** Ruffian reviewed on Amazon in the United Kingdom on 27 January 2021 - A truly heartwarming, interesting, story with a wonderful narrative. Unquestionably a splendid read

A Solitude of Stars: With deft turns of phrase and an imagination that would make Philip K. Dick jealous, Gilson foresees a dystopian future, the seeds of which are definitely being sown right now. The story is a chilling glimpse of what may come to pass, warmed by a thread of love that raises the narrative beyond despair. I found the stories disturbing and breath-taking in equal measure. The Apparat and Dirigiste tribes are ranging across our solar system seeking peace by waging war, raising the question; is humanity actually capable of peace? A riveting read. - *Rob Swan, The Write Factor*

Songs of Bliss gripped me from the start - I had to read right to the end. Loved the humour. Impressed by the surprising empathy that I felt for rather - on the face of it - unlikeable characters. Look forward to seeing it in print. - *Maighdean-Mhara, commenting on Authonomy*

I just wanted to thank you once more for your help acquiring this beautiful collection. It's found a new home at the top of my library. I've already stumbled onto some wonderful stories in a couple of the collections, and I can't wait to get more. Have a wonderful holiday and a great new year... - *Richer Daniel Laporte, California, December 2021*

Tales From The Land Of Saints & Scholars

Melodies In Black Ink: A collection of darkly captivating short tales, each inspired by the melodies that move us, the lyrics that linger, and the stories hidden between the notes.

Gilson (editor of the international Fireside Stories series) offers a dark, poignant collection of genre-crossing stories, all inspired by songs, that explore the fragile intersections of love, loss, resilience, and the shadows we carry. Ranging from children with superpowers to accounts of blossoming love, abusive relationships, unexpected pregnancies, and the isolating rhythm of a machine-driven society, Gilson's stories capture raw textures of the human experience in a key suggested by their musical inspirations, which include lushly brooding tracks from Kate Bush, This Mortal Coil, Angel Olsen, The Cure, and Youssou N'Dour (the sublime "7 Seconds," a duet with Neneh Cherry.) Gilson has a gift for moment-to-moment storytelling that grips and then lingers, like Gorilla Glue stuck to one's fingertips, resisting even the harshest solvents of reason.

Life goes wrong in unpredictable yet resonant ways throughout these 26 compact tales, and Gilson's vivid portrayals of scenery and emotion make it easy to lose oneself in these narratives, drowning in a wave of feeling that refuses to let go. From the Scottish Highlands to space travel to the blood-soaked earth of Danish-Viking battlefields—told from the perspective of Ulfhednar and his sacred wolf, Ulric—these stories span wide imaginative terrain. Despite some big ideas and SF elements, characterization is compelling. "The Jakey and the Nae Chancer" introduces Elliot and Fiona, who have perfected the art of detachment, the latter of whom "was almost certain that her heart was too delicate to risk breaking again." One of the most heart-wrenching stories, "Be Well," is inspired by a devastating loss. It's a piece that does more than tug at the heart, it reaches in and seizes hold with unrelenting intensity.

Adding a unique dimension, each story concludes with a toast to the song and artist that inspired it, an invitation to experience these briskly potent stories on another sensory level, with a soundtrack tying words to melody, emotion to rhythm. Melodies in Black Ink is not light reading—but it is deeply moving, with haunting emotional rewards.

Searing, surprising stories of urgent feeling, inspired by beloved songs.

Tales From The Land Of Saints & Scholars

The US Review of Books
Professional Reviews for the People

Melodies in Black Ink: This work is not just another set of tales linked together by a myriad of characters who sometimes appear in more than one narrative. In fact, this is much more than just another short story collection. It is also a reflective, musical journey. Accompanying each story is an explanation of the song that inspired the writing. Most impressive is the wide expanse of musical genres, artists, and songs included in this book. From Wardruna to Metric to Blue Oyster Cult to Dot Allison, the book's audience will experience a musical journey unlike any other. The incorporation of the notes discussing each inspirational song provides an informative background. It also provides historical context, along with the author's personal anecdotes, about each song.

What makes this book even more realistic is its honest, vulnerable, and sometimes gritty portrayal of the characters and their existences. One story in which all of these themes and characteristics culminate is "Going Underground." It is a story in which even the main character's name, Daniel Grimes, reflects the character's harsh, gritty environment and existence, as well as the difficult decisions Daniel must make. Daniel embodies rebellion against the status quo after having lived a life in which he originally "played by the rules. All it got him were ration credits and a little coin, enough to rent a bedsit and eat slop." "Going Underground" is a daring story with a dystopian tone. Deepening that dystopian tone is the fact that the author cleverly disguises the story's time period, and the tale can be read as either occurring in the past, the present, or the very near future.

Music lovers will appreciate this book because of the role music plays in each and every story. The stories, too, are a testament to not only the power of music but also of the necessity of interdisciplinary studies and the humanities. The stories are a novel type of ekphrastic writing in that, rather than responding to visual art, the stories are responses to music. The fluid, poetic writing in each story mirrors the magic and lyricism inherent in the songs the author utilizes. These stories are powerful, emotional, and moving. Most of all, they are beautifully and unquestionably human.

RECOMMENDED by the US Review

Book review by Nicole Yurcaba

www.ingramcontent.com/pod-product-compliance
Lightning Source LLC
Chambersburg PA
CBHW030257080526
44584CB00012B/346